Stemming the Torrent

Expression and control in the Victorian discourses on emotions, 1830–1872

GESA STEDMAN
Centre for British Studies, Humboldt-Universität Berlin

Routledge
Taylor & Francis Group
LONDON AND NEW YORK

First published 2002 by Ashgate Publishing

Reissued 2018 by Routledge
2 Park Square, Milton Park, Abingdon, Oxon OX14 4RN
711 Third Avenue, New York, NY 10017, USA

Routledge is an imprint of the Taylor & Francis Group, an informa business

A Library of Congress record exists under LC control number: 2001099651

ISBN 13: 978-1-138-74156-0 (hbk)
ISBN 13: 978-1-138-74154-6 (pbk)
ISBN 13: 978-1-315-18279-7 (ebk)

STEMMING THE TORRENT

In this new study, Gesa Stedman mines the vein of emotion in Victorian writing to unearth new insights into the ways literature responded to the dramatic social and political changes then taking place.

Through an examination of the history of key Victorian emotion words, the major topics that dominate the discourses on emotions in this era, and the central fictional and non-fictional 'paradigm scenarios' which constitute these discourses, Stedman shows how slowly written representations of the 'passions' change in the 19th century. She argues that in texts about feelings, Victorian authors seem to attempt to delay or halt on a discursive level what can no longer be stopped on any other level of their culture and society.

Reading fictional texts alongside non-fictional works, this study highlights the tensions between the need of 19th-century writers to control 'storms of passion' and their effects, and their need to express feelings. Contemporary research from various disciplines such as sociology, ethnology and history inform this study, which juxtaposes canonical material such as Dickens' *Hard Times*, Charlotte Brontë's *Shirley* and Germaine de Staël's *Corinne* with popular novels and non-fictional texts such as *The Education of the Heart*, by Sarah Ellis, and Darwin's *The Expression of Emotion in Man and Animals*. The analysis deals with emotions applying to both genders, but includes a special section examining the representation of emotion in relation to women.

Stemming the Torrent provides new insights into the literature of the period, and brings to light important new material for the scholars interested in the philosophy and psychology of emotions.

For my parents and for Nils

'Thus passed the hours till I had reached my fourteenth year: thus grew up feelings, in our mutual hearts, which, had fate placed the barrier between us that at one time seemed inevitable, might but have been remembered in after years as the offspring of childish quarrels and idle jealousy. As it was, they were destined to go on like some mountain stream, which, gay and brawling in the summer sunshine, frets and foams in sparkling activity against every obstacle that it meets, but does harm to nothing; till, when the rain falls on the summits above, it is joined on its course by a thousand accessory streams, grows dark and furious, powerful and overwhelming, and rushes down, a torrent, over the land below, sweeping away peace, and happiness, and prosperity, in its angry course.'

G.P.R. James, 'Remorse'. *A Book of the Passions* (1838-39).

Contents

List of Figures

Acknowledgements

In George Black's *The Family Health Book* (1892), the passions can be found between the entries on 'partridges' and 'pastry'. This seems the most suitable place for them, since a lot of 'pastry' was needed to produce the special kind of 'pie' that I have been made to eat throughout the work for this study on the passions: humble pie. When I first started, I had no idea how much material and immaterial support would be needed to complete this book and it is with real gratitude and humility that I acknowledge my debt to the following people and institutions:

To the *Deutsche Forschungsgemeinschaft*, the *Sonderforschungsbereich 'Literatur und Anthropologie'* (Konstanz) and the *Berliner Senatsverwaltung für Arbeit, Berufliche Bildung und Frauen* (*Förderprogramm Frauenforschung*) for their generous funding.

To Professor Dr Jürgen Schlaeger (Berlin) for taking me on board in the first place and not making me walk the plank (although he probably sometimes wished he had), and most of all for teaching me to go beyond description.

To Professor Valentine Cunningham (Oxford) for much-needed advice and encouragement at the right moment.

To Professor Dr Christiane Eisenberg (Berlin), Dr Kate Flint (Oxford) and Professor Dr Walter Göbel (Stuttgart) for valuable bibliographical hints.

To the members of Professor Dr Margarete Zimmermann's research group (Berlin) for welcoming me among them, for many stimulating discussions and most of all for showing me the way when I had lost it.

To my research group on emotions, consisting of Dr Jana Gohrisch (Berlin), Dr Marion Müller (Oxford/Bonn) and Katharina Quabeck (Berlin), for insights, inspiration, laughter, proof-reading, re-ordering my sprawling material, generally putting up with me, each being indispensable in their own individual way and for proving that even in academia colleagues can turn into friends.

To Anke Börsel, Corinna Radke and Catherine Smith (Berlin) for their sense of humour, their careful proof-reading and their friendship; special thanks to Anke (and her student colleagues) for their patient book-carting. And thanks to everyone else at the Centre for British Studies for leaving me alone when I most needed it (most of the time), and showing an interest in spite of my frequent absences.

To Professor Joan DeJean (Pennsylvania), Professor Dr Peter Drexler (Potsdam) and to Professor Dr Gustav Klaus (Rostock) for their valuable advice on academic publishing.

To the staff at the Bodleian Library (Oxford) and the British Library (London) for their help and their kindness.

To my editor Erika Gaffney and all the staff at Ashgate for their patient support.

To my parents Monika Stedman and Michael Stedman, who each in their separate way let me get on with things and never stopped believing in my abilities. Their support has been invaluable in many ways.

To all my friends and family who have listened to my complaints and never lost hope that the book would be finished. Special thanks to Mary Lyons (Jersey/Oxford) for providing me with a home from home in Oxford, and for many enjoyable and stimulating discussions.

To two special people without whose help this project would have failed: to Margarete Zimmermann, whose generosity and unique combination of friendship and food for thought inspired me and made me go on when I had already given up (more than once), and to Nils Kummert, who was intelligent enough to keep his sense of humour and set me right when the Victorian 'storms of passion' threatened to capsize me, intellectually or otherwise.

For permission to reproduce images and texts, I thank the following publishers and institutions:

The British Library, London. Musée d'art et d'histoire, Ville de Genève. Tate, London. The Walters Art Museum, Baltimore. AMS Press, New York. Blackwell Publishing, Oxford. Cambridge University Press, Cambridge. Clarendon Press, Oxford. Columbia University Press, New York. HarperCollins Publishers Ltd, London. Haynes Publishing, Sparkford. ITPS, Andover. Oxford University Press, Oxford. Palgrave Publishers Ltd., Basingstoke. Penguin, Harmondsworth. Rutgers University Press, Piscataway. Taylor and Francis, Andover. University of Wisconsin Press, Madison, Wisconsin. Virago Press, London. All efforts have been made to contact copyright holders.

G.S.

1 My leaves cannot contayne in them the large discourse: Introduction

Paradigm scenarios: Emotions and Literature

According to John Keble's *Lectures on Poetry* (1832-41), poetry functions as 'a kind of medicine divinely bestowed upon man: which gives healing relief to secret mental emotion, yet without detriment to modest reserve: and, while giving scope to enthusiasm, yet rules it with order and due control'.[1] It is this dialectic of the expression of the emotions and the necessity to control them, of 'enthusiasm' and 'reserve', of 'healing relief' and 'order', and its relation to literature which is the focal point of this book.

The connection between emotions and literature is of course not a specifically Victorian concern, but one that had agitated generations of writers and thinkers before the advent of 19th-century mass culture. But although the problem seems to transcend historical periods,[2] there seems little point in analysing the emotions outside their historical and discursive context since they and the debates concerning their adequate representation are both subject to historical change. Prior to entering the minefield of emotions theory and the history of feelings, some general remarks regarding texts and emotions are called for.[3]

---

1 John Keble (1912), *Keble's Lectures on Poetry, 1832-41*, transl. by Edward Kershaw Francis, 2 vols., Clarendon Press, Oxford, lecture I, p. 22.

2 On the relation of emotionality, genre and control cf. Valentine Cunningham (1999), 'Readers Beside Themselves: Particular Pleasures and Generic Controls', in Jürgen Schlaeger and Gesa Stedman (eds), *Representations of Emotions*, Gunter Narr, Tübingen, pp. 43-57.

3 The philosophical discussion of emotional reactions to fictional texts is not a very fruitful one. Not only does it rest on a simple concept of reading as identification, it is also conducted with no concern for actual historical reactions to specific texts. For an overview of this debate cf. Margit Sutrop (1999), 'Sympathy, Imagination, and the Readers' Emotional Response to Fiction', in Schlaeger and Stedman (eds),

As readers we can find representational reservoirs of emotions in texts, stored there for our collective cultural memory[4] and available for specific uses which each century and each generation may define anew. Textual representations of feelings can be compared to what Ronald de Sousa has called 'paradigm scenarios ... [which are] drawn from our daily life as small children' and 'later reinforced by the stories, art, and culture to which we are exposed ...'.[5] As readers, one can learn from these paradigm scenarios which provide examples of emotional behaviour and experience. Consequently, texts can function as intentional or unintentional conduct books, a purpose of which Victorian writers and readers were well aware. In texts, a 'space' may be created in which emotions can be compensated which cannot be expressed in 'real' life. Establishing ideals, for instance the concept of the nation which became so popular during the 19th century, is also helped by visual and verbal representations. Furthermore, texts allow the invention of new or different emotion concepts which can later even transcend their textual origin and move out into 'reality', as may have been the case during the Romantic period.[6] Whether one can rely on texts as useful sources for historical analysis of actual emotional experience is a question I would like to keep till later.[7] Doubtlessly, texts can demonstrate

---

Representations, pp. 29-42. Cf. also Henrike F. Alfes (1995), *Literatur und Gefühl. Emotionale Aspekte literarischen Schreibens und Lesens*, Westdeutscher Verlag, Opladen, for a further systematic rather than historical approach to emotion and literature.

4 On the relation of the body, emotions and cultural memory cf. Aleida Assmann (1999), *Erinnerungsräume. Formen und Wandlungen des kulturellen Gedächtnisses*, C.H. Beck, Munich, p. 20.

5 Cf. Ronald de Sousa (1980), 'The Rationality of Emotions', in Amélie Oksenberg Rorty (ed), *Explaining Emotions*, University of California Press, Berkeley etc., pp. 127-151, quotation p. 142. In like manner social interactionists conceive of emotions as worked out and dramatised in a 'script' while social constructionists like Rom Harré speak of 'standard dramatic scenarios'. Cf. John R. Gillis (1988), 'From Ritual to Romance. Toward an Alternative History of Love', in Carol Z. Stearns and Peter N. Stearns (eds), *Emotion and Social Change: Toward a New Psychohistory*, Holmes and Meier, New York/Oxford, pp. 87-121, quotation p. 89, and Rom Harré (1986), 'An Outline of the Social Constructionist Viewpoint', in id. (ed), *The Social Construction of Emotions*, Basil Blackwell, Oxford, pp. 2-14, quotation p. 13.

6 Sometimes the texts seem to be producing their subject, as Michel Foucault has shown for the discourses on sexuality, i.e. writing about the feelings and interpreting them may actually help to create these emotions. Cf. Michel Foucault (1991), *Der Wille zum Wissen. Sexualität und Wahrheit 1*, Suhrkamp, Frankfurt a.M. [French original 1976], and Foucault ([7]1995), *Archäologie des Wissens*, Suhrkamp, Frankfurt a.M. [French Original 1969].

7 This is the assumption on which rests Norbert Elias's study, a work which I still

'feeling rules'[8] explicitly, and their possible effects can be shown, thus providing contemporary readers with guidelines, and later scholars with an insight into the emotional ideals of an historical period. Finally, in a culture which bases its teaching of knowledge and values on representations such as art and literature, the influence of texts and images on the development of an emotional habitus is of great importance. That Victorian writers were conscious of the special part that texts could play can be illustrated by a revealingly textual metaphor, used by the Scottish psychologist Alexander Bain in his seminal study *The Emotions and the Will* (1859), to explain his concept of internalised order: 'conscience ... reproduces, in the maturity of the mind, a facsimile of the system of government as practised around us'.[9]

The concept of habitus, developed by Pierre Bourdieu, who adapted it from Norbert Elias and Erwin Panofsky, implies an embodied emotional ideal which will be visible even in the smallest and seemingly insignificant bodily actions and can itself generate emotional conduct. Thus, habitus does not only refer to conscious or unconscious mental notions and processes which structure people's attitudes and conduct,[10] but also to bodily action, inextricably linked to emotional experience and behaviour.[11]

---

consider to be an important analysis of historical cultures of feeling, in spite of recent criticism. Cf. Norbert Elias ([19]1995), *Über den Prozeß der Zivilisation*, 2 vols., Suhrkamp, Frankfurt a.M. [1936]. For the arguments directed against Elias cf. Ralf Baumgart/Volker Eichener ([2]1997), *Norbert Elias zur Einführung*, Junius, Hamburg, in particular p. 87ff.

8 Arlie Russell-Hochschild (1983) developed this concept in her influential study, *The Managed Heart. Commercialization of Human Feeling*, University of California Press, Berkeley, Cal. etc., p. 56ff. It designates social norms of emotional behaviour. Being happy at a marriage and expressing grief at a funeral are two examples of feeling rules. However, these rules only explain what one is supposed to feel (and how to express this emotion), not the actual feelings involved in a given, culturally defined and variable situation.

9 Alexander Bain ([2]1865) [1859], *The Emotions and the Will*, Longmans & Co., London, p. 283.

10 Bourdieu's concept of habitus – although not originally a historiographic category – can be related to the French tradition of *histoire des mentalités*. His concept of embodied mental dispositions and his focus on material objects and behaviour which reflect and structure these dispositions can be compared to the concept of *imaginaire*, which also looks at the collective function of visual, verbal and material forms of representations. For a discussion of the problems of *histoire des mentalités* and the concept of *l'imaginaire* see below, note 47, and the overview by Sabine Jöckel (1987), 'Die 'histoire des mentalités': Baustein einer historisch-soziologischen Literaturwissenschaft', in *Romanistische Zeitschrift für Literaturgeschichte*, vol. 172, pp. 146-173.

11 On the concept of habitus cf. Pierre Bourdieu (1985), *Outline of a Theory of Practice*,

As a more specific alternative to the ill-defined idea of a collective identity, derived as it is from the concept of individual identity,[12] habitus links the 'individual' and his or her feelings and behaviour (and their representations) with the collective dimension. As Bourdieu explains:

> In order to define the relations between class, habitus and the organic individuality which can never be entirely removed from sociological discourse, ... habitus could be considered as a subjective but not individual system of internalized structures, schemes of perception, conception, and action common to all members of the same group or class and constituting the precondition for all objectification and apperception: and the objective co-ordination of practices and sharing a world-view could be founded on the perfect impersonality and interchangeability of singular practices and views.[13]

Lyon and Barbalet also emphasise the role of the body which is more than just the passive recipient of or medium for the emotions, but a vital source of social agency:

> An adequate understanding of social agency requires a concept of embodied agency. ... Emotion has a role in social agency as it significantly guides and prepares the organism for social action through which social relations are generated. The body cannot be seen merely as subject to external forces; the emotions which move the person through bodily processes must be understood as a source of agency: social actors are embodied.[14]

How the general notion of the embodied habitus can be profitably used for

---

transl. by Richard Nice, Cambridge UP, Cambridge [1977] [French original 1972]. Catherine Lutz and Lila Abu-Lughod (eds) (1990) exemplify the relation between embodiment, habitus and emotions in their seminal collection of essays, *Language and the Politics of Emotion*, Cambridge UP, Cambridge, 'Introduction', p. 12f. See also Hans-Ulrich Wehler (2000), 'Emotionen in der Geschichte: Sind soziale Klassen auch emotionale Klassen?', in id., *Umbruch und Kontinuität. Essays zum 20. Jahrhundert*, C.H. Beck, Munich, pp. 251-64.

12 For an overview of recent debates on personal and collective identity, and the uses of these concepts, see Peter Wagner (1999), 'Fest-Stellungen. Beobachtungen zur sozialwissenschaftlichen Diskussion über Identität', pp. 44-72 and Jürgen Straub (1999), 'Personale und kollektive Identität. Zur Analyse eines theoretischen Begriffs', pp. 73-104, both in Aleida Assmann and Heidrun Friese (eds), *Identitäten. Erinnerung, Geschichte, Identität*, vol. 3, Suhrkamp, Frankfurt a.M.

13 Bourdieu (1985), *Outline*, p. 86.

14 M. Lyon and J.M. Barbalet (1994), 'Society's body: emotion and the "somatization" of social theory', in Thomas J. Csordas (ed), *Embodiment and Experience. The Existential Ground of Culture and Self*, Cambridge UP, Cambridge, pp. 48-66, quotation p. 50.

literary and cultural analysis will be illustrated in the course of this study. What may at first seem a concept characterised by rigidity and consequently one opposed to historical change, as some historians have criticised, turns out to be an exceptionally useful heuristic tool to explain why the Victorian discourses on emotions are distinguished more by continuity than by change.[15]

A set of questions follows from the above:

- Which part does the body play in Victorian texts on the emotions, and how does it relate to the central concern of expression and control of the feelings?
- How do the individual body and the feelings bear upon the body politic in the 19th century?
- Which role does language play for these concerns?
- Which 'space' do Victorian writers accord the feelings, and how is this related to the development of the habitus of the emerging cultural leaders of the 19th century (the middle classes)?
- What do 19th-century writers say about feeling and literature?
- Which kinds of paradigm scenarios do they create in fictional and non-fictional texts?
- What function do these paradigm scenarios have for the creation and maintenance of the middle class habitus?

And finally, a problem which informs all inquiries into 19th-century culture:

- How do the Victorian discourses on emotions relate to historical continuity and change?

The aim of such an approach is to make visible how the discourses on emotions worked during the Victorian period, and which functions they

---

[15] For an overview of the advantages and problems of historical analysis inspired by Bourdieu see Sven Reichardt (1997), 'Bourdieu für Historiker? Ein kultursoziologisches Angebot an die Sozialgeschichte', in Thomas Mergel and Thomas Welskopp (eds), *Geschichte zwischen Kultur und Gesellschaft. Beiträge zur Theoriedebatte*, C.H. Beck, Munich, pp. 71-93 and Hans-Ulrich Wehler (1998), 'Pierre Bourdieu. Das Zentrum seines Werks', in id., *Die Herausforderung der Kulturgeschichte*, C.H. Beck, Munich, pp. 15-44.

may have fulfilled.

In my use of the term 'discourse' I have conflated two of its most frequently used meanings. In the more traditional use of the term, 'discourse' can refer to a set of texts or debates which focus on a specific subject. Following Michel Foucault's coinage of 'discourse', an additional level has become prominent in recent years. In this sense of the word, 'discourse' refers to the unconscious rules and strategies which govern debates of a given topic, ordering what can and what cannot be said about it, and in some cases even 'creating' the topic in the first place. This approach allows me to explain those texts which explicitly focus on the emotions as well as the underlying rules which make these explicit discussions possible.[16]

But before taking a closer look at the discourses on emotions in the first half of the 19th century, two more general problems need to be addressed: what are emotions and how can one analyse the history of feelings on the basis of literary texts?

Ontological illusions? Theories of Emotion

Interest in the emotions has once again come to the fore during the last two decades. Ongoing debates range over a variety of questions, none of which have been satisfactorily answered yet. These academic discussions of the emotions are dominated by a set of binary distinctions, as Catherine A. Lutz and Geoffrey M. White have shown.[17] Many of these basic dichotomies delineating the field of emotion research are not specific to the subject. They need to be confronted for most academic undertakings and illustrate how central the emotions are not only to human behaviour but also to general epistemological debates about such issues as relativism versus universalism, idealism versus materialism, or 'nature' versus 'culture'. Many of these debates originated in the 18th and 19th centuries and some modern approaches to the emotions seem surprisingly

---

16 Cf. Sarah Mills (1998), *Discourse*, Routledge, London, Michel Foucault (1996) [1991], *Die Ordnung des Diskurses*, Fischer, Frankfurt a.M., [French original 1972], and Foucault (^{7}1995), *Archäologie des Wissens*, and Lutz and Abu-Lughod (1990), 'Introduction'.

17 Cf. Catherine A. Lutz and Geoffrey M. White (1986), 'The Anthropology of Emotions', in *Annual Review of Anthropology*, vol. 15, pp. 405-436.

similar to Victorian discussions of the feelings.[18]

Emotions are either seen as material substances, e.g. as physiological phenomena, or as mental value judgements, with no material basis at all. Related to this is the discussion whether emotions are socially constructed or whether they are invariable physiological occurrences that are part of 'nature', not 'culture'. In some older 20th-century theories, emotion is still viewed as the counterpart of reason, and, depending on the approach, is either seen as a more authentic part of human experience than reason seems to be, or vice versa. More recent models consider emotion and reason as inextricably linked and equally valid modes of human experience.[19] Another important debate concentrates on the alleged universality and invariability of the emotions, strongly opposed by the opposite camp which defends its view of the emotions as relative occurrences differing from culture to culture.[20] Closely related to this problem is the discussion of so-called basic emotions, believed to be shared by all cultures.[21]

---

18 Charles Darwin's *The Expression of Emotion in Man and Animals* (1872) is a case in point. His use of questionnaires and photographs, sent out to British missionaries, was replicated by Paul Ekman more than a century later, who also used photographs of facial expressions to prove his idea of the universality of emotions. Ethological emotion research in general is heavily indebted to Darwin's study and in some cases does not seem to go beyond Darwin's ideas. Cf. Paul Ekman's 'Introduction' to Charles Darwin ([3]1998), *The Expression of the Emotions in Man and Animals*, Harper Collins, London [1872], pp. xxi-xxxvi. See also Ann Cvetkovich (1992), *Mixed Feelings. Feminism, Mass Culture, and Victorian Sensationalism*, Rutgers UP, New Brunswick, N.J., for the relation between 19th-century theories of feeling and modern (feminist) politics, in particular the introduction, 'The Politics of Affect'.

19 For an overview of this debate cf. Richard A. Shweder (1984), 'Anthropology's Romantic Rebellion Against the Enlightenment, or There's More to Thinking Than Reason and Evidence', in R.A. Shweder and Robert A. LeVine (eds), *Culture Theory. Essays on Mind, Self, and Emotion*, Cambridge UP, Cambridge, N.Y., pp. 27-66. See also Dylan Evans (2001), *Emotion. The Science of Sentiment*, Oxford UP, Oxford, in particular 'The head and the heart', pp. 112-144.

20 Defenders and opponents of constructionism and relativism discuss this problem in an article and responses to it published in *Current Anthropology*, vol. 38 (3), pp. 327-351, William M. Reddy (June 1997), 'Against Constructionism. The Historical Ethnography of Emotions'.

21 Cf. Lutz and White (1986), 'The Anthropology of Emotions', and Michael Lewis and Jeannette M. Haviland (1993), 'Preface' in id. (eds), *Handbook of Emotions*, The Guilford Press, New York/London, pp. ix-x. The so-called 'basic emotions' will not be discussed in this study, nor do I wish to offer any solutions for the problem. From a cultural historical perspective, the mere existence of certain feelings is much less relevant than their cultural meanings and manner of representation.

Many emotion theories suffer from serious deficiencies: some are based on the analysis of contemporary phenomena which are then used as a basis for general and ahistorical or at least not period-specific conclusions and models of emotionality.[22] A similar lack of interest in historical matters can be observed in many psychological publications, and more critical perspectives, to be found for instance in Klaus-Jürgen Bruder's approach to the feelings, are only slowly being developed, and usually at the margins of the discipline.[23] For an analysis of literary developments from a historical perspective, ahistorical emotion models have only a very limited use.

Equally problematic are definitions which ignore or exclude important elements of the discourses on emotions. The social foundation of emotions, their constructed and constructive, i.e. emotion- and behaviour-generating 'nature', the change of feelings and their representations over time, and issues such as the relation of gender and feeling which vary across cultures as opposed to allegedly universal emotional tendencies, are frequently overlooked in emotion theories. Instead, writers consciously or unconsciously choose a normative approach. So-called negative emotions are distinguished from so-called positive ones, without declaring from which point of view they are considered to be so. Some authors do not even seem to notice that they are expressing value judgements by using these categorisations. More often than not, theories highlight individual emotional experience at the expense of its social foundation. Even some sociological theories of emotion conceptualise the social element inherent in the feelings as the relation between *alter* and *ego*. Such models rely on a dichotomy between 'individual' and 'society', terms justly criticised by Norbert Elias because they imply a radical difference between two

---

22 Heinz-Günter Vester (1991) for instance uses prototypical emotions in his sociological investigation *Emotion, Gesellschaft und Kultur. Grundzüge einer soziologischen Theorie der Emotionen*, Westdeutscher Verlag, Opladen to draw general conclusions concerning a society's emotional climate without taking into account the period- and culture-dependent nature of these protoypical emotions. Cf. also Evans (2001), *Emotion. The Science of Sentiment*, p. 22ff., for a rather cavalier approach to emotional change.

23 For an example of psychology's dominant ahistorical approaches to emotion cf. K.T. Strongman ([3]1993), *The Psychology of Emotion*, John Wiley and Sons, Chichester etc. For a more critical perspective cf. Klaus-Jürgen Bruder (1993), 'Psychologie der Emotion. Der psychologische Diskurs über die Gefühle', in id., *Subjektivität und Postmoderne. Der Diskurs der Psychologie*, Suhrkamp, Frankfurt a.M., pp. 167-201. Cf. also Shula Sommers (1988), 'Understanding Emotions: Some Interdisciplinary Considerations', in Carol Z. Stearns and Peter N. Stearns (eds), *Social Change*, pp. 23-38 on the need to integrate history and psychology.

interdependent aspects of human experience. In summary, I am inclined to agree with Rom Harré who calls the simplistic emotion models 'intellectually anorexic accounts' and 'ontological illusions'.[24]

Without attempting an exact definition of the emotions, I have decided to base my investigation of the Victorian discourses on the feelings on the following trans-disciplinary approach: emotions are not an essence or a substance but culturally and historically relative; they require an analysis which takes their discursive contexts into account. This does not, however, imply overlooking or excluding their possible physical basis. Moreover, emotions are constructed by society, but they combine two levels, that of the 'individual' and 'society'. Individuals (physically) experience emotions but they can never access them without first acquiring knowledge of the social relevance, and appropriateness of certain feelings; thus, the social can never be absent from any kind of emotional experience and its representation.[25] The social aspect includes not only the problem of evaluating one's own and other's emotions – emotions are always inextricably linked to a society's moral order[26] – but also the role of emotional socialisation processes and the relation of individual and collective control. It is this social and moral context which make written and visual paradigm scenarios so relevant for the study of the feelings.[27]

In spite of the fact that the term 'emotion' frequently connotes a series of 'undesirable' aspects, such as weakness, irrationality, femininity, and

---

24 Cf. e.g. Vester (1991), *Emotion, Gesellschaft und Kultur*, p. 27, for the uncritical use of the terms 'positive' and 'negative' emotions. Both Jürgen Gerhards (1986), 'Soziologie der Emotionen. Ein Literaturbericht', in *Kölner Zeitschrift für Soziologie und Sozialpsychologie*, vol. 38, pp. 760-771, and Theodore Kemper, 'Sociological Models in the Explanation of Emotions', in Lewis and Haviland (eds) (1993), *Handbook*, pp. 41-51, work with traditionally differentiated concepts of the individual and society. See also Harré (1986), 'An Outline', p. 9.

25 For a social constructionist view of the emotions and their potential to generate relations, judgements etc. see the essays in Harré (ed) (1986), *The Social Construction of Emotions*.

26 Op. cit., p. 6.

27 Cf. also Lutz and Abu-Lughod's approach, Lutz and Abu-Lughod (1990), 'Introduction'. On the important issue of gender and emotion, cf. Russell-Hochschild (1983), *The Managed Heart*, and Catherine Lutz (1990), 'Engendered Emotion: Gender, Power, and the Rhetoric of Emotional Control in American Discourse', in Lutz and Abu-Lughod (eds), *Language and the Politics of Emotion*, pp. 69-91, and most recently Catherine Lutz (2002), 'Emotion and Feminist Theories', in Ingrid Kasten, Gesa Stedman, Margarete Zimmermann (eds), *Kulturen der Gefühle in Mittelalter und Früher Neuzeit* (Querelles. Jahrbuch für Frauenforschung vol. 7), Metzler, Stuttgart/Weimar, pp. 104-121.

loss of control,[28] I have used it throughout as it is impossible to find or to create a word encompassing all important aspects without evoking the above-mentioned value judgements.[29]

Et voilà donc un beau sujet: Texts and the History of Feelings

The French historian Lucien Febvre issued a rallying cry for the historical study of emotions in the early 1940s, pleading the cause for this 'attractive subject'. Historians of the *Annales* school followed his recommendations up to a point. While they began to investigate what has become known as *histoire des mentalités*, focusing on such topics as death, fear, private life, and childhood, their British colleagues refrained from similar undertakings. Apart from Norbert Elias's seminal work which only became influential in the second part of the 20th century, decades after it had first been written, the feelings were not considered worthy objects of historical research. But in spite of the knowledge of the difference between the medieval and the Romantic concepts of love, or 18th-century sensibility and post-modern emotionality and the consequent possibility of differing emotional experiences[30] historians have only quite recently taken a fresh look at this *beau sujet*, leaving behind them the view that the emotions are easily accessible, universal, and therefore uninteresting invariant substances.[31]

---

28 Cf. Catherine Lutz's analysis of both sets of contradictory connotations associated with the term 'emotion': on the one hand we find pejorative notions such as lack of control, weakness, irrationality, and femininity. The second set of values on the other hand develops romantic ideas of the emotions as life-giving energy supposedly saving us from alienation. See Lutz (1990), 'Engendered Emotion'.

29 For stylistic reasons I have occasionally supplemented 'emotion' by 'feeling'.

30 Cf. e.g. Peter Dinzelbacher (1993), 'Emotionen', in *Das andere Mittelalter. Emotionen, Rituale und Kontraste*, Kunsthalle Krems, pp. 101-110, Niklas Luhman (1982) and his systems-theory analysis *Liebe als Passion*, Suhrkamp, Frankfurt a.M., Heinz-Günter Vester (1999), 'Emotions in Postemotional Culture', in Schlaeger and Stedman (eds), *Representations*, pp. 19-27, as well as Gillis (1988), 'From Ritual to Romance'. Gillis is justified in his warning against a concept of the emotions which rests largely on 19th-century assumptions and is then used in anachronistic fashion as the standard against which earlier emotion culture is measured.

31 Recent developments show that the emotions are gaining in importance not only for literary critics but for historians as well. For the classic *Annales* approach cf. Lucien Febvre (1953) [1941], 'Comment reconstituer la vie affective d'autrefois? La sensibilité et l'histoire', in id., *Combats pour l'histoire*, Librairie Armand Colin, Paris, pp. 221-239, repr. from *Annales d'Histoire Sociale*, vol. 3, and Roger Chartier et al. (eds) (1987), *La sensibilité dans l'histoire*, Gérard Monfort, Brionne. For more recent

Conceptualising the feelings as culturally relative without a fixed trans-historical and trans-cultural base has shown how much they are subject to historical change. Thus, the term 'emotion' can only serve as an inadequate word for forms of human experience which differ from period to period.

One reason which may have hindered historians in approaching the emotions more readily is the difficulty of finding adequate source material for the analysis of mental and emotional processes. As with other historical problems, one faces the question of how one can reconstruct emotional behaviour and experience of the past with the help of visual and verbal sources, even if one does not want to attempt an objectivist analysis inspired by Ranke's notion of *wie es eigentlich gewesen*.[32] But is it possible to read more from the sources than sets of feeling rules? The distinction introduced by the historians Carol and Peter Stearns is helpful here: they differentiate between emotional experience and emotionology, i.e. actual emotions as opposed to feeling rules and standards, which may differ considerably from feelings as actually experienced in a given period.[33] This raises the question whether a text-based analysis of a period's emotionology can ever yield an adequate idea of actual emotional experience and behaviour. Some historians who work with texts seem to overlook the fact that literary texts in particular frequently have no intention of being 'true' to life.[34] Thus it is necessary to assume a

---

overviews see Carol Z. Stearns and Peter N. Stearns (1988), 'Introduction', *Social Change*, and Peter N. Stearns (1993), 'History of Emotions: The Issue of Change', in Lewis and Haviland (eds), *Handbook*, pp. 17-28, and Ute Frevert (2000), 'Angst vor Gefühlen? Die Geschichtsmächtigkeit von Emotionen im 20. Jahrhundert', in Paul Nolte et al. (eds), *Perspektiven der Gesellschaftsgeschichte*, Munich, C.H. Beck, pp. 95-111.

32 On the relation of objectivism and historicism cf. Otto Gerhard Oexle (1984), 'Geschichtswissenschaft im Zeichen des Historismus. Bemerkungen zum Standort der Geschichtsforschung', in *Historische Zeitschrift*, vol. 238, pp. 17-55.

33 See Peter N. Stearns with Carol Z. Stearns (1985), 'Emotionology: Clarifying the History of Emotions and Emotional Standards', in *American Historical Review*, vol. 90, pp. 813-836.

34 Cf. Stearns and Stearns (1988), 'Introduction' on this problem. In the same volume, different attempts are made to use fictional and non-fictional texts for historical analyses. However, from the point of view of literary studies, these attempts do not go far enough in acknowledging the 'constructed' character of texts and their use of literary techniques. Norbert Elias's study (and those of his followers) also sometimes betray an overly simplified notion of literary texts and the possibility of overcoming the discrepancy between a culture's emotionology and actual emotional experience. For a more promising example of the convergence between history proper and literary studies see Anne-Charlott Trepp's recent analysis of middle class feelings in Hamburg in which she shows a welcome awareness of literature's influence on autobiographical writing.

discrepancy between a text's claim to truthfulness and accuracy and 'real' historical behaviour. Nevertheless, even as a literary-cultural scholar one can on occasion speculate as to the actual, extra-textual emotional experience with the help of social history, the history of mentalities, and non-literary sources,[35] although the danger remains that one discovers no more than one's own specific concerns in a given text or image.[36] However, the focus of this study clearly lies on the emotionology of the Victorian period, since the analysis is largely text-based. And in spite of post-structuralist tendencies which have influenced literary studies and historiography alike, and in the most extreme case deny any difference between the textual and non-textual, between the discursive and the non-discursive, I would like to uphold this difference. Determining historically what functions discourses may have had is only possible if one relates these discourses to a non-discursive realm, even though this might in turn be only accessible with the help of another discourse, i.e. written or visual sources.

Opting for an entirely ahistorical approach to the emotions, as some literary critics seem to advocate for the 19th century, cannot be an appropriate response to the imponderable theoretical tensions briefly hinted at above.[37] Neither is the sole reliance on the history of ideas very helpful, since if one takes seriously the concept of the emotions as embodied in the individual as well as the social 'body', it is insufficient to analyse no more than literary and philosophical concepts of the feelings.[38] A further problem lies in the prevalence of a common sense model of the emotions which many literary critics adhere to, disregarding the advances

---

Trepp (1996), *Sanfte Männlichkeit und selbständige Weiblichkeit. Frauen und Männer im Hamburger Bürgertum zwischen 1770 und 1840*, Vandenhoeck and Ruprecht, Göttingen.

35 On recent historiographic developments see Roger Chartier (1995), 'L'Histoire culturelle entre "Linguistic Turn" et Retour au Sujet', in H. Lehmann (ed), *Wege zu einer neuen Kulturgeschichte. Mit Beiträgen von Rudolf Vierhaus und Roger Chartier*, Wallstein Verlag Göttingen, pp. 29-58.

36 See Gillis (1988), 'From Ritual to Romance'.

37 Cf. e.g. Barbara Hardy (1986) [1985], *Forms of Feeling in Victorian Fiction*, Methuen, London, as well as Barbara Korte's (1993) study which deals with a subject related to the emotions, namely non-verbal communication and literature: *Körpersprache in der Literatur. Theorie und Geschichte am Beispiel englischer Erzählprosa*, Francke, Tübingen.

38 An example for a restricted focus on the history of ideas, analysed only on the basis of canonised authors and texts, is Fred Kaplan's (1987) study *Sacred Tears. Sentimentality in Victorian Literature*, Princeton UP, Princeton.

that emotions theory has made under the influence of anthropology, sociology and history.[39] What I therefore wish to retain from the advances made in emotions historiography and theory is the distinction between a period's emotional standard and emotional experience, as well as the emphasis on historical relativity. What I would wish to shed is the on occasion simplistic approach to literary texts. The awareness and knowledge of the complexity of (literary) texts and the sensitiveness to language is on the other hand the most important element I would want to keep from literary studies on the emotions. What can be safely left behind is their frequent ignorance of or at least disinterest in historical matters and in concerns which transcend the canon.

No one investigating the 19th-century discourses on emotions can ignore Peter Gay's multi-volume investigation into Victorian psychohistory, *The Bourgeois Experience. From Victoria to Freud* (1984-1998). His series is simultaneously an insurmountable obstacle and a welcome matrix against which one can set off an analysis based on quite different concepts. With his title, Gay clearly signals where his interest lies: Freudian psychoanalysis forms the backbone of his historical studies. His range and interpretation of sources both visual and verbal is impressive and can never be replicated by a rather more humble and less experienced author of a first book-length study. But I would argue with Carol and Peter Stearns that a psychoanalytical approach to emotions history is not the most interesting path to go down when trying to make sense of the Victorian discourses on the feelings.[40]

Peter Gay of course takes up Norbert Elias's justified criticism of ahistorical psychoanalytical terminology, based as it is on the notion of an enclosed, separate core within the individual which can be analysed without taking its (historical) context into account.[41] He rejects reductionist psychohistory but nevertheless argues for sex and aggression as the fundamental driving forces of human behaviour. Applying psychoanalytic

---

39 Examples for the use of emotion concepts lacking complexity are Kaplan's and Hardy's studies, as well as the following two works: Michael Bell (1983), *The Sentiment of Reality: Truth of Feeling in the European Novel*, Unwin, London, and Wolfgang Herrlinger (1987), *Sentimentalismus und Postsentimentalismus. Studien zum englischen Roman bis zur Mitte des 19. Jahrhunderts*, Niemeyer, Tübingen.

40 Although one cannot accuse Gay of having dealt 'with change as a process ... mechanically derived from a smattering of evidence combined with theory', I would agree with Stearns and Stearns that psychohistory rests too much on a static concept of the human psyche. See Stearns and Stearns (1988), 'Introduction', in particular p. 4.

41 Cf. Elias ([19]1995), *Über den Prozeß*, p. lxvii.

concepts to the period during which they were developed is not as anachronistic as using the same concepts for much earlier periods, but I would still doubt the effectiveness of such an approach. The danger of drawing foregone conclusions from the material seems to me to be considerable if a system which is inherently ahistorical is adapted to historical research. An example may illustrate this: Gay explains psychoanalytically the presence of the two central emotion metaphors of the 'current' and the 'flow' of feelings, which one of his key witnesses called Mabel Loomis Todd uses. He focuses on the alleged sexual nature of these metaphors and reads them as expressions of Todd's individuality and her unusual sexual awareness.[42] But what he overlooks is the fact that these metaphors are the most conventional expressions for the emotions which can be found in the Victorian discourses on the feelings. Rather than reading them as representative of her urgent sex drive, I would want to place these metaphors in their wider discursive context. What would emerge is almost the opposite of Gay's findings: 'currents' of feeling are banal expressions, virtually dead metaphors, used as a kind of short-hand and indicative of a writer's lack of originality, or his or her wish to remain within the boundaries of the discourses on emotions, not an attempt to verbalise an insistent and individual sex drive.

Although I have myself used the terms 'middle classes' and 'Victorian' as comprehensive labels and am aware of the need to differentiate between different middle class, regional, and religious cultures, Gay's sweeping approach to middle class culture across Europe and including North America seems rather too bold.[43] For all the similarities between these cultures, their differences perhaps require that greater attention be paid to 'national' discourses on emotions before their comparison can be safely attempted. Pierre Bourdieu's study of social distinction in 20th-century France has brought the national limits and peculiarities of middle class culture sharply into focus, and this would apply equally to middle class

---

42 Peter Gay (1984), *Education of the Senses* (*The Bourgeois Experience*, vol. 1), Oxford UP, New York/Oxford, p. 76.

43 Gay defends this approach by highlighting the similarities between the different countries and the movement of ideas and inventions across national boundaries. Such a generalised method overlooks the specific elements of the discourses on the emotions, e.g. the explicit and frequent distinction the English writers make between 'French feeling', as they call it, and English emotionality. But cf. Peter Gay (1998), *Pleasure Wars* (*The Bourgeois Experience*, vol. 5), W.W. Norton and Co., New York/London, p. 22f.

culture of the past.[44] I have therefore attempted something at the same time much more limited than Gay's series – a study of English discourses on emotions in the 19th century, with a few Celtic voices thrown in. And something which is more open to the workings of these discourses: my heuristic tools try to uncover not the specific Victorian forms of ahistorical instinctual drives, but rather something which implies historical difference, not similarity between the Victorians and us (driven by the same urges, only expressed differently) but an attempt to realise the Victorians' own terms and ways of dealing with the feelings. Although my concepts have mostly also been developed in the late 20th century and therefore imply an anachronistic approach to past events and representations, they appear to me to be more open to such past forms of dealings with the feelings. And finally, as a literary historian, I would not dare to attempt a reconstruction of actual emotional experience but have naturally limited myself to the emotionological level.

The large discourse, or the Choice of Texts and its Consequences

But the focus on Victorian emotionology also has its difficulties. Deciding which texts and images to select is one such problem. Literary critics investigating Victorian emotional culture have concentrated mainly on canonised texts, focusing particularly on Victorian novels.[45] While it is

---

44 Again, Trepp's contextualised and detailed approach to emotions history in 19th-century Hamburg can be quoted here. Cf. Trepp (1996), *Sanfte Männlichkeit*.

45 The set of studies mentioned in notes 37-39 can be cited as examples for works which rely entirely on canonical texts. A greater tolerance towards popular or non-fictional material can be found in accounts transcending traditional approaches to literary studies, e.g. in Elaine Showalter's (1987) and Helen Small's (1996) respective studies on madness in 19th-century culture, The Female Malady: Women, Madness and English Culture, 1830-1980, Virago, London and *Love's Madness. Madness, the Novel and Female Insanity, 1800-1865*, Clarendon Press, Oxford and more recently in Jane Wood (2001), *Passion and Pathology in Victorian Fiction*, Oxford UP, Oxford. Sally Shuttleworth's two studies on Victorian psychology in relation to the works of George Eliot and Charlotte Brontë are further examples of a contextualised approach to literature which does not hesitate to read popular health guides alongside canonical authors. See Shuttleworth (1984), *George Eliot and Nineteenth-Century Science: The Make-Believe of a Beginning*, Cambridge UP, Cambridge and id. (1996), *Charlotte Brontë and Nineteenth-Century Psychology*, Cambridge UP, Cambridge. Cvetkovich (1992), *Mixed Feelings*, also focuses on a genre which has not gained canonical status yet: sensation fiction. Adela Pinch's (1996) *Strange Fits of Passion. Epistemologies of Emotion, Hume to Austen*, Stanford UP, Stanford, focuses on the period prior to the one

helpful to draw on these studies, 19th-century discourses on emotions also invite the investigation of a broader textual basis.[46] Many canonical authors such as Charles Dickens, the Brontë-sisters, or George Eliot were influential for the collective *imaginaire*, the long tradition of deeply ingrained mental images expressed in texts and pictures which are constitutive for the Victorian middle class habitus.[47] They must therefore be included in any study of the Victorian discourses on the feelings. But other genres such as conduct books or scientific (and pseudo-scientific) treatises were equally influential. Rather than limiting the discussion of 19th-century feelings to fictional works, the Victorian discourses on emotions need to be described as an enormous array of texts in which different concepts from various genres interpenetrate one another. What Nancy Armstrong and Leonard Tennenhouse have rightly claimed (only) for female conduct books is equally true of 19th-century non-fictional texts on the feelings:

> despite remarkable parallels between the literature of conduct and the conduct of literature, literary histories rarely if ever contain references to the literature of female conduct, and even more rarely are conduct books for women allowed to contribute to our notion of cultural history.[48]

I have concentrated on and also reads canonical authors such as Hume and Austen 'alongside' Charlotte Smith, Ann Radcliffe and sources on the death of Princess Charlotte. But although Pinch works within a historical framework, 'literary' analyses of the texts dominate the book and philosophical concerns (where do the emotions come from?) seem to transcend what she emphasises, namely the historically specific 'epistemologies' of feeling in the late 18th and early 19th century. Nevertheless, her study is often stimulating and it is so precisely because it juxtaposes unusual material with well-known texts.

46 In his article 'The Victorian Sensibility', in *Victorian Studies*, vol. 7 (1), pp. 67-97, William A. Madden (1963-64) focuses on what he calls the 'first-rate literature of the Victorian period' because according to him this can be used as direct evidence of 'Victorian sensibility' (p. 69). On his final page, however, he suggests that it might be useful to study the topic 'in fields other than literature' (p. 97).

47 This concept was developed by Jacques Le Goff to broaden historical research by including a wider range of sources, in order to enable research into collective mental structures. *L'imaginaire* looks at the values that make people act as well as the 'objects' which are part of it, i.e. texts, images, architecture etc. '*L'imaginaire nourrit et fait agir l'homme. C'est un phénomène collectif, social, historique. Une histoire sans l'imaginaire, c'est une histoire mutilée, désincarnée*'. Cf. Jacques Le Goff (1985), 'Préface', in id., *L'imaginaire médieval. Essais*, Gallimard, Paris, pp. I-XXI, quotation p. VII, and for a critical assessment cf. Otto Gerhard Oexle (1990), 'Das Andere, die Unterschiede, das Ganze. Jacques Le Goffs Bild des Europäischen Mittelalters', in *Francia. Forschungen zur westeuropäischen Geschichte*, vol. 17 (1), pp. 140-158.

48 Nany Armstrong and Leonard Tennenhouse (1987), 'The literature of conduct, the

This study therefore focuses on the different kinds of explicit discourses on emotions,[49] as well as drawing to a lesser extent on visual material.[50] Since the discourses on emotions in this period are dominated by middle class writers and readers, and the issues they found most pressing, I have largely relied on publications written by and directed at middle class or occasionally lower middle class readers and writers.[51]

I have had to choose from two possible approaches: I could have written either a study of the place and function of individual emotions such as love or joy, anger and grief, and their representations in the Victorian discourses on the feelings. Or, and this is what I have actually attempted, a second option would have been an overview of the workings of the 19th-century discourses on emotions in general. The decision for such a comprehensive approach can be explained by two related reasons: before one can focus on any individual sub-discourses, some knowledge of the general rules is necessary so that any conclusions one may care to draw can be validated. And in order to decide which individual emotions were particularly important to the Victorians, I needed to discover how they systematised the

---

conduct of literature, and the politics of desire: an introduction', in id. (eds), *The Ideology of Conduct. Essays on Literature and the History of Sexuality*, Methuen, New York etc., pp. 1-24, quotation p. 3. For the use of 'minor' texts as expressive of a period's dominant ideas, topics, images and values, see also Sabine Jöckel (1984), *'Nouvelle histoire' und Literaturwissenschaft*, Schäuble, Rheinfelden, in particular pp. 239-242.

49 Lutz and Abu-Lughod distinguish between a 'discourse on emotion' which explicitly deals with the topic, and an 'emotional discourse', a term which refers to the affective content or effect of a text or an utterance. Since the scope of this study would not allow the balanced analysis of both types of discourse, I have mostly limited my analysis to the 'discourse on emotion', i.e. to the explicit discussion of the emotions in fictional and non-fictional texts. Cf. Lutz and Abu-Lughod (1990), 'Introduction', p. 10.

50 The 19th century is not only a period in which literature became a mass commodity, it is also a time when visual culture underwent significant change influencing artistic representations of the feelings. For a recent study on the relation of visual culture and Victorian literature cf. Carol T. Christ/John O. Jordan (eds) (1998), *Victorian Literature and the Victorian Visual Imagination*, University of California Press, Berkeley, Cal. See also Kate Flint (2001), *The Victorians and the Visual Imagination*, Cambridge UP, Cambridge, Julie F. Codell (1992), 'Sentiment, the Highest Attribute of Art: The Socio-Poetics of Feeling', in *Dickens Studies Annual*, vol. 21, pp. 233-251 and Gesa Stedman (2000), 'Pleasurable Pictures – The Delights of Visual Excess', in *REAL*, vol. 16, pp. 149-162.

51 'Middle class' and 'lower class' are of course shorthand expressions for much more complex forms of social stratification. For a discussion of these terms and what they refer to, cf. F.M.L. Thompson (1988), *The Rise of Respectable Society: A Social History of Victorian Britain, 1830-1900*, Fontana, London, p. 16ff. and chapter 4 of this study.

whole field. Admittedly, the pleasure of having a whole field before me also encouraged me to attempt a bird's eye view of Victorian emotionology, rather than a close-up of what have turned out to be the specific obsessions of the Victorian writers on the feelings: affection, selfishness, pride, and anger.

In order to arrive at such a comprehensive view it was necessary to use not only a trans-disciplinary approach but also a broad text- and source-basis. As the discourses on emotions are never restricted to merely one type of text but always comprise a hybrid mixture of different topics (morality, health, religion, politics etc.) and their respective genres it would have been inappropriate to limit the analysis to only one such genre. The catalogue of the British Library lists hundreds of entries with titles using 'emotion', 'passion', 'sentiment' etc. for the period analysed here.[52] One can find popular versions of *Sense and Sensibility* in novels such as *Passion and Principle*; conduct books teaching the *Education of the Heart*; scientific studies investigating *Mind and Emotion in Relation to Health and Disease*; poems and lectures on *The Poetry of the Feelings*, and precursors of coffee table books sporting titles such as *The Sentiments of Flowers* or *Gems of Beauty ... Engravings of the Passions*. I have selected representative examples of all these genres. Their diversity is itself an expression of the topic's complex nature, or as Elizabeth Barrett superscribes her long poem 'An Essay on Mind' (1826) with the Spenser-quotation heading this chapter: it is a discourse too 'large' to be contained in just one study.

Although I have included both texts by male and female authors in this study, the novels I have analysed are mainly written by women. The reasons for this are two-fold: firstly, texts from almost all other genres I have studied, with the exception of conduct books, were written by male authors who dominated the literary field of non-fiction in the 19th century. Because I wanted to include what women writers thought about the emotions, I had to use the genre in which they were prominent in the Victorian period, to gain access to their views. But more importantly perhaps, the Victorian discourses on emotions themselves argue the case

[52] The discourses on emotions include more than just texts which explicitly name the feelings in their title. However, due to the amount of available material, one way of selecting appropriate texts has been the search for keywords in the title, i.e. emotion, passion, sentiment, feeling, and affection. I have nevertheless included other relevant works, even though the titles may not initially indicate any relation to the discourses on emotions.

for women writers (albeit in paradoxical fashion). Because women were thought to be more emotional than men some (male and female) writers thought they should also write about them, to fulfil their roles as superior 'educators of the heart'. The final chapter on emotional paradigm scenarios focuses largely on novels written by women and shows how women made use of the separate spheres argument to push the boundaries of the discourses on emotions.

The most various types of texts share fundamental characteristics and concerns, requiring an approach encompassing these similarities, without, of course, overlooking significant differences between, e.g., a popular health guide, a serious scientific study, and a novel. These differences do not, however, justify relegating the non-fictional works to the murky notion of 'cultural context'.[53] Both types of texts form part of the 'large' discourses on emotions and non-fictional texts are closely related to fictional ones, for reasons to be discussed later.

Distinguishing fiction from non-fiction is a notoriously difficult task. I have decided upon a pragmatic approach. Since attempts to find absolute distinctions between both types of texts have consistently failed, it might be more profitable to use a scale model. While it may be possible to classify a text intuitively as prototypically fictional or non-fictional, the majority will lie somewhere in between and evince either more or fewer characteristics of the one or the other prototype. Characteristics of texts (sometimes differentiated according to 'signals' and 'features' of fictionality) are not inherent and cannot be fixed once and for all. Whether a text is written and then read as fiction or non-fiction depends on the context in which it is produced and consumed. The different readership and the uses to which they are put distinguish fictional from non-fictional texts, while their usual differentiating feature, referentiality, has come to play a somewhat subordinate role in recent discussions of fictionality. In the 19th century, the book-market did distinguish between fiction and non-fiction. Novels and poetry were reviewed in one section in periodicals, and works of non-fiction were discussed in another part. But periodicals reviewed

---

53 For this problem cf. Tony Bennett (1990), *Outside Literature*, Routledge, London/New York, Jean Starobinski (1974), 'La littérature. Le texte et l'interprète', in Jacques Le Goff and Pierre Nora (eds), *Faire de l'histoire*, vol. 2, Gallimard, Paris, pp. 225-244 and the view shared by many New Historicists that '... literary and non-literary "texts" circulate inseparably ...', as Harold A. Veeser (1989) put it in his introduction to the essay collection *The New Historicism*, Routledge, London/New York, pp. ix-xvi, quotation p. xi.

both types of text in one volume, and publishing houses, e.g. the Longman firms in London, had fiction and non-fiction on their list. Historically, the overlap between both types of texts can be explained by the overall didacticism which is so characteristic of much Victorian book production, fictional or non-fictional. Aims and readership of many publications used for this book are related. Nevertheless, a doctor or a scientist writing for a specialist and a general public is not the same as a novelist producing mass fiction. For a start, their educational background and resources would have been different. And even though they may have shared a general didactic aim, novelists were obviously tied more to this objective because of the precarious reputation of their preferred genre. That referentiality played an important part in the Victorian period, even though it may have lost its uses as a distinguishing feature of texts for modern readers, is obvious from the criticism that reviewers directed at novelists who produced 'impossible' characters and unlikely plots. The success of Dickens's notoriously improbable plots goes some way against this: obviously, readers liked some unlikely plots but not others, or rather: if characterisation was ineffectual and the writing got out of control, then improbable plots were criticised.

For the purposes of this book, the similarities between fictional and non-fictional texts are most important. The shared use of language and metaphor, the recurrence of typical plot structures and devices count more than the differences. In particular since the differences between an allegedly 'true' medical case story presented in a dramatic mode, and a 'fictional' sub-plot in a novel intended to teach the reader the same moral, namely a balanced approach to the feelings, recede into the background as soon as the texts' function becomes the central object of interest.[54]

In each chapter, I have set a few key texts in relation to the general rules governing the discourse, with the aim of providing sufficient contextualisation for each individual text, explaining its links with the discourses on emotions as a whole, and distinguishing between discursive patterns and an individual text which may subvert or affirm these patterns. Important elements and analytical categories which make up these patterns are shared metaphors, the role of the body, narrative patterns and devices, recurrent types of character and plot, and most of all the overall problem of

---

[54] For an overview of the debate on fiction and non-fiction, and the suggestion of a scale model to distinguish the two, see Klaus W. Hempfer (1990), 'Zu einigen Problemen einer Fiktionstheorie', in *Zeitschrift für französische Sprache und Literatur*, vol. 100, pp. 109-137.

emotional expression and control. Such a movement between a more abstract or general level, and a more detailed analysis of a given text allows an individual work to come to life without simply using it to illustrate an argument. Conversely, placing individual works in a context of general discursive patterns allows an understanding of the rules of the discourse which may work 'behind' an author's back but might easily be overlooked if a more traditional author-and-text approach is chosen. Moreover, such an alternation between 'close-ups' and 'long-shots' opens up a vista both on general historical developments and on period-specific characteristics of the discourses on emotions.

Because the texts which constitute the Victorian discourses on the feelings share so many features, I have sometimes presented only a summary analysis of a given topic, e.g. the use of recurrent metaphors or similar plots, so as not to tire the reader with endless and repetitive page references. Whenever this is the case, the similarities by far outweigh the differences one can find in the texts. In one case, I have also desisted from presenting a complete analysis: Alexander Bain's various editions of *The Emotions and the Will* are too voluminous to be examined adequately and at length, but in order to make up for the neglect of certain of his chapters, I have used it throughout as a general reference text against which I have tested my hypotheses. That is the reason for the scattered appearances of *The Emotions and the Will* in this study.

Wherever possible, information on a text's publishing history has been included because this illustrates who had access to the text and helps to contextualise historically my analysis of the discourses on emotions. To quote John Sutherland: 'There is ... no Victorian novel ... which was not materially influenced by the publishing system, for good or ill.'[55] This, I would argue, is equally true not just of novels but of any text.[56]

---

55 John Sutherland (1976), *Victorian Novelists and Publishers*, Athlone Press, London, p. 6.

56 Because publishing history and the individual history of authors are closely linked, I have also added bio-bibliographical notes on all but a very few authors, collected in the appendix. Biographies of the following authors (some of which are only mentioned briefly) have not been included: Matthew Arnold, Jane Austen, Elizabeth Barrett Browning, Charlotte Brontë, Thomas Carlyle, Joseph Conrad, Charles Darwin, Charles Dickens, George Eliot, Felicia Hemans, John Keble, Letitia Elizabeth Landon, George Henry Lewes, John Stuart Mill, Samuel Smiles, Herbert Spencer, and William Wordsworth.

The twin forces of continuity and change: Periodisation

Another notoriously difficult problem to be broached is the question of how best to divide the 19th century into sub-periods. For the purposes of this book, a rigid division is not very helpful.[57] Although social and political developments can be distinguished and I would not want to argue for complete continuity throughout the long 19th century, a fairly neutral period division into 'early', 'mid' and 'late' 19th century seems to work best. These adjectives relate most of all to the century's decades, and are not meant to refer to any specific characteristics of these decades. The discourses on emotions are marked so much by discursive continuity that any fixed division of the century would run counter to my findings. Following Marc Bloch, it is the object of historical inquiry which should provide the period division we choose rather than any consideration external to this object.[58] But the scope of this study is nevertheless limited. The majority of my texts fall into the period between 1830 and 1872, with some references to earlier publications if they proved to be influential. Charles Darwin's study *The Expression of the Emotions in Man and Animals* was published in 1872. It constitutes a new departure and was to be a seminal text for the years to come. Although it still contains some moral judgements and references to fictional texts, it sets a new agenda: evolution and physiology are the key terms which were to become influential for both fictional and non-fictional texts on the emotions. Darwin's materialist study, with its minute attention to the body and juxtaposition of humans and animals, was read widely by fellow scientists and writers of fiction. But for all the paradigmatic quality of his study, change in the discourses on emotions should not be overemphasised. A constant fixation with historical change identifies us as victims of an

---

57 Samuel Chew and Richard Altick suggest a division into 'early' and 'late' Victorianism in Samuel Chew and Richard Altick (^{2}1967), *The Nineteenth Century and After (1789-1939)* (A Literary History of England, vol. 4, ed by Albert Croll Baugh), Appleton-Century-Crofts, New York, p. 1279. See also Madden (1963-64), 'Victorian Sensibility', for a discussion of period divisions. The term 'Victorian' is used in this study although it may imply too unified an approach to a century which saw exceptional and rapid change and diversity in living and working conditions. Nevertheless it is possible to establish a coherent notion of the Victorian discourses on emotions which justifies such a unifying expression. For stylistic reasons I use it interchangeably with the expression '19th century'.

58 'C'est à ces phénomènes mêmes qu'il convient de demander leurs propres périodes'. Marc Bloch (1997), *Apologie pour l'histoire ou Métier d'historien*, ed by Etienne Bloch, Armand Collin, Paris [1993] [1941], p. 150.

exaggerated modernism which cannot view stasis or relative lack of transformation within a culture or society as interesting in itself. In this book, therefore, I have stressed the absence of change within the discourses on emotions more than transformation and have read this relative lack of change as expressive of the dilemmas which beset the Victorians. Further studies will show if and when a transition between the 19th and the 20th centuries occurred.[59]

Since the discourses on the feelings are closely related to topical political events such as the danger of revolutionary masses losing control of their 'passions', a promising period seemed to be the first half of the 19th century with its considerable political, social, and cultural unrest. But the first half of the 19th century is not as innovative in inventing new emotion concepts as preceding centuries, e.g. the late medieval and early modern (re)discovery of the self and its relation to the 'passions'[60] or the 18th-century 'invention' of a special 'aesthetic' organ and a moral sense.[61] What is characteristic of the discourses on emotions is also reflected in the wider social sphere. As the social historian F.M.L. Thompson puts it:

> ... Reform essentially glanced backward with an approving eye on the traditional order which it sought to buttress, and the railway pointed forward into the unknown territory of urbanized and industrialized society. Therein lies the kernel of the message: not that 1830 was some decisive turning-point and outstanding landmark in social history, but that it stood in a particularly prominent way at the crossroads between the traditional and the new, neatly demonstrating the twin forces of continuity and change that are always at work in society.[62]

---

59 Cf. Wood (2001), *Passion and Pathology*, on the increasing dominance of medical and physiological explanations at the expense of moral and philosophical ones in the course of the 19th century.

60 Cf. Marion Müller (1999), *'These Savage Beasts Become Domestick': The Discourse of the Passions in Early Modern England with Special Reference to Non-fictional Texts*, D.Phil. Thesis, unpublished ms., University of Oxford.

61 Cf. Jürgen Schlaeger (1999), 'The Politics of Taste', in Schlaeger and Stedman (eds), *Representations*, p. 77ff. For 18th-century developments see also Walter Göbel (1996), 'Conflicting Definitions of the Culture of Sensibility', in Jürgen Klein and Dirk Vanderbeke (eds), *Anglistentag 1995 Greifswald. Proceedings. XVII*, Max Niemeyer Verlag, Tübingen, pp. 93-104 who also argues for a 'micro' approach to emotions history, focusing on shorter time spans, Klaus P. Hansen's (1990) collection of essays *Empfindsamkeiten* (Passauer Interdisziplinäre Kolloquien, vol. 2), Wissenschaftsverlag Richard Rothe, Passau and Janet Todd (1986), *Sensibility: An Introduction*, Methuen, London.

62 Thompson (1988), *The Rise of Respectable Society*, p. 13.

The Victorian discourses on emotions discuss concerns which predate the 19th century, thereby showing how much these discourses are commanded less by rapid change but are rather a phenomenon of *longue durée*. The fondness of 18th-century authors for benevolence and 'moral sentiments' are taken up by their Victorian successors, as are an interest in controlling the passions of crowds following the French Revolution, and the Romantic fascination with feeling as a means of 'authentic' individuality and a requirement for (poetic) genius, as well as the anxious reaction against Romanticism. Nevertheless, occasional but significant departures did occur in the 19th century. Questions of gender rose higher on the public agenda with the close association of the emotions and the separate spheres debate which climaxed in the 1830s and 40s; with the advent of mass culture and as one consequence of industrialisation the obsession with individual and public health moved centre stage in the discussion of the emotions and the body, both individual and social; the new mode of dealing with the feelings in a strictly materialist context of evolutionary physiology was heralded by Charles Darwin; a specifically middle class habitus was created and maintained by using the emotions as a means of social distinction; the staple ingredients of the discourses on emotions such as morality and religion received lengthy attention in relation to this habitus; and the fashionable notion of the English nation's alleged superiority gained considerably in status and was used to simultaneously subvert and affirm the notion of a stable 'English' middle class habitus. These seemingly unrelated and varying concerns, closely linked to the Victorian obsession with sexuality, madness, and health, come together in the central problematic which governs this period's discourses on the feelings: how to provide for an (imaginative) space for the emotions while simultaneously remaining in control of them.

2 Emotion vocabularies: The History and Usage of Key Emotion Words

The language of the passions: 19th-Century Emotion Words

One way of entering the intricate maze of the Victorian discourses on emotions is to take a look at the history and use of recurrent key emotion words.[1] After some general remarks on 'the language of the passions' in the 19th century, there follows an account of the etymological history of the six most frequently used emotion words – affection, feeling, emotion, passion, sensibility and sentiment – on the basis of their respective entries in the Oxford English Dictionary and a number of other sources.[2] By

---

[1] Cf. Raymond Williams (1988) [1983] [1976], 'Introduction', in id., *Keywords. A Vocabulary of Culture and Society*. rev. and exp. ed., Fontana Press, London p. 15.

[2] For the short overview of each term's history I have compared the relevant entry in the *OED* with the entries in the following dictionaries and encyclopaedias, merely a selection and not a comprehensive list, and with representative examples from the most important genres dominant in the 19th-century discourses on emotion (cf. chapter 1): *Encyclopædia: or, an Universal Dictionary of Arts and Sciences (Chambers)*, R. and W. Chambers, London 1728; *The Complete Dictionary of Arts and Sciences in Which the Whole Circle of Human Learning is Explained ... (Croker's Dictionary)*, J. Wilson etc., London etc. 1766; *Encyclopædia Britannica*, A. Bell and C. Macfarquhar, Edinburgh [3]1788-1797; Richard Reece (1808), *A Practical Dictionary of Domestic Medicine Comprising the Latest Discoveries Relative to the Causes, Treatment, and Prevention of Diseases*, Longman, Hurst, Rees, and Orme, London; *The Oxford Encyclopædia; or, Dictionary of Arts, Sciences, and General Literature*, printed for Thomas Kelley, Oxford/London 1828; *The Penny Cyclopædia of The Society for the Diffusion of Useful Knowledge*, Charles Knight, London 1833-58; *Encyclopædia Britannica*, A. and C. Black, Edinburgh [7]1830-42; *Encyclopædia Britannica*, A. and C. Black, Edinburgh [8]1853-1860; *The Household Encyclopædia; or Family Dictionary on Everything Connected with Housekeeping and Domestic Medicine ...*, 2 vols., W. Kent, London 1858; *Chambers's Encyclopædia. A Dictionary of Universal Knowledge for the People ...*, W. and R. Chambers, London 1862; *Chambers's English Dictionary. Pronouncing, Explanatory, and Etymological ...* W. and R. Chambers, London/Edinburgh 1872; D. Hack Tuke (ed) (1892), *A Dictionary of Psychological Medicine ...*, J. and A. Churchill,

comparing these sources with my corpus of texts, I have been able to establish the frequency of use of these keywords and the genres in which they tend to appear, the words' most common semantic contexts and semantic shifts in the discourses on emotions. The keywords in their specific semantic surroundings work as 'veiled instructions', as miniature feeling rules. As discursively contextualised lexeme combinations the keywords perform what the central paradigm scenario in Victorian texts on the emotions is about: the ambivalent nature of emotional expression and control, continuity and change.[3]

Many of the six keywords are still in (everyday) use at the beginning of the 21st century. A first task therefore lies in establishing the distinction between 19th-century meanings and contexts of use as opposed to our contemporary understanding of these terms.[4] The linguistic overlap is exacerbated by the fact that most Victorian writers used the majority of the above-mentioned words synonymously. This makes it even harder to differentiate between them, and it entails the danger of forgetting entirely that the meanings of the words were subject to change. The following passage, taken from Charles Bell's popular *The Anatomy and Philosophy of Expression as Connected with the Fine Arts* (1806/44), is a typical example for the synonymous use of key emotion words:

> In the *affections* which we call *passions* or *emotions*, there is an influence which points to the breast as the part where they are felt. Some have asserted that they are seated in the bowels; and the *sensations* I am about to describe have been

---

London; George Black (1892), *The Family Health Book*, Ward, Lock & Co, London; James Sully (1892), *Outlines of Psychology*, new ed., revised and largely rewritten, Longmans, Green, and Co., London; F. Ryland (^{7}1897), *Psychology. An Introductory Manual for the Use of Students*, revised and largely rewritten, George Bell and Sons, London.

3 The expression 'veiled instruction' is taken from James R. Averill (1990), 'Inner feelings, works of the flesh, the beast within, diseases of the mind, driving force, and putting on a show: Six Metaphors of Emotion and Their Theoretical Extensions', in David E. Leary (ed), *Metaphors in the History of Psychology*, Cambridge UP, Cambridge, pp. 104-132, quotation p. 119. Cf. also Helmut Bonheim (1999), 'Die Variable Geschlecht im Wortschatz der Emotionen', in Andrea Gutenberg and Ralf Schneider (eds), *Gender – Culture – Poetics. Zur Geschlechterforschung in der Literatur- und Kulturwissenschaft (Festschrift für Natascha Würzbach)*, WVT, Trier, pp. 31-46 and Williams, *Keywords*, p. 21f.

4 Although I am aware that 'word', 'term', and 'lexeme' are not true synonyms I will use them as such in this chapter.

arrayed as proofs that the *affections* exist in the body. But that, I affirm, is impossible. They are *conditions of the mind*, and cannot be seated in the body, although they both influence and are influenced by it.[5] (My emphasis, G.S.)

I am inclined to agree with the Reverend H.L. Mansel, author of the article on 'Metaphysics' in the eighth edition of the *Encyclopædia Britannica* (1857), when he complains about this practice:

> Hitherto we have used the words *passion* and *emotion* as synonymous. ... To distinguish, indeed, between these terms, in strict accordance either with philosophical or general usage, is out of the question; for scarcely any two writers or speakers are in all respects consistent with each other. Sometimes emotion is a species of passion; sometimes passion is a species of emotion; sometimes the two terms are used as exactly synonymous; and at others the word *passion* is used to designate a violent degree of emotion.[6]

A further difficulty one encounters in 19th-century discourses on the emotions, a phenomenon which can still be observed in 20th-century texts on the feelings,[7] is the pronounced tendency to 'fix' the feelings by

---

5 Charles Bell (^{3}1844) [1806], *The Anatomy and Philosophy of Expression as Connected with the Fine Arts*, John Murray, London, p. 84. Bell is aware of the ambiguity of the terms 'emotion', 'passion' and 'sentiment', and therefore decides to limit his investigation to 'mental excitement' which results in physical expression (p. 145). But since he then proceeds to use the keywords interchangeably again to designate all kinds of emotional states, this insight is lost. Further examples of synonymous use can be found in Alexander Bain's (^{2}1865) [1859] *The Emotions and the Will*, Longmans & Co., London, e.g. on p. 70, p. 96 and p. 101. This kind of word use is not restricted to non-fictional texts. One can observe a similar technique of word clustering in novels which also often use several emotion words in close proximity, e.g. in the following passage from Dinah Mulock Craik's (1996) [1850] novel *Olive*, Oxford UP, Oxford: 'And they were so young and *impassioned*, so quickly wed and so soon parted, that this *emotion* had no time to deepen into that soul-united *affection* which is independent of outward semblance ...' (p. 14). (My emphasis, G.S.). Further examples: Geraldine Jewsbury (1994) [1848], *The Half-Sisters*, Oxford UP, Oxford/New York, p. 65, p. 91, p. 223, p. 320.

6 *The Encyclopædia Britannica* (^{8}1857), vol. 14, p. 579.

7 20th-century definitions can be just as inconsistent or arbitrary as 19th-century examples. The only aspect that these attempts at classification reveal is how difficult it is to give a sound theoretical base to the 'scientific' analysis of the emotions. Cf. e.g. the otherwise useful overview of sociological theories of the emotions by Peggy A. Thoits (1989), 'The Sociology of Emotions', in *American Review of Sociology*, vol. 15, pp. 317-341. She attempts to determine emotionality by using different categories,

defining and classifying them. Attempting to come to terms with the emotions by inventing sets of definitions and classes of feelings is a practice which has been a staple ingredient of the discourses on emotions through the ages.[8] The arbitrary distinctions drawn between feelings, emotions, affections, passions, and sentiments make it difficult to untangle the 19th-century use of key emotion words. They also indicate how problematic it has always been to express in words what seems simultaneously to exceed and to subvert verbal representation. The excessive nature of these classification exercises, which are not restricted to the emotions, can be explained by the increasingly positivist and objectivist tendencies in 19th-century science.[9]

Different classification methods can be found in various genres. Proceeding from the Aristotelian concept of pleasure and pain, Alexander Bain's serious scientific investigation *The Emotions and the Will* (1859) distinguishes eleven so-called 'families of emotions', all containing 'pleasures and pains ... just as the natural orders of plants may each contain food and poison, sweet aromas and nauseating stinks'.[10] A more popular work is Robert Tyas's *The Sentiments of Flowers* (1836), which contains the enormous and self-defeating amount of over 200 different 'sentiments' and their respective floral representations, thus putting the viability of Tyas's method of classification into question. In similar fashion, the professor for elocution and vocal physiology, Alexander Melville Bell, lists everything from abhorrence, absence, and acquiescence to warmth, warning, yielding, and zealousness in his book of elocutionary exercises entitled *The Language of the Passions* (1852). The literary extracts are intended as examples for emotions whose expression needs to be

---

distinguishing feelings and affects from moods and sentiments. The latter are alleged to be more specific terms which refer to lasting and less intensive emotions and to socially constructed perception patterns (p. 318f.).

8 Cf. Marion Müller (1999), *'These Savage Beasts Become Domestick': The Discourse of the Passions in Early Modern England with Special Reference to Non-fictional Texts*, D.Phil. Thesis, University of Oxford, unpublished ms., on the medieval and early modern discourses on emotions and its debt to Greek and Roman notions of the feelings, in particular chapter 1 'Homo interior / Homo exterior', pp. 22-70.

9 See Lorraine Daston (1998), 'Die Kultur der wissenschaftlichen Objektivität', in Otto Gerhard Oexle (ed), *Naturwissenschaft, Geisteswissenschaft, Kulturwissenschaft: Einheit – Gegensatz – Komplementarität?*, Wallstein Verlag, Göttingen, pp. 9-39 on the development of 19th-century science and its dependence on 'objectivity'.

10 Bain (^{2}1865), *The Emotions and the Will*, p. 39f.

practised.[11] Many more such examples of classification methods can be found and quite obviously they help little towards a clearer concept of the emotions but say much about the pressing concerns Victorian writers had to come to terms with whenever they broached emotional topics. The attempts at establishing clear-cut boundaries between specific emotions, the wide-spread tendency to establish hierarchies of feeling, and the – from a modern perspective – often pseudo-scientific manner in which these largely ineffective classification exercises are undertaken are important elements of the central expression-and-control paradigm in the Victorian discourses on emotions.[12] While the definitions and 'dry nomenclature'[13] function as an attempt at controlling the emotions on the discursive or referential level, their excessive nature equally signifies the futility of such an exercise: it seems impossible to tie the emotions down linguistically, apparently distinct meanings are blurred and the initial attempt at separating them is thwarted because the words are all used to explain each other, thus collapsing all the linguistic and conceptual boundaries which were initially set up to differentiate them.[14]

---

11 Another author obsessed with classification is Charles Bray. In the various editions of his educational treatise *The Education of the Feelings*, first published in 1838, he changes his phrenological classification system several times and seems to be undecided how to establish a hierarchy of feelings.

12 Charles Darwin (1872) takes up Spencer's 'definition' of feelings, sensations and emotions in *The Expression of the Emotions in Man and Animals*, John Murray, London. According to Darwin's concept of Spencerian emotion, emotions are synonymous with feelings, while sensations are said to be 'generated in our corporeal framework' (p. 27). But the following discussion of 'emotions' shows that their physical basis is Darwin's main point of interest, indicating that he does not in fact distinguish emotion, feeling and sensation. In *The Education of the Feelings*, printed for Taylor & Walton, London, and Adam & Charles Black, Edinburgh, Charles Bray (^{1}1838) e.g. speaks of 'higher feelings' and 'superior faculties' which, although less dangerous than mere passion, still require control from the 'intellect' and 'obedience to the will of God' (p. 93). In his chapter on the feelings in *The Study of Sociology*, Kegan Paul, Trench & Co, London, Herbert Spencer (^{13}1887) also sets up a hierarchy of 'moral sentiments' with justice as the most elevated and abstract emotion, unattainable to women because they are said to be influenced too much by feeling (p. 374ff.).

13 Charles Bray finally abandons the excessive account of phrenological 'sentiments' in the third edition of his treatise, arguing that such a 'dry nomenclature' makes the text too difficult to understand for a general readership. Cf. Bray (^{3}1860), *The Education of the Feelings*, Longman & Co., London, p. 68.

14 A small number of authors seemed to have been aware of the problem and explicitly refer to the difficulties inherent in any definition. Nevertheless, their subsequent explanations usually then revert to established synonymous use of emotion words, as is

My keyword analysis has brought to light that Victorian writers were less innovatory than their predecessors. Instead of coining new words for the feelings, they continued to use every emotion word which had come into existence by the 19th century. Thus one finds the older term 'passion' alongside 'feeling' or 'emotion', making the words appear to be virtually interchangeable. Only when one pays attention to the keywords in their semantic surroundings can one detect differences between them. This linguistic fact indicates the relative continuity which marks the discourses on emotions in the 19th century. Whether linguistic continuity can also be read as an indication of the continuity of actual emotional experience and behaviour is a question difficult to answer without support from further, extra-linguistic sources.[15] But for all the appearance of sameness, in the

---

the case in the article on 'passion' in the seventh edition of the *Encyclopædia Britannica* (1830-42), which acknowledges the imprecise meaning of the word and then goes on to use 'feeling of the mind', 'affection' and 'passion' as virtual synonyms, and adding to the confusion by also using 'desires' and 'dispositions' as further emotion words to explain the meaning of 'passion'. It is only the late-19th-century psychologists James Sully and Frank Ryland who, in their respective text books, openly acknowledge the impossibility of distinguishing clearly between the different emotion words. Sully (1892), *Outlines of Psychology*, p. 351, and Ryland (1897), *Psychology*, p. 214, p. 228, p. 234ff. In the third edition to *The Senses and the Intellect*, Longmans, Green, and Co., London, Alexander Bain (1868) discusses the problem of definitions, and explains that he discarded 'emotion' as his generic term, to be replaced by 'feeling', but that he continued to use 'emotional' as the adjective for both, thus adding to the confusion (Appendix, p. 668).

15 John R. Gillis (1988), 'From Ritual to Romance. Toward an Alternative History of Love', in Carol Z. Stearns and Peter N. Stearns (eds), *Emotion and Social Change: Toward a New Psychohistory*, Holmes & Meier, New York/Oxford, pp. 87-121, and Joan DeJean (1997), 'A Short History of the Heart', in id. *Ancients Against Moderns: Culture Wars and the Making of a Fin de Siècle*, University of Chicago Press, Chicago, pp. 80-123, as well as Helmut Bonheim (1980), 'Word Invention and the History of Affect', in Gunter Brettschneider and Christian Lehmann (eds), *Wege zur Universalienforschung (Festschrift für Hansjakob Seiler)*, Gunter Narr, Tübingen, pp. 521-528, all explictly state that in their opinion changes in a period's emotionology imply a change in actual emotional perception and behaviour. Rom Harré (1986), 'An Outline of the Social Constructionist Viewpoint', in id. (ed), *The Social Construction of Emotions*, Basil Blackwell, Oxford, pp. 2-14 seems to be of a similar opinion when he says that from the culturally diverse emotional vocabularies follows the diversity of emotions themselves (p. 10). I would fully agree with the latter statement on the diversity of emotions; whether such a simple link can, however, be established between emotion vocabularies and actual perception and behaviour is another matter. Cf. Heiner Schultz (1979), 'Begriffsgeschichte und Argumentationsgeschichte', in Reinhart Koselleck (ed), *Historische Semantik und Begriffsgeschichte*, Klett-Cotta, Stuttgart, pp. 43-74, and

Victorian discourses on the feelings the six keywords are not only used with subtle shades of meaning, one can even detect slight semantic shifts in comparison to 18th-century usage.

19th-century attempts at defining and classifying the emotions do not help much in determining the meaning and usage of the six keywords enumerated above. But Victorian 'emotion vocabularies' (Harré) can be differentiated from earlier and later usage by looking less at individual emotion words but rather at their semantic contexts and the ways certain lexemes are combined.[16] Linguistic patterns of usage, word clusters, and consciously or unconsciously applied discursive rules emerge which, although they may only differ slightly from each other and from earlier patterns, reveal which emotion concepts dominated in the period. Metaphors are of particular relevance in this context, as will become clearer in this and the following chapter.

Such a broader approach to *Begriffsgeschichte* shows how semantic shifts occur, and how semantic elements which are no longer relevant for an individual word can still be present in the wider discursive context in which one encounters the term. Thus, although the word 'emotion' has by the early 19th century long shed its older meaning of political upheaval, this notion is subliminally present in the 19th-century discourses on emotions because the threat of revolutionary emotional masses is constantly evoked whenever the dangers of unbridled passion are mentioned. The reason for this lies in the need for social distinction which the Victorian opinion makers, the middle classes, assert again and again, by characterising everybody 'below' them as a dangerous and impassioned 'mob'.

But even such a contextualised analysis naturally entails certain methodological problems, inherent in all attempts at *Begriffsgeschichte*.[17]

Williams's (1988) 'Introduction' to *Keywords*, pp. 11-26 on the problem of word change and conceptual and behavioural change, as well as Williams's contention that 'language [does not] simply reflect [ ] the processes of society and history. On the contrary, ... some important social and historical processes occur *within* language ...' ('Introduction', *Keywords*, p. 22).

16 Harré (1986), 'An Outline', p. 4f., and DeJean (1997), 'A Short History', also suggest the concept of 'clustering'. Both authors are obviously indebted to Raymond Williams's (1988) seminal *Keywords* which introduces the term 'cluster' and stresses the 'interconnections' between words (p. 22) but only DeJean explicitly states this.

17 On the methodological problems see Schultz (1979), 'Begriffsgeschichte'. For a recent discussion cf. Franz-Hubert Robling (1995), 'Probleme begriffsgeschichtlicher

Analysing the history of a given word does not automatically provide an insight into the related concept. This can only be achieved by contextualising the word in its more immediate semantic surroundings, as well as taking into account the wider discursive context that a term is found in (author/narrator, genre, readership). My selection of texts, i.e. a comparison between dictionary articles with scientific, popular non-fictional, and fictional texts, would perhaps normally be considered insufficient, since less formal usage of words (in letters and diaries and the like) has not been taken into account. Lastly, the discourses on emotions contain more than just six key emotion words so that an analysis of such terms as benevolence, pity, pride, or love, would be equally valid and relevant to this study's over-all topic.[18] In general, an analysis of keywords will only provide an insight into explicit discussions of certain feelings, but will not help towards an understanding of a text's or an author's implicit concept of the emotions, possibly contained in passages which do not use any of the keywords. Again, it is emotion metaphors, in particular those which do not use any of the six emotion words, which can be more revealing than the keywords used in isolation.

In spite of these reservations and the acknowledgement that much work remains to be done in terms of quantity and quality of the analysis, some insights can be gained from the history and use of the following six key emotions words.

Forschung beim Historischen Wörterbuch der Rhetorik', in *Archiv für Begriffs-geschichte*, vol. 38, pp. 9-22, and for a critical approach to historical semantics cf. Anna Wierzbicka (1986), 'Human Emotions: Universal or Culture-Specific?', in *American Anthropologist*, vol. 88, pp. 584-594.

18 In fictional texts in particular discussions of emotional behaviour are not restricted to certain keywords. Instead, metaphors or rarer emotion words are used to render the texts more interesting and varied. This variety, however, depends on the authors' ability to write, i.e. a popular novel relying to a large extent on common phrases such as the novel *Passion and Principle* (1842/53) shows less linguistic diversity than Charlotte Brontë's (1849) *Shirley*. That the use of metaphors and original turns of phrase is not restricted to fictional texts can for instance be illustrated by the poetic quality of Bain's (1859) *The Emotions and the Will*.

Social and historical processes occur within language: The History of Six Key Emotion Words

The two oldest terms in my selection of emotion words are the lexemes 'feeling' and 'passion'. According to the *OED* the former goes back to the early 12th century, denoting the faculty or power by which one feels. It is therefore not surprising that on the basis of a rough count 'feeling' is the word which one encounters most frequently in any 19th-century text on the emotions, followed by 'emotion', 'affection' and 'passion'. 'Sentiment' and 'sensibility' are used more rarely, and often with more specific meanings.[19]

As this brief etymological section will show, the early modern era and especially the 18th century were crucial periods during which semantic shifts and expansions of meaning for key emotion terms took place.[20] Although some Victorian dictionaries, handbooks or guides directed at the general public continued to define and use emotion words in an 18th-century manner, some significant departures are notable. While the seventh edition of the *Encyclopædia Britannica* (1830-42) still contains entries for most emotion words and also largely follows earlier editions, the eighth edition (1853-60) retains only the brief definition for 'affection' and radically cuts the articles on 'emotion', 'passion', 'sensibility' and 'sentiment'. Compared to the 18th-century editions this shows that the emphasis has shifted by the mid-19th century. The emotions and especially their successful (self)control were, although still an important topic, no longer of such pressing concern to all writers and dictionary compilers that they required separate articles but could be dealt with in

19 I have not attempted an accurate, statistically valid count of the six keywords since such a positivist approach would not only be as self-defeating as the 19th-century passion for endless classificatory schemes; as a decontextualized undertaking it would not yield sufficient insights into the Victorian discourses on emotions. For an account of the related changes of key emotion words in French see DeJean (1997), 'A Short History', in particular pp. 78-82.

20 Emotion historians have questioned the emphasis on 'watersheds' like the early modern period and the 18th century. Although the case for new departures and breaks with tradition, on both the emotionological and experiential level, can be overstated, the history of emotion words does seem to support the claims for key periods in which the discourses on emotions underwent visible change. Cf. Carol Z. Stearns and Peter N. Stearns (1988), 'Introduction', in id. (eds), *Emotion and Social Change: Toward a New Psychohistory*, Holmes & Meier, New York/Oxford, pp. 1-21, in particular pp. 1-6, Gillis (1988), 'From Ritual to Romance', pp. 87-121.

general overviews, for instance on 'metaphysics'.[21]

The reasons for word change are notoriously difficult to pinpoint and are often informed more by speculation than by certainty. It nevertheless seems plausible that feeling became the more prominent term in 19th-century usage because the importance of the self, of internal states, and of sensation became more and more pronounced throughout the 19th century. The influence of physiological and materialist accounts of the emotions required a word encompassing the aspect of 'sensation', inherent in the word feeling. An emphasis more on interiority than on passive impressions working on the individual externally, as implied by the word passion, called for a term allowing for just that kind of interior, allegedly individual psychological state. And finally, the religious overtones evoked by the word passion perhaps needed to be replaced by a more secular word in view of 19th-century religious doubts, which had already set in during the 18th century but which became more prominent after the turn of the century. The move towards a more and more secularised society, in spite of all evidence to the contrary which the popularity of the Oxford Movement and the influence of Nonconformism seem to imply, may have supported such linguistic change. That the term 'emotion' increases in usage in the 19th century may have been a consequence of its 'scientific' ring. This is probably due to its Latin etymology which lends a text (or its author) greater scientific credibility. It is also the newest emotion word in my set of keywords which can be used interchangeably with the other three, feeling, affection, and passion, and therefore perhaps needed longer to enter general usage. It only occurs with any great frequency in 19th-century scientific texts but since science was on the rise during the Victorian era, this may have helped the word on the way to its modern status as a generic term.

---

21 A further example of a greater confidence in writing about the emotions are the entries for my set of keywords in *Chambers's Encyclopædia* (1862) which, following Alexander Bain's lead, focus largely on emotion and expression in the context of pain and pleasure and no longer concentrate on the dangers of uncontrolled emotion. 'Passion' does not appear as an entry, 'feeling' refers to the main article on 'emotion' and while 'sensibility' is defined exclusively as a physiological term, 'sentiment' and 'sentimentality' do not merit separate entries.

Feeling

The above-mentioned meaning of 'feeling' as the faculty or power by which one feels is from the 14th century onwards supplemented by the notion of physical sensation or perception through the sense of touch or the general sensibility of the body. It is this meaning of the word which predominates in 18th- and 19th-century dictionaries and encyclopaedias. The *physical aspect*, also present in other emotion words, plays a significant part because it is the basis for the association between emotion and disease.

In the 15th century, a new meaning encompassing the condition of being emotionally affected can be identified. From that period onwards, the word acquires various different *'psychological' meanings*, e.g. it can refer to an emotion itself, in expressions such as 'a feeling of fear'. 'Feeling' meaning the emotions, susceptibilities, and sympathies in a collective sense only comes to prominence in the late 18th century. It is therefore not surprising that this semantic element only appears relatively late in 19th-century dictionaries and encyclopaedias. 'Feeling' rarely merits a separate entry but is nevertheless used as an explanatory term for 'passion', e.g. in the seventh edition of the *Encyclopædia Britannica* (1830-42). But it is in this psychological sense that the word is used most frequently in 19th-century health guides, conduct books, and novels.

The word began to be used as a *generic term* comprising sensation, desire, and emotion but excluding perception and thought in the early 19th century. This use predominates in 19th-century scientific texts dealing with the emotions. Most of these meanings remained current throughout the 19th century. The exception is the use of feeling as a synonym for *'opinion'* which only occurs very rarely, an example of a semantic shift where the partial meaning of the word does not reappear in the wider discursive context.

Emotion

The term 'emotion' appears more often in scientific texts in the 19th century than it does in fictional texts. It is nevertheless not a rare word, and, like 'feeling' and 'passion', it is used in a general sense to describe emotional states. It is a word which can only be traced back to the late 16th and early 17th century, and, in accordance with its etymology, the Latin term *movere*, it at first referred to a '*moving out*', to a migration or the transference from one place to another. The meaning of emotion as a 'moving, stirring, *agitation* in a physical sense', a late 17th-century addition, although obsolete today, is still sometimes used in early 19th-century texts. The transfer of meaning to the political sphere which I have already mentioned first occurs in the late 16th century.

Emotion as a *synonym for feeling and passion*, denoting a disturbance of mind, is a meaning which is most frequently encountered in 19th-century texts on the emotions and can be traced back to the mid-17th century. It is this sense on which Dr Johnson's dictionary (1755) focuses, the first to devote a separate entry to the term in my selection of dictionaries. The third and seventh editions of the *Encyclopædia Britannica* also concentrate their entries on the notion of an 'internal motion or agitation of the mind' but distinguish this from passions as being less strong and not followed by 'desire'. But again, the physical danger inherent in the discourses on emotions is emphasised.

The more specific *psychological meaning* of the term emotion seems to be, a rare occurrence, a 19th-century 'invention' and can be found mainly in 19th-century scientific texts. In this sense, emotion means mental feeling or affection and is distinguished from cognitive or volitional states of consciousness. The fact that many dictionaries (e.g. *The Household Encyclopædia* or the eighth edition of the *Encyclopædia Britannica*) do not devote separate entries to the word but nevertheless use it in their explanations of the passions is another illustration of the semantic proximity between most of the terms in my set of keywords.

Affection

The two meanings of affection, the one denoting a *representation of feeling*, the other being a *synonym of disease*, are both present in 19th-century texts on the emotions and in some cases, their meanings overlap. But the most general meaning of the term which relates it to the word 'passion' refers to the *idea of being affected or acted upon* or influenced by someone or something (mid-17th century). Being mentally moved or affected is a meaning which goes back as far as the 13th century, while the notion of an affection being a representation of a feeling or an emotion can be found in the early 17th century.

Earlier meanings *oppose affection to reason* in a similar manner to passion or lust but this use has become obsolete by the early 19th century at the latest, just as the idea of affection meaning a general state of mind or a *disposition* is no longer common. The notion of an affection signifying an *inclination* or a penchant for something or somebody can be traced back to the 14th century while the idea of affection denoting *animosity* or at least biased feeling is first found in the late 15th and mid-16th centuries respectively. These meanings seem to have become obsolete by the 19th century. Affection referring to a *bodily state* or an influence can be found in the early 16th century, as can the use of affection as another term for disease. Although in most dictionaries analysed here, writers focus more on the meaning of affection as inclination, they all mention its synonymous use as another term for disease, thus indicating how closely they associate the emotions with disease. The word is used in the same sense in 19th-century health guides while novelists mainly use 'affection' in the sense of feeling or attachment. The sense of affection as affectation is now obsolete but is still sometimes present in 19th-century usage, thus indicating the possibility of 'faking' feeling.

Passion

The fourth most frequent term to be encountered in 19th-century texts on the emotions is the word 'passion', used almost as often as affection and emotion. Its earliest meaning referred to the sufferings of pain and was at first exclusively used to denote *Christ's suffering* on the cross (12th century onwards). The general sense of suffering or affliction became obsolete before the 19th century and most 19th-century dictionary articles do not focus on the religious background of the term. But again this semantic shift is compensated for, in a way, by the religious elements to be found in the discourses on emotion as a whole, a topic discussed at greater length in the following chapters. Nevertheless, for some readers the religious meaning may have remained uppermost in their minds for a longer period than the history of the word 'passion' suggests.

'Passion' signifying a painful affection or a *disorder of the body* or some part of it was a meaning which originated in the late 14th century. This word use seems to have been common throughout the following centuries and can be found in 19th-century usage, again linking passion with illness, a dominant trend in Victorian texts. The notion of *passivity*, inherent in the term's etymology, as implied in the notion of passion denoting a condition of being acted upon by an external agency, is similar to the word 'affection'. This notion can be traced back to mid-14th-century sources and was still prevalent in the early 19th century. 'Passion' as an 'affection of the mind', as an *overpowering emotion*, the word's most important meaning in 19th-century texts, also came into use in the mid-14th century.

The important relation between passion and literature is illustrated by the fact that in their articles on the passions 18th-century dictionaries and encyclopaedias devote long passages to the role of literature. It is a subject which many Victorian treatises on the emotions and conduct books discuss as well.

Passion as another word for *strong sexual attraction*, sometimes rendered in the lexeme combination 'tender passion', the latter one of the few instances in which 'passion' is used in an unambiguously positive context in Victorian texts, first appears in the late 16th century. Finally, passion as another word for *anger* (early 16th century) is a meaning which is frequent in 19th-century texts whenever the alleged destructive character of passion is invoked. Writers of health guides use passion as their keyword, and this continues throughout the period studied here, in spite of the diminishing importance of the term for the discourse as a whole. Authors of sensation novels focusing on the effects of violent emotion also use the word passion as their most common keyword.

Sentiment

Sentiment first referred to a *personal experience* or one's own feeling (14th century), a meaning now obsolete but still present in 19th-century discourse. Sentiment as sensation, a *physical feeling*, or knowledge due to vague sensation also dates back to the 14th century and can very occasionally be found in 19th-century texts. Its meaning as *intellectual or emotional perception* can be dated to the same period while the notion of a mental attitude or *opinion* is a later development (early 17th century). This use is less frequent in the 19th century, again a semantic shift resulting in a specific meaning disappearing, but it does occasionally appear in novels.[22]

---

[22] E.g. in Charlotte Brontë's *Shirley* (1849) and in Rhoda Broughton's *Not Wisely But Too Well* (1867).

More common is the use of sentiment denoting a '*mental feeling*' or an emotion, the term's most frequent use in a variety of 19th-century genres. In the 17th and 18th centuries, sentiment often referred more specifically to love. From the mid-18th century onwards it could also refer to a *thought or reflection coloured by or proceeding from emotion*, while its more specific use by phrenologists as a *name for the faculties* concerned with emotion is of course a late 18th- and early 19th-century addition.[23] The phrenological use of the term extended specifically phrenological texts as can be illustrated for instance by S.O. Beeton's conduct book *Family Etiquette*. Beeton bases the section on 'Expression of Senses and Faculties' on the different 'sentiments' as defined by the phrenologists.[24]

The now chiefly derisive use of the term referring to an *excess of refined and tender emotion* dates back to the late 18th century and in the adjective 'sentimental' often carries this negative connotation in Victorian texts. The term's diminishing importance can be observed in the *Encyclopædia Britannica* which contains a long article on the sentiments (in particular in their relation to literature) in its third edition (1788-1797) but does not devote a separate entry at all to the word in its seventh and eighth editions. The same is true of *Chambers's Encyclopædia* (1862) while its counterpart, *Chambers's Dictionary* (1872), explains the term in the manner described above but then lists 'sentimental', 'sentimentalism' and 'sentimentality', thus focusing the attention on the affectation of 'fine feeling' rather than on the older meaning of 'a thought occasioned by feeling' or a feeling itself. Again, the problem of inauthentic feeling is stressed.

---

23 Bray's phrenological text *The Education of the Feelings* uses feeling as his keyword and restricts the use of the term sentiment to a very few instances. Either the word denotes some of the faculties the phrenologists considered important (in a table he copied with little alterations from George Combe, distinguishing 'propensities' which humans share with animals, from 'sentiments' denoting social feelings, and the 'intellectual faculties') or it is used for 'emotions' which Bray values more highly than others, e.g. justice, religious feelings etc.

24 Cf. S.O. Beeton (c. 1868), *Family Etiquette: A Complete Guide to Conversation, Parties, Travel, and the Toilette, with Hints on Domestic Affairs*, Ward, Lock, and Tyler, London, pp. 47-53.

Sensibility

A term with an even more specific meaning and one which is used only rarely until the middle of the 18th century is 'sensibility'. Its early meaning (14th century) as the *capability of sensual perception* is rare and now obsolete, but the meaning of the word as power of sensation or perception, or the *response of organs to stimuli* (early 15th century), is a use which can be found in 19th-century texts, especially in health guides. Its main meaning as the power or *faculty of feeling*, the capacity of sensation and emotion as distinguished from cognition and will, which first comes into use in the early 19th century, or the slightly earlier meaning as *emotional consciousness* (mid-18th century) are more important for Victorian texts.

A more specific meaning, but one relevant to the discourses on emotions, is the 18th- and 19th-century meaning of the term as a capacity for *refined emotion*, delicate sensitiveness of taste, readiness to feel compassion and be moved by the pathetic in literature or art. It is this aspect and its social elements, i.e. seeing sensibility as a mark of social distinction, which is a focus of many dictionary articles up to the middle of the 19th century and it is also this meaning which is most often used in other 19th-century texts. Again a convergence can be observed between the word's physiological meaning denoting perception and its social, aesthetic and moral aspects which make it an important, if rarer, term in 19th-century discourses on emotions.[25]

This brief overview has shown what authors of dictionary articles dealing with the emotions were mainly concerned with: the relation of body and mind, the notion of emotion as a kind of disease, the necessity of emotional expression which sits uneasily alongside the danger of inauthentic feeling or fake affection, and the possibility of using key emotion words to give verbal shape to apparently non-verbal, psychological phenomena. It is important to note that all these motifs originated long before Victorian writers entered the scene. In spite of the semantic shifts explained above, the discussion of pre-19th-century topics illustrates the relative continuity characteristic of the discourses on emotions in the 19th century.

---

[25] Cf. Williams's (1988) analysis of the latter two terms in *Keywords*, in particular for the social implications and the connections between the words.

Veiled instruction: Key Emotion Words and 19th-Century Semantic Contexts

Semantic shifts and changes in preference for certain individual keywords do not preclude recurrent lexeme combinations expressing familiar obsessions in the set of keywords as a whole: a dominant motif is the fear of losing control and the dangers to physical and mental health that the emotions are alleged to present to the individual and society, in addition to the shared conventions that govern the use of keywords, as well as their near-synonymous usage. Whether this semantic overlap (with the exception of sensibility which does not work as a synonym) can be read as the inability to delineate a discursive field, an 'object' of investigation, or rather as a positive assertion is debatable. Did Victorian authors fail to set up clear definitions because it was unnecessary? Or is it perhaps a futile exercise regardless of historical moments, one that even contemporary scholars have not performed in a satisfactory way? I am inclined towards the latter answer, although it might imply an 'essentialist' definition of emotion as inherently undefinable. Perhaps the reason for the unsatisfactory Victorian classification schemes lie in their rigidity which often disallow 'mixed emotions' (Bain) and blurred boundaries. These fuzzy borders can then only be expressed unintentionally, as it were, by the proximity of key emotion words.

The first of the conventions that determine the use of all keywords is their appearance in either a pejorative or 'positive' semantic context, the organising principle for such a binary distinction being the notion of pleasure and pain, the two categories into which all emotions are said to fall.[26] The pejorative 'selfish feeling' appears alongside 'pleasurable feelings', and 'sweetest feelings' can turn up in the same text as 'destructive feeling'. An 18th-century engraving, 'Weeping & Joy' from Timothy Bobbin's *The Passions Humourously Delineated* (1773), a series of caricatures popular during the 19th century, may serve to illustrate this fondness for the binary distinction between pleasure and pain as well as their inseparableness (fig. 2.1).[27]

---

26 Some authors also allow a third category, that of 'mixed emotion', which contains elements of both pleasure and pain. Cf. Bain (^{2}1865), *The Emotions and the Will*, p. 11.

27 'Timothy Bobbin' is the pseudonym of John Collier, a Lancashire writer. *The Passions Humourously Delineated* was republished with slight changes in 1810 and again in 1858. Cf. Diana Donald and Brian Maidment, *Human Passions Delineated. An*

The psychological meaning of an emotion word often overlaps with its medical or physiological meaning, thus linking the emotions and the body. Many authors set up a hierarchy of emotions and use expressions such as 'the lower passions', 'our best feelings' or 'the highest sentiments', always implying a kind of progression from 'bad' to 'good' feeling, indicating how heavily the discourses on emotions are imbued with morality. Although this element has always influenced the discourses on emotions, the impact of 18th-century moral philosophy and its focus on the feelings must have played an important role in this respect. Alexander Bain's discussion of 'the ethical emotions' to which he devotes a complete chapter illustrates this: he engages with all the important 18th-century positions, still the obvious starting point for a mid-19th-century debate on feeling and morality.

A further shared convention governing the use of key emotion words is the central dialectic of expression and control, another basic distinction which organises all thinking and writing on the emotions, from dictionary articles to health guides and novels. It gives rise to such phrases as 'the cultivation and management of feelings', 'master the emotions' or 'the power of the body to control these affections'.

A strategy which one can observe for most of the keywords is their metaphoric use in anthropomorphic or even personified turns of phrase, e.g. in the idea that the passions are 'capricious' or in a sentence such as 'passion will draw in its horns' once it is under control. The use of the words is determined not so much by their specific individual meanings but more by the underlying concepts of emotion that were prevalent at the time.[28] Conceptualising the emotions metaphorically as a natural weather phenomenon like a storm produces notions of the passions as the 'gales of life', the 'stormy interludes of intemperate passions', 'tumultuous' and 'impetuous feeling'. This naturalises passion and implies that control of them is as difficult to achieve as the management of nature.

The notion of the emotions as a kind of 'pressure cooker', creating energy and heat,[29] produces such combinations as 'warmth of feeling',

---

Exploration of the Work of Tim Bobbin, Hanborough Parrot, Oxford 1990.

28 Personifications and metaphorical expressions of the emotions can be traced back a long way. Cf. Averill (1990), 'Six metaphors of emotion'.

29 The modern (American) variant of this emotion concept is analysed by George Lakoff and Mark Johnson (1980) in their seminal book on metaphors, *Metaphors We Live By*, Chicago UP, Chicago.

'seething emotion' and, on a slightly less intensive scale, 'the warmth and glow' that the affections can 'excite'. Again the 'dangerous' side of the feelings is highlighted, because they can produce energy like fire or heat, needing constant vigilance if they are not to create havoc. But the 'positive' aspects of this kind of energy may also be implied, since the absence of all energy, and the absence of all feeling, is usually not the answer to the expression-and-control problem which Victorian writers preferred.

The third most important metaphor of emotion which sees feeling as a movement, an agitation (of the mind), results in the third set of expressions, again shared by most of the keywords: one finds phrases such as 'agitated by feeling', emotion defined as 'an internal motion' or the 'affections of the mind', as well as the passions being explained as 'motions and agitations of the soul' or appearing as the 'surging unrest of a passionate spirit'. The emphasis on movement is not only related to the concept of feeling as energy requiring an outlet, but also to the body as the expressive medium of emotion.

Although I have emphasised the shared conventions of use, I would not wish to minimise the differences in this set of keywords. Thus one encounters 'affection' in its medical meaning as disease, and by transference, as disease of the mind ('affection of the mind') in health guides and medical treatises, while in fiction it is used largely as a positive term, denoting family feeling, neatly summarised in the popular expression 'the domestic affections'.[30] It is used mainly for relations between friends or parents and children and can be distinguished from 'passion' in that it is a more stable emotion and carries almost no sexual connotations. In the popular combinations 'tender affection' or 'gentle affection' it also carries a certain gender bias, since it is often used for the relations of women, either amongst themselves, or with their offspring. It also designates the feelings married couples experience after the period of (possibly) passionate courtship is over. In this sense it is a positive term while the notion of affection as a disturbance of the mind comes closer to passion and implies a similarly pejorative connotation.

Passion occasionally appears in a positive semantic context, e.g. as

[30] Cf. Felicia Hemans's and Charles Mackay's respective poetry collections and their virtually identical titles. F. Hemans (1812), *The Domestic Affections and Other Poems*, T. Cadell, London; Charles Mackay (1858 etc.), *The Home Affections*, George Routledge, London.

'tender passion', but combinations with adjectives giving it a negative aspect, such as 'destructive passion', 'violent passion', 'evil passion' or the 'baneful tendency of passion' are more common. Although it can also appear in a near-synonymous sequence with feeling, emotion or affection, it is the term which carries the heaviest semantic load and thus determines the largely negative connotations with which it is associated. Personifications, similes and metaphors, although also possible with the other keywords, are most often formed with the word passion. Likewise, the dangers of the lack of control, although they are sometimes implied in the context of emotion or feeling, are most prominent in expressions using 'passion' or 'passionate'. It is therefore not surprising that the genre which prefers this term to all others is that of the medical text or health guide which usually emphasises the dangerous effects of the passions on the body. This is also one of the notions that seems to be the most long-lasting: the late 19th-century *Family Health Book* (1892) lifts a whole passage on the passions as the 'gales of life' from Richard Reece's exposition on the passions, to be found in his *Practical Dictionary of Domestic Medicine* (1808), and quotes it verbatim – but without acknowledging the source.

Both emotion and feeling differ from passion in that they denote 'deep' feeling, while passion is seen to be 'capricious', more sudden and less permanent. Both emotion and feeling can be used positively and negatively, 'tender emotion' and 'fine feeling' can occur alongside 'painful emotion' and 'morbid feeling'.

And finally, sentiment and sensibility, the words used most rarely in 19th-century texts. Again, a negative context is possible for both of them, e.g. in expressions such as 'the undue exertions of the sentiments' or 'morbid sensibility'. More frequent, however, are combinations such as 'the higher sentiments', 'religious sentiments' and 'noble sentiments'. It is only the adjective 'sentimental' which carries a decidedly pejorative meaning in the 19th century and is associated with false feeling, affectation and excessive emotionality, as in 'effusion of sentimentality' or 'susceptible and sentimental'. It is nevertheless a term which depends much on its context and the hierarchy of emotion words a specific text or author has set up; it is neither as neutral as feeling or emotion, nor as automatically negative a term as passion.

Sensibility is a word used even less frequently than sentiment, and it is the one term which cannot serve as a synonym for any of the other keywords. It is quite definitely associated with refinement, opposed to coarseness and vulgarity, but this can also take on a negative meaning when it is associated with excessive emotionality, as in the phrase 'persons who are feeble, and possessed of much sensibility' which is associated with 'sickly sensibility'. Even when its original and seemingly neutral meaning of perception or sensation overlaps with its emotional meaning, the term has a slight gender bias, in that its association with emotional refinement and taste is in this period – albeit only by implication – considered the prerogative of women.

When the six key emotion words are placed in their semantic and textual context it becomes obvious that the words do not merely, or perhaps not even predominantly, serve as vehicles of expression for specific emotion concepts. To a large extent, they fulfil a performative role: by juxtaposing certain adjectives and nouns, lexeme combinations such as 'tender affection' or 'violent passion' indicate that to be passionate implies a certain vehemence, and to be affectionate in a family context is necessarily associated with tenderness. The words and phrases produce, or are intended to produce, an effect on their readers which transcends the discursive realm and may influence their actual behaviour and emotional experience. Thus one can conclude that the keywords in their semantic and discursive context function as feeling rules, signalling what kind of emotional experience and subsequent behaviour is appropriate in a given situation. Just as the discourses on emotion as a whole do more than just represent an already existing subject, the emotions, the use of keywords and phrases does not simply reflect pre-existing notions about the feelings: it may have actually brought about emotional experience which was either unknown prior to that specific use of a keyword, or at least not as common.

A topic which bridges the gap between linguistic contexts and the general motifs and rules of the discourse is that of metaphor. Entirely metaphorical concepts of the emotions, such as the heart or the breast as the seat of the feelings, go beyond the set of keywords. They will take us to the central concerns of the Victorian discourses on emotions and are therefore discussed separately in the following chapter which investigates the relation between the feelings and the body.

3 I could not speak the feeling: Emotions and the Body

Expression is to passion what language is to thought: Emotional Expression

In her poem later entitled 'Alone I sat; the summer day' (1837), Emily Brontë's poetic persona voices her frustration at not being able to express in words what goes on inside her:

> Alone I sat; the summer day
> Had died in smiling light away;
> I saw it die, I watched it fade
> From misty hill and breezeless glade:
>
> And thoughts in my soul were gushing,
> And my heart bowed beneath their power;
> And tears within my eyes were rushing
> Because I could not speak the feeling ... .[1]

Brontë makes use of the traditional 'inexpressibility motif'[2] which gains particular importance in the course of the 19th century. The ability to express the inexpressible – the emotions – is seen to be a vital capacity, not just a matter of poetic talent, but something which is necessary to the preservation of individual and – by implication – social health. Although post-Romantic Victorians acknowledge this necessity they worry about the

---

[1] Quotation taken from C.W. Hatfield (ed) (1941), *The Complete Poems of Emily Jane Brontë*, Columbia UP, New York, p. 48. The second part of the poem seems to demand an autobiographical reading because of its focus on a (failed or unacknowledged) writer's frustration of having written in vain – a problem which many women writers encountered and which helps to contextualise historically Emily Brontë's use of this traditional motif.

[2] Barbara Hardy has rightly identified this motif, first described by E.R. Curtius, as a common feature of the discourses on emotions as a whole; but as she does not contextualise it historically this observation loses its critical edge. Cf. Barbara Hardy (1986) [1985], *Forms of Feeling in Victorian Fiction*, Methuen, London, p. 12f.

consequences of uncontrolled emotional expression. This gives rise to the tensions and the unease so typical of Victorian texts on the feelings.

But the short Brontë quotation does more than give poetic shape to the difficulty of 'speaking the feelings'. Brontë also uses a common emotion concept, that of emotion seen as 'inner feeling' needing some kind of external expression and she moves the body centre stage as the medium of expression ('my heart bowed', 'tears within my eyes were rushing'). The quotation is an example of the central paradox behind the notion of 'not being able to speak the feeling'. The apparent 'failure' of language which allegedly cannot give adequate shape to an emotional state is compensated for by a linguistic device. Metaphor does in fact 'speak the feeling' via a description of the body, which seems to replace verbal with non-verbal expression.

In this chapter, an account of the role of emotional expression and the need for its control is followed by an analysis of the different individual and social functions attributed to the emotional body in 19th-century fictional and non-fictional texts. Emotion metaphors based on the body are important in this context because they bridge the gap between that which seems to exceed expression (the feelings, the body) and that which can be explicitly stated. Distinctive features of the discourses on emotions in the 19th century such as discursive control and recurrent body and emotion metaphors and images are explained by the social function they had: creating discursive stability and providing feeling rules. After a broader overview of these issues based on several popular and 'serious' non-fictional and some fictional texts, a 'close-up' of Charlotte Brontë's novel *Shirley* (1849) explores in greater detail the dialectic relation between individual and social expression and control.

Charles Bell's *The Anatomy and Philosophy of Expression as Connected with the Fine Arts* provides a useful introduction to the major topics important for the discussion of expression. It is a text which became very influential in the Victorian period although it was already published in 1806.[3] The book was so popular that by 1877 it had run to seven editions and even attracted the interest of the Queen.[4] In an intriguing mixture of

3 The quotations in the following section are taken from the third and enlarged edition, published posthumously by John Murray in 1844. The first edition was entitled *Essays on the Anatomy of Expression in Painting* and appeared in June 1806, a second edition was published in 1824 and a fourth one in 1847. A fifth edition was published in Bohn's artist series in 1865, followed by another two editions in 1872 and 1877.

4 Bell's study was also read by numerous artists, among them the Pre-Raphaelites. The

physiology, art criticism and popular science which draws on the long history of physiognomy,[5] the Scottish physiologist and nerve specialist Charles Bell discusses the relation between body and mind made visible by emotional expression:

> In the human countenance, under the influence of passion, there are characters expressed, and changes of features produced, which it is impossible to explain on the notion of a direct operation of the mind upon the features. ...
>
> Since we are dwellers in a material world it is necessary that the spirit should be connected with it by an organised body, without which it could neither feel nor re-act, nor manifest itself in any way. It is a fundamental law of our nature that the mind shall have its powers developed through the influence of the body; ... (p. 82f.).

In familiar binary terms, Bell states that '[t]he emotions and passions, grounded on these great classes of sensation, ... derive their most important traits of expression from the general tone of pleasure or of pain' (p. 153f.). And although he also discusses the possible detrimental effects of these painful emotions, he focuses on emotional expression as a form of the beautiful. Expression, he says, 'raises affection' (p. 20) and:

> Human sentiments prevailing in the expression of a face, will always make it agreeable or lovely. Expression is even of more consequence than shape: it will

---

article on Bell in the *Dictionary of National Biography* (henceforth: *DNB*) not only names the Queen, the artists Flaxman and Fuseli but also 'the Nabob of Arcot [who] had a copy in red morocco and satin' as avid readers. These names indicate that the book must have been read by a well-off readership rather than by the average middle class reader who would not have been able to afford a book priced at 52*s* 6*d* (1824), 21*s* (1847) and 16*s* in 1872. Only the mid-century edition would have come closer to the price range of prospective middle class readers at only 5*s* in 1877 (*English Catalogue*, 1863-72, 1872-80), if we take Simon Eliot's price categories as standards of comparison: low prices up to 3*s* 6*d*, medium between 3*s* 7*d* and 10*s* and high prices over 10*s*. Cf. Simon Eliot (1995), 'Some Trends in British Book Production, 1800-1919', in John O. Jordan and Robert L. Patten (eds), *Literature in the Marketplace. Nineteenth-Century British Publishing and Reading Practices*, Cambridge UP, Cambridge, pp. 19-43. For Bell's influence on the Pre-Raphaelites see Julie F. Codell (1986), 'Expression Over Beauty: Facial Expression, Body Language, and Circumstantiality in the Paintings of the Pre-Raphaelite Brotherhood', in *Victorian Studies*, vol. 29 (2), pp. 255-290.

[5] For an overview of the history of physiognomy and the changes it undergoes between the 15th and early 19th century cf. Jean-Jacques Courtine and Claudine Haroche (1988), *L'Histoire du visage. Exprimer et taire ses émotions XVe – début XIXe siècle*, Rivages, Paris.

> light up features otherwise heavy; it will make us forget all but the quality of the mind. (p. 60)

It is this expressive beauty which distinguishes human beings from animals, an issue with which Bell struggles. On the one hand, his research into the workings of the nervous system has led him to make numerous comparisons between humans and animals. On the other hand Christianity requires a strict distinction between 'men' and 'brutes'. It is therefore not surprising that he discusses this relation again and again, advocating the avoidance of animal-like qualities in paintings and establishing a hierarchy of feelings in order to uphold the Christian notion of man's superiority. Although both animals and humans share certain muscles, it is their difference which is important, as well as those muscles 'which indicate emotions and sympathies of which the lower animals are not susceptible; and as they are peculiar to man, they may be considered as the index of mental energy, in opposition to mere animal expression' (p. 136f.). '[M]ere animal expression' is described as 'low' and without dignity, whereas mental activities and emotional expressions which he considers to be peculiar to human beings are rated more highly. Two worries can be sensed here: firstly, the presence of what James R. Averill and C. Solomon have called the 'myth' of the passions belonging somehow to the dangerous and uncontrollable realm of the 'animal' and therefore to the potentially destructive body.[6] Secondly, the threat to orthodox religious belief posed by the discovery that humans and animals share many physiological characteristics which adds to the unease that is symptomatic of the text.[7]

---

6 J.R. Averill (1990), 'Inner feelings, works of the flesh, the beast within, diseases of the mind, driving force, and putting on a show: Six Metaphors of Emotion and Their Theoretical Extensions', in David E. Leary (ed), *Metaphors in the History of Psychology*, Cambridge UP, Cambridge, pp. 104-132, in particular p. 108.

7 In his treatise on the education of the feelings Charles Bray also discusses the relation between humans and animals. His phrenological classification schemes explicitly state which of the 'sentiments' or 'animal propensities' are shared by both humans and animals. But he is careful to emphasise that humans should restrain their 'selfish feelings ... which are shared by the brute creation' and should cultivate instead 'those feelings, proper to man alone, which cause him to make his own interest subservient to that of the whole race'. Bray ([1]1838), *Education of the Feelings*, printed for Taylor & Walton, London, and Adam & Charles Black, Edinburgh, p. 12f., p. 18. Popular health guides are even more explicit in their advocacy of the difference between humans and animals and the need to suppress the 'baser passions' which both share. Cf. e.g. anon. (1858), *Health for the Household: Based on a Knowledge of Air, Water, Food, Clothing, Drink, and the Training of the Mind*, Jarrold and Son, London, 'The Gain of a

Bell shows greater confidence when he states that expression is universal, given to us by 'nature':

> To see every one hushed to the softest breathing of sympathy with the silent expression of the actress, exhibits all mankind held together by one universal feeling: and that feeling, excited by expression, so deeply laid in our nature, as to have influence, without being obvious to reason. (p. 89f.)

Emotional expression obviously has a social function, it 'is bestowed as a boon, a mark of superior intelligence, and a source of enjoyment; and ... its very nature is to excite sympathy; ... it radiates, and is understood by all; ... it is the bond of the human family' (p. 145).[8]

On the level of the individual, expression serves as a kind of safety valve, as John Keble (1792-1866), the influential poet and Oxford Movement clergyman and another ardent advocate of emotional expression, explains:

> To begin with, then, we are all so framed by nature that we experience great relief, when carried away by any strong current of thought or feeling, if we are at last able, whether by speech or gesture, or in any other way, to find an expression for it. This is most clearly seen in the case of those who, even when alone, mutter and croon to themselves, under the influence of strong emotion.[9]

Keble also speaks of the 'gift of tears' which serves as relief

---

well-trained Mind', p. 10: 'All the higher animals have strong BRUTE PROPENSITIES in them, but *they* have also more or less clear glimmerings of *Reason*, to soften and bend those headstrong inclinations'.

8 In her novel *The Ruling Passion*, Richard Bentley, London, Rainey Hawthorne [= Charlotte Elizabeth Riddell] (1857) stresses this social function of (verbal or non-verbal) emotional expression: 'if there be no confidence, there cannot be complete affection; if we do not speak of our feelings, how can we understand each other? ...', (vol. 3, p. 13).

9 John Keble (1912), *Lectures on Poetry 1832-41*, transl. by Edward Kershaw Francis, 2 vols., Clarendon Press, Oxford, vol. I, lecture I, p. 19. Keble was Oxford professor of poetry from 1831-41 and held his lectures in Latin. Their influence was therefore restricted to an academic readership. His ideas can nevertheless be linked to a wider discussion of the relation between expression and poetry, analysed by Isobel Armstrong (1977) in her essay 'The Role and the Treatment of Emotion in Victorian Criticism of Poetry', in *Victorian Periodicals Newsletter*, vol. 10 (1), pp. 3-16. For a discussion of Keble's theory of poetry based on the notion of truthful emotional expression see chapter 5.

from extreme emotional tension.[10]

Behind the idea that strong emotion calls for expression lies the notion that the body and the face mirror the 'true' character and emotional state of a person, a concept which once again became popular because of the wide dissemination of the work by the 18th-century Swiss physiognomist Johann Caspar Lavater, whose texts remained in circulation during the 19th century.[11] Emotional expression is understood to be a means of reading a person's mind. Bell sees this in a positive light:

> Are we not now authorised to say, that expression is to passion what language is to thought: that as without words to represent ideas, the reasoning faculties of man could not be fully exercised, so there could be no violence or excess of passion merely in the mind, and independent of the action of the body? As our thoughts are embodied and the reasoning powers developed by the instrument of speech, the passions or emotions have also a corresponding organ to give them a determined character and force. The bodily frame, though secondary and inferior, comes in aid of the mind; and the faculties owe their development as much to the operation of the instruments of expression as to the impressions of the outward sense. (p. 197)

By contrast, the absence of emotional expression may imply the absence of feeling, e.g., in the case of Mr Helstone, an important character in Charlotte Brontë's novel *Shirley*, a text on which the final section of this chapter focuses. Mr Helstone epitomises the seemingly unemotional man, a type of (male) character which one frequently encounters in Victorian novels: his 'dry-eyed and sober' mourning for his wife is considered scandalous because he does not adhere to the prescribed rules of emotional expression.[12]

---

10 Keble (1912), *Lectures*, vol. I, lecture XVI, p. 327. The idea of relief for unspeakable emotion is echoed by numerous novelists, when characters 'having no other language, ... speak in burning tears ...', Sarah Ellis (1846), *Temper and Temperament; or, Varieties of Character*, 2 vols., Fisher, Son & Co., London, vol. 1, p. 162. In *The Ruling Passion* the omniscient narrator explicitly comments on the use of tears, in particular for women: 'what would women, who cannot go forth into the world and forget their sorrows in occupation and active exertion, do without tears ...' (vol. 1, p. 213f.).

11 Cf. Courtine and Haroche (1988), *L'Histoire du visage*, who link this renewed interest in physiognomy to the rise of individualism, and in the 19th century, to the need of naturalising and safely identifying the different social classes (p. 144ff.). On Lavater's influence in England see John Graham (1961), 'Lavater's *Physiognomy* in England', in *Journal of the History of Ideas*, vol. 22, pp. 561-572.

12 Charlotte Brontë (1985) [1849], *Shirley. A Tale*, Penguin, Harmondsworth, p. 82. The character of Shirley Keeldar, one of the two female protagonists of the novel, is an

The main reasons which made emotional expression so important for the Victorians can be summarised as follows: it serves as relief, it is a medium of human sympathy, it is expressive of the beautiful and therefore pleasing, it enables the reading of another person's mind, it proves the links between body and mind, and, with slightly more difficulty, it serves as a mark of distinction between humans and animals. But what about the dangers of emotional expression, never far from a Victorian's mind? And why has 'reading the face' and emotional expression once again become an important issue? Charles Bell is explicit on the first of these points:

> As the actions and expressions of the body betray the emotions of the heart, we may be startled and forewarned, as it were, by the reflection of ourselves, and at the same time *learn to control our passions by restraining their expression*. ... The powers of language are so great, and minister in so superior a manner to reason and the higher faculties of the mind, that the language of expression, which attends the development of these powers, is in a manner superseded; good taste and good manners retain it in habitual subordination. We esteem and honour that man most who subdues the passions which directly refer to himself, and cultivates those which have their source in benevolence – who resists his own gratification, and enters warmly by sympathy into what others feel – who despises direct pleasures, and cultivates those enjoyments in which he participates with others. (p. 198f.) (My emphasis, G.S.)

Note the keywords 'good taste and good manners', the advocacy of restraint with regard to selfishness and the stress laid on benevolence and sympathy. All these elements are crucial for the middle class habitus, in the process of being forged during the 19th century, but their origin is obviously older. The importance of a number of concepts developed in the 18th century, already explained in the context of key Victorian emotion words, is obvious in these passages. Bell's argument that the intensity of feeling may change if its expression is restrained prefigures Russell-Hochschild's concept of the feeling rule, drawing a distinction between an emotion and its outward display which need not necessarily be commensurate with one another.

---

exception in that she is described as an emotional character whose face nevertheless remains inscrutable to the observer. This adds to her complexity but can also be explained by the relative obtuseness of her observer with regard to women: 'Mr Yorke ... gazed at her much puzzled. He could not divine what her look signified; whether she spoke in earnest or in jest: there was purpose and feeling, banter and scoff playing, mingled, on her mobile lineaments' (p. 359).

Keble values expression but his attention is nevertheless also focused on the necessity of 'order and due control' (vol. I, lecture I, p. 22), once the feelings have found their way into speech or gesture. He criticises men speaking 'unseasonably and inappropriately of [their] own inner feelings' (vol. I, lecture V, p. 69) and instead recommends 'modest reserve – I might even compare it to the modest blush of a country maiden – which is shown by those who write from the heart' (vol. I, lecture V, p. 84). The urgent need to 'stem the torrent of excessive emotion'[13] is also emphasised in a metaphorical passage, highlighting the familiar link between illness and emotion which can only be managed with the help of poetry:

> Forthwith the fevered anxieties and ponderings which were spreading hither and thither like a flood, are now controlled and confined to a single channel: thither are directed or naturally flow all that crowds into the mind from all sides: and as Imagination strives to draw them together, while consciously or unconsciously she gives them outline and ornament, men gradually become their own physicians and do not resent the change that comes over them. (vol. I, lecture IV, p. 59)

Emotional expression, in spite of its value and necessity, is obviously also considered dangerous, something to be kept within strict boundaries, in particular with regard to the 'selfish feelings' or 'violent passion', two emotional states meriting the strongest disapproval in Victorian texts on the feelings.[14]

The central paradox between emotional expression and control of the feelings, explained in the opening paragraphs of this chapter, can thus be found on two levels. The individual simultaneously laments the inability to express his or her feelings, and by thus lamenting, gives expression to just these allegedly inexpressible emotions. Once again the performative role of language can be observed. In social terms, the need to suppress overt or extravagant feelings is concurrent with the opposite need for social control. It is necessary to be 'legible', i.e. people have to be able to judge each other's characters and social background at a glance. This ability is

---

13 Alexander Bain (^{2}1865) is another author who focuses explicitly on the need to control the emotions and finds many similar phrases metaphorically conceptualising the feelings as 'currents', 'fountains' etc. which need to be stopped, re-routed or calmed. The quotation is taken from *The Emotions and the Will*, p. 204.

14 See for example Charles Bray (1838 etc.), *The Education of the Feelings*, Mary Ann Stodart (1840), *Every Day Duties*, and Sarah Ellis (1869), *The Education of the Heart: Woman's Best Work.*

particularly important in a mass society with considerable social mobility. However, it is dangerous to be too obvious in one's external signals of interior movements and expression of character. In the 19th century, individualisation had advanced significantly and the cult of privacy – albeit a highly organised privacy – had reached new heights. Being too open-hearted and willing to express one's emotions without any restraint whatsoever was not in keeping with this cult. But since the absence of all emotional expression not only implied the unhealthy absence of all feeling, but also rendered it impossible to judge what kind of class an individual belonged to, and what type of character he or she represented, the Victorians found themselves confronted with an almost unsolvable dilemma. This dilemma is the reason why authors of texts on the emotions oscillate between the call for total emotional control and the sometimes only grudgingly admitted individual and social necessity of emotional expression.[15]

Charles Darwin's scientific study *The Expression of the Emotions in Man and Animals*, published by John Murray in 1872, also focuses on expression. It was a text which, like many of the author's other writings, would exert considerable influence on subsequent discussions of the emotions and on Victorian thought in general.[16] It is possible to

[15] Cf. Courtine and Haroche (1988), *Histoire du visage*, p. 147f. and p. 272ff. on this central paradox and the specific form it takes in the 19th century. See also Richard Sennett (1974), *The Fall of Public Man*, Alfred J. Knopf, New York.

[16] On its first day of publication the book sold the surprising number of 5,267 copies, compared to an average print-run for a non-fictional book of about 750 to 1000 copies. Overall, 9,000 copies were sold in the first four months but sales slackened after the initial rush. The first edition, priced at 12*s*, was so large that no second edition appeared during the author's lifetime (1809-1882) but only in 1889, edited by his son Francis Darwin. A third edition, incorporating all Darwin's notes he wanted included in subsequent editions, has recently been published by Paul Ekman (1998), Harper Collins, London. The following analysis is nevertheless based on the first edition, since this is the one mid-19th-century readers would have used For a comparison of the three editions cf. Ekman, Apendix II, to the third edition. For the publication history of the book cf. *DNB* and Paul Ekman's preface and introduction to the third edition. A largely negative review of *The Expression* by Thomas Spencer Baynes (April 1873) in the *Edinburgh Review* (pp. 492-528), also testifies to the enormous influence that any publication by Darwin had. Although Baynes accuses Darwin of being vague, unscientific, intolerant, ignorant and unable to distinguish between physiology and psychology, as well as disregarding the difference between humans and animals, he describes Darwin and his followers as numerous and compares them to a religious sect of considerable force. Baynes praises Charles Bell's approach, approving not only Bell's allegedly more suitable language and style, and the study of paintings and sculpture for

contextualise it by drawing attention to the similarities with and, more importantly, to the differences to Charles Bell's work (1806). These point to the slow and barely detectable developments within the discourses on emotions between the early and mid-19th century which can be observed in spite of the overwhelming impression of discursive continuity that the analysis of Victorian keywords in the preceding chapter has brought to light.[17]

Darwin's text illustrates a shift of emphasis which has occurred by the middle of the century. His whole approach attempts to be purely scientific. Not only does he reject Bell's and his predecessors' use of art in their discussion of emotional expression as useless (p. 14f.), his own study is based neither on introspection, nor on the analysis of painted images. Instead, he used observation (of his own children), questionnaires sent out to missionaries, and photographs of the insane to come to more 'objective' conclusions as to the nature of the emotions (p. 13ff.). This approach was the basis for ethological research undertaken in the 20th century.[18] Although the notion of inner feeling needing an expressive outlet is still present, this is not Darwin's predominant interest. Nor does he worry about distinguishing men and animals. On the contrary, his examples anthropomorphise animals, thus closing the gap between humans and non-humans rather than widening it, as Bell and writers of popular health guides attempted to do. He defends the observation of animals by stating that their expressions are not 'conventional' and the person who observes is not 'biased' as he would be if human beings were the main object of scientific study (p. 17). Darwin is able to do this because his whole analysis presents man and the emotions as quite a different object, compared to Bell. Man has become an organism, consisting only of physiological phenomena, and his inner being is no longer the focus of attention. Neither is the social context of emotion or its religious nature *per se* of interest to Darwin. He observes religious practices with the same detachment with which he observes frogs. Yet moral issues are never completely absent from his study, however much he may have wanted to exclude any considerations that go beyond physiology. Sentences such as

---

his analysis, but, crucially, that Bell maintained the difference between humans and animals.

17 Courtine and Haroche (1988) even speak of 'une rupture majeure' (*L'Histoire du visage*, p. 270) that Darwin's text constitutes in comparison with the earlier tradition of physiognomy and studies of emotional expression.

18 Cf. Ekman (1998), 'Introduction to the third edition', p. xxivff.

the following – 'No emotion is stronger than maternal love' (p. 78) – make their normative appearance, and when things get too complicated, Darwin reverts to quoting Shakespeare because his own categories are unable to capture the complex nature of certain emotions such as jealousy which cannot be described in the usual physiological manner but require anthropomorphisation as e.g. in 'the green-eyed monster' (p. 262).[19]

Overall, one can detect a far greater confidence in Darwin's treatment of the subject. As his prior publications had already established evolution as the dominant although not uncontested paradigm for scientific study, it follows that he places his observations in an evolutionary context (p. 12f.).[20] From this he concludes that emotional expression is inherited – although possibly it is first learned and then passed on – and largely universal (p. 352 and p. 17): 'It seemed probable that the habit of expressing our feelings by certain movements, though now rendered innate, had been in some manner gradually acquired' (p. 19). He also argues that emotions barely exist without their physical expression (p. 31f.) – a far cry from such popular mentalist accounts as the one written by the reputable Scottish doctor John Abercrombie in 1833, entitled *The Philosophy of the Moral Feelings*, which focuses almost entirely on the mental aspect of emotion, and tries to exclude the body.[21] But although the body is not in

---

19 The use of literary examples as illustrations is criticised by a late-19th-century evolutionist writer on the emotions. Hiram M. Stanley (1895) considers this technique 'unscientific', thus echoing Darwin's own criticism of Bell's analyses of paintings. *Studies in the Evolutionary Psychology of Feeling*, Swan Sonnenschein, London, p. 2: 'But to refer to Shakespeare or Goethe as psychological authorities, or in illustration or proof of psychological laws, is generally a doubtful procedure. The literary and artistic treatment of human nature is quite distinct from the scientific, and literature and art cannot be said to be of much more value for psychology than for physics, chemistry, or biology ...'. The role of literary examples and of narrative in non-fictional texts on the emotions is discussed in greater detail in chapter 5.

20 For an overview of Darwinism and its opponents, cf. Peter J. Bowler (1992), 'Darwinism and Victorian Values: Threat or Opportunity?', in *Proceedings of the British Academy*, vol. 78, pp. 129-147.

21 John Abercrombie's treatise was also published by John Murray and judging from the number of editions it ran to (a second edition appeared as early as 1834 and its seventh edition in 1846), it must have been a popular text. The entry on Abercrombie in the *DNB* also supports this. Perhaps the treatise's success can be explained by the mode that the book was written in: a mode looking back to older mentalist treatments of the emotions, rather than to the future where the problematic relation of the newly developed notions of evolution threatening religious beliefs awaited the readers of more materialist accounts. William Cooke Taylor (4 May 1833), however, an American lawyer and critic of American literature, medicine and science, who reviewed the book

itself a problem in Darwin's text, the body as well as the emotions are still carefully circumscribed and controlled on the discursive level. They are placed in a strictly scientific framework, complete with definitions, a discussion of academic precursors, and on a deeper level of discourse, the adherence to certain discursive rules (classification, genderisation, moralisation) which make the complexity of the topic manageable and also indicate the continued need for boundaries with which the emotions can be controlled. But the necessity of repressing the feelings is not discussed as much as it is in earlier texts on the feelings, so that sentences such as the following – 'The insane notoriously give way to all their emotions with little or no restraint ...' (p. 155) are comparatively rare.

In conclusion one can say that although expression is still important in the 1870s, the emphasis has shifted. What agitates writers in the earlier decades of the century – moral issues, the dangers of lack of self-control, and the threat of an amorphous and inscrutable mass rising in mad passion – seems to have become slightly less important. Human beings are reduced to a physiological organism and their explicit social control which earlier writers of fiction and non-fiction advocated has been replaced by 'mere' discursive control. As Courtine and Haroche state, the history of expression is not the same through the centuries and even for a comparatively short period spanning only the first half of the 19th century one can detect a development, if only a relatively slow one:

> Les marques gravées que relève Cardan, les figures des passions que peint Le Brun, le vif mouvement des sentiments que veut saisir Lavater, le réflexe des émotions qu'observe Darwin, les symptômes d'un langage s'exprimant sur le corps que Freud écoute, ne sont pas des signes de même nature, ne permettent pas le même type d'interprétation. Ils ne supposent ni la même position pour qui les observe, ni la même identité de qui les produit. (p. 270)[22]

---

in *The Athenæum*, No. 288, is highly critical of the publication and describes it as 'little more than a collection of assertions, and there are few and feeble attempts to support them' (p. 278). Taylor laments the absence of 'a popular introduction to the study of ethics in our language', and recommends an encyclopaedia article as suitable reading, while he obviously does not consider Abercrombie's volume to be useful or instructive for '[y]oung men [who] are taught everything but their duties as men and citizens, and the obligations that bind them to society' in universities and 'public seminaries' (loc. cit.).

22 The engraved marks emphasised by Cardan, the faces of passion painted by Le Brun, the vivid movement of the feelings which Lavater tries to catch, the reflex of emotions Darwin observes, the symptoms of a language expressing itself through the body that Freud listens to are not signs of the same nature, they do not permit the same kind of

The rotting carcass versus The utmost pitch of attainable delight: Representing the Body

The concept of expression is based on the body. Its image and function(s) are so prominent in the Victorian discourses on emotions that they deserve a detailed discussion. Recent research into the history of the body, inspired in particular by feminist theory, has radically questioned the notion of a stable body.[23] It can no longer be conceptualised as a 'mechanism' whose physical properties do not change and can thus be viewed as a fixed 'medium' producing the same physical sensations and sexual identities throughout the ages.[24] Even if a certain scepticism is called for when extremists define the body as entirely constructed and thus open for all kinds of re-interpretations, one must allow for the possibility of change and historically contextualised notions of the body. In the 19th century the body is a focal point for a number of discourses and contemporary anxieties such as individual and social health, political control, insanity, sexuality, and gender. This makes it impossible to discuss the relation between the body and the emotions as a merely physiological connection free from the influences of such contemporary debates and obsessions.

It is at this point that traditional 20th-century psychological accounts of the relation between the body and the emotions can throw only little light on Victorian emotionology, let alone on 'actual' 19th-century emotions. A more constructivist concept is called for which permits the highlighting of the decidedly metaphorical nature of 19th-century images of the body.

In spite of the idea of an immutable body governed by the humours which one generally encounters in Victorian texts, in particular in health

---

interpretation. They presuppose neither the same position for the observer nor the same identity for those who produce these signs. (My translation, G.S.)

23 Roy Porter (1991) summarises the dangers of unsophisticated body concepts: 'Scholars have warned that it would be grossly simplistic to assume that the human body has timelessly existed as an unproblematic natural object with universal needs and wants, variously affected by culture and society (in one age, "repressed", in another, "liberated", etc.). Such a crass nature/culture division would obviously be unhelpful; and it would be misconceived – and ironical! – to give the old mind/body dualism a new lease of life by attempting to study the ("biological") history of the body independently of ("cultural") considerations of experience and expression in language and ideology.' 'History of the Body', in Peter Burke (ed), *New Perspectives on Historical Writing*, Polity Press, Cambridge, pp. 206-232, quotation p. 208.

24 For an overview of recent trends concerning the concept and the history of the body cf. Maren Lorenz (2000), *Leibhaftige Vergangenheit. Einführung in die Körpergeschichte*, edition diskord, Tübingen.

guides, many texts do not only contain one concept of the body. Authors also differ considerably amongst themselves concerning the symbolic value that they accord it. One can find at least two notions of the body in 19th-century texts, a 'pure' and an 'impure' one, echoing the idea of 'positive' and 'negative' emotions, either pertaining to 'pleasure' or to 'pain'. Although many authors are fond of these simple dichotomies, some were aware of 'mixed emotions'. But the frequent reference to pleasure and pain as an either/or-category indicates that the desire for definite boundaries was perhaps greater than the ability to acknowledge the complexity of the issue. Interestingly, novelists, even popular ones, often showed a greater awareness of pleasurable pain and painful pleasure in their fictional representations of feeling.

In relation to the emotions, a further distinction can be made: on the one hand, authors discuss the body as a means of characterisation (of 'national' or fictional characters) and describe it as an immobile, passive 'mirror' of personality, or what they call 'temper and temperament', including not only intrinsic physical properties but also extrinsic ones, namely dress.[25] The character of the protagonist in the first of Sarah Ellis's stories in *Temper and Temperament*, Horace Grant, is for instance described by his large and massive body which is too sleepy for exertion. His 'black' looks (p. 16) and his early inertia is explained by the absence of passionate energy: 'It was not passion which called forth this expression of countenance in the boy, for he had scarcely sufficient energy to be called passionate. It was like the stirring of some deep and latent fire, that might in after-life awaken into passion; ...' (p. 16f.)[26]

On the other hand, the body appears as an active force in many descriptions of actual emotional behaviour, expressive of specific feelings.[27] Fictional texts in particular make use of the expressive role of

---

25 Charles Dickens is perhaps the author who is most famous for his often humorous descriptions of physical features as expressive of character, e.g. Gradgrind's square forehead which suits his excessively rational approach. In her conduct book *Every Day Duties*, Seeley, London, p. 99, Mary Ann Stodart (1840) explains that dress serves as an 'index to the mind' and advises women to choose their servants very carefully and to beware of domestic staff which lays too great a store by outward appearances.

26 Ellis (1846), *Temper and Temperament*. Horace Grant's apparent inertia is a result of being pampered and educated to become selfish, characteristics which will lead to an unsuitable marriage and the loss of his wife in childbirth through neglect, occurrences for which he atones in due course, in spite of what Ellis calls a 'constitutional tendency of character' (p. 5).

27 Two traditions intersect here: that of physiognomy which focuses on the morphology of man, and that which is more interested in the movement of emotional expression in the

the body in non-verbal interactions between characters,[28] e.g. in a seductive dance scene between the protagonist from F.E.M. Notley's novel *Olive Varcoe* and the man who loves her but at first decides to marry someone who seems more suitable:

> He put his arm around her; he took her hand in his; the glossy coils of hair rested on his breast: they could not reach his shoulder. He forgot Eleanor Maristow, and the dance grew faster and faster, as she sang in a low voice a wild Russian melody to Mazurka time. (p. 5)

Both the more static and descriptive concept of the body and the body-in-movement-concept in non-verbal communication are conflated in fictional and non-fictional accounts of madness and hysteria which were considered partly the result of a specific physical make-up, and partly the consequence of certain emotional actions.

A favourite notion of the body is that of a 'wasting' organism whose energy needs protection, e.g. by moderating the emotions.[29] Both joy and anger or fear are said to provoke 'sudden death' because of the violent transport of feeling which expends all physical energy.[30] Medical treatises

---

body and the face. Cf. Courtine and Haroche (1988), *Histoire du visage*, p. 30 and p. 132ff.

28 Barbara Korte has published a study on non-verbal communication in fictional texts. Although she observes an increase in non-verbal communication in Victorian novels, her analysis is largely systematic rather than historical and is thus of only limited value for my own work since no explanations or reasons are given for her observations. Korte herself acknowledges the necessity of further period-specific studies which use a broader text base, linking fiction to other historical discourses. Cf. Korte (1993), *Körpersprache in der Literatur. Theorie und Geschichte am Beispiel englischer Erzählprosa*, Francke, Tübingen, p. 255f.

29 Charles Bray (1836), *The Education of the Body. An Address to the Working Classes*, printed by Henry Merridew, Coventry, p. 6.

30 This is a common notion which we find in 18th- and 19th-century dictionaries and in Victorian health guides, and one of the fairly rare points on which all writers seem to agree. Cf. e.g. the article on the 'passions' from Richard Reece's (1808) *Practical Dictionary of Domestic Medicine*, Longman, Hurst, Rees, and Orme, London: 'excessive joy, however, is often attended with severe evils; instantaneous death has occurred from the immediate and rapid tumult produced on the spirits by its unexpected occurrence'. It is this section which reappears unchanged in George Black's (1892) *Family Health Book*, Ward, Lock & Co., London, and similar passages can be found in numerous other texts, e.g. in the anonymous *Household Encyclopaedia* (1858), 2 vols., W. Kent & Co. etc., London etc., which states unequivocally under the heading 'passions' that '[s]udden and excessive joy may prove extremely hurtful .... Nay, it may become dangerous by causing expansion or laceration of the vessels, spitting of blood,

on the emotions as well as health guides concentrate not on health but on disease ('the rotting carcass'[31]), yet the notion of the danger of passion for the individual and the social body is not restricted to these genres, as the following analysis of Charlotte Brontë's novel *Shirley* (1849) will show. The anonymous author of a conduct book for young men, *The Young Man's Mentor* (1842), succinctly summarises this view: 'The debility of your body robs your heart and mind of their energy; and the want of vigour in the mind and soul subjects the body to the most disgraceful propensities, and the most baneful passions' (p. 14). A particular danger exists if one indulges in an 'excess of luxury' or 'morbid sensibility'[32] and if one forgets to 'come with an heart sifted and cleansed from worldly and carnal affections and desires ...'.[33] The Christian concept of the body as canonically inferior to mind and the source of sin permeates such passages.[34] However, less pejorative images of the body can also be found in various genres. Not only in idealised metaphors of the heart, explained below, but also in discussions of the pleasures of physical health and happiness – 'the utmost pitch of attainable delight'[35] – and the danger of emotional repression. As well as horrific tales of disease and death one finds the notion of the sleeping 'mortal body',[36] and not only paroxysms of rage and 'storms of passion' debilitating the body, but also 'electric throbbings of internal joy [which] vibrate the harpstring of his heart'.[37] In particular in Alexander Bain's *The Emotions and the Will* both types of body images can be found. His frequent emphasis on physical pleasure underlying all kinds of emotions can be explained by his so-called 'hedonist' attitude which conceptualises the majority of physical processes as pleasure. But Bain is aware that the notion of all emotions pertaining either to pleasure or to pain is not the only way of describing the feelings.

---

fevers, deprivation of understanding, swooning, and even sudden death'.

31 A.J.X. Hart (1869), *Catholic Psychology*, n.p., London, p. 96f.

32 Sarah Ellis (1869), *The Education of the Heart: Woman's Best Work*, Hodder and Stoughton, London, p. 156, p. 124.

33 M.A. Stodart (1840), *Every Day Duties*, p. 7, quoting the book of the Homilies.

34 Porter (1991), 'History of the Body', p. 213.

35 Bain (^{2}1865), *The Emotions and the Will*, p. 44: 'The first thrill of the virgin fibres of the brain, gives the utmost pitch of attainable delight'.

36 Charles Bray (^{1}1838) explains death as 'that gentle sleep, which dissolves our mortal body, and perhaps reposes the spirit, intervening between its earthly and heavenly career', quoting from the *Monthly Repository* in *The Education of the Feelings*, p. 93.

37 J.H. Powell (1853), *The Poetry of the Feeling and Poetry of Diction. A Lecture*, Geo. De Fraine, Chronicle and Gazette Office, Aylesbury, p. 6. His lecture is analysed in greater detail in chapters 4 and 5.

And when he likens the emotions to 'destroying Vandals' (p. 23) physical pleasure is obviously not his main priority.

It is remarkable that the impure, corrupted body merits metaphorical treatment less frequently than the notion of the body as a source of pleasure which gives rise to elaborate conceits. This may be due to the tendency to 'aetherialise' the body, as Roy Porter has explained:

> Alongside the disciplining of the body [in the 18th century], indeed, one might almost say, the fulfilment of that disciplining, was the desire to render the body effectively aetherialised and invisible, and thereby to throw the emphasis upon the mind.[38]

On the whole it is the danger of the body and the passions that writers on the emotions are obsessed with, a tendency which can be illustrated by the following illustration, taken from an advertisement for 'Fennings' Adult Cooling Powder', from Alfred Fennings's *Everybody's Doctor* (1864), a medical guide (fig. 3.1). 'Fennings' Cooling Powder' is recommended against indigestion, colds, rheumatism, erysipelas, eruptions, fevers, and diseases arising from 'unhealthy Heats of the System'. Since for Victorian medical experts these 'heats' are not only caused by physical ailments, but can result from indulgence in the passions, this anthropomorphised representation of the 'heats' (the many-headed dragon) and the fight against them might equally be read as a visual metaphor of the struggle against overwhelming feeling. Note the archaic and 'naturalising' imagery (the bearded semi-naked man wielding a cudgel) which associates disease (and by transference: passion) with timeless fights against primordial beasts.

The obsessive manner with which writers treat the relation between disease and emotion, body and feeling, is itself an indication of the anxiety that the subject could provoke, in spite of a gradual shift towards greater confidence by the middle of the century which can be observed in scientific studies on the emotions (Bain, Spencer, Darwin). And disease is not restricted to the individual: the relation between individual, social and moral health is frequently foregrounded, as the following quotation, from the anonymous health guide *Health for the Million* (1858), illustrates:

---

[38] Roy Porter (1991), 'Bodies of Thought: Thoughts about the Body in Eighteenth-Century England', in Joan H. Pittock and Andrew Wear (eds), *Interpretation and Cultural History*, Macmillan, Basingstoke/London, pp. 82-108, quotation p. 91.

> ... 'the health of a community is an almost unfailing index of its morals.' No one can wonder at this who considers how physical suffering irritates the temper, depresses energy, deadens hope, induces recklessness, and, in short, poisons life. ...
>
> Good and bad health are, therefore, most assuredly, both cause and effect of good and bad morals.[39]

In a similarly revealing passage, Charles Bray twice uses a word closely associated with disease – contagion – to explain the relation between morality and the emotions: in his conduct book *Education of the Feelings* he speaks of the danger of a 'contaminated moral atmosphere' which may make young people 'catch... the contagion'.[40] The importance of the body can be illustrated in another passage from the same text: 'And when it is considered how contagious are all the feelings of our nature, whether good or evil ... it is evident that the well-being of society is affected in no slight degree by the regard which is paid to the outward decencies and amenities of life.'[41] The word contagion, although common in the discourses on emotions to describe the effect of emotional rhetoric on groups of people, also overlaps with a contemporary issue. It conjures up the image of Josephine Butler's mid-century campaign against the 'Contagious Diseases Acts'. These acts did not only embody the Victorian sexual double standard which allowed men to gain sexual experience while repression or even the absence of any physical desire was demanded of and attributed to women. The acts also emphasise once again the relation between individual morality and social health (implied in the 'social' image of

---

39 The quotation in the first line is attributed to Harriet Martineau. Anon (1858), *Health for the Million, including Hints on the Physical Training of Youth and the Treatment of Invalids and Old Age: With Observations on Unhealthy Employments*, Kent & Co., London, p. xxii.

40 Bray ([3]1860), *The Education of the Feelings*, p. 29. The notion of 'contagious' emotions which is also explained in Bain's ([2]1865), *The Emotions and the Will* (p. 158), and mentioned in Charles Mackay's (1841 etc.) account of *Memoirs of Extraordinary Delusions*, Richard Bentley, London, p. 2, also known as 'Madness of Crowds', can be traced not only to the 18th century but also to texts on rhetoric in which the workings of *movere* are based on this medico-social concept of the emotions. For the 18th-century discussion cf. Erika Fischer-Lichte (2000), 'The Body as Sign and as Experience: On the Effect of Theatre Performance', in *REAL*, vol. 16, pp. 117-131, and for the earlier versions of this popular notion cf. Marion Müller (1999), *'These Savage Beasts Become Domestick': The Discourse of the Passions in Early Modern England With Special Reference to Non-Fictional Texts*, D.Phil. Thesis, unpublished ms., University of Oxford, chapter 1, '*Homo interior / homo exterior*', pp. 22-70.

41 Bray ([3]1860), *The Education of the Feelings*, p. 140.

contagion), as well as indicating how obsessively Victorian society focused on (women's) bodies.[42]

This focus was still more obvious in a problem related even more closely to the emotions than the dangers of venereal disease: madness, or 'the morbid emotions of women', as one medical tract summarises its discussion of mainly female diseases concentrating on hysteria and its derivatives.[43] The standard concept of excessive emotionality leading to madness is succinctly put by the anonymous doctor who wrote the health tract *The Best Methods of Improving and Preserving Health and Invigorating Life* (c. 1832): 'It is fortunate for man, that when old-age arrives, his passions lose much of their strength, otherwise they would much shorten life, and even bring on insanity.'[44] Another anonymous health guide – *Hand-Book of Health and Physiology* (1863),[45] published as a part of Cassell's popular general knowledge series – explains the relation of body and mind in similar fashion. First of all, physical pain and weakness are emphasised, before the mental effects are stressed. Keywords are nervousness, restlessness, complaining, groundless fears, excitement, violence, discontent, inertia, and despondency – all of which designate behavioural consequences rather than physical ones. Obviously, the anonymous author has the social effects of 'excessive sensibility' in mind (inertia implying indulgence and the wilful absence of occupation), rather than the individual sufferings of a person so affected. The association of women, mental disturbance and the womb is a common one in the 19th century (and in previous centuries):

> The diseases that depend upon *disturbances* in the several functions of the nerves include every kind of *morbid feeling*; and in all cases the *pain* and *weakness* caused by disease are felt by the nerves communicating between the part affected and the seat of sensation in the brain. Indeed, every form of disease and every physical injury may be said to affect the mind; ... Still it has been found exceedingly difficult to define '*nervousness*', commonly so called.

---

42 Cf. Barbara Caine (1997), *English Feminism 1780-1980*, Oxford UP, Oxford, pp. 108-10.

43 Walter M.B. Johnson (1850), *The Morbid Emotions of Women; Their Origin, Tendencies, and Treatment*, Simpkin, Marshall and Co., London.

44 Anon (c. 1832), *The Best Methods of Improving and Preserving Health and Invigorating Life. By a London Physician*, C. Kerbey, London, p. 35.

45 Anon (1863), *Hand-Book of Health and Physiology: A General View of the Physical Structure of Man, and of the Means of Preserving the Several Functions of the Body in Healthy Activity*, Cassell's, London.

> Persons so affected are easily *excited* or *depressed*; they are physically and morally *timid*; watchful of their own sensations and feelings; prone to view everything that concerns them in the worst aspect; starting at every slight noise; *restless*, *complaining*, and *impatient*; full of groundless *fears*; their *excitement* sometimes tending to *violence*, their impatience to angry discontent, and their *inertia* to *despondency*. That there are moral causes for such a morbid condition is certain, and among these may be reckoned such *deeply felt emotions as disturb the action of the brain*; and, in females, causes connected with the womb and its functions. But the cause is more frequently a physical one, arising from that intimate connection between the nerves and the blood-vessels that we have briefly described.[46] (My emphasis, G.S.)

That the mind can be 'debilitated' if the senses are 'indulged' in[47] is an opinion which one most often encounters in more or less explicit discussions of sex and masturbation. William Cooke, a doctor who first wrote about *Mind and the Emotions considered in Relation to Health and Disease* (1839) and later re-published a longer version as a kind of physician's memoir and manifesto – *A Commentary of Medical and Moral Life* (1852) – has no qualms about making the familiar link between masturbation and 'extreme nervous excitability'. Note the melodramatic tale of a young gentleman who commits suicide after having weakened himself by indulging in 'secret vice'. That notions of class are associated with sex and the body is obvious from the connection Cooke makes between corrupted teenagers and sexually rapacious servants:

> Young persons as they arrive at maturity are often the subjects of extreme nervous excitability or depression. ... These symptoms are not unfrequently connected with habits of secret vice. Russel mentions the calamitous case of a young gentleman of rank and fortune, who became so weakened by his addiction to the habit alluded to, that he lost all enjoyment of life, sunk under despondency, and drowned himself. Every person concerned in the education and training of youth of either sex, should feel the importance of using all possible means of preventing their minds from being corrupted by impure addresses to their imaginations. It is desirable, for this reason, that children as they advance in years, should not associate unnecessarily, or sleep with,

---

46 Anon (c. 1863), *Hand-Book of Health and Physiology* (Cassell's Elementary Handbooks), Cassell, Petter, and Galpin, London, p. 36f.

47 Bray (^{1}1838), *Education of the Feelings*, p. 10.

domestics, or with any person older than themselves, if there is the least reason to fear their want of delicacy, or of their just sense of propriety. ...[48]

Although both sexes are in danger of being corrupted by sexual activities, it is women who are most at risk from becoming insane because they are said to have 'a more exalted sensibility and stronger feelings and passions ...'.[49] The conviction that physical differences between the sexes result in two different emotional characters, and the consequences for society and gender roles, is extremely widespread. It provides the basis for the so-called separate spheres debate, another discourse with which the discourses on emotions overlap. The idea that it is the difference in their physical make-up that makes women prone to more violent emotions and consequently in danger of becoming insane is in keeping with the admittance figures of Victorian asylums: the majority of asylum patients were women. And although some asylum doctors were evidently aware of the social causes of insanity (e.g. extreme poverty), the majority believed female madness could be explained by the female reproductive system which had to remain under strict control so as not to provoke hysteria. As the Doctor Robert Brudenell Carter wrote in his study of hysteria in 1852:

> It is reasonable to expect that an emotion, which is strongly felt by great numbers of people but whose natural manifestations are constantly repressed in compliance with the usages of society, will be the one whose morbid effects are most frequently witnessed. This anticipation is abundantly borne out by facts; the sexual passion in women being that which most accurately fulfills the prescribed conditions, and whose injurious influence upon the organism is most common and familiar.[50]

This is an instance in which the image of the body – that of the woman at the beck and call of her physical frame – had direct consequences for the treatment of actual (women's) bodies. Although Victorian asylum doctors have become famous for their less brutal treatment of their inmates (replacing shackling with so-called 'moral management'), they nevertheless still coerced their patients and this had direct consequences

---

48 William Cooke (1852), *A Commentary of Medical and Moral Life; or Mind and the Emotions, Considered in Relation to Health, Disease, and Religion*, Longman, Brown, & Co., London, p. 250.

49 [Robert Tyas?] (1840), *The Hand-Book of Health*, Robert Tyas, London, p. 15.

50 Quoted in Elaine Showalter (1987), *The Female Malady: Women, Madness and English Culture, 1830-1980*, Virago, London, p. 132.

for them in terms of activities, dress etc.[51]

As Catherine Gallagher has shown, even the Malthusian notion of the healthy body was considered to have negative consequences for society. In reversal of the dominant view of the diseased body threatening social order, as exemplified by the texts read for this study, the healthy body was regarded as a danger because it led to an increase in the rate of reproduction and could result in overcrowding, thus depleting social resources. This is just another example of the great anxiety associated with the body, with health, and with social order closely related to both.[52] The overlap between these discourses within the discourses on emotions emphasises not only the latter's hybrid nature. It also indicates the centrality of the emotions for 19th-century literature and culture as well as once again highlighting the complexity of the issue: the discourses on emotions always move between the individual and society, the body and the mind, and between abandonment and control.

The successful pamphlet *The Philosophy of the Sexes, or Every Woman's Book*, written by the radical working-class reformer Richard Carlile (1790-1843) and published in 1826, is a rare example of an oppositional voice, and significantly it is a working class one. In this pamphlet on birth-control, Carlile argues for a kind of gender equality with regard to sexual feelings. He begins by criticising the tendency of writers on the emotions to idealise the passions in personifications and metaphors of the heart which results in ignorance on the part of the lovers (p. 6). According to Carlile, '[i]t is a barbarous custom that forbids the maid to make an advance in love' and calls to 'Young women! assume an equality, plead your passions when you feel it, and to those to whom it may apply' (p. 7). He explains that although women and men may differ in terms of their external appearance, they are alike with regard to sexual passion which must not at any cost be suppressed:

---

51 Madness in men would probably have been seen as a threat to their masculine identity, because of the close association of insanity or hysteria with women. Cf. Valentine Cunningham (2000), 'The Poetry and Poetics of Violent Feelings', in *REAL*, vol. 16, pp. 43-57, for the analysis of a famous Victorian male 'case' – Tennyson – and its relation to Victorian discourse.

52 Catherine Gallagher (1987), 'The Body Versus the Social Body in the Works of Thomas Malthus and Henry Mayhew', in Catherine Gallagher and Thomas Laqueur (eds), *The Making of the Modern Body. Sexuality and Society in the 19th Century*, University of California Press, Berkeley, pp. 83-106.

> Impediments to natural enjoyments bring on the more violent paroxysms of the fit, and it may be truly inferred, that LOVE is A DISEASE: a disease delightful in its cure, but distressing and disastrous if not cured. ... It is a passion, not criminal in the indulgence; but criminality attaches where the indulgence is withheld; because health, and even life is endangered. (p. 11ff.)

Carlile does not wish to 'advocate indiscriminate intercourse' (p. 15) but if 'Chlorosis' is to be avoided, particularly in women who cannot resort to what the men have at their disposal – prostitutes – 'Love must be gratified, or its victim pines and dies' (p. 16). He supports this opinion with examples from other cultures (p. 21ff.) and asks for a different marriage practice and that women who take lovers should 'neither be degraded nor brutalized, nor made miserable in consequence thereof, as they now are ...' (p. 24). Consequently, Carlile recommends the use of contraception (his favoured method, although he lists several, is the contraceptive sponge for women) (p. 26ff.). This would not only increase the pleasure since no worries of unwanted pregnancies would hinder intercourse (p. 31), no sins such as masturbation would have to be committed (p. 30) and poverty abated, since no couple would have to have more children than they could maintain, and no one needed to have illegitimate children either (p. 36f.). He defends his pamphlet against the possible accusation of being 'like one of those vile, mischievous, misleading, and fraudulent books, commonly on sale for the gratification of ignorantly diseased appetites' (p. 37). He can therefore describe his publication as a work of 'physical, philosophical, and moral instruction' to be read by 'every man, woman, and child at the age of puberty' (p. 38). In a later version, Carlile apparently toned down the emphasis on (female) sexual pleasure and stressed the uses of contraception for the control of the population but it is nevertheless interesting to note that he turns the familiar argument of women's 'excessive sensibility' as the cause for various diseases on its head. In Carlile's opinion, the absence of sexual gratification for both women and men, not their physiological difference is the cause for mental (and physical) illness. That women may suffer from this more easily than men is explained in cultural terms: they cannot use prostitutes or take lovers without being stigmatised (p. 16). But although other writers would take up birth-control as an issue, Carlile's publication must be considered the exception rather than the rule. His is a rare case of a dissenting voice in the discourses on emotion, since his focus on the pleasures which the body can accord rather than on its relation to disease is unusual.

Most of the texts discussed here do not of course give any indication of actual bodily behaviour and perception.[53] Again, one finds the rules of the game laid out for readers who were supposed to follow the guidelines set out by the authors. Whether readers actually conformed to these rules is another matter. Nevertheless, from the case studies included in texts written by doctors, and from physiologists' examples one can gather that certain symptoms and modes of behaviour were common, and others considered extraordinary or inappropriate. In fictional texts, the acting out and embodiment of feeling rules indicate that certain forms of bodily expression were acceptable or even fashionable. The much-discussed blushing and fainting of female characters is a case in point.[54] Female characters in fictional texts seem more often to act out their emotionality, in particular in seemingly uncontrolled or violent scenes, than male characters. This is of course in keeping with the view that women were more emotional, less controlled than men. Male characters may, on occasion and at critical moments, cry or gnash their teeth, blush or walk up and down a room but in many cases, these are either effeminate men or those who cannot control their 'ruling passion' (pride or greed), and thus express their general immodesty and lack of self-mastery. In *Shirley*, Robert Moore is only allowed to weep when he has been severely weakened by illness and Reginald Ireby in *The Ruling Passion* – although he constantly expresses his emotions with his body – only has 'negative' emotions to express (pride and hate). In such scenes, the body is used as the expressive medium of 'the lesser passions' and indicates the danger of uncontrolled emotion. Non-fictional texts also use many examples in which women play a central role, in particular hysterical women whose interesting symptoms and endless physical characteristics obviously fascinate the – probably largely male – authors.

---

53 Porter (1991) is justified in warning against the danger of 'floating off into the stratosphere of discourse analysis, and neglecting the more everyday and tangible materials available' ('History of the Body', p. 210) when analysing the history of the body. This study can however do no more than correlate historian's findings with textual analysis, e.g. relating the discursive construction of hysteria with the actual treatment of 'insane' women in Victorian asylums. It would nevertheless be desirable for future (transdisciplinary) research projects to reverse the perspective in order to find out more about 19th-century emotions, rather than merely analysing the period's emotionology.

54 Shirley Keeldar mocks this tendency in *Shirley* when Mr Helstone asks her what she would do if the house were attacked. She answers 'Don't know – faint, perhaps – fall down, and have to be picked up again ...' (p. 326). In a confrontational scene between herself, her uncle and Louis Moore she is too weak to remain upright but significantly does not faint, again exemplifying her own strength and the author's wish to abstain from convention (p. 582).

It is important to distinguish the moments and reasons for the body being foregrounded. It is used for the illustration of excessive passion and the danger that this presents to physical, and consequently to mental, well-being. Non-verbal communication, based as it is on the body, also heightens the intensity of critical moments because the description of physical symptoms gives rise to images which may have had a greater effect on readers than mere dialogue. But most importantly, body images also illustrate that a certain habitus, be it aristocratic (proud) or middle class (charitable, humble) is always embodied, in addition to its gendered nature which explains the different physical reactions attributed to women and men.

In non-fictional texts the body is mainly used for the purposes of illustration. Bodily symptoms are described to explain the differences between emotions, or to emphasise the physical dangers of uncontrolled emotionality. Since the body is unquestionably the site, basis, or even the cause of the feelings, its prominence is not surprising, particularly in view of the fact that purely mentalist accounts of the feelings became less important and more materialist and physiological ones appear to have become more widespread throughout the 19th century.

In fictional texts, the body comes in where language seems to fail, i.e. when the inexpressibility motif seems to threaten a person's ability to express his or her feelings. The character's verbal language fails and is replaced by non-verbal forms of communication. These scenes often coincide with crucial moments in the narrative, e.g. in Charles Dickens's *Great Expectations* (1860-61). The protagonist Pip falls dangerously ill after a series of disastrous events and disappointments. Only after this period of mute, but explicit expression of a crisis through the medium of the body is he finally able to accept life as a grown-up (without 'great expectations') when he is restored to health.[55] Many similar scenes occur in popular and 'serious' novels alike and it is often those scenes on which illustrators of Victorian novels focus their attention.[56] It is the non-verbal moments or at least those moments in which the body plays a central role which are depicted in these images. Again, the more static style for the expression of character or moods through images of the body and clothing can be observed, and a greater emphasis on physical movement in scenes

[55] Charles Dickens (1993) [1860-61], *Great Expectations*, Oxford UP, Oxford, chapter XVIII.

[56] Cf. Athena Vrettos (1995), *Somatic Fictions. Imagining Illness in Victorian Culture*, Stanford UP, Stanford.

representing a crisis, e.g. in the following two engravings, taken from G.P.R. James's novel *A Book of the Passions* (1838-39). The first image uses the static style of expression although the story is highly melodramatic, while the second one illustrates one of the critical moments in a tale of jealousy (fig. 3.2) and (fig. 3.3).[57]

It is important to note that decisive moments in the narrative are frequently described in a manner – and illustrated as such – reminiscent of tableau-scenes in melodramas. In these scenes, the dramatic action is frozen for a moment and all characters remain in one expressive position, giving the audience the chance to take in the impact of the preceding scene.[58] This decidedly non-verbal technique, which Peter Brooks has called 'mute', uses the body as a vehicle for the expression of the dramatic crisis and its emotional effects.[59] One can observe a considerable overlap between several media here: written texts, theatrical practice, illustrations of novels, popular prints, and 'serious' painting.[60]

These images of critical moments seem at first glance wholly representative of excess and in some cases of transgression: language fails and the body is the sole medium of emotional expression, taking some form of uncontrolled and violent action (fainting, crying, death, murder etc.) which appears to fly in the face of the ubiquitous rule that governs the discourses on emotions: control. Yet at closer inspection, the conventional character of these excessive images soon becomes apparent. Although the

---

57 'Leonora' tells the story of Count Henry's passion for the said Leonora. His love for his brother Ferdinand's bride leads to Ferdinand's accidental death, and ultimately, to Leonora's end. The story is entitled 'Remorse' and is obviously intended as a strong warning against brotherly rivalry, passion and revenge. The second image, 'Jealousy', is taken from the title page of James's *A Book of the Passions* and depicts a scene in which the hero rescues his love from being thrown by her horse. The text explains that she is on the verge of fainting in his arms. Laura is an only daughter who falls in love with a count whom she suspects of having a secret affair. Her father mistakes the other woman for his son-in-law's lover and kills her. It turns out that she was merely the count's sister. The count also dies during the altercation, leaving Laura in despair. After her death which causes him to lose his faith, her father goes to live as a recluse on a Swiss island where he happens to encounter the first-person narrator of the story who provides the frame for these melodramatic events.

58 Cf. Johann N. Schmidt (1986), 'Tableau, Panorama, Diorama', in id., Ästhetik des Melodramas. Studien zu einem Genre populären Theaters im England des 19. Jahrhunderts, Carl Winter, Heidelberg, pp. 302-314, and Peter Brooks (1976), 'The text of muteness', in id., The Melodramatic Imagination. Balzac, Henry James, Melodrama and the Mode of Excess, Yale UP, New Haven/London, pp. 56-80.

59 Brooks (1976), loc. cit.

60 Julian Treuherz (1993), *Victorian Painting*, Thames and Hudson, London, p. 107f.

potentially dangerous, boundless and unpredictable body takes pride of place in these images, it is not allowed to play this part unchecked. Firstly, gender relations are rarely subverted in these visual representations. It is usually women who faint or fall, and are caught by men. For women to faint or to cry is not a transgression at all, but rather expected behaviour which draws on the idea of their 'excessive sensibility' allegedly making them more disposed to experience violent emotions. Secondly, these tableau-style images are derived from a genre (melodrama) which, although it evokes scenes of sex and crime, places them firmly in a moral framework which distinguishes clearly between right and wrong, pleasure and pain, gain and punishment. And these dramatic and narrative frameworks are not even absent from 'mere' pictures because the taste for moralising, narrative images ensured their presence in any kind of pictorial representation.[61] Finally, conventional gestures made these images predictable and less shocking in their effect. Overall, then, one is inclined to read this type of apparent bodily excess as a very controlled, conventionalised physicality which was probably more pleasing than actually threatening.[62]

This type of controlled, conventionalised excess is echoed in the use of language in fictional and non-fictional texts alike. One does not find totally uncontrolled bodies, requiring obvious and physical restraint. Rather, the dichotomous treatment of the body as either pathologised or highly idealised – the corrupted and the pure heart which Abercrombie speaks of (p. 59, p. 157) – is again indicative of the importance of discursive control. By giving the body a definite, conventionalised shape – be it a metaphorical or a physiological and 'scientific' shape – its potential danger can be contained, while its uses as a means of communication, of character expression, and as a necessary medium for the expression of the inexpressible need not be questioned. Writers of fictional as well as of non-fictional texts go to considerable lengths to use the body as a medium of expression, a device to indicate character and race distinctions, as the site and cause of gender differences, and as a focal point for their social and political concerns such as middle class identity, social health, and order.

---

61 Cf. Treuherz (1993), op. cit., p. 21f., p. 34f. This tradition can also be traced back to the 18th century but it became more dominant in the 19th century and the ascendancy of middle class didactic and moralistic taste. Cf. William Vaughan (1999), *British Painting. The Golden Age from Hogarth to Turner*, Thames and Hudson, London, p. 10.

62 See Gesa Stedman (2000), 'Pleasurable Pictures – The Delights of Visual Excess', in *REAL*, vol. 16, pp. 149-162 for a more detailed discussion of this argument.

One of the most important elements of such discursive control which works in conjunction with conventional pictorial images of the body is the use of body metaphors for the emotions. The following section therefore looks at the relation between language, emotion and the body and its cultural function situated between discursive stability and excess.

Strokes of identity: Language, Emotion, and the Body

Charles Bell compares emotional expression to language, highlighting the link between verbal and non-verbal forms of communicating emotion. An instance which bridges the gap between verbal and non-verbal expression on the level of narration or discourse is that of metaphor. Metaphors of emotion most often use the body as their target or source, thereby verbalising the body. This technique of 'letting the body speak' is an important feature of all texts on the emotions and is by no means restricted to fictional texts. Bain's *The Emotions and the Will* illustrates this. His descriptions of emotions are often metaphorical, at times they even seem poetic, e.g. when he speaks of the 'current' (p. 102) or the 'fountain' (p. 121) of feeling, or when he likens the emotions resulting from success in sporting activities to moments 'separated by intervals of suspense and emotional stillness, like brilliant stars over the azure spaces' (p. 153). This may be due to his background as professor not only of logic but also of English. But even though his metaphors may at times be more original than those we find in health guides and treatises by his lesser-known fellow authors, their presence in itself should not come as a surprise. As Mark Johnson and George Lakoff, as well as David E. Leary have argued, metaphors are present in all kinds of texts, sometimes in rather conventional form, and exert considerable influence on the way in which the world is conceptualised.[63] Complex phenomena such as the emotions can also be said to 'demand' metaphoric treatment because their complexity would otherwise prove too difficult to be captured verbally. Alexander Bain explains the use of metaphor, or what he calls 'those strokes of identity whereby an abstruse or obscure notion is rendered lucid by some familiar parallel' (p. 166), in the following, characteristically 'hedonistic' manner: 'The mind, labouring and struggling to understand

[63] Cf. George Lakoff and Mark Johnson (1980), *Metaphors We Live By*, Chicago UP, Chicago, and David E. Leary (1990), 'Psyche's Muse: The Role of Metaphor in the History of Psychology', in id. (ed), *Metaphors in the History of Psychology*, Cambridge UP, Cambridge, pp. 1-78, in particular p. 2.

what is difficult, is suddenly illuminated by the help of the well-chosen analogy, and enjoys buoyant reaction. Such is the pleasure and felicitous exposition' (p. 166).

The analysis of my corpus of texts[64] has shown that not only the use of keywords is characterised by continuity. Favourite Victorian metaphors for the emotions are equally well-established and emphasise discursive stability rather than innovation. Apart from this stability, their performative function, comparable to that of the key emotion words, as idealising and didactic verbal feeling rules is also easily discernible.

In 19th-century texts, the most common emotion metaphor is that of the breast or the heart as the seat of all feeling. A second metaphorical conception, linking emotionality with 'natural' phenomena such as the weather or water, but also, crucially, with the body, is that of the emotions as a 'fountain', a 'current' or a 'torrent'. The heart can appear as the 'human' or 'universal' heart on the one hand, or on the other, as the more specific 'feminine' or 'woman's' heart, but only very rarely as an explicitly male one. In both these cases, the dominant concept of the heart is that of a 'container': the heart can boil, it can be warm, it can be a fountain, ready to overflow, it can be full or overcharged, and one can pour out one's heart. By extension, feelings are often represented as 'floods of happiness', 'fountains of love' or 'torrents of passion'.[65] A related spatial metaphor sees the heart as a space: the 'core' of the heart or the 'inmost' heart is the dwelling place of true religion or true feeling, and the 'desert places' of the heart signify the absence of emotion. This type of metaphor functions as a metonymy of the concept of the individual and the person which had come to be the norm: that of an inner 'core', virtually inaccessible, whose outward expression could never be identical with its 'true' and totally individual nature.[66] In other words: this is the central metaphor giving shape to the inexpressibility motif explained at the outset of this chapter.[67]

In general, the heart is seen as the source of creativity and writing, of

---

64 In the section that follows no individual sources are given because the observations hold true for all the texts that I have read, justifying such a summary approach.

65 Cf. R.A. Erickson (1997), *The Language of the Heart, 1600-1750*, University of Pennsylvania Press, Philadelphia, p. 14f. on the link between the two dominant metaphors.

66 Cf. Norbert Elias ([19]1995) [1936], *Über den Prozeß der Zivilisation*, 2 vols., Suhrkamp, Frankfurt a.M., p. LVIff., and Courtine and Haroche (1988), *L'Histoire du visage*, p. 144ff.

67 These spatial metaphors and the interest in 'internal', seemingly inaccessible human depths are reflected in the Victorian fascination with all things (para)psychological.

religious feeling, and of emotion contrasted with reason, metaphorically housed in the 'head' which is opposed to the 'heart'. The heart also functions as a metonymy either for feeling in general, or for a person, producing personifications such as the 'reigning' heart, the heart as 'master' or the 'unsuspecting' heart. The heart can live a life of its own, it softens, melts, thrills, expands, trembles, swells or, more negatively, it can be hurt by a pang, it can be pierced, it stings and rankles. The notion of movement within the heart – indicative of the history of the word emotion as *movere* – is present in the double metaphor of the heart as the seat of true feeling conceptualised as a musical instrument, whose chords can vibrate, or whose strings are plucked. Finally, lexeme combinations such as 'open-hearted', 'hard-hearted', 'soft-hearted' etc. are used for the psychological characterisation of literary characters. The idea that the heart reveals the character of a person is also present in the metaphor of the heart which can be 'read', representing the heart as a book in which a person's character and emotions are inscribed. This concept produces slight confusion in that the act of reading is associated with reason, thus making the heart not only the seat of feeling but also linking it to more cognitive processes. However, all these variants of the heart metaphor share the use of the body as a medium to express what seems to exceed verbal representation.

Heart metaphors are not restricted to fictional texts, even health guides which normally rely on a strictly physiological definition of the heart as an important organ endangered by excessive emotionality, sometimes juxtapose the physiological meaning of the word with its metaphorical extension, thus producing a linguistic confusion which I have already explained in the overlap between the medical and the emotional meaning of the word 'affection'.[68]

All these excessively idealised notions of the heart have a long tradition: ancient texts saw the heart as the seat of the soul while Christian thought introduced the spatial metaphor of the heart as a 'house' and later developments (Harvey, Descartes) made the heart resemble a mechanism such as a clock.[69] The notion of the heart as a musical instrument became

---

68 Cf. in particular the overlap of metaphorical and medical meanings of the heart in William Cooke (1839), *Mind and Emotions Considered in Relation to Health and Disease*, Longman & Co., London and the second and much longer edition, W. Cooke (1852), *A Commentary of Medical and Moral Life*.

69 Cf. Barbara Duden, (1995), 'Anmerkungen zur Kulturgeschichte des Herzens', in Faridah Akashe-Böhme (ed), *Von der Auffälligkeit des Leibes*, Suhrkamp, Frankfurt

so popular that it provoked satirical treatment in the 19th century.[70] The fact that so many writers used these common metaphors, some of them so widespread that they can almost be considered dead metaphors, can perhaps best be explained by their cultural function.

Popular metaphors serve as a kind of shorthand which makes the complexity of emotionality manageable and in a fictional text it allows readers easier access to a character's psychological make-up. But most importantly such a metaphorical continuity indicates stability in a society which was anything but stable. Cultural and textual continuity could thus help provide a sense of coherence, of links with Christian tradition and past centuries which did not exist on any but the discursive level. Yet in another paradoxical twist, the sheer excess and abundance of idealising metaphors belies the assertion that 'where the middle classes exert political power it is the surreptitious victory of thrift over extravagance, of simplicity over ornament, of austerity over frivolity' that dominates taste and culture.[71] By trying to exert discursive control, the use of metaphor, just like the use of excessive classification and definition of key emotion words, subverts its purpose and becomes expressive not of controlled feelings, but of their opposite: the potentially boundless nature of all emotions.[72]

The body as the site for individual and social expression and control of

---

a.M., pp. 130-141, in particular p. 135, Erickson (1997), *The Language of the Heart*, p. 4, and Joan DeJean (1997), 'A Short History of the Human Heart', in id., *Ancients Against Moderns: Culture Wars and the Making of a Fin de Siècle*, University of Chicago Press, Chicago, pp. 80-123, in particular p. 108ff.

70 Cf. Gesa Stedman (2000), '"Private" Passions in Public Places – Women's Poetry on the Feelings', in Sabine Coelsch-Foisner and Holger Klein (eds), *Private and Public Voices in Victorian Poetry* (Studies in English and Comparative Literature, vol. 16), Stauffenburg Verlag, Tübingen, pp. 149-160 and Ina Schabert (1997), *Englische Literaturgeschichte aus der Sicht der Geschlechterforschung*, Alfred Kröner, Stuttgart, p. 468f.

71 Philippe Perrot (October 1987) argues along these lines in his article 'La richesse cachée: pour une généalogie de l'austerité des apparences', in *Communications*, vol. 46, pp. 157-179, quotation p. 158: '... partout où la bourgeoisie exerce un pouvoir politique, c'est la sourde victoire de l'épargne sur le gaspillage, de la simplicité sur l'ornement, de l'austerité sur le frivole' (My translation, G.S.).

72 Since my study works only with textual material which either falls into the category of fiction or is characterised by related features (notably narrative) and not with any kind of sources which would offer insights into 'actual' emotions or the history of the body, it is impossible to follow Barbara Duden's (1995) suggestion. She conceptualises the heart as more than metaphor in her concept of the heart as a cultural model which governs experience and action ('praxisleitendes *Erlebnis*'). See her article 'Anmerkungen zur Kulturgeschichte des Herzens', in particular p. 130f.

the feelings is one of the fundamental topics in Charlotte Brontë's novel *Shirley* (1849). The novel will serve as my key text for the next section which concentrates on how the body and the body politic work together in a fictional text which combines several important strands of the Victorian discourses on emotions.

No passionate link? Body and Body Politic in Charlotte Brontë's novel *Shirley*

Ever since George Henry Lewes accused Charlotte Brontë of having written a disjointed novel with 'no passionate link' between its two constitutive elements[73] – the two love plots and the rebellion plot – have critics grappled with *Shirley*, the author's second novel which followed her first astonishing success, *Jane Eyre* (1847), in 1849.[74] Lewes showed himself singularly biased in his review. It is written from the perspective of a man who criticises the novel which he (rightly) believed to have been produced by a woman on the basis of a different standard than one he would apply to texts stemming from a man's pen. Charlotte Brontë was worried that this would happen, since her male pseudonym 'Currer Bell' had begun to be questioned, and was consequently deeply hurt that a personal acquaintance could publish such a vindictive review exposing her as a woman writer allegedly 'unworthy' of her sex.[75]

It was this literary criticism – the accusation of having created a disunited text – which would endure.[76] In his more sympathetic treatment,

---

73 'There is no passionate link; nor is there any artistic fusion or intergrowth, by which one part evolves itself from another'. George Henry Lewes (January 1850), 'Currer Bell's Shirley', in Barbara Timm Gates (ed), *Critical Essays on Charlotte Brontë*, G.K. Hall & Co. Boston, Mass., pp. 217-223, quotation p. 217. First published in *Edinburgh Review*, vol. 91.

74 Charlotte Brontë (1985) [1974] [1849], *Shirley*, Penguin, Harmondsworth, p. 17f. All page references refer to this edition.

75 Charlotte Brontë famously sent a spirited reply to Lewes, with whom she had earlier corresponded regularly. It hurt her most that he exposed her as a woman writer, a fact not yet known by many besides him, although it was already a matter of speculation. See Lewes (January 1850), 'Currer Bell's Shirley', p. 221. For the author's response cf. anon. (1980) [1933], *The Brontës. Their Lives, Friendships and Correspondence*, Basil Blackwell, Oxford, 2 vols., vol. 3 [3], p. 67: she writes to Lewes (January 1850): 'I can be on my guard against my enemies, but God deliver me from my friends!'

76 The reviews seem to have been favourable except for criticism of her treatment of the clergy which provides no more than a kind of comic sub-plot, yet heightened Victorian

Asa Briggs analyses the historical context of the novel – the early 19th-century rebellions of mill workers in Northern England – in its relation to what he calls the 'private theme' of the two love stories, but nevertheless maintains that the novel falls into two seemingly unrelated parts.[77] Following Sally Shuttleworth's opinion that in *Shirley* 'the circulating economies of psychological and social life are directly interwoven',[78] my analysis moves away from the conventional view of the novel as interesting but flawed, by re-reading its daring 'passionate link' between love plot and historical plot in the light of the discourses on emotions. What Brontë achieves in *Shirley* is remarkable: she manages to tie together all the most important topics of the Victorian discourses on emotions – religion, gender, social order, individual and social expression and control of the feelings – and relates the dangers of individual emotional repression to its possible social consequences. She shows that complete repression is not the answer to the problem of expression and control, and offers a multivocal debate of four major emotion concepts in the novel. After working through friendship, marriage of convenience without love, and benevolence as compensation for love, she finally arrives

---

sensitivity to religious matters was offended by her satirical treatment of ineffective, indulgent and intellectually inferior curates. Although *Shirley* was not quite such a runaway success as *Jane Eyre*, it did prove popular enough for its 20,000 copies to sell out within nine months. And by 1897, the novel had gone to nine editions, including an early cheaper one, as part of the 'Life and Works' series published by Smith and Elder in 1872-73, with *Shirley* as the second volume, priced at 5*s*. Cf. Juliet Barker (1994), *The Brontës*, Weidenfeld & Nicolson, London, p. 610ff., p. 810 and the *English Catalogue*. For the author's comments on the reviews cf. anon. (1980), *The Brontës*, vol. 1 [3], p. 35, p. 42, p. 45.

77 Asa Briggs (1958), 'Private and Social Themes in *Shirley*', in *Brontë Society Transactions*, pp. 203-19. Briggs speaks of a 'fatal absence of focus which prevents it from being a successful novel', p. 218. This view can still be found in an otherwise interesting analysis by Sandra M. Gilbert and Susan Gubar (1984) [1974], 'The Genesis of Hunger, According to *Shirley*', in id., *The Madwoman in the Attic. The Woman Writer and the Nineteenth-Century Literary Imagination*, Yale UP, New Haven/London, pp. 372-398.

78 Sally Shuttleworth (1996), *Charlotte Brontë and Ninteenth-Century Psychology*, Cambridge UP, Cambridge, p. 183. For an overview of further modern reactions to *Shirley*, cf. Judith and Andrew Hook's (1985) introduction to *Shirley*, Harmondsworth, Penguin, pp. 7-32, in particular p. 28ff. and Arnold Shapiro (winter 1968), 'Public Themes and Private Lives: Social Criticism in *Shirley*', in Timm Gates (ed), *Critical Essays*, pp. 223-232, repr. from *Papers on Language and Literature*, vol. 4 (1), pp. 74-84. Terry Eagleton (1975), *Myths of Power. A Marxist Study of the Brontës*, Macmillan, Basingstoke/London, in particular chapter 3, pp. 45-60, also analyses the convergence of the public and the private themes of the novel.

at a concept of heterosexual love-as-friendship which has left passion behind and carries with it the promise of private and public happiness for all. In the union between Caroline Helstone and Robert Moore, and in the marriage between Shirley Keeldar and Louis Moore, Brontë arrives at the representation of a 'passionate link' between the private and the public, the individual body and the body politic, thereby illustrating how closely related these allegedly 'separate spheres' were for a Victorian writer.

In *Shirley*, the reader is offered different perspectives since the novel incorporates several narrators. An omniscient, overt but heterodiegetic first person narrator is sometimes supplemented by first person accounts or soliloquies by main characters, as well as by written sections, in particular those penned by Louis Moore. His autobiographical notebook allows the reader a privileged insight into the lover's state of mind and serves as a counter perspective to the largely female view that predominates in the novel. In addition, lengthy literary quotations constitute a further level of discourse so that the novel can be seen as a complex and multivocal text, which, in spite of apparent closure at the end, invites the reader to come to his or her own conclusions regarding the main issues that the novel discusses. This is particularly true since the text is based on dialogue and dispute, thus allowing the reader a view of more than one side of an argument. The novel incorporates different levels of direct and indirect characterisation and comment, and although the sympathies of the narrator obviously lie with the opinions expressed by the female protagonists, in particular concerning social questions, contradictory views also get a hearing. In addition, several differing protagonists as well as concepts of love, life and politics are offered which makes *Shirley* much less heavily didactic than the average Victorian novel, which would not ironically shy away from a final moral, as the narrator in *Shirley* does: 'The story is told. I think I now see the judicious reader putting on his spectacles to look for the moral. It would be an insult to his sagacity to offer directions. I only say, God speed him in the quest!' (p. 599).

Three elements are crucial in this novel which conceptualises the 'body as the cross-roads between self and society'[79]: the treatment of emotional expression and control in a fictional setting, the interrelation between what at first appears to be private feeling and society, and the confrontation of the expression-and-control paradigm with contemporary gender debates.

Although *Shirley* begins with the setting for the political plot, I would

---

[79] Porter (1991), 'History of the Body', p. 207.

like to reverse this order and introduce the two female protagonists first. This should not be understood as a subtle move to reinstate the love plot as the main theme of the novel. But in order to understand the social and political implications of the two models that Caroline Helstone and Shirley Keeldar represent it is necessary to start with the individual body and character before its connection with the body politic can be explained. What can be analysed separately in such an investigation must nevertheless be considered inextricably linked in the text (and the discourses on emotions as a whole).

Charlotte Brontë chose to contrast two women in *Shirley*, a literary strategy popularised by Jane Austen and Germaine de Staël, whose importance as a person and as an intertextual source is discussed at greater length in chapter 5. Charlotte Brontë professed to a dislike of Jane Austen – significantly because she thought her writing devoid of 'passion',[80] defined by Brontë as 'what throbs fast and full', that is: as a bodily occurrence. Brontë sets her own treatment of emotion off from Austen's allegedly dispassionate approach and thus claims a space for her own manner of 'narrating the heart' as an embodied emotional habitus. Nevertheless, Brontë's ploy of distributing two aspects of emotionality onto two characters is reminiscent of Austen's *Sense and Sensibility* (1811) and its contrasting pair of heroines, Marianne and Elinor Dashwood, who represent the dangers of too much and too little emotion and expression. By using this method of characterisation, Brontë is able to describe in detail two different approaches to emotion. With Caroline, she illustrates the dangers and the futility of individual repression. With Shirley, she shows that expression does not necessarily lead to happiness either. The relations that both characters have with their future husbands form the centre of the 'passionate link' between the individual body as the medium

80 '... the Passions are perfectly unknown to her; she rejects even a speaking acquaintance with that stormy Sisterhood; even to the Feelings she vouchsafes no more than an occasional graceful but distant recognition. Too frequent converse with them would ruffle the smooth elegance of her progress. Her business is not half so much with the human heart as with the human eyes, mouth, hand and feet; what sees keenly, speaks aptly, moves flexibly, it suits her to study, but what throbs fast and full, though hidden, what the blood rushes through, what is the unseen seat of Life and the sentient target of death – *this* Miss Austen ignores; she no more, with her mind's eye, beholds the heart of her race than each man, with bodily vision sees the heart in his heaving breast. Jane Austen was a complete and most sensible lady, but a very incomplete, and rather insensible (*not senseless*) woman, if this is heresy – I cannot help it.' Charlotte Brontë (12 April 1850) in a letter to W.S. Williams, in anon. (1980), *The Brontës*, vol. 2 [3], p. 99.

of emotional expression, and the social body which directly depends upon it. Both protagonists also serve as the author's 'leading ladies' for her fictional debates of the four emotion concepts which form this link, already mentioned above: friendship, loveless marriage of convenience, benevolence as compensation for the absence of love, and finally love-as-friendship in marriage.

Caroline is the first of the two protagonists to be introduced in *Shirley*. The reader is presented with an initial impression of her through the eyes of her older cousin Hortense Moore who thinks that she '"is not perfect, ... there is much to be desired in her"'. Hortense's characterisation of Caroline also throws some light on her own bent of mind:

> '... Caroline, then, is defective; ... There is about her an occasional something – a reserve, I think – which I do not quite like, because it is not sufficiently girlish and submissive; ... In time, I doubt not, I shall make her uniformly sedate and decorous, without being unaccountably pensive. I ever disapprove what is not intelligible.' (p. 95)

Hortense specifically intends not only to teach Caroline '"a system, a method of thought, a set of opinions ..."' but also '"the perfect control and guidance of her feelings"' (p. 96). As we shall see, too much control will have an adverse effect on Caroline. She is the protagonist used by Brontë to illustrate one of the four emotion concepts that are enacted, embodied and discussed in *Shirley*. Early on Caroline begins thinking about the absence of love characteristic of the life of an 'old maid': '"I have to live, perhaps, till seventy years. As far as I know, I have good health: half a century of existence may lie before me. How am I to occupy it? ... What was I created for, I wonder? Where is my place in the world?"' (p. 190).[81]

[81] Sally Shuttleworth (1996) bases her discussion of *Shirley* on the parallel that she sets up between the 'woman question' on the one hand and the problem of industrial modernisation and the plight of the workers on the other (*Charlotte Brontë*, p. 184f.) This analogy seems slightly forced and I find her argument more convincing when she relates the description of Caroline's decline to contemporary Victorian debates on health and disease (e.g. p. 186). Although she is right in stressing the overlap between the Victorian discourses on social health, on the working classes and on psychology, this does not necessarily imply that Caroline is the 'site' where these three discourses meet. I would stress the importance of the discussions in the novel of the relation between expression and control of emotionality, and its social causes and consequences, rather than making the plight of the workers – something which Brontë only writes about in a worried and ambivalent manner (cf. the description of the 'mob') – the point where the 'private' and the 'public' intersect.

Her restricted outlook on life is a result of her precarious situation at home. Her uncle Helstone considers women in general and Caroline in particular to be rather weak creatures who quickly get on his nerves. He is virtually incapable of showing any affection and leaves her to her own devices. Caroline's education is unsystematic and makes her feel inferior (p. 103). When her uncle forbids her to see the Moores, and her lessons with Hortense have to stop, Caroline does her best to keep herself occupied by sewing and reading the few books from her uncle's library which she is able to read, not knowing any Greek or Latin (p. 376). Her limited experience has also made Caroline shy of society and she intensely dislikes receiving the visits of the three unattractive and silly curates, or the 'pattern ladies', as the fashionable female society of the area is ironically termed by the narrator (p. 132f.). The latter describes Caroline herself in the following manner:

> ... her face was expressive and gentle; her eyes were handsome, and gifted at times with a winning beam that stole into the heart, with a language that spoke softly to the affections. ...
>
> So much for Caroline Helstone's appearance; as to her character or intellect, if she had any, they must speak for themselves in due time. (p. 102)

She does indeed speak for herself and a certain lack of submissiveness shines through (p. 110ff.). When she is happy, this becomes visible in her face:

> Her cheek had a colour, her eyes a light, her countenance an expression ... which would have made even plain features striking ... Each lineament was turned with grace; the whole aspect was pleasing. At the present moment – animated, interested, touched – she might be called beautiful ... . (p. 119)

When she still feels sure of Robert's affection, this state of youthful hope is presented in a sensuous description:

> ... the door bolted, her white dressing-gown assumed, her long hair loosened and falling thick, soft, and wavy to her waist, and as, resting from the task of combing it out, she leaned her cheek on her hand and fixed her eyes on the carpet, before her rose, and close around her drew, the visions we see at eighteen years. (p. 122)

Her feelings at this stage are easily divined (p. 109) but this expressiveness will rapidly fall away once she perceives a change in Robert's behaviour towards her (p. 127, p. 129). When she has understood that Robert does not intend to marry her, she tries to suppress all signs of emotion, a feat she usually succeeds in (p. 130).

She acquiesces when her uncle orders her to break off her relationship with Hortense, and thus with Robert. She submits to his rule without rebelling, because she feels rejected by Robert, and even avoids looking at him in church: 'it was both too much pain and too much pleasure to look: it excited too much emotion; and that it was all wasted emotion, she had learned well to comprehend' (p. 187). Painfully, she comes to the conclusion that where her feelings dwell on him, his do not on her (p. 188). Caroline fights against her intense feelings of love and although this soon becomes obvious in her physical aspect, she maintains that nothing is wrong with her except the need for change (p. 200, p. 203). And although she fears that Robert and Shirley are becoming involved with one another, which makes her feel left out like a bystander at a banquet (p. 239, p. 254), she continues to control her feelings: 'None could affirm that she had trembled or blushed, that her heart had quaked, or her nerves thrilled: none could prove emotion ...' (p. 251), and defends her rejection of making a display of her feelings (p. 313). These feelings nevertheless become obvious during the attack on the mill, when Shirley only just restrains her from coming to Robert's rescue (p. 333). She subverts the stereotype of the submissive young woman at this stage, a fact that Robert and Shirley comment on during a discussion following the attack (p. 352). Caroline is a complex character who is not represented as the archetypal 'angel in the house'.

Although her friendship with Shirley, her growing intimacy with Mrs Pryor, and her charitable activities sustain her for a while, Caroline nevertheless soon falls ill (p. 399, p. 401) and becomes weaker and weaker, only to be saved by Mrs Pryor's attention and the revelation that she is Caroline's mother. Caroline is much changed. Only when Robert himself has undergone a transformation during his illness caused by his shotgun wound and understands how dear she is to him, does she improve not just in physical but in mental health as well (p. 557). Her slightly passive character is once again revealed during Robert's proposal (p. 561) and when she – mistakenly – fears that through marriage she will not be able to live with her mother. In telling language, she is described as 'nestling' to him and he addresses her as 'my dove' (p. 595). Louis remarks upon her nature in another passage of indirect characterisation which contrasts Shirley and Caroline: '"What a difference there is between S. and that pearl C. H.! Caroline, I fancy, is the soul of conscientious punctuality and nice exactitude ...'" (p. 490).

This contrast is remarked upon several times. In most respects Shirley is virtually the exact opposite of Caroline in terms of temper and looks.[82] Their friendship is based on equality of taste rather than character or social background. Each serves as the contrastive mirror of the other protagonist. But just as Caroline is not merely passive and weak, but can also be spirited and persevering, so Shirley is not always strong and temperamental. Both characters are ambivalent and thus occasionally subvert the conventional dichotomy between the 'angel in the house' and the strong heroine.[83]

As soon as the two protagonists meet for the first time, they are compared by the narrator who at first points out their similarities but then emphasises the contrast. Shirley's exterior mirrors her internal qualities: she is more open than Caroline and less shy, yet for all her greater expression of feeling she is not easily 'read': 'Her features were distinguished ... mobile they were and speaking; but their changes were not to be understood, nor their language interpreted all at once' (p. 211f.).

The narrator gives another impression of the contrast between the two young women when they prepare for the Whitsuntide church fête, stressing their difference in character: Caroline is punctual and neat while Shirley is indolent with the heat and cannot be brought to look tidy, not even with Caroline's help (p. 292). But the contrast lies deeper than appearances: Shirley, although 'warmhearted and sympathetic' is not shaken by emotional experiences as Caroline is (p. 341). And where Caroline is shy, Shirley is open. When Mr Helstone and Caroline visit her and she meets the latter for the first time she welcomes them cheerfully and without any hesitation (p. 210). Hers is a happy nature (p. 237), she is impulsive (p.

---

82 Gilbert and Gubar (1984), 'Genesis', p. 382f., and Eagleton (1975), *Myths of Power*, p. 58, see Shirley as Caroline's *alter ego* who embodies everything that Caroline herself does not allow herself to be. Shirley has also been interpreted as a fictionalised Emily Brontë, e.g. by Elizabeth Gaskell (1997) [1906] [1857], *The Life of Charlotte Brontë*, J.M. Dent, London, p. 198ff., and Judith and Andrew Hook (1985), 'Introduction', p. 22. Both these interpretations, although justified, detract from the emphasis placed on the contrast between the two female protagonists and on the different ways they deal with their feelings. While Caroline seems to lean more towards the control side of the expression-and-control paradigm, Shirley tends more towards expression although she also hides some of her feelings (notably her fear of having become infected with rabies and her love for Louis).

83 For an overview of 'typical' Victorian heroines, cf. Merryn Williams (1985), *Women in the English Novel, 1800-1900*, Macmillan, London, in particular pp. 34-36.

245) and of a kindly disposition (p. 270, p. 295). In spite of her social status, her thoughts do not run merely on business and money (p. 230). While Caroline is worried by her lack of education and occupation, Shirley is much more content in her everyday activities, which afford her a wider scope of employment (p. 372f.).

She is described as quick-tempered (p. 275) and her countenance shows 'a ruffled and darkened brow, curled lip, and incensed eye' (after having thrown out one of the curates, p. 287) but she is quick to atone for her outbursts, e.g. when she hurts Mrs Pryor by accusing her of being unwelcoming and unhelpful after the attack on Robert's Mill (p. 349).

Shirley's emotional reactions are less visible than Caroline's, before Caroline succeeds in suppressing them, that is, and as has been mentioned, they are not always easy to interpret either (p. 359, p. 374). Although Shirley expresses anger, other feelings are 'evinced in her own peculiar fashion. When deeply moved, by serious fears or joys, she was not garrulous. The strong emotion was rarely suffered to influence her tongue, and even her eye refused it more than a furtive and fitful conquest' (p. 426). This does not, however, occur because Shirley does not possess any feelings. On the contrary, as Caroline explains to Robert in familiar metaphorical language: '"I have found her chary in showing her feelings; but when they rush out, river-like, and pass full and powerful before you, – almost without leave from her – you gaze, wonder, you admire, and – I think – love her"'. She goes on to state that she has been allowed to see Shirley's '"heart's core"' (p. 559) and in a blazon-like style, describes it as follows: '"Like a shrine, – for it was holy; like snow, – for it was pure; like flame, – for it was warm; like death, – for it was strong"' (p. 560).

Shirley's air of authority (p. 333) and her courage are not only commented on, e.g. by Mr Helstone (p. 267), they are visible in her acts. She even longs for adventures and something to defend or fight for – '"I almost long for danger; for a faith – a land – or, at least, a lover to defend"' (p. 299) – and when Robert offers her marriage, her anger makes her quite formidable, as he later explains to Yorke: '"By the Lord! Yorke – she rose – she grew tall – she expanded and refined almost to flame: there was a trembling all through her, as in live coal, when its vivid vermilion is hottest. ..."' (p. 499f.). This side of her nature is emphasised particularly in the first half of the novel, and is slightly corrected when a new facet is added by Louis's written account.

Before Shirley is seen through the eyes of her former tutor, she appears as a fearless, and even slightly transgressive female character. The most striking passages are those in which Shirley assumes the role of 'Captain Keeldar'. Although this role is only playfully taken up, it was quite daring on the part of Charlotte Brontë to include such blatantly androgynous passages. Even though Shirley never actually cross-dresses, and her feminine beauty is never questioned, these ironic passages subvert the notion of fixed gender roles. Her little cousin Henry stresses the fact that she is no amazon (p. 471), but that is precisely the role which she seems to assume.

Together with the multivocal discussions of women, their nature and role, the androgynous appearance of 'Captain Keeldar' serves as an enactment of the possibilities that would lie open to women, were they allowed to assume different roles, e.g. the role of heir and lord of the manor, instead of waiting to be married off to someone, as Shirley very nearly is forced to do by her uncle Sympson. This striking contrast to Caroline's largely conventional femininity is stressed (p. 390). Shirley speaks of herself as 'Captain Keeldar' (p. 247f.) and is criticised strongly for it by Mrs Pryor (p. 217). She is encouraged in her playful act by Robert Moore (p. 250) and by Mr Helstone who asks Mrs Pryor to

> '... take care of *this future magistrate, this churchwarden* in perspective, *this captain of yeomanry, this young squire* of Briarfield, in a word: don't let him exert himself too much: don't let him break his neck in *hunting*: especially, let him mind how he *rides* down that dangerous hill near the Hollow'. (p. 215) (My emphasis, G.S.)

Although Shirley and Helstone continue in this vein and take up this style of conversation at later stages as well, the irony of this list of male (aristocratic) occupations is not lost on the reader when contrasted with Caroline's numerous pleas for useful occupation. By drawing attention to the contrast between an imaginary 'Captain Keeldar' and Shirley's (and Caroline's) actual position, their relatively limited roles are once again emphasised.

Nevertheless, it is this part of the 'grave but gallant little cavalier' (p. 211) which makes it possible for Shirley to converse with Robert on equal terms and enables her to save his business by investing in his affairs (p. 243, p. 254). But this image of the strong, independent and temperamental being receives its first slight dent when Robert's notoriously misogynous assistant Joe Scott, who thinks women should follow St Paul's rules and compares Shirley to a 'chattering pie' (p. 320ff.), describes the inattentive manner in which she conducts these business conversations: '"she hears no more o' Mr Moore's talk nor if he spake Hebrew"' (p. 324). This may or may not be true – but Shirley's character is revealed to be far more ambivalent than Caroline's when Louis Moore appears on the scene. He accompanies his pupil Henry Sympson and his family. Shirley used to live with her uncle's family and thus profited from Louis's instruction – another difference which sets her off socially from Caroline whose patchy education has already been described. A first indication that Shirley is not always as strong and self-reliant as the image of 'Captain Keeldar' implies comes with the incident of the dog-bite which provokes an unfounded panic in Shirley. She can only overcome this with Louis's help (p. 479f.). His account of her behaviour – although perhaps not wholly reliable since he is in love with her and may therefore be biased – throws a new light on her character. He sees her as sometimes childlike (p. 488), and in her capricious behaviour towards him (p. 432f.) she does seem less assured than she usually is. And in prior discussions of love or marriage she has indicated herself that it is not a husband she can baby whom she is seeking, but someone who will be able to master her. In a surprising inversion of the image of 'Captain Keeldar' she appears almost masochistic in her wish to be led. Again through Louis's eyes the necessity to 'tame' her, and indeed his choice of words for her – '"[s]ister of the spotted, bright, quick, fiery leopard"' (p. 574) and '"[p]antheress"' (p. 584) – indicate a relation of animal and keeper. In the end, Shirley lets herself be conquered and Louis sheds enough of his pride – derived from his socially inferior position – to publicly acknowledge his feelings for her. But it is nevertheless Shirley who proposes to him.

Shirley undergoes a more striking change than Caroline, and it is the love for a man which causes this change. On the whole, though, it is the spirited Shirley who dominates the novel, and her daring assumption of an androgynous role – albeit only in passing – leaves a greater impression than her later transformation, more in accordance with the role of a docile wife. The fact that she gives up all her rights as mistress of Fieldhead so that Louis is once and for all forced to take up his position as master finalises the transition and the delivery of all power. This type of narrative closure was common in Victorian novels and was largely required by their readers. The transformation of the protagonist who gives the novel its title does not seem to have convinced all of them, though: George Henry Lewes sharply criticised the transgressive aspects in Shirley's character – this side of her seems to have left a greater impression on him than her later switch to more conventional femininity.[84]

Troubled power relations bordering on masochism are an aspect of Charlotte Brontë's work which can also be found in *Villette* (1853) and *The Professor* (1857)[85] and which continue to disturb readers and critics.[86] The masochistic woman who desires a 'professor' as her partner is a worrying image, in particular for feminist critics. But the opportunities that these learned men open up for the female characters ought not to be underestimated in a period during which women were either self-taught or at the hands of more or less qualified tutors. An intellectually challenging partner, even if he could only be imagined as a superior figure, who was willing to engage with them intellectually, is more than the average Victorian heroine could bargain for and is in itself unusual and found more often in novels written by women (e.g. in George Eliot's novels) than by men. That Shirley chooses Louis on the basis of his character's merits is a further point of defence of this narrative twist whose considerable significance will be better understood in the light of the paradigmatic emotion concepts which Caroline's and Shirley's respective experiences serve to illustrate.

As I have already briefly mentioned, the novel contains four different emotion concepts – explicit discussions of emotional habitus – all of which are inextricably and by definition bound up with social norms. Firstly, tender affection, to be found in friendship and family relations. This concept is illustrated mainly by the relationship between Caroline and Shirley, and in the later stages of the novel by Mrs Pryor and Caroline. Secondly, the total absence of feeling in marriages of convenience, hinted at rather than illustrated in the debates focusing on Shirley's future and in Robert's plans to marry her for money. Thirdly, benevolence may function as compensation for spinsterhood, as exemplified in Miss Mann and Miss Ainley, and discussed by Caroline who does not manage to achieve emotional serenity by applying this concept to her own situation. And finally passionate love, which may end in marriage of mutual consent but only if passion is worked through and turned into love-as-friendship which

84 While criticising Shirley, Lewes at the same time succumbs to her appeal: 'Shirley, if she did not occasionally use language one would rather not hear from the lips of a lady, and did not occasionally display something in her behaviour, which, with every allowance for Yorkshire plainness, does imply want of breeding, – Shirley, we say, would be irresistible'. Lewes (1850), 'Currer Bell's Shirley', p. 220.

85 *The Professor* was written in 1846 but published posthumously in 1857.

86 Gilbert and Gubar (1984), 'Genesis', p. 393ff., Eagleton (1975), *Myths of Power*, p. 57.

does no longer pose the threat that violent passion may do. These four concepts are varied throughout the novel and are discussed at length. All of them are closely related to gender issues and thus are intrinsically social in nature. The one concept which is never shown in its darker side is friendship, while the possible negative outcome of spinsterhood, unrequited passion or incompatibility in marriage receive explicit attention from both narrator and protagonists. This again echoes the notion that all emotions and their experience are linked to pleasure and pain, although *Shirley* illustrates that both aspects are usually present in any emotional experience and thus make the novel a more complex text than the scientific treatises which depend on clear-cut boundaries between pleasure and pain.

All concepts and their variants share the fact that they are embodied, as the definition of habitus explained in the first chapter implies. They are expressed in non-verbal forms of communication such as tears or gestures and develop characteristic forms of bodily posture, behaviour and state (of health).

Arguably one of the most important concepts in the hierarchy that the novel sets up is friendship, exemplified by the relationship of the two female protagonists.[87] For Caroline, her newly developed friendship with Shirley is the first sign of hope, although in the end it will not suffice to restore her physical, moral and social well-being – her mother and a lover and husband are required for such a restoration. For Shirley, the benefit appears to be slightly less visible, but it is Caroline's quiet nature and orderliness which check Shirley's temper and occasional laxity of manner. Although she is less lonely than Caroline due to her more privileged social position, she also profits from Caroline's presence because they share interests and taste, as opposed to the shallow occupations of the 'pattern girls' (p. 131ff., p. 231, p. 375) which both have to spend time with as hostesses. For both young women, the mutual discussions of friendship, love, marriage and gender relations help to clarify their positions and to

---

[87] Tess Cosslett (1988), *Woman to Woman: Female Friendship in Victorian Fiction*, Harvester Press, Brighton, includes an interesting discussion of *Shirley* in her study. She claims that the model represented by Caroline and Shirley differs from the majority of fictional friendships in Victorian novels. Although it is here that the woman writer engages with cultural prescriptions of femininity (p. 4), it also breaks with the convention that female friendship assimilates women to marriage and with the dominant concept of friendship as a re-enactment of the mother-daughter relationship (p. 13). She attributes to the friendship between Caroline and Shirley a 'central structuring role' of the whole novel (p. 116) which stands in strong opposition to the disruptive quality that characterises the majority of male-male relationships in the novel (p. 120).

come to terms with their respective feelings for Robert and Louis. Each serves as the sounding-board and corrective force of the other. Their friendship is described as an explicitly feminine realm – in spite of Shirley's assumed androgynous role as 'Captain Keeldar' – and is characterised by equality (p. 23).

Shirley and Caroline both agree that the presence of men can disturb their intimacy: '"If they are of the wrong sort, like your Malones, and your young Sykes, and Wynnes, irritation takes the place of serenity. If they are of the right sort, there is still a change – I can hardly tell what change, one easy to feel, difficult to describe"' (p. 221).[88] Yet what will cloud their mutual attachment is precisely the presence of a gentleman, and the illusion he is under that Shirley loves him, as well as the consequences that this has for Caroline. But the strength of their friendship is illustrated by the fact that it deepens and continues, and can be relied upon in a crisis, namely the 'defence' of Briarmains during the night of the machine breakers' attack, and by their explicit discussions of the problem (p. 263).[89]

The evening before the 'mob' attacks the mill, Helstone asks Shirley to look after Briarmains and Caroline, which Shirley comments on: '"I promise you then to stay with Caroline", replied Shirley. "As you say, we shall enjoy each other's society: we will not be separated to-night. Now, rejoin your old friend, and fear nothing for us"' (p. 326). Shirley and Caroline are not quite as equal as is alleged. It is less their social position – even though that comes into it – but their different temperaments which might push the discerning reader towards an interpretation which attributes to Shirley the 'male' and to Caroline the 'female' role implied in this passage.[90] However, any danger of reading anything else into their friendship than just that – friendly affection – is allayed by the presence of an equally important emotion concept: that of heterosexual love.

Love is explicitly contrasted with affection – that emotion reserved for friends and family.[91] In a moving plea, Caroline defends her 'English'

---

88 See Cosslett (1988), *Woman to Woman*, on the symbolic significance of this feminine world (p. 123ff.).

89 It is slightly curious and inconsistent that Shirley is largely absent during Caroline's severe illness, but this is required by the plot so that Mrs Pryor's maternal role can be brought more to the fore.

90 In *Myths of Power*, Eagleton (1975) comes to similar conclusions when he characterises their relationship as 'latently sexual'. Cf. also Gilbert and Gubar (1984), 'Genesis', p. 381, for a similar interpretation.

91 In the use of this word (affection) Brontë adheres to the implicit rules of the discourses on emotions which reserve the term for just those relationships.

concept of affectionate friendship as opposed to passionate love in her refutation of Shirley's accusation of being negligent in her emotional expression towards her:

> 'Shirley, I never had a sister – you never had a sister; but it flashes on me at this moment how sisters feel towards each other. Affection twined with their life, which no shocks of feeling can uproot, which little quarrels only trample an instant that it may spring more freshly when the pressure is removed; affection that no passion can ultimately outrival, with which even love itself cannot do more than compete in force and truth. Love hurts us so, Shirley: it is so tormenting, so racking, and it burns away our strength with its flame, in affection, is no pain and no fire, only sustenance and balm. I am supported and soothed when you – that is, *you only*, are near, Shirley ...'. (p. 265)

In this passage, Caroline is made to contrast passion and love, characterised by fire, burning and racking pain, with affection which gives sustenance and balm. While passion is described as a threat to the existence of those who love, since it consumes all energy, affection is represented as a life-sustaining force, thereby placing it above passion. But in this quotation, an idea from an earlier paragraph is also taken up. Here, the narrator describes Caroline's face as awakening 'not only the calm sentiment of esteem, the distant one of admiration; but some feeling more tender, genial, intimate: friendship, perhaps – affection, interest' (p. 119).

'Tender affection' is the keyword here. It is a word derived from the French[92] and faintly reminiscent of a highly popular and innovative 17th-century emotion concept developed by the French author Madelaine de Scudéry (1608-1701) in her best-selling novel *Clélie* (1654) and the famous geographical representation of the *précieux* concept of tender love, the *carte de tendre*.[93] It is unknown whether Charlotte Brontë actually knew

---

92 Cf. the *OED* for the word's etymology.

93 My attention was drawn to this connection by Joan DeJean (1997), who also discusses *Clélie* and the *carte de tendre* in 'A Short History of the Human Heart', in id., *Ancients Against Moderns: Culture Wars and the Making of a Fin de Siècle*, University of Chicago Press, Chicago, pp. 80-123, p. 83ff. This is just one of the literary models which Brontë uses to subvert conventional sexual images in literature as well as 'courtship roles and myths', as Gilbert and Gubar (1984) call them, 'Genesis', p. 395. But I would contradict their opinion that Brontë did not have any 'subversive' literary model at hand to do this. This depends on the definition of subversion: if the ironic treatment of marriage in Jane Austen's novels or the inherently misogamist texts by Madeleine de Scudéry are allowed to fall into this category, then *Shirley* can be considered as subversive a novel as it could be in the first half of the 19th century. As

this novel or comparable texts by the same author – in one of her letters she tantalisingly mentions a crate of forty French books which have recently arrived in her native Haworth for her to read without giving further details as to the titles and authors.[94] But apart from the fact that Scudéry's influence can be traced throughout the centuries, Brontë both knew and read Julia Kavanagh,[95] a writer who was familiar with the work of Madeleine de Scudéry. Although Kavanagh considered the *carte de tendre* to be *Clélie*'s greatest flaw, she nevertheless testifies to Madeleine de Scudéry's enormous influence in her description of the 'school' of writing which Scudéry initiated and whose traces can be found in sensation novels in Kavanagh's time:

> The young, the imaginative, the impulsive, may have been charmed with her stories, ... they may have liked, too, the earthquakes, the carrying off of damsels, the shipwrecks, and the pirates; that school still lives, and though it has learned to look more real, it is pretty much what it was in Mademoiselle de Scudéry's days; but for the older, the wiser, and the sadder readers, whom this accomplished lady also had to please, what a mine of delight must those long discourses on human passions and feelings, on the manners, ridicules, and follies of men and women, those episodes of coquettes, flirts, and jealous or dissatisfied lovers, have afforded.[96]

Even though Kavanagh's study was published after Charlotte Brontë's death, familiarity with Madeleine de Scudéry's work can be assumed not

---

Gilbert and Gubar (1984) rightly acknowledge, the novel's ending is based upon 'an almost cynical excess of concession to narrative conventions' (p. 396) – a narrative device which in itself can be judged subversive.

94 Cf. anon. (1980), *The Brontës*, vol. 1 [1], p. 214f. and Enid Duthie (1975), *The Foreign Vision of Charlotte Brontë*, Methuen, London.

95 Cf. anon. (1980), *The Brontës*, vol. 1 [2], p. 185, vol. 3 [3], p. 88, p. 118, p. 203 on her correspondence and meetings with Julia Kavanagh.

96 Julia Kavanagh (1862), *French Women of Letters: Biographical Sketches*, Hurst and Blackett, London, p. 133f. That Scudéry was still known in the 19th century can also be proved by a play, written by H.J. Coke (c. 1880), entitled *Mademoiselle de Scudéry. A Drama in Five Acts*, published by Samuel French, London and New York, by a 19th-century translation of Scudéry's novel *Artamène ou Le grand cyrus*, which appeared in 1858 in a French imprint from Caen, translated by Francis Gifford, and by her presence in an anthology of French literature: anon. (ed) (1867), *Half-Hours With the Best French Authors. Short Passages From Some of the Most Celebrated Prose Writers. Translated Into English ...*, Seeley, Jackson, and Halliday, London, p. 83. Nevertheless, the biographical headnote to the extract by Scudéry states that her novels do not 'possess much attraction for the modern reader', although they were admired during her lifetime.

only because of the latter's popularity over the centuries but because of specific intertextual links between *Shirley* and Scudéry's texts. These can be found in the depreciation of passion in favour of friendship and love based on 'inclination', as well as in the criticism of the marriage of convenience and the absence of 'esteem' and friendship. And it is in particular in those passages with Kavanagh praises, namely, the 'long discourses on human passions and feelings', that one can find the closest parallels between Scudéry and Brontë.

Although the notion of *amitié tendre* is a heterosexual concept, used to describe a model of the relations between men and women, it can also be applied to friendship between women, based on similar ideals, namely the absence of passion and the importance of mutual trust, respect and affection. Almost everything is present in tender friendship that one would normally expect in love, except the violence of passion[97] – affection 'outrivals' passion, as Caroline explains.

It is surely not by accident that Shirley's expression of love for Louis is not only based on the Victorian ideal of love as mutual support and companionship, but also uses the originally *précieux* notion of choice for women who select their husbands (if they marry at all) on the basis of their character. According to his note-book, Shirley demanded the following of Louis when she proposed to him:

> '... I do not ask you to take off my shoulders all the cares and duties of property; but I ask you to share the burden, and to show me how to sustain my part well. Your judgement is well-balanced; your heart is kind; your principles are sound. ... Be my companion through life; be my guide where I am ignorant: be my master where I am faulty, be my friend always!' (p. 580)

When she explains to her uncle how she will choose a husband, Shirley also uses the *précieux* keyword 'esteem' to describe her criterion for love (and marriage) (p. 444). Interestingly, Brontë rates 'esteem' higher than Alexander Bain in *The Emotions and the Will*. For Bain, esteem is the

---

[97] Cf. Roswitha Böhm (1998), 'Vom *code galant* zum *code tendre*. Freundschaftsentwürfe im Kreis der Madame de Sévigné', in Sabine Eickenrodt and Cettina Rapisarda (eds), *Freundschaft im Gespräch* (Querelles. Jahrbuch für Frauenforschung, vol. 3), Metzler, Stuttgart/Weimar, pp. 125-136, and for a description and discussion of the *carte de tendre* and its key concepts (respect, courtesy, male subjection, tenderness, esteem, gratitude) and implications, cf. Renate Baader (1986), *Dames de lettres. Autorinnen des preziösen hocharistokratischen und 'modernen' Salons (1649-1698): Mlle de Scudéry – Mlle de Montpensier – Mme d'Aulnoy*, Metzler, Stuttgart, pp. 107ff.

feeling roused when a person possesses 'useful qualities' which do not excite admiration (p. 88). For him esteem is not 'a first-class emotion in respect to contributing to our happiness' (p. 89), although it does contribute to social bonds and human sympathy (p. 90). Perhaps Brontë chose it nevertheless as her positive concept to be opposed to violent and dangerous passion because for her respect and trust were more important qualities than any characteristic which would 'excite', be it admiration or passion or any other potentially uncontrollable feeling. Her concept of esteem holds a strong social promise, which 'blind' passion, directed only at one individual person, cannot fulfil.

However, Charlotte Brontë does not go quite as far as her *précieux* predecessors: it is not the man who becomes the servant of the lady, but Shirley who delivers all power to Louis. In the end, the aristocratic and chivalrous ideal which emphasises women's superiority is 'victorianised' and the concept of 19th-century gender relations with women as the helpers and supporters of their husbands, and as mothers, is reinstated.

Caroline's idea of companionship with Robert is far closer to the conventional 19th-century concept of the wife as the husband's helpmeet. Although at first she explains her emotion as 'friendship', she soon realises that her feelings for Robert are of a different nature. But when Robert implicitly rejects her very obliquely expressed feelings of love she falls back on the idea of family affection and friendship. He does the same: his greeting is characterised as 'cousin-like, brother-like, friend-like, anything but lover-like' (p. 127). Robert and Caroline keep up a sort of pretence: he rejects her feelings which he has perceived and advises her 'to exclude one who does not profess to have any higher aim in life than that of patching up his broken fortune, and wiping clean from his bourgeois scutcheon the foul stain of bankruptcy' (p. 144). Caroline has understood: '"I know it is your duty to try to get on, and that it won't do for you to be romantic; but in future you must not misunderstand me, if I seem friendly ..."' (p. 144f.). In this passage, family affection and friendship is contrasted with romance whose associations with 'melodrama' and 'passion' are bluntly put forward by the narrator at the beginning of the novel:

> If you think ... that anything like a romance is preparing for you, reader, you never were more mistaken. Do you anticipate sentiment, and poetry, and reverie? Do you expect passion, and stimulus, and melodrama? Calm your expectations; reduce them to a lowly standard ... (p. 39)[98]

98 This paragraph is alleged to be in response to a criticism voiced by G.H. Lewes, who

Here, love is viewed pejoratively as pure romance, or as sentimentalism, a variety of the love concept which receives short shrift in *Shirley* (p. 176, p. 284).[99]

For much of the novel, love appears as a negative force giving rise to all kinds of bodily and social problems. Only when the protagonists manage to acknowledge their feelings for their respective future partners, and a life of love-as-friendship is made possible, does this change. Since the resolution of the plot takes up less space than the representation of the emotional conflicts leading up to this finale, the emphasis on love as problematic, as a battlefield which potentially endangers individual and social health if it is not directed at the right person(s), may have had more impact on the readers than the 'happy ending'.

When Robert first perceives his feelings for Caroline after their pleasant evening sharing their interest in literature, he becomes 'grave, almost morose' and decides: '"This won't do! There's weakness – there's downright ruin in all this. However", he added, dropping his voice, "the frenzy is quite temporary. I know it very well: I have had it before. It will be gone to-morrow"' (p. 120). The conventional pejorative view of passionate love as a 'frenzy', a danger in need of control, is an old motif

---

thought *Jane Eyre* too melodramatic. In answer to this criticism, Charlotte Brontë explained in her letter dated 6 November 1847 that her first publishers criticised her for her lack of 'startling incident' which made her change her style of writing, although at first she had 'determined to take Nature and Truth as my sole guides, and to follow to their very footprints; I restrained imagination, eschewed romance, repressed excitement; over-bright colouring, too, I avoided, and sought to produce something which should be soft, grave, and true'. Anon (1980), *The Brontës*, vol. 1 [1], p. 152.

99 The word 'sentimental' is used to describe the Reverend Hall and his penchant for being slightly 'romantic'. Caroline and Hall exchange flowers – in friendship – and both ironise this (p. 284). In an earlier passage, 'sentimentalism' and 'sentiment' are discussed even more explicitly: Mark Yorke, in a conversation with Robert Moore and his parents about Caroline and the latter's comment that Robert was '"not sentimental"', explains the word: '"... For your benefit, Mr Moore, I've been looking up the word "sentimental" in the dictionary, and I find it to mean "tinctured with sentiment". On examining further, "sentiment" is explained to be, thought, idea, notion. A sentimental man, then, is one who has thoughts, ideas, notions; an unsentimental man is one destitute of thought, idea, or notion"' (p. 176). Rose Yorke comes to Robert's defence: '"There are different kinds of thoughts, ideas, and notions", said she, "good and bad: sentimental must refer to the bad, or Miss Helstone must have taken it in that sense, for she was not blaming Mr Moore; she was defending him"' (p. 177). This conversation puts the multifaceted nature of love in a nut-shell, anticipates the novel's conflict and serves as one of the many examples for extended and explicit debates of the different emotion concepts to be found in *Shirley*.

which can be found in numerous health guides, sometimes employing the image of the 'vortex' of passion which Robert's brother uses to characterise his feelings for Shirley. Loss of moral, intellectual and physical control are associated with this image. '"No one who looks at my slow face can guess the vortex sometimes whirling in my heart, and engulfing thought, and wrecking prudence"' (p. 569).[100] Prudence is needed by the good business man as well as the virtuous young woman, while physical health is the basis for all individual and social projects, since its absence would hinder the lover of fulfilling his or her social role (as mother, as businessman and father, or as considerate brother). Finally, loss of reason, often also associated with physical causes, would result not only in a failure to embody these roles. It would also lead to a total break-down of human intercourse since a person in a 'frenzy', or one who has been swallowed by the 'vortex' is not just an ineffective brother or business man, but rather a 'useless' human being in general, unable to communicate meaningfully with anyone.

But the dangers of love have to be learned, as the narrator explains in an allegorical description of Caroline's experience which begins with the naive hope of requited feelings. The passage contains numerous personifications of feeling. While hope is feminised and said to 'smile on us', and experience is said to offer necessary and 'purifying and invigorating lessons', love is masculine and associated with pain. The metaphors associated with this pain induced by a 'man' carry sexual overtones (quiver, arrows, penetrate). But the wound which the Cupid's 'arrows' opens is 'like a thrill of new life', a painful beginning, an initiation on the physical and symbolic level.

> Hope, when she smiles on us, and promises happiness to-morrow, is implicitly believed;– Love, when he comes wandering like a lost angel to our door, is at once admitted, welcomed, embraced: his quiver is not seen, if his arrows penetrate, their wound is like a thrill of new life: there are no fears of poison, none of the barb which no leech's hand can extract: that perilous passion – an agony ever in some of its phases, with many, an agony throughout – is believed to be an unqualified good: in short, at eighteen, the school of Experience is to be entered, and her humbling, crushing, grinding, but yet purifying and invigorating lessons are yet to be learnt. (p. 121f.)

---

100 He uses the image again shortly afterwards, in his description of the scene in which Shirley and Louis acknowledge their feelings for each other: '"... The world swims and changes round me. The sun is a dizzying scarlet blaze; the sky a violet vortex whirling over me"' (p. 579).

The pejorative use of 'passion', and its association with illness – 'agony' merges the physical and the symbolic level contained in this passage. This association will be taken up again and again in the description of Caroline's slow physical decline. The harshness of unrequited love is couched in vivid terms by the narrator, whose commentary and address to the (female) reader links emotionality and gender in the following passage. While a thwarted male lover may express his disappointment, a woman may not because this would bring 'shame and anguish, inward remorse for self-treachery' upon her. Such 'unnatural' behaviour for women is no option for Caroline because another personified feeling would appear to 'repay' her for her transgression: self-contempt. The preservation of an intact self is too important to endanger it by openly expressing one's feelings. Therefore, the narrator recommends control which will even conquer the pain induced by the 'scorpion's' poison:

> Take the matter as you find it: ask no questions; utter no remonstrances: it is your best wisdom. You expected bread, and you have got a stone: break your teeth on it and don't shriek because the nerves are martyrized: do not doubt that your mental stomach – if you have such a thing – is strong as an ostrich's – the stone will digest. You held out your hand for an egg, and fate put into it a scorpion. Show no consternation: close your fingers firmly upon the gift; let it sting through your palm. Never mind: in time, after your hand and arm have swelled and quivered long with torture, the squeezed scorpion will die, and you will have learned the great lesson how to endure without a sob. (p. 128)

Again, the connection between emotion and physical suffering is highlighted, thus explicitly linking passion and the body. The negative concept of love is embodied as physical illness and in Caroline's case it is also linked with depression. As the analysis of Shirley Keeldar has shown, the overtones of masochism are not unusual in Charlotte Brontë's work.

Caroline endangers her health because of her determination to repress her feelings of love, which she determines to replace with mere cousin-like friendship. And since 'she will be her own governor, and resolve to subdue and bring under guidance the disturbed realm of her emotions' (p. 130) she suffers – if mainly 'mutely' (p. 189) and visible only through her physical frame and her face (p. 255). No one quite understands this change – partly because Caroline attempts not to express her feelings and plans to find useful employment which will help not only to overcome her love for Robert but the pressing problem inextricably bound up with it: her lack of occupation. More intensely than ever does she try to create a plan to keep herself occupied, and while involved in the unloved activity of needlework, she cannot always keep her emotions under control, 'but this sign of emotion was rare, and quickly effaced: the sharp pang passed, the dimness cleared from her vision; she would re-thread her needle, re-arrange tuck and trimming, and work on' (p. 244). Caroline goes so far as to take pride in her ability to repress her feelings (p. 251). In the end, this results in her falling seriously ill. Her sickness is likened to the results of violent weather, emanating from the 'East' whose 'poison' affects 'white Western isles'. The contrast evoked here is one between the unsullied English 'virgin' and the experienced and 'tainted' 'other' whose power suddenly bursts upon the unsuspecting 'virgin' like a new Lazarus:

> The future sometimes seems to sob a low warning of the events it is bringing us, like some gathering though yet remote storm, which, in tones of the wind, in flushings of the firmament, in clouds strangely torn, announces a blast strong to strew the sea with wrecks; or commissioned to bring in fog the yellow taint of pestilence, covering white Western isles with the poisoned exhalations of the East, dimming the lattices of English homes with the breath of Indian plague. At other times this Future bursts suddenly, as if a rock had rent, and in it a grave had opened, whence issues the body of one that slept. Ere you are aware, you stand face to face with a shrouded and unthought-of Calamity – a new Lazarus. (p. 399)

No doubt is expressed concerning the reason for Caroline's illness: 'mental excitement'. Her sickness will 'taint' her and come upon her like an 'unthought-of Calamity', like a natural disaster against which she is unable to defend herself, because her long emotional struggle has made her vulnerable to the effects of 'miasma' and other unwholesome vapours:

> Probably ... some sweet, poisoned breeze, redolent of honeydew and miasma, had passed into her lungs and veins, and finding there already a fever of mental excitement, and a languor of long conflict and habitual sadness, had fanned the spark to flame, and left a well-lit fire behind it. (p. 399)

Although the quoted passage seems to emphasise the negative effects of this illness in physical terms (lungs, veins, fever), the contradictory words used to describe the 'breeze' imply the presence of both pleasure and pain, of expression and control. While the breeze is simultaneously sweet and poisoned, associated with both honeydew and miasma, the 'fever' makes Caroline excited and languid and both together result in a 'well-lit fire', a symbol which may be read as energy-consuming and as life-giving at the same time, just like the central emotion metaphor of the 'pressure cooker' type which focuses on the same set of contradictory elements.

The description of Caroline's near fatal illness shares with popular health guides the conviction that emotional turmoil leads to sickness and mental suffering, possibly even madness. The brain fever-trope is closely associated with an emotional crisis and once again the body is made to express what cannot be verbalised.[101]

But what about the positive outcomes of love? Affirmations of love can be found in *Shirley*, and in the final resolution of the two love plots, the individual body is briefly allowed to be the expressive medium of the healthy effects of love, possibly because the dangers of love or rather the dangers of suppressed love and misdirected feelings were more important to Brontë than the pleasures it can afford. Again, the embodiment of feeling becomes visible when Caroline's physical change is described to represent her changed outlook on life and her successful mastery of love-as-friendship. While lack of requited love results in depression and in a crushed and drooping aspect, 'tasting the cordial of heart's-ease' leads to an upward movement, a surge of energy which has direct consequences for her body: 'All about her seemed elastic; depression, fear, forlorness, were withdrawn: no longer crushed, and saddened, and slow, and drooping, she looked like one who had tasted the cordial of heart's-ease, and been lifted on the wing of hope' (p. 557).

In a conversation on the advantages and disadvantages of marriage, Shirley describes love in general terms, again contrasting it with passion, and without referring to a specific person. She opposes the lasting effects of harmonious and tender, faithful affection with short-lived passion: '"I don't think we should trust to what they call passion at all, Caroline. I believe it is a mere fire of dry sticks, blazing up and vanishing ..."'. The set

---

[101] Cf. Emily Brontë's use of this trope in *Wuthering Heights* (1847) where her heroine Cathy suffers from this 'illness' whenever her wishes are opposed and her love for Heathcliff is threatened. Gilbert and Gubar (1984) suggest that Caroline is suffering from *anorexia nervosa*, 'Genesis', p. 390. Although this is an illness which links mental suffering and the body, and some of Caroline's symptoms (e.g. extreme weakness) fit this 'diagnosis', it appears too specific an analysis and slightly ahistorical as well. I would question the necessity of 'diagnosing' a fictional character whose illness is largely meant to be symbolic. Cf. also Kucich's Foucauldian analysis of Caroline's attempts at repression which he interprets as expressive and productive. John Kucich (winter 1985), 'Passionate Reserve and Reserved Passion in the Works of Charlotte Brontë', in Timm Gates (ed), *Critical Essays*, pp. 68-88, quotation p. 68, repr. from *ELH*, vol. 52, pp. 913-37.

of characteristics she ascribes to an unnamed male person (obviously she is thinking of Louis) emphasises kindness, patience, the absence of flattery but nevertheless a liking for women, truthfulness, filial and brotherly affection and the absence of selfishness, and these she sets up as the ideal features of a future husband (p. 224). Caroline's credo of love is similar, but she stresses the difference between 'vulgar associations' and love which is pure and should not be associated with shame (p. 313).[102]

But on the whole the depreciation of sentimentality and romance, and the frightening story of Caroline's pining and decline serve as a severe warning against the dangers of love, corresponding with Walter Cooke's warning against 'love sickness' in *Mind and Emotion in Relation to Health and Disease* (1839) which he counts as one of the 'depressing emotions', among fear and grief (p. 15ff.), contrasting them with the 'exciting emotions' such as anger, pride, vanity and ambition (p. 7ff.). In the later extended version (1852), Cooke explains what effect love, the 'master-emotion' (p. 125), may have. After first briefly mentioning the 'long train of other benevolent emotions' (p. 125) which may be the result of love, he focuses on its possible danger, in particular for women and uses strong language (inferior passions, derangement, pervert the judgement) to make his point:

> These causes may be found in the misplaced affections of young persons, clandestine intimacies (founded usually in passions inferior to love), thwarted or disappointed love. From any one of these causes it may occur that there are derangements which impair digestion, disturb sleep, pervert the judgement, and endanger all the healthy actions. ... Sophisticated love sometimes transforms a young person from loveliness, openness, suavity, and cheerfulness, into reserve, mysteriousness, untruthfulness, and moroseness. (p. 127)

Shirley differs from the average health guide in the connection between emotionality and its social aspects, most obvious in the discussion of marriage and its opposite, spinsterhood. Charlotte Brontë does not only devote a whole chapter to 'old maids' (chapter 10) but includes numerous discussions of single women and spinsterhood as well. She takes up a

---

102 Caroline again defends her views when Mrs Yorke accuses her of being '"sentimental"' and '"being guided by impulse"' and '"influenced by ... feelings"'. '"Of course, I should often be influenced by my feelings: they were given me to that end. Whom my feelings teach me to love, I *must* and *shall* love; and I hope, if ever I have a husband and children, my feelings will induce me to love them. I hope, in that case, all my impulses will be strong in compelling me to love"' (p. 387).

contemporary debate, in part inspired by the relatively large number of unmarried women.[103] The conventional view of single women as lonely, without purpose in life and 'cankered' (p. 193) is put forward, e.g. by Robert Moore (p. 197), but Caroline soon learns that her neighbours Miss Mann and Miss Ainley, although idiosyncratic, have made the most of their socially stigmatised position. She develops respect for the way they have overcome their difficulties, the lack of occupation and the consequences of poverty. Although they are despised by others and considered socially useless, they have found a role – something that Caroline herself craves. Nevertheless, when she first perceives the physical changes that her position and unrequited love have wrought upon her, she is afraid of finding '"signs of an old maid about"' her (p. 192).

'Old maids' look different from married women, their physical frames serve as negative embodiments of this unsought for emotion concept: the absence of love. Thus the aptly named Miss Mann sits 'primly and somewhat grimly-tidy in a cushioned rocking-chair, her hands busied with some knitting: this was her favourite work, as it required the least exertion. ... to avoid excitement was one of Miss Mann's aims in life ...' (p. 193f.). Nevertheless, these women fill the gap with another emotion which compensates, up to a point, the absence of the implied ideal of heterosexual love: benevolence.[104] By being wholly unselfish and by devoting their energy to others, they profit from the power that benevolence gives them: '... Caroline became aware of the power a most serene, unselfish, and benignant mind could exercise over those to whom it was developed' (p. 196).[105]

She resolves to make this selfless diligence her model, but she cannot

---

103 Middle class women often remained unmarried because men married comparatively late (in their thirties) since they had to acquire enough income to afford starting a family or went out to the colonies and thus 'depleted' the number of available young men. And of course some women did not marry because they did not wish to do so. Cf. Joan Perkin (1988), *Women and Marriage in Nineteenth-Century England*, Routledge, London, p. 226ff., and Shirley Foster (1985), *Victorian Women's Fiction: Marriage, Freedom and the Individual*, Croom Helm, Beckenham, p. 6f.

104 Needless to say, this ideal is part of the legacy of the 18th-century philosophy of moral sentiments and one of the many instances in which Victorian writers revert to 18th-century emotion concepts.

105 My attention was drawn to the profitable outcome of benevolence for the 'sister of Charity', as Miss Ainley is called in *Shirley* (p. 197), contrasted with 'a Lady Bountiful', a caricature of the middle class Victorian do-gooder, by a paper that Bronwyn Rivers presented at the Victorian Graduate Research Seminar at the English Faculty (University of Oxford) on 25 May 1999.

imagine living such a lonely life and decides that she needs some sort of serious occupation that goes further than nursing the poor and the sick, an occupation which for all its importance does not fulfil her emotional and intellectual needs. She can only hope to 'stem and keep down anguish' for a short time by these occupations, the 'current' of feeling needs a stronger outlet and this outlet is obviously a husband (and children) which are required, implied by the adjective 'barren' which characterises her childless and unmarried state, as well as symbolising her emotional lack:

> Yet I must speak truth; these efforts brought her neither health of body nor continued peace of mind: with them all, she wasted, grew more joyless and more wan; ... Winter seemed conquering her spring: her mind's soil and its treasures were freezing gradually to barren stagnation. (p. 199)

Caroline is aware that her want of occupation is linked to her sex. Not only is the only male counterpart to remain unmarried in the novel (apart from Reverend Helstone who has tried marriage and disliked it), the Reverend Hall. He is a happy bachelor well looked after by his equally happy unmarried but learned sister, an obvious indication how lack of occupation (other than household work) and being single go together in the case of women.[106] She also understands that it would be easier if she were a boy (p. 104). Shirley and Caroline both agree that the lack of occupation tires them and although she thinks that labour alone does not make human beings happy, Caroline is convinced that '"it can give varieties of pain, and prevent us from breaking our hearts with a singly tyrant master-torture. Besides, successful labour has its recompense; a vacant, weary, lonely, hopeless life has none"' (p. 235). Interestingly, she uses the concept of the 'tyrant master-torture', a variant of the 'master emotion' which Cooke equates with love. And it is not the pleasure which she concentrates on, but rather the variety that an occupation would offer her, as well as pain.

Caroline comes up with the idea of becoming a governess but not only is her uncle violently opposed to the idea, the terrible experience that Mrs Pryor gives a vivid account of discourages her as well (p. 363). Again, the physical consequences of this plight are emphasised and the danger to the

---

[106] Managing a father's or brother's household was a typical task for single women but since Caroline has no brother to look after or sister to live with, she cannot follow Margaret Hall's or Hortense Moore's example. And the latter is also not an entirely positive role model. Although knowledgeable, she is intractable and strict, self-indulgent and does not come close to the selfless ideal that Miss Ainley represents. Cf. Perkin (1988), *Women and Marriage*, p. 227.

self that the 'inward storm' of feeling may pose:

> But the lady's whole frame seemed shaken: she sat down, bent her head to her knee, and wept aloud. Nothing could console her till the inward storm had had its way. *At last the agony subsided of itself.* ... and by the time they reached Fieldhead, *she had re-entered into herself: the outside was, as usual, still and shy.* (p. 369) (My emphasis, G.S.)

Caroline rails against the fate of having nothing to occupy her (p. 376f.) and utters a plea for better education, addressed at the 'Men of England', to help overcome the plight of 'sour old maids' who are 'envious, backbiting, wretched, because life is a desert to them'. At the same time she explains her ideal view of women whose roles she limits to that of the companion, the nurse and the 'prop':

> '... Fathers! cannot you alter these things? ... You would wish to be proud of your daughters and not to blush for them – then seek for them an interest and an occupation which shall raise them above the flirt, the manœuvrer, the mischief-making tale-bearer. Keep your girls' minds narrow and fettered – they will still be a plague and a care, sometimes a disgrace to you: cultivate them – give them scope and work – they will be your gayest companions in health; your tenderest nurses in sickness; your most faithful prop in age'. (p. 378f.)

What, then, remains for Caroline (and with slightly less urgency: for Shirley), if benevolence as compensation for spinsterhood, the position of a governess as a substitute for a more rewarding occupation, and love itself are all impossible? Until Caroline's love, Shirley's rejection and his illness have convinced Robert and he has changed from being solely interested in his business problems, she is 'forced' into physical decline. Only with marriage, the legitimate shape that the concept of mutual love-as-affection may take, will she be restored to mental and bodily well-being. However, marriage is not in itself an ideal, as the multivocal discussions of that institution in the novel illustrate.[107] These discourses within the novel produce a sense of 'openness', of a topic offered to the readers from which they may draw their own conclusions. The juxtaposition of the different attitudes towards marriage also create an ironic distance because some of

---

107 Cf. Perkin (1988) on the 'Crusade Against Marriage', *Women and Marriage*, pp. 207-232 and F.M.L. Thompson (1988), *The Rise of Respectable Society: A Social History of Victorian Britain, 1830-1900*, Fontana, London, in particular the chapter on marriage, pp. 85-113.

the speakers are shown up to be narrow-minded and in need of 'enlightenment'.

Apart from the author's own thoughts about marriage (she married late in life and rejected two earlier suitors), two possible influences on the novel's manifold discussions of marriage can be identified: the contemporary misogamist debate, influenced by free-thinkers such as Robert Owen, St Simon and Fourier, and again the 17th-century French tradition of *précieux* anti-marriage texts. Although Charlotte Brontë's Tory politics are a world apart from early socialist opinions, she nevertheless may have been aware of these views of marriage and sympathised with them. But since she seems to have drawn on an older literary tradition for her concept of 'tender affection', it is equally possible that she also drew inspiration from Madeleine de Scudéry for her discussion of marriage. Since *préciosité* was an aristocratic movement to begin with, perhaps the notion of chivalric love and choice for women even suited her political opinions better. In any case, her readers would have interpreted the discussion of marriage in *Shirley* as a contribution to contemporary debates, whatever the original intertextual inspiration may have been.

The most outspoken advocate against marriage is Caroline's uncle Helstone, whose own experience has hardened him against women in general and marriage in particular (p. 82f., p. 124, p. 166). The ideas put forth by Mr Yorke and his son Martin are not much more sophisticated and are moreover coloured by misogyny (p. 175f.). Malone, one of the unsuccessful curates, launches a similar invective against marriage, at least against a certain type of 'love-making' based on a 'mere matter of sentiment' and on 'some fantastic tie of feeling'. He thinks a marriage of convenience is the answer to the problem (p. 56). Even Robert Moore, whose attitude towards women is much more positive than e.g. Helstone's, is initially against marriage, associating frivolity and conventionality with it (p. 57f.). In a discussion with Mr Yorke, who hints at a possible match with Shirley or some other wealthy lady, Moore is even more adamantly opposed to contemplating marriage which he thinks is utopian and silly, since it cannot be reconciled to his business needs. Poverty and the absence of love are linked for him, obstructing any thought of marriage (p. 180).

Another type of marriage, reserved for the upper echelons of society, is the marriage of convenience, which Malone recommends to Moore. This is also Shirley's possible fate, if her former guardian and uncle Sympson has his way: '... his mission was clear, and he intended to discharge it conscientiously: he anxiously desired to have his niece married; to make for her a suitable match; give her in charge to a proper husband, and wash his hands of her for ever' (p. 443). Against the horror of a loveless but 'suitable' match with a sentimental sonneteer of the Philip Nunnely-variety (p. 446f.) or a coarse but rich 'gentleman' such as Samuel Fawthrop Wynne (p. 444), Shirley sets her credo of marriage-for-love: '"Before I marry, I am resolved to esteem – to admire – to *love*"' (loc. cit.). Her uncle accuses her of madness and later attributes her strange ideas to the French novels she has allegedly read: '"Your mind is poisoned with French novels. You have imbibed French principles"' (p. 513).[108] Their quarrel becomes more heated and Shirley explains to her uncle that she walks '"by another creed, light, faith, and hope"' than he does. This shocks him, since he sees blasphemy in her utterance and accuses her of being an '"atheist"'. This makes Shirley's hackles rise even more and induces her to accuse her uncle in his turn as governed by the '"god"' of the '"World"' which she denounces as a demon who forces men and women into '"unnatural"' matches. Her use of images makes it clear that for her all '"domestic vice"', the absence of feeling and even death find their origins in this type of marriage:

> 'In my eyes, you too, if not an infidel, are an idolater ... . Sir, your god, your great Bel, your fish-tailed Dagon, rises before me as a demon. ... He binds the young to the old, the strong to the imbecile. ... In his realm there is hatred ... – there is disgust –... – there is treachery ... – there is vice ... . All that surrounds him hastens to decay: all declines and degenerates under his sceptre. *Your* god is a masked Death. ... I am anchored on a resolve you cannot shake. My heart, my conscience shall dispose of my hand – *they only*. Know this at last.' (p. 518f.)

Marriage without love, in other words, is an empty form which cannot provide occupation or a suitable 'home for the heart'. But in *Shirley*, love nevertheless only finds its correlative in marriage and only when both Louis and Robert have acknowledged their feelings is marriage a possibility, even if it transgresses social norms, as is the case with Shirley and Louis. And only then will love result in positive consequences, for the individual body, as Caroline's example shows, and the social body, the community as a whole. This is the crucial move that Charlotte Brontë makes, this is where the 'passionate link' is created. The fact that Robert

[108] This direct reference to French novels might be an allusion to Madeleine de Scudéry's misogamist inclinations.

does not at first want to return Caroline's love is by no means simply a matter of domestic relevance but has consequences for his treatment of workers, his business methods and his whole outlook on his social role.

All four major emotion concepts in *Shirley* are inherently social.[109] Affection is expected of and reserved for friends and family; and its absence, as in the relation between Helstone and his niece, may lead to negative consequences for the individual. Friendship, although rated highly in the novel, is nevertheless not sufficient as a form of life, in particular for young women. Spinsterhood, although a possible destiny promising benevolence as a compensation, and the absence of selfish feeling, is not sufficient for Shirley and Caroline. In order to avert the danger of society's ridicule, marriage is a requirement for both. However, a union based on incompatible tempers, or worse still, solely on financial prospects, is no solution because this would imply the absence of love. It is love on which marriage must be based, not the passionate variety but 'tender affection', companionship, the husband and wife as friends. By repressing love, individual illness may occur, thus endangering the chance to fulfil the required social role as wife and mother.

But unrepressed feeling, the abandonment of all emotional control, can also result in social danger: that of the violent 'mob', attacking at random and upsetting social peace. This can lead to 'a sort of moral earthquake [which was] felt heaving under the hills of the northern counties' (p. 62). And although Caroline at one point criticises labelling '"all poor working people under the general and insulting name of "the mob"' (p. 118), this is the main impression that the narrator and the verdict of other characters impart to the reader. Helstone even goes so far as to call the rioters 'vermin' (p. 73) and when it comes to the attack on Robert's mill, the description of the narrator makes them appear as disembodied and non-human on the one hand (p. 329) and as the primordial danger on the other:

> A yell followed this demonstration – a rioters' yell – a North-of-England – a Yorkshire – a West-Riding – a West-Riding-clothing-district-of-Yorkshire rioters' yell. You never heard that sound, perhaps, reader? So much the better

[109] The first indication that love affairs are intertwined with social matters is given in an account of Sarah, Robert Moore's servant, and her two prospective lovers, Moses Barraclough and Fred Murgatroyd. Moore is able to prepare himself against the first 'visit' to his mill by disaffected workers because the jealous Murgatroyd reports on Barraclough's plans to attack another mill-owner's property and to send a deputation to Moore's Hollow Mill (p. 150). A seemingly private conflict between two jealous lovers is shown to have direct political consequences.

> for your ears – perhaps for your heart; since, if it rends the air in hate to yourself, or to the men or principles you approve, the interests to which you wish well, Wrath wakens to the cry of Hate: the Lion shakes his mane, and rises to the howl of the Hyena: Caste stands up, ireful, against Caste; and the indignant, wronged spirit of the Middle Rank bears down in zeal and scorn on the famished and furious mass of the Operative Class. It is difficult to be tolerant – difficult to be just – in such moments. (p. 335)

Animal imagery is used to describe what happens when 'the fighting animal was roused in every one of those men there struggling together, and was for the time quite paramount above the rational human being' (p. 336). 'Negative' passions are couched in familiar terms and appear in the form of an allegory, half animal, half human: '... Discord, broken loose in the night from control, had beaten the ground with his stamping hoofs, and left it waste and pulverized ...' (p. 338).[110]

But the gravest consequences nevertheless occur when individual repression, that is excessive control, leads to political mistakes. Robert is convinced that his main task lies not with love but with business and politics (p. 56, p. 61, p. 155f., p. 355). Caroline's attempts at teaching him not only love but humility initially fail. His pride and his sole focus in life, making his mill a commercial success, lead to political upheaval. Because of his hard stance he upsets the workers. Not his political conviction is faulted by the narrator but his manner of presenting it to his workers. Being humiliated by Shirley and his complete prostration after having been shot – significantly not by one of his workers but by a raving 'leveller', the outsider and Antinomian Mike Hartley (p. 48, p. 50, p. 589) –, teach him that success and business are not the only objectives in life. As he confesses to Mr Yorke immediately before being shot '"The machinery of all my nature [is wrong]; the whole enginery of this human mill: the boiler, which I take to be the heart, is fit to burst"' (p. 496). A marriage of convenience with respect but no love on his part, such as a union with Shirley would have been, serving his business interests but not his emotional needs, is revealed to be a mistake. He comes to the conclusion that '"never more will I mention marriage to a woman, unless I feel love. Henceforth, Credit and Commerce may take care of themselves"' (p. 501). Putting pride (p. 319f.) and ambition first, and being selfish, is soundly

---

[110] The description and characterisation of William Farren contrasts with the image of the disembodied mob. His honesty and respectability are frequently stressed (p. 156ff.), he represents one of the 'deserving poor' and profits from Caroline Helstone's and the Reverend Hall's sympathy (p. 421).

disqualified in *Shirley*. Robert is humbled, falls sick, and in his weakness acknowledges his true needs and feelings. Once he puts his business second, and his love for Caroline first, social peace can reign, not without the help of a general lessening of tension through the developments on the wider political scene (p. 590f.).[111] Two mistakes are thus averted: a union with Shirley which would have had disastrous consequences for Caroline, Louis and for Robert and Shirley. And more importantly: humility which Robert's newly 'educated heart'[112] has learned means that his concerns are now no longer only with his own business prospects. Although modernisation is an irreversible development in *Shirley*, mill-owner and workers come to a compromise:

> 'Caroline, the houseless, the starving, the unemployed, shall come to Hollow's mill from far and near; and Joe Scott shall give them work, and Louis Moore, Esq., shall let them a tenement, and Mrs Gill shall mete them a portion till the first pay-day. ... Such a Sunday-school as you will have, Cary! such collections as you will get! such a day-school as you and Shirley, and Miss Ainley, will have to manage between you! The mill shall find salaries for a master and mistress, and the Squire and the Clothier shall give a treat once a-quarter.' (p. 598ff.)

It is obvious that this utopian compromise is a direct result of Caroline's softening influence, as well as of the repeal of the Orders in Council:

> "Now, I can take more workmen; give better wages; lay wiser and more liberal plans; do some good, be less selfish: *now*, Caroline, I can have a house – a home which I can truly call mine – and *now* –" He paused; for his deep voice was checked. "And *now*", he resumed – "now I can think of marriage; *now* I can seek a wife." (p. 594)[113]

---

111 The Orders in Council, issued by the Privy Council and part of the British government's anti-Napoleonic campaign, were lifted, once again allowing free trade between Britain and the Continent and America.

112 This type of 'education of the heart' is one of the most important and most frequent plots to be encountered in the discourses on emotions.

113 Gilbert and Gubar (1984), 'Genesis', p. 398, view the ending as the victory of 'men and their industrial patriarchy'. I would strongly contradict this view: the compromise is only possible after Robert's feelings have been allowed to emerge, otherwise his selfishness would have kept him from true success as a master. Gilbert and Gubar are however right in that neither industrialism nor sexual relations are allowed to remain a contested, ambivalent area. The only tension that is present in the novel's final paragraphs is one between a romantic view of the past and a slight criticism of the industrialised future.

Less generally dangerous results would have come about if Shirley had repressed her feelings for Louis or if he had refused to marry her because of her social status. But again, not only individual unhappiness for both would have been the consequence. Shirley's property and income would have fallen into the hands of a 'gentleman' with no interest in the poor. And Louis would not have become the benevolent proprietor of Fieldhead that the last part of *Shirley* envisages: an educated country gentleman of not only refined taste but of sound moral judgement as well, thus amalgamating middle class values and education with aristocratic power as 'the least presumptuous, the kindest master that ever was ...' (p. 593).[114] Terry Eagleton explains the effects of the compromise as 'an extraordinarily contradictory amalgam of smouldering rebelliousness and prim conventionalism, gushing Romantic fantasy and canny hard-headedness, quivering sensibility and blunt rationality'.[115]

Robert's and Caroline's differently motivated attempts at repression are associated with a social problem in the one case and an allegedly 'private' problem in the other. It is no accident that the consequences of repression on the woman's part seem to be played out on the level of the individual body, while those on the man's part endanger the body politic. *Shirley* serves as an example of the close relation between the discourses on emotion and the so-called separate spheres debate, already mentioned in the context of women and madness. Associating men with the public and women with the private sphere was a common notion in 19th-century discourse. In a way, the individual body and the body politic would find a further connection in the overlap between the discourses on emotion and the separate spheres debate which made the body the cause and the site for social differentiation into two gendered spheres. The following chapter looks at the connection between this overlap and at religion and social order. What will emerge is the importance that religion, order, and gender had for the creation and maintenance of a specifically middle class habitus.

---

[114] DeJean stresses this 'mixing of ranks' which the *précieux* salon writers of the 17th century advocated with their new ideal of marriage based on friendship and esteem and not on convenience. What was a political challenge in the 17th and 18th century had become a more common probability in the 19th century during which middle class and upper class ranks mixed more frequently (mainly through the marriage of younger aristocratic sons with middle class women and their entry into one of the professions). Cf. Joan DeJean (1991), *Tender Geographies. Women and the Origin of the Novel in France*, Columbia UP, New York, p. 88 and p. 90.

[115] Terry Eagleton (1990), 'Class, Power and Charlotte Brontë', in Timm Gates (ed), *Critical Essays*, pp. 50-60, quotation p. 51.

Fig. 2.1 ‘Weeping & Joy’. Timothy Bobbin. *The Passions Humourously Delineated* (1810/1858) [1773]

FENNINGS'

ADULT COOLING POWDERS.

These famous COOLING POWDERS, are the best Medicine to correct the disordering ACIDITIES of INDIGESTION, the saline impurities of COLDS, RHEUMATISM, ERYSIPELAS, ERUPTIONS, &c., and are the finest blood-coolers for all body-scorching FEVERS, and DISEASES arising from unhealthy HEATS of the System.

FENNINGS' ADULT COOLING POWDERS, form one of those rare Medicaments which, without weakening the body in the least, will cool the fever-burnt blood, and lower to a healthy standard the quickly-throbbing pulse.

A dose taken at bedtime with a basin of gruel, immediately a cold is caught, will mostly subdue all feverish symptoms, and cure the cold in a single night.

Sold by all respectable Chemists, in Boxes, at 1s. 1½d. and 2s. 9d., with Directions. The large size Boxes, 2s. 9d., contain three times the quantity of the small Boxes.

FENNINGS'

STOMACHIC MIXTURE

WILL PREVENT OR QUICKLY CURE,

TYPHUS OR LOW FEVER, DIPHTHERIA, CHOLERA, SCARLET FEVER, INFLUENZA, DYSENTERY, BOWEL COMPLAINTS, SORE THROATS, GRIPING PAINS, WINDY SPASMS, BILE, &c.

This unfailing Medicine to cure, seldom requires a second dose. A dose taken twice a week, is a sure safeguard against the Cholera, Dysentery, Typhus or Low Fever, Scarlet Fever, and other malignant disorders if in the house or neighbourhood.

Sold in Stamped Bottles with full directions, 1s. 1½d. each. Family Bottles (great saving), 2½s. each.

Fig. 3.1 Advertisement for 'Fennings' Adult Cooling Powder'. Alfred Fennings. *Everybody's Doctor* (1864)

Fig. 3.2 'Leonora'. G.P.R. James. *A Book of the Passions* (1838-39)

Fig. 3.3 'Jealousy'. G.P.R. James, *A Book of the Passions* (1838-39)

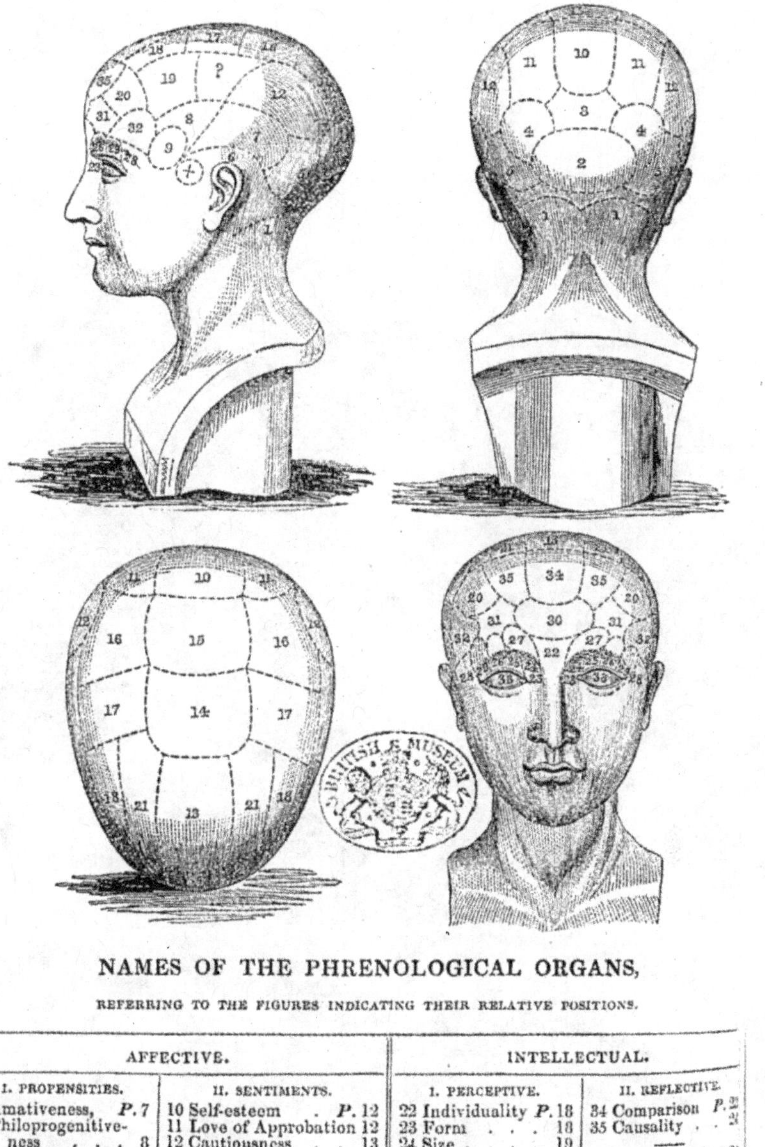

NAMES OF THE PHRENOLOGICAL ORGANS,

REFERRING TO THE FIGURES INDICATING THEIR RELATIVE POSITIONS.

AFFECTIVE.		INTELLECTUAL.	
I. PROPENSITIES.	II. SENTIMENTS.	I. PERCEPTIVE.	II. REFLECTIVE.
1 Amativeness, *P.* 7	10 Self-esteem . *P.* 12	22 Individuality *P.* 18	34 Comparison *P.* 2…
2 Philoprogenitive-ness . . . 8	11 Love of Approbation 12	23 Form . . . 18	35 Causality . .
3 Concentrativeness 8	12 Cautiousness . . 13	24 Size 19	
4 Adhesiveness . 9	13 Benevolence . . 13	25 Weight . . 19	Modes of Activity
5 Combativeness . 9	14 Veneration . . . 14	26 Colouring . . 19	Practical Directions . . .
…structiveness 9	15 Firmness 14	27 Locality . . 20	Combinations .
…entiveness 10	16 Conscientiousness 15	28 Number . . 20	Materialism . .
…iveness . 10	17 Hope 16	29 Order . . . 20	
…iveness 11	18 Wonder 16	30 Eventuality . 21	
…veness 11	19 Locality 16	31 Time . . . 21	
	? Unasertained.	32 Tune : . . 21	
	20 Wit or Mirthfulness 17	33 Language . . 22	
	21 Imitation . . . 17		

Fig. 4.1 'Names of the Phrenological Organs'. George Combe, *Outlines of Phrenology* ([5]1835)

Fig. 4.2 **'Affection'. E.T. Parris, *Gems of Beauty, Displayed in a Series of Twelve Highly Finished Engravings of the Passions* (1838)**

Fig. 5.1 'Portrait de Germaine de Staël en Corinne au cap Misène'. Elisabeth-Louise Vigée-Lebrun (1809)

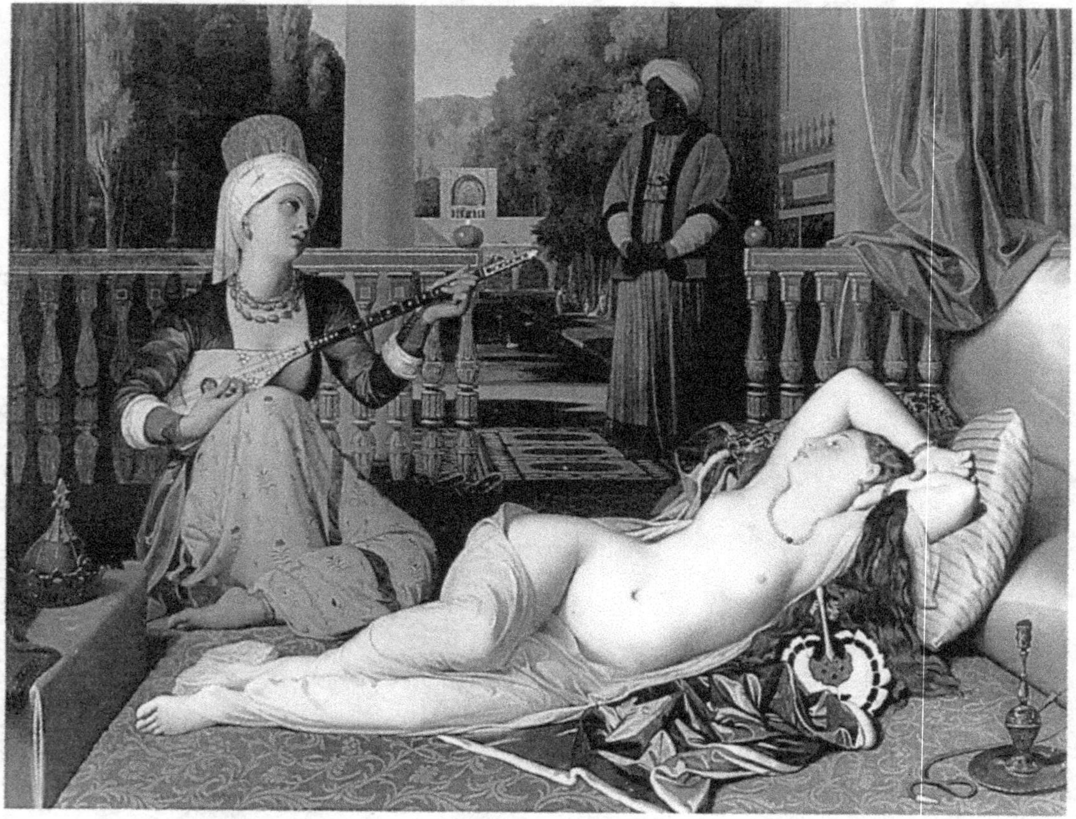

Fig. 5.2 'Odalisque with Slave'. Jean-Auguste-Dominique Ingres (1842)

Fig. 5.3 'Ophelia'. Sir John Everett Millais (1851-52)

4 The local moral order: Emotions and the Development of a Middle Class Habitus

The emotions are always coupled with what Rom Harré has called the 'local moral order' of a given society.[1] In the 19th century, this moral order consists of the moral, social and religious assumptions of that part of society which was – to use Bourdieu's terminology – to accumulate the greatest cultural capital: the middle classes. That the discourses on emotions have such a social dimension has already become visible in the discussion of the role of the body and of emotional expression for both the individual and for society. Many Victorian writers explicitly emphasise the necessity of managing one's emotions and thereby maintaining social order. But apart from these prominent and explicit discussions the majority of 19th-century authors also establish implicit boundaries in their works: the discourses on emotions are themselves controlled by rarely questioned recurrent moral, social, and religious assumptions.

Although the 'middle class' label encompasses a broad range of possible occupations,[2] certain cultural values were shared by an increasing

---

1 Rom Harré considers emotions such as envy, jealousy, spleen, spite etc. as those feelings which can only be understood with reference to the local moral order, constituting a prerequisite for the existence of these emotions 'in the cognitive repertoire of the community'. I would extend the concept of the moral order and its influence on a society's approach to emotionality to all emotions, not just the ones Harré lists. Harré (1986), 'An Outline of the Social Constructionist Viewpoint', in id. (ed), *The Social Construction of Emotions*, Basil Blackwell, Oxford, pp. 2-14, quotation p. 6.

2 In his social history of England, *The Rise of Respectable Society: A Social History of Victorian Britain, 1830-1900*, Fontana, London, F.M.L. Thompson (1988) calls the middle classes 'a very mixed bag' (p. 16), thereby emphasising their heterogeneity. Nevertheless, recent studies have shown that in spite of economic differences which also influenced social practice, middle class values can be identified which unified members of the different occupational groups belonging to the middle classes. Cf. Gunilla-Friederike Budde (1994), *Auf dem Weg ins Bürgerleben. Kindheit und Erziehung in deutschen und englischen Bürgerfamilien 1840-1914*, Vandenhoeck & Ruprecht, Göttingen, p. 15ff. and Leonore Davidoff and Catherine Hall (1987), *Family Fortunes.*

number of Victorians. It is precisely these values (and the social and cultural practices ensuing from them) which were to constitute the Victorian middle class habitus. Historians have questioned the rise of the middle classes and the impact that they had on 19th-century culture and society because of their close ties with the gentry.[3] But at least for the literary field their prominence is incontestable. And if a topic becomes as pressing as the expression and control of the emotions do in the 19th century, it is only to be expected that the emerging public opinion makers would deal with the problem at length. But the readership of middle class authors extended their own social background since their objective included the reform of the working classes. This didactic aim is nowhere more obvious than in novels, conduct books and advice manuals which play a prominent role in the Victorian discourses on emotions.[4] They

---

Men and Women of the English Middle Class, 1780-1850, Hutchinson, London etc., in particular pp. 13-35.

3 Cf. the debate sparked off by Martin J. Wiener (1992) [1981], *English Culture and the Decline of the Industrial Spirit, 1850-1980*, Penguin, London. Although Wiener is surely right in stressing the convergence between the middle and the upper classes in the 19th century, the need to distinguish oneself and the increasing self-confidence in the assertion of middle class values can be observed in many 19th-century texts, not least in Matthew Arnold's rhetorical deconstruction of middle class self-importance in *Culture and Anarchy*. Nineteenth-century texts on the feelings almost always assert some of the values associated with the middle classes. For a comparative analysis of these values (and practices) cf. Budde (1994), *Auf dem Weg*. An overview of the relations between the middle and the upper classes in Europe can be found in Werner Mosse (1995), 'Adel und Bürgertum im Europa des 19. Jahrhunderts. Eine vergleichende Betrachtung', in Jürgen Kocka (ed), *Bürgertum im 19. Jahrhundert*, vol. 3 (*Verbürgerlichung, Recht und Politik*), Vandenhoeck & Ruprecht, Göttingen, pp. 9-47. For a refutation of Wiener's argument and further details on the social and political background of the middle classes see Eric J. Hobsbawm (1995), 'Die englische *middle class* 1780-1920', in Jürgen Kocka (ed), *Bürgertum im 19. Jahrhundert*, vol. 1 (*Einheit und Vielfalt Europas*), Vandenhoeck & Ruprecht, Göttingen, pp. 85-112. Cf. also Peter Gay (1998), *Pleasure Wars* (*The Bourgeois Experience*, vol. 5), W.W. Norton & Co., New York/London, 'Introduction', pp. 3-23.

4 The importance of the feelings in the 19th-century can be gauged from the many genres which dealt with emotional sincerity and the correct application of feeling rules. Although the emotions have always been present in many different types of texts, the 19th century is perhaps the first century in which they appear as objects of mass culture. The reason for so many authors focusing on the emotions lies precisely in the worry that this type of mass culture provoked. If the majority of people are suddenly thought to have gained political and cultural influence (which they did not, of course, for a long time actually achieve), their behaviour requires control, and one of the means to accomplish this could be found in didactic literature of all kinds.

provide the textual basis for the following investigation of the place the feelings occupy within Victorian middle class culture. After briefly relating emotionality and the middle class tendency to social distinction, I will look at the three discursive mainstays of the Victorian middle class habitus in relation to the feelings: religion, social order, and gender.

Many 19th-century authors use feelings as a pivot for their project of creating a stable middle class habitus. What they deem to be correct and authentic emotional behaviour is contrasted with aristocratic pride and lack of true feeling on the one hand. On the other hand it is lower class immorality and the dangers of the impassioned 'mob', or 'the motley group of the idle, the reckless, and the imitative that swarm in the alleys and broadways of a metropolis'[5] from which they want to set themselves off.[6] Thus the early-19th century author Elizabeth Bonhote uses her long poem *Feeling, or, Sketches from Life; A Desultory Poem* (1810) to tell the story of an impoverished aristocratic woman who decides to earn her own keep by painting and writing. She associates feeling with middle class initiative and self-help, as opposed to the power of 'stiff, cold, feudal pride / O'erwhelm[ing] all FEELING in its hateful tide' and the dangers of 'luxury'[7]:

> But, oh, what FEELING struggled in his breast!
> As he her spirit and her worth confest,
> And how he blest that bold reflective mind
> That dar'd fulfil what FEELING had designed;
> And throw the prejudice of *birth* aside,
> And burst *thy bonds*, hereditary pride![8]

---

5 In his *Memoirs of Extraordinary Popular Delusions*, 3 vols., Richard Bentley, London quotation p. 323, Charles Mackay (1841) deals with numerous cases of 'crowd madness' or 'moral epidemics', as he calls them (p. v), e.g. 'Popular Follies in Great Cities' which describes among other issues how catch-phrases become popular.

6 Hobsbawm (1995), 'Die englische *middle class*', has identified a development in this process of social distinction. In his opinion, the early part of the century is characterised by the efforts of the middle classes to set themselves off against the aristocracy, while the later 19th century is marked more by their attempts to stress the difference between themselves and the lower classes.

7 [Elizabeth Bonhote] (1810), *Feeling*, Manners & Miller, Edinburgh, Longman, Hurst, Rees & Orme, London, p. 64, p. 112.

8 Op. cit., p. 86. Although in his *Commentary of Medical and Moral Life; or Mind and the Emotions, Considered in Relation to Health, Disease, and Religion*, Longman, Brown, & Co., London, William Cooke (1852) at first asserts that pride can be observed

Charlotte Brontë can associate feeling and proper manners in similar fashion when she surrounds Caroline Helstone with her Sunday school pupils, who have adopted the values that Caroline has taught them although they are mere country girls:

> Peasant girls as they were, they had too much of her own English sensibility to be guilty of the coarse error: they stood round her still, civil, friendly, receiving her slight smiles, and rather hurried efforts to converse, with a good feeling and good breeding: the last quality being the result of the first, which soon set her at her ease.[9]

And in Mrs Stringer's long poem *The Chain of Affection; A Moral Poem* (c. 1830),[10] the story of a young prisoner is told, who was forced to forge a deed in the name of his employer and is now awaiting his execution. He is reformed with the help of charitable ladies who visit him and teach him to die 'by Heaven's blessing':

> 'I erred against my country's upright
>   laws,
> Where justice reigns triumphant in
>   the cause.
> In pleasure's paths I careless us'd
>   to stray,

in all classes (p. 150), he then goes on to explain that as one of the so-called 'exciting emotions', producing dangerous moral and physical effects, it is to be observed particularly in 'the higher and fashionable circles. Among these elevated personages there is not generally that healthful vigour which is to be found in humbler life. There is more excitability and less power, and the vital actions are more readily disturbed; under these circumstances the proper cultivation of the emotions is of vast importance'. He is quick to defend those aristocrats who do not fall under this category, but continues with the following assertion: 'But it is equally certain that to a lamentable extent, especially so far as ladies are concerned, beauty and accomplishments are so sedulously studied, that pride and vanity grow luxuriantly, to the production of some most injurious physical effects' (p. 152).

9 Charlotte Brontë (1985) [1849], *Shirley. A Tale*, Penguin, Harmondsworth, p. 308.

10 The poem was published as *The Chain of Affection; A Moral Poem: and Other Poems. By A Lady*, printed for J. Darnill, Richmond. The publication date (1830) has been inferred from the dated engraving by J.S. Alpenny on the inner leaf, showing a young man kneeling in a cell and clasping a Bible to his breast. The date as well as the author attribution follow the catalogue of the British Library. I have been unable to discover any further biographical details.

Regardless of the snares that strew'd
the way'.[11]

In *The Philosophy of the Moral Feelings* (1833), John Abercrombie voices his corresponding conviction that 'the unthinking classes of society' stand in need of good examples:

> ... when any of these [persons in situations of rank and public eminence] are found manifesting disregard to sacred things, or giving an air of fashion to what is calculated to corrupt the moral principles of the unthinking classes of society. ... and it becomes them seriously to consider, whether they may not thus be sowing among the ignorant multitude the seeds of tumult, revolution, and anarchy.[12]

Only when the working classes accept the middle class set of values – piety, thrift, chastity, temperance – and the excesses of aristocratic pride or passion have been averted is it no longer necessary to emphasise social distinction. Nevertheless, 19th-century middle class texts on the emotions often betray the tensions between this didactic aim – reform of the lower classes – and the middle class writers' need to distinguish themselves from those above and below them. In addition, some writers on the emotions also criticise what they perceive to be dangerous social and moral developments within middle class culture itself: selfishness and materialism.[13] This kind of pessimistic outlook on society reflects the difficulties and contradictions that are characteristic of Victorian attempts at creating a stable middle class habitus. Matthew Arnold's critical assessment of everything that is typical for the middle classes in the 19th century is a case in point. Although he also attacks the aristocracy and the

---

11 [Mrs Stringer] (c. 1830), *The Chain of Affection*, p. 18, p. 17.

12 John Abercrombie (1833), *The Philosophy of the Moral Feelings*, John Murray, London, p. 60.

13 Albert O. Hirschman has shown that material interest was not always an object of middle class criticism, considered as an obstacle to feeling. On the contrary, when capitalism and the middle classes began to emerge, interest and commerce developed into a positive concept which was thought to control the passions and help civilise society. By the 19th century, this view had changed completely: too much commercial activity was disparaged as dehumanising and a sole focus on material interest was more and more judged to be uncivilised or at least uncultured. See A.O. Hirschman (1977), *The Passions and the Interests. Political Arguments for Capitalism before its Triumph*, Princeton UP, Princeton.

lower classes for their various misdemeanours, it is the middle classes themselves – his own background – that he ironises and criticises most. By engaging in a kind of rhetorical dialogue with his detractors (or those he sets up as such), Arnold emphasises the process, the emergence, of a middle class habitus and the fact that what may in retrospect appear as monolithic, linear or straight-forward was in fact a contested area with debates focusing on different educational, religious, moral and political values.[14]

The emotions can serve as a point of distinction because of their importance for the development of such an habitus. Thus, religion is based on and likened to feeling, as the following discussion shows, thereby creating a permitted space for the emotions. In addition, certain religious values (benevolence, the absence of selfishness and pride) might just as well be termed emotional states. And thrift, chastity and temperance rely on the control of certain 'passions', e.g. gluttony and voluptuosness, faint echoes of the seven deadly sins. But feeling is also needed for an ordered society, not least for a society ordered along strict gender divisions. In other words: the emotions underpin all the elements that make up the ideal middle class habitus which mainstream Victorian writers propagate.

Religion: floods of tenderness and sympathy or, The mortification of every selfish passion

Religion is the broadest framework which sets the terms for the Victorian middle class habitus. With the exception of Charles Darwin, virtually all authors studied in this book agree on some basic Christian creed and their theological differences are not always easily discernible. It is more a question of degree if one compares Mary Ann Stodart's ranting against '[t]he thick clouds of Popery'[15] with Charles Bray's mildly agnostic

---

[14] I have decided against a detailed discussion of Arnold's *Culture and Anarchy* for two reasons: partly because it is so well known that a further account of its main arguments would serve little purpose. And partly because Matthew Arnold belongs to the critical élite of the 19th century and was, in a way, ahead of his time. He was already distancing himself from values and practices which were still shared by the majority of the middle classes. He can therefore only speak *ex negativo* for the type of text and author which I am most interested in. But cf. Gay (1998), *Pleasure Wars*, on 'bourgeoisophobes', pp. 24-32.

[15] Mary Ann Stodart (1840), *Every Day Duties*, G. Seeley, London, p. 163.

Christianity or with Alexander Bain's detached analysis of religious feelings. I intend to focus on the similarities among them in order to explain the shared values and implicit rules that are specific for the Victorian discourses on emotions.[16] The examples I have chosen are to be read as just that: examples. Although the following quotations may be the most emphatically expressed passages I have selected, those I have not quoted still fit the same emotional-intellectual frame.

In his *Hymns for the Christian Church and Home* (1840 etc.), the Unitarian clergyman James Martineau explains the natural relation between true emotion and true devotion:

> Worship is an attitude which our nature assumes, not *for a purpose*, but *from an emotion*. Whenever it is genuine, it is the natural and spontaneous utterance of a mind possessed by the conception of the infinite relations in which we stand, and aspiring towards a point of view worthy of their solemnity. And though it breathes forth the deepest and greatest of desires, it is essentially an end, and not a means; and, like the embrace of friendship, or the kiss of domestic affection, loses all its meaning, when adopted from conviction of its reasonableness, or with a view to personal advantage. Those who ask, or who would explain, *what it is for*, – whether disposed to regard it as serviceable for persuading God or for benefiting man, – have as absolutely lost its true spirit, as the mother would forget her nature, if she were to regulate her caresses by expediency. The plaints of a sacred sorrow, the cry of penitence, the vow of duty, the brilliancy of praise, shed forth, like the laughter and the tears of infancy, from a heart conscious of nothing else, are examples of the true and primitive devotion.[17]

Like many other Victorian authors, Martineau contrasts insincere emotions and a rationalistic interest in 'personal advantage', as it is e.g. evinced by the curates whom Charlotte Brontë lampoons in *Shirley*, with true feeling emanating from the heart. Only those feelings which are neither conventional nor directed by expediency can be 'true' and can serve as the basis of devotion. In the hierarchy of desire, friendship, and domestic affection, religion is likened to desire, but only as a desire which has no

16 Analysing the various approaches to the emotions in different religious groups in the 19th century – an undertaking that lies beyond the scope of this study – would be a useful point of departure for future research.

17 James Martineau (^{5}1846) [1840], *Hymns for the Christian Church and Home. Collected and Edited by J.M.*, printed for the editor, and sold by Chapman, Brothers, London, p. v.

personal aim. What at first seems to be dangerously close to physical desire and thus would allow the emotions to go unchecked, proves at closer inspection to be less paradoxical. Martineau approves of true emotionality and by regarding the feelings as the source of devotion he grants them a place. But by locating them in a religious framework circumscribed by 'penitence' and 'duty', he ensures their implicit control. And even the language of desire is quickly converted into 'the embrace of friendship' and 'the kiss of domestic affection', again subordinating feeling to implicit control. With this convergence of the discourses on emotions with religious discourse, a space is created for the feelings at the same time as their possible impact is limited.

It is this overlap between emotionality and religious belief which allows the Ulster poet and conduct book writer Mary Ann Stodart to use a highly expressive and poetic language for her description of the devotional duties of young women in her conduct book *Every Day Duties: In Letters to a Young Lady* (1840): 'What we long for, is heart-religion, coming from the heart, and travelling to the heart, clothed not in carefully chosen and well-selected words, but in the glowing, inimitable language which the heart spontaneously gives.'[18] Fellow conduct book writer and teacher Sarah Ellis, brought up as a Quaker and later turned Congregationalist, even speaks of the 'floods of tenderness and sympathy' with which God 'has enriched the hearts of His faithful servants', thus using the two central metaphors of emotion for a description of religious feeling.[19]

John Abercrombie links the notion of the heart as the seat of true religious feeling to a Christian view of moral behaviour:

> True religion is seated in the heart, and sends out from thence a purifying influence over the whole character. ... It aims not at an ostentatious display of principles, but a steady exhibition of fruits. *Qualities which it cultivates with especial care, are humility, and charity, and mercy, – the mortification of every selfish passion, and the denial of every selfish indulgence.* (My emphasis, G.S.)[20]

18 M.A. Stodart (1840), *Every Day Duties: In Letters to a Young Lady*, G. Seeley, London, p. 206. According to *Allibone's Dictionary* the book was already in its fourth edition in 1857.

19 Sarah Ellis (1869), *The Education of the Heart: Woman's Best Work*, Hodder and Stoughton, London, p. 220f.

20 Abercrombie (1833), *Philosophy of the Moral Feelings*, p. 197f.

Religious feeling will make the individual conform to certain rules of behaviour, namely the absence of 'every selfish passion' and the cultivation of those moral principles deemed to be desirable: humility, charity, benevolence, and sincerity. This concept can be found in a case story in Cooke's *Mind and the Emotions in Relation to Health and Disease* (1839/1852) which he likes enough to mention it twice. It illustrates Cooke's conviction that

> Divine revelation provides for mankind as wanderers from the path of righteousness, and for their being restored by a progressive work, admirably adapted to the development of those sentiments and emotions which ennoble our nature, and lead to the most beneficent actions.[21]

In a later passage, Cooke emphasises the universality of Christianity which 'recognizes no distinction of persons, but produces similar effects on the poor illiterate man as on the rich and educated ...'. These effects are explicitly described not only as moral but also as physical in their impact:

> ... the tendency of the christian [sic] religion is to exalt all those faculties of mind, and all those moral feelings that elevate character and promote health, usefulness, and happiness; and to repress those exercises of mind, and those moral feelings (or excesses or perversions of feeling,) which produce distress, defame the character, and impair health.[22]

The narrative Cooke includes in both versions of his treatise is quoted at length here because it represents several important elements typical for the discourses on emotions: the concept of the loving married wife and mother, waiting in the home, the sanctuary, for her husband to return from the outside world; middle class pride in their wealth; the relation between 'passion' and health (or disease); the danger of excessive emotion, in particular for women; and finally the redeeming quality of faith in God. Cooke tells the story of a 'delicate, intelligent, and pleasing woman', fairly recently married, whose husband drowns in a bathing accident just when the happy couple plan to move into their new house with their daughter. This 'case' illustrates the necessity of controlling an emotion which the

---

[21] W. Cooke (1852), *A Commentary of Medical and Moral Life; or Mind and the Emotions, Considered in Relation to Health, Disease, and Religion*, Longman, Brown, & Co., London, p. 9.

[22] Op. cit., p. 17, p. 16f.

Victorians cultivated in elaborate rituals – namely, grief – perhaps because the high mortality rate forced them to do so.

> She had prepared her breakfast, and then placed herself in the window, with her infant in her arms, to catch the first glimpse and give those expressions of welcome which had so often delighted the husband and father. She sat and watched in eager and long expectation. Lively and pleasing hope sunk into suspense, and then into painful apprehensions. Messengers had been sent but brought no tidings, for the friends had prudently sent for the brother of the deceased to make the sad communication. His unexpected appearance and distressed countenance told the tale. She fell into violent paroxysms of hysteria. For some days life was doubtful. She shed no tears. The liver secreted no bile. The kidneys ceased to act. The skin was dry. I never witnessed a case in which there was such a suspension of secretion and life be spared. Her lamentations were severe. The names of "widow" – "husband", which she often repeated, never failed to rend her wounded heart. But even at this period her piety maintained the struggle, and soon gained an extraordinary ascendance. "Grief", she would say, "struggles with resignation. I have sustained a great loss, but I am sure it is all right". At times she had delightful experience of the consolations of the gospel, and would express herself as having greater discoveries of the mercy of God than she had ever before known. Recovery was slow, but I am firmly persuaded that had she been entirely destitute of the hopes and consolations of the gospel she must have sunk beneath the awful catastrophe.[23]

The novel *The Ruling Passion* (1857), written by the popular fiction writer Rainey Hawthorne, and published in three volumes by Richard Bentley, one of the most important London publishing houses, fictionalises the feeling rules endorsed by Abercrombie and Cooke in a conventional novelistic setting.[24] *The Ruling Passion* may serve as an example of how religious values form the basis of the Victorian middle class habitus not because it is exceptional, but rather because it is commonplace in terms of

---

23 Cooke, W. (1839), *Mind and Emotions Considered in Relation to Health and Disease*, Longman & Co., London, p. 45.

24 *The English Catalogue* only mentions this three volume-edition, priced at 31*s* 6*d*. It is possible that the novel's rather complicated legal plot and the fact that the author loses sight of her women characters for long stretches of time made it less appealing to her readers so that no cheaper one volume-edition could be justified. Yet she was known for her accurate descriptions and knowledge of what the author of the *DNB*-entry calls 'commerce' and many of her other novels were successful.

plot, characterisation, and narration. Such a text can be considered a kind of conventional interface, where the several strands of the discourses on emotions meet.[25]

The Ruling Passion tells a story of pride, greed and the legal battle over the country house Briarton, in possession of the Ireby family. The novel draws on numerous Victorian conventions: the legally complicated inheritance plot is combined with an orphan-romance, the invalid motif is embodied by an 'angel in the house', crafty lawyers are outdone by honest ones, the country is set against the bustling, materialist city, and the protagonist Reginald Ireby (note his telling name, derived from the word 'ire') is made to acknowledge his immoral ways and reforms before he dies. Hawthorne clearly borrowed the governess motif from the Brontës (Constance's coach trip is reminiscent of a similar voyage in Charlotte Brontë's *Jane Eyre*), attempts a Dickensian legal conundrum, and uses an orphaned- and dependent-sister plot inspired by Jane Austen's *Sense and Sensibility* as a background story. Her stock characters (angelic women, dreadful headmistresses, cunning lawyers, unreasonable old men, proud and passionate youths, shrews etc.) undergo little or no development, and if they do, this is not shown but only told, in the final passage which explains Reginald's (and to a lesser extent, his sister Constance's) reform. The novel is narrated from the point of view of a traditional omniscient, heterodiegetic and moralistic narrator and except for a few scenic passages, descriptive narration and rather unsubtle direct characterisation is the norm. But it is precisely because of its conventionality, extending also to language, emotion metaphors and the way the body is used as an expressive medium, that I have chosen to make *The Ruling Passion* a key text in this chapter – something which its aesthetic qualities would not otherwise merit.[26] It is an example of the many Victorian narratives which

---

25 Hawthorne seems also to have been familiar with popular psychological theories: her narrator comments on the lawyer Walter Martock's face in physiognomical terms (2, p. 22f.) and muses on the power of association (3, p. 85f.).

26 The review of *The Ruling Passion* in *The Athenæum*, No. 1573, 19 December 1857, p. 1586, is justified in its criticism of the novel. It is interesting to note that Geraldine Jewsbury, who wrote it, did not realise who the author and in particular of what sex s/he was. 'There is a good deal of talent shown in this novel, but it is not well amalgamated; the incidents are arbitrary and depend too evidently on the author's will; the characters are less human beings than fancy portraits. The result does not give the reader the impression of reality, and the effect is on the whole more fatiguing than pleasant. The story is clogged by long-winded reflections and observations too obvious to need

steer their readers through a complicated moral maze,[27] at the end of which they should have understood that 'principle, not passion, must be their guide through life, if they would hope for peace in it, for tranquillity at death; ...' (3, p. 277).[28]

Reginald only arrives at this conviction after a life guided not by those Christian values enumerated by Abercrombie, but rather by their opposites: greed, pride, revenge, and violent passion. And furthermore, deceit and insincerity, intemperance, impiety, and selfishness are also embodied by a number of other (minor) characters in the novel. General Ireby and his sons Delavelle and Reginald are driven by possessiveness and greed. Materialism is the order of the day (1, p. 82f.) and it is difficult for Ireby and Delavelle not to listen to 'that cunning voice ... which lures man on so imperceptibly to destruction – ere, in one word, temptation was yielded to, and became a sin!' (1, p. 63). The narrator makes it clear throughout the novel that greed and pride as the sole guiding emotions lead to sin, and finally, to death. In such a society, interested solely in obtaining material gain, it is not surprising that insincere feelings are common. Delavelle's feelings for his son and the emotional consequences are described as 'the forced fondness of manner, not the earnest love of the heart; it was the affection of words, and proceeded from determination, not the love of deeds, proceeding from the soul. The child's heart withered in the uncongenial atmosphere' (3, p. 227). And in a revealing passage, one of

---

extension. The situations are some of them very good, and the character of Reginald Ireby, the younger brother, is well conceived. ... exasperated by his wrongs, and without the strength necessary either to control circumstances or to submit to them, he brings nothing but evil on himself and those dependant on him; but he is too entirely provoking, and the reader soon ceases to feel either pity or sympathy for him. His two sisters are touchingly drawn, in their helplessness and confiding trust in this very broken reed, their brother, whom they love and forgive in a way that would be difficult to heroines in real life. "The Ruling Passion" would have been better called Monomania: it consists in Reginald's determination to obtain at once both his rights and his revenge. ... The author has not the skill to regulate the power which he unquestionably possesses. He draws without models, and has not sufficient knowledge of human nature to dispense with them. "The Ruling Passion" is not a pleasant novel, but the author has more ability than he has brought to bear on the present work' (p. 1586).

27 A similar example is Dinah Mulock Craik's novel *Olive* (1850), which in aesthetic terms is only marginally more interesting than *The Ruling Passion*. A part of the plot is based on a similar 'conversion' story, where a clergyman who has lost his faith is slowly brought back to believing in God with the help of the angelic (but otherwise more resourceful) Olive after whom the novel was named.

28 The first number in brackets always refers to the respective volume of the novel.

the protagonists of the legal sub-plot, Thomas D'Evelyn, illustrates the ever-present danger of emotional hypocrisy and insincerity when feeling rules are adhered to without being felt. Significantly, this occurs in a scene of mourning, as common in Victorian novels as in society, and it appears that grief is an emotion particularly difficult to express in a manner sanctioned by society:

> '... there is a mourning of manner which is considered quite as essential as black gloves and a crape hatband; and provided these two, manner and dress, I mean, be attended to, the deeper mourning of the heart is never thought of. Yet the poor, who weep for their relatives in ragged coats, and coloured dresses, sorrow more, perhaps, than we do'. (3, p. 71f.)

In familiar metaphorical guise, the narrator comments on the absence of truth and the consequences this has for 'the human heart':

> It may be ... that at the bottom of that unfathomable well, the human heart, the precious gem is lying; but, unhappily, so many falsehoods are heaped on the top of it; so many jarring interests and false views of expediency, and evil passions, choke up the fountain from whence it ought to gush clear and bright; so much which turns out subsequently to be but worthless tinsel instead of pure gold is palmed upon us in its place; that at length we almost come reluctantly to admit the idea, either that truth has forsaken her old haunts altogether, or that she sleeps so very far down that it is merely waste of time looking for her. (1, p. 81)

This state of affairs is seen as a result of a kind of alienation, which allows D'Evelyn to advise his younger colleague Martock to '... lay aside sensibility and sentimentality; ay, and if it be possible, common sympathy with your fellows. If you just can get rid of these three incumbrances, your success is certain; if not —' (2, p. 19). Martock, of course, does not follow this advice, and is one of the most positively drawn characters of the whole novel. But before comparing the novel's immoral characters with their idealised counterparts, another comment by the narrator will throw some light on the social problem which the novel focuses on, namely the dangerous absence of 'positive' feelings:

> How little we know of each other, even of those most closely connected with us by ties of relationship, or love, or friendship ... .
>
> It is well perhaps for human beings to believe they know the secret histories and feelings of their fellows, *for the delusion keeps alive sympathy, which*

> *otherwise might perish altogether for want of aliment*; but often it seems curious to pause and reflect for a moment, on our utter ignorance of what a world of sensations may be peopling the heart of our nearest friend, while we are all unconscious of the fact. (2, p. 90f.) (My emphasis, G.S.)

Reginald's passion and pride are perhaps to be preferred to the rather cold-hearted lawyer D'Evelyn, or his greedy half-brother Delavelle, but it is the two sisters and Walter Martock who embody the most positive emotions in *The Ruling Passion* and who function as models for the novel's readers. Reginald's impetuous (1, p. 213), passionate (1, p. 221, p. 244) and revengeful nature and his hate are stronger than love (3, p. 179) and make him more suited to live with the Indians than in England (3, p. 223); it also makes him age prematurely and in the end leads to his death (3, p. 266f.), thus punishing him for his 'vindictive, passionate feeling' (2, p. 193). And although Delavelle appears to be at first rather unremarkable (1, p. 39) and even shows some filial affection for his father (1, p. 62), his hate for the General's second wife (1, p. 98) and his love of money and power are stronger (1, p. 196). What haunts the men of the Ireby family is summarised by D'Evelyn, the lawyer, as follows:

> '... General Ireby insisted on leaving his property absurdly; or perhaps it were better to say unjustly, for more absurdly than to Reginald, his youngest son, he could not possibly devise it. In one word, father, first-born, second-born, and for aught I know to the contrary, grand-children, are all alike, ridiculous, haughty, unmanageable, and yet still unsteady. Possessed with one leading notion, Briarton, they think it is the only thing worth having or keeping in life. Briarton was the General's mania; it is his sons'. (2, p. 14f.)

Although Constance resembles Reginald most, her alleged impetuosity is never properly described. Instead, her positive influence on her brother (1, p. 208), her resolution to help the family by going out to work (2, p. 47) and the close ties she enjoys with her sister are stressed. That she is said to have 'reformed' at the end of the novel parallels Reginald's transformation into a repentant, wiser person. Nevertheless, Constance occupies a kind of middle ground between Reginald, whose repentance comes too late for his survival (at least on earth), and his other sister Marian, thus making her the character with which the readers could most easily identify – flawed, but not fatally so, and not too other-worldly to be completely unrealistic. The latter description fits her sister Marian who is the epitome of the morally and emotionally superior 'angel in the house'. She is soft and fragile (1, p. 55) and able to influence her brother, if not to lasting effect:

> The young man was at length softened. That which no remonstrance, nor reasoning, nor proffers of service had been able to effect, was accomplished by a few words spoken from the heart, and consequently appealing directly to it. Tears of mingled pride, anger, and affection sprang to his eyes, as the tones of that young, clear, yet subdued and melancholy, voice thrilled to his soul; .... (2, p. 34)

But it is the character differences between Reginald and Marian that lead to the accident which fatally injures her – he cannot understand her feelings which would allow her to take money from Delavelle to help them in their impoverished situation (2, p. 268). Marian bears her sufferings virtually without complaint (3, p. 57) and spends her final days poor but happy, helping Constance to look after the children she is charged with. The source of this angelic behaviour, as well as of Constance's more worldly nature, is the love of God: '... for it was the same God who watched over their steps in the town as in the country. ... And this conviction comforted the hearts of the girls in times of heavy sorrow, and enabled them to endure the load wherewith it had seemed good unto Him to burden them' (1, p. 279).[29]

The Ruling Passion is an example of that type of didactic novel which does not intend to teach its readers specific religious practices or points of doctrine, but which wants to encourage a certain latitudinarian Christian attitude of submission, humanity, and benevolence as opposed to selfishness. It is a fictional expression of that 'code of belief and ethics, followed by Christians and unbelievers alike' which can be called evangelical in its emphasis on personal atonement and conversion.[30] And in spite of a conventional apology for the moral supplied at the end, the narrator does not hesitate to spell out this didactic aim which *The Ruling*

---

29 In case the readers should think that 'goodness' is restricted to women, two positive male figures – albeit rather sketchily drawn ones – also figure in *The Ruling Passion*: Ernehulst, Constance's husband, described as a gentleman speaking 'the king's English' (2, p. 81) and Walter Martock, the upright lawyer who advises Reginald not to succumb to passion, i.e. not to attempt breaking the will disinheriting him, and who remains unmarried because he cannot contemplate replacing his first love (Marian) (3, p. 285f.).

30 J.F.C. Harrison (1971), *The Early Victorians, 1832-1851*, Weidenfeld and Nicolson, London, p. 133.

Passion shares with health guides warning against the dangers of uncontrolled passion such as anger and pride:

> ... I say, if you are disposed to make an unrighteous will, ... – walk some leisure-day into Doctors' Commons, and read the original testament of General Delavelle Ireby, of Briarton, in —shire ... and think of its result; and if, moreover, you feel evil feelings and vindictive passions, and unattainable wishes rising in your bosom ... oh! reader ... remember no tale – no matter how humble its purport, no matter how feebly told – is written without an object: and it is earnestly to be hoped, that something, some good plan ... may be implanted or awakened, even from the perusal of this now concluded story of the Ruling Passion. (3, p. 289f.)

Social Order: The imitation within ourselves of the government without us

Teaching Christian values and experiencing religious feelings allowed the individual a certain space for his or her emotionality, if only one permitting the cultivation of such 'positive' emotions as sympathy or benevolence. But religion also served another purpose: that of social control. In *The Emotions and the Will* Alexander Bain describes his idea of the effects of religious feelings which he approvingly classifies as a 'Tender Sentiment', provided it does not consist of the 'grossest and most grovelling superstitions ... where terror prints its deepest mark'[31]:

> Sentiment often lends itself to aid the duty of social obedience, whose real foundations is in the highest degree practical or utilitarian. The sanctity and divine right of monarchs and dynasties are scarcely extinct as feelings in the present day. Indeed, it is frequently said, that without the help of the religious sentiment, civil order could not be maintained.[32]

The aim of the Victorian discourses on emotions and the focal point of most texts used here is the creation and preservation of a specific habitus based on 'civil order'. Again and again, authors call for emotional and therefore social order but these explicit demands are also supplemented by implicit rules representing order on the discursive level. In the fourth

---

[31] A. Bain (^{2}1865) [1859], *The Emotions and the Will*, Longmans & Co., London, p. 91.
[32] Op. cit., footnote p. 278.

edition of Charles Bray's successful educational manual *The Education of the Feelings*, published in 1872, these two modes converge. The subsequent passage does not only express middle class pride in material advancement, but also explicitly recommends 'orderly habits', symbolised on the discursive level by Bray's post office metaphor:

> Nothing is more important in education than teaching orderly habits. There should be a place for everything, and everything in its place ... .
> The Post Office is the best example we have at present of what order or organisation can effect. ... The world at present, comparatively, is a complete Chaos, but we have only to follow this example of the Post Office, and introduce Order, and all may then receive those external advantages of civilisation which hitherto have been confined to a favoured few. ([4]1872, p. 138)

Further examples of the overlap between explicit calls for social order and their discursive embodiment will follow, but first an account of the main ideas on which Bray bases his advice manual.

In spite of the religious crisis which he experienced as a young man and his reputation as the leading Coventry free-thinker, Bray constantly invokes God as well as the values exemplified above in *The Education of the Feelings*. Christianity is his individual and social standard of feeling and behaviour, which he hopes will in time result in an ideal social order.[33] Bray acknowledged that *The Education of the Feelings* owes a considerable debt to his wife and her eldest sister Sara Hennell, and their experience with children.[34] The text alternates explanations with narrative examples, either taken from the Unitarian magazine *The Monthly Repository*, or based on the author's own experience. It is not addressed to people who have studied education but intended for 'those, whose opportunities have as yet been limited for acquiring such knowledge'

---

33 For details of his crisis of faith and the consequences this had for his marriage, see Bray's (c. 1884) autobiography, *Phases of Opinion and Experience During a Long Life: An Autobiography*, Longmans, Green and Co., London, p. 15ff.

34 Bray (c. 1884), op. cit., p. 52. Bray was obviously guided by the Unitarian's liberal approach to education, which in its turn had been influenced by Pestalozzi's ideas and in particular by Pestalozzi's emphasis on physical and moral as well as intellectual education, his interest in the individual child and its natural development, as well his as religious tolerance. See Ruth Watts, (1998) *Gender, Power and the Unitarians in England 1760-1860*, Longman, London/New York, p. 113f.

(¹1838, n. p.). *The Education of the Feelings* aims

> To urge the great importance of MORAL EDUCATION – to shew the bearing of a few great truths upon it – to point out the NATURAL LAWS which the Creator has established, by which the feelings are to be trained and cultivated .... (¹1838, preface, n. p.)[35]

'Training' or 'management', and 'cultivation' of the feelings – in other words: control and expression – are the two keywords which appear again and again and are intended as the means which will create the greatest happiness for all, Bray's overall utilitarian aim. *The Education of the Feelings* ran to four English and one unauthorised American edition and was so popular that from its second edition onwards it was published by the various Longman-firms in London.[36] A reviewer in the *Westminster Review* (1850) praised the second edition in the following words: 'With unaffected simplicity, and in a clear, manly, healthfully vigorous moral tone has Mr. Bray executed the task he set himself, and has produced a book of small size, but of great merit and utility, and containing much excellent remark.'[37] The different editions chart the development that Bray

35 The first edition dating from 1838 appeared anonymously or at least without mentioning the author's name.

36 Bray comments on the various editions of *The Education of the Feelings* in his autobiography and explains that he withdrew the phrenological terminology to simplify the book. He also mentions the unauthorised American edition (1881) published by S.R. Wells and Co., New York: 'This is Phrenologically illustrated by heads in which different organs are large or small. It has been done without consulting me; but I am sufficiently paid by the good that it may do, and the compliment implied' (p. 52f.).

37 The review which appeared under the heading 'Education' in vol. 52 in 1850, pp. 615-617, is signed 'C.S.H.' I have been unable to trace the author's identity, as even the *Wellesley Index to Victorian Periodicals* contains no more than the bare initials. The review is favourable, and is written in a tone which resembles Bray's own manner, using naturalising metaphors of growth and development for the education of children. The only slight hint of criticism is directed at phrenology but its 'educational precepts' are praised (p. 616). A second and much longer review of Bray's most important writings, by St George William Joseph Stock (1879), appeared in *The Westminster Review*, vol. 111 o.s., pp. 488-506. Although Stock is critical of Bray's sceptical approach to philosophy, he also has some praise for him: 'Whatever judgement may be formed of Mr. Bray's philosophical powers, we make acquaintance with him here as a good man; for no one can read this little book and fail to esteem the author' (p. 493). In her letters, George Eliot comments favourably on *The Education of the Feelings*: 'I don't know of any sort of work more needed among the educators', she writes to Sara Sophia Hennell in a letter dated 22 November 1872 and in a letter to Bray himself she

as well as Victorian society underwent. They can also serve both as conventional examples of the views dominating texts on the emotions and as illustrations of more marginalised attitudes.

How then are children to be educated, according to Charles Bray? In his opinion, 'man' can be distinguished from animals by 'the proportion in which his feelings are under the control of his reflective powers ...' ([1]1838, p. 14). If he 'cultivates' these properly, he will be happy, happiness being defined as the 'happiness of all mankind' ([1]1838, p. 18). What endangers happiness as well as the influence of reason is selfishness and the danger of 'excess and abuse' ([1]1838, p. 20). But:

> The union of self-control with the benevolent feelings is the point at which we should aim; this accomplished, a child will delight to yield his own gratification of appetite to that of others, and find an ample recompense in the consciousness of being the giver of pleasure and conqueror of self. ([1]1838, p. 40f.)

This state can be reached only by restraint of some feelings and strengthening of others. Bray does not recommend complete submission of the emotions, on the contrary, he calls for the 'cultivation and guidance' of certain feelings ([1]1838, p. 29). But he is in no doubt as to which passions are 'evil': 'greediness, stupid surrender of the understanding, vanity, lying, and hypocrisy' ([1]1838, p. 39). Conquering these selfish feelings is associated with pleasure ([1]1838, p. 95) and can be attained if the teacher – the 'judicious trainer of the feelings' ([1]1838, p. 54) – does not only instruct, but shows children by example what goals they are to aim at ([1]1838, p. 3ff.).

Like Matthew Arnold, Rainey Hawthorne or Charles Dickens, e.g. in *Dombey and Son* (1847-48) or *Hard Times* (1854), Bray criticises materialism.[38] In his opinion, insufficient 'conquest' of selfishness and the

---

comments on the 1860-edition: 'We shall certainly read the parts you suggest in the 'Education of the Feelings' – and I dare say *I* shall read a good deal more of it, liking to turn over the leaves of a book which I read first in our old drawing-room at Foleshill ...', in Gordon S. Haight (ed) (1954-55), *The George Eliot Letters*, Yale UP, New Haven/London, vol. 5, p. 329 and vol. 3, p. 324 respectively.

38 Cf. e.g. Matthew Arnold (February 1866) [1987] [1970], 'My Countrymen', in P.J. Keating (ed), *Matthew Arnold. Selected Prose*, Penguin, London, pp. 175-201, in particular p. 190f. This essay was first printed in the *Cornhill Magazine*. It is a response to an article from the *Saturday Review* entitled 'Mr Matthew Arnold and his Countrymen' (3 December 1864), which in its turn is a reaction to Arnold's 'The

emphasis that is laid on 'acquisitiveness' are the cause of 'most of the prevalent evils of society at the present day' ([1]1838, p. 73). He strongly objects to this since only self-gratification and not the happiness of all people are the object of such a materialist outlook on life which moreover opposes the Bible ([1]1838, p. 74). What should be taught is not the 'love of possession' but the acquisition of things which may provide happiness ([1]1838, p. 75). Yet if the 'law of God' is observed just as the aim to provide happiness for all is kept in mind society may prosper, as the progressivist Bray believes, and selfishness and the ensuing materialism will be diminished in their influence on society.[39]

Up to this point, Bray's ideas are similar to many other middle class writers' views. He uses a system of popular science, phrenology, as the 'scientific' basis for his advice, whose significance will be explained below, and recommends general Christian principles and rules of behaviour. But there are two aspects where Bray differs from his more conservative fellow authors such as Sarah Ellis or Mary Ann Stodart: in his concept of childhood and in his political convictions.

Even in the first edition of *The Education of the Feelings*, before Bray became interested in workers' co-operatives and Robert Owen's communitarian project,[40] his treatment of the working classes is sympathetic if ambiguous.

> ... man in his moral and intellectual capacity is still in his infancy, for he is still trusting for his enjoyment to the feelings of his inferior nature. ...
>
> Let but the principles of our constitution be understood – *let but education rest upon a proper basis, and the petty distinctions of a savage age, which form the present scale of society, will be abolished.* Man will then be estimated according to his supremacy in *those things which distinguish him from the brutes – for moral feeling and intellect.*
>
> ... he will likewise perceive that *the only way to obviate the evils of society, is not to level all distinctions,* which would be impossible, *but to make all happy by such regulations as shall afford to every one time for moral and intellectual*

Function of Criticism'.

39 Abercrombie (1833) expresses a similar hope for the future: 'Amid much weakness, therefore, and many infirmities, his [man's] moral improvement goes forward. Faint and feeble at first, as the earliest dawn of the morning, it becomes brighter and steadier as it proceeds in its course, and, "as the shining light, shineth more and more unto the perfect day"'. *The Philosophy of the Moral Feelings*, p. 244.

40 Bray (c. 1884), *Phases of Opinion*, p. 58ff.

> *cultivation*, and the consequent moral and intellectual enjoyment. (^{1}1838, p. 194f.)[41]

Although he speaks of 'a savage age', Bray still upholds social distinctions, i.e. class differences, and addresses the individual as the agent of social change which is clearly envisaged as reform and not as revolution. This focus on the individual is in accordance with the dominant notion that the state should not intervene but that every person should rise in society on the basis of his or her own merit. In the 1860-edition, Bray is more explicit in his social analysis – he uses the term 'bondage' to describe the plight of 'three-fourths of humanity' (^{3}1860, p. 31). But although his tone is more radical and the political passages are more numerous, he still wavers in his recommendations as to how this state of affairs which he clearly perceives as a danger to individual and social well-being ought to be overcome. Bray acknowledges the greater political influence that is the result of what he calls 'the spirit of democracy' but expresses a typically middle class fear of the 'mediocrity' of lower class values and behaviour. Recommending education for the lower classes to save them from the influence of 'public opinion', conforms with the paternalistic views of most middle class writers and expresses a similar desire in the author to distinguish himself from the lower classes. Bray goes on to criticise eleemosynary charity and recommends self-help à la Samuel Smiles[42] before acknowledging – albeit grudgingly – the new-found power of the working classes:

> To insist upon the only means which are really efficacious to raise the conditions of the poor, – providence, prudence, forethought, economy, education, – and to help the poor to help themselves, is not the popular course. ... But everywhere *the spirit of democracy is on the increase*, and all men, whether consciously or not, are aiding it by their exertions; ... public opinion becomes more powerful and irresistible, and *in proportion as it thus becomes more powerful is it lowered to the mental and moral level of the increasing multitude from whence that power is derived.* No doubt this is good upon the whole, as the world is made for the happiness of all, not of a class; but,

41 My emphasis, G.S.

42 Bray (^{4}1872) explicitly mentions Samuel Smiles in the fourth edition of *The Education of the Feelings*: 'The teacher also will be expected to furnish illustrations of the duties inculcated, since little more than principles can be expected in a small work like the present. Mr. Samuel Smiles' books on "Character", "Self-Help" &c., will be found useful for this purpose' (p. iv f.).

> nevertheless, it everywhere tends to exalt mediocrity and to make popular that only which is capable of being understood and appreciated, not by the highest minds and intellects, but the lowest. (^{3}1860, p. 53f.) (My emphasis, G.S.)

Bray struggles with the need to distinguish himself, as a member of the commercial middle classes, from those below him whose increasing public influence he recognises. But the familiar worry about 'the misrule of fashion', – upper class luxury – which immediately follows the passage quoted above, is also evident, thus indicating how precarious the 'middle position' was felt to be, a position that is characteristic of the middle classes in the 19th century. Nevertheless, Bray's sympathies with those classes which his fellow authors prefer to label as the dangerous, amorphous 'mob' or the 'obscure and insignificant multitude'[43] are obvious when he describes them as 'slaves'. Significantly, Bray was also against capital punishment: '... Capital Punishment is an error, and much of our penal code is based upon injustice' (^{3}1860, p. 90).

Where Charles Bray definitely moves beyond the implicit conventions of the discourses on emotions is in his views of childhood. He does not call for simple repression of all those feelings which adults deem to be excessive in children. Although he praises modesty in children, his main objective is to make teachers and parents train and cultivate certain emotions, while reducing the impact of all selfish feelings. This notion of cultivation and management, not of repression, is accompanied by a concept of childhood which stresses freedom and self-expression, rather than mere rule-governed behaviour. Here, he tends more towards the expressive side of the expression-and-control paradigm.[44] In Bray's

43 This expression is used in the conduct book anon. (1842), *The Young Man's Mentor, On His Entrance Into Life; With Rules for His General Conduct After Leaving School. The Whole Intended to Assist in Forming and Strengthening the Intellectual and Moral Character of Youth and Manhood*, T.M. Cradock, London. The author recommends self-education and self-help for mental, moral and religious improvement so that the 'young man' may raise himself above others (p. 7). The target audience of this programme of self-improvement aimed at social distinction is described as reaching 'from the embryo merchant and manufacturer down to the humbler mechanic and assistant tradesman' (p. 6).

44 Such views do not appear to have been the norm in Victorian middle class education and the experience of childhood seems to have been characterised by strict rules, as can be gathered from Budde's (1994) analysis of middle class life in England and Germany during the 19th century, *Auf dem Weg*, p. 116ff. Cf. also Anne Digby and Peter Searby (1981), *Children, School and Society in Nineteenth-Century England*,

opinion, each child is different and therefore requires individual treatment. He advises the application of just 'one great rule': 'to be ourselves what we would wish our children to be' ([2]1849, preface, p. i). He also asks that children should not be 'snatche[d] ... hastily away' from their occupations all the time ([1]1838, p. 47) and demands of parents and teachers that they show respect towards their children. These should be taught by gentleness and kindness and directed rather than restrained ([1]1838, p. 54). Since in Bray's view feelings develop according to certain stages – first the 'selfish or animal feelings and the perceptive faculties', then 'the moral feelings' and then 'the reasoning powers' – this gradual development should be assisted and not forced ([1]1838, p. 187). He warns against the dangers of making children study too hard ([1]1838, p. 188f) and advises parents to teach children to rely on their own resources ([1]1838, p. 191). The aim of this is to make 'the season of childhood that which it ought to be, the season of happiness' ([1]1838, p. 190). Parents should not fear spoiling their children by making them too happy. And even 'bursts of passion' should not be repressed because this may result in sulkiness ([3]1860, p. 134). Instead: 'Let the child's limbs and affections have full play and free scope, and let our endeavour be to assist the natural growth and enter fully into his mind and spirit' ([3]1860, p. 133). This happiness may be endangered when parents are excessively authoritarian, an attitude which Bray criticises:

> Some parents and teachers have themselves the love of authority so strong, that they would actually prefer that a child should do right because they command it, than of its own accord; ... Their aim seems to be less that of teaching a child to walk alone, than to strengthen the leading-strings which attach it to themselves. ([1]1838, p. 96)

He then goes on to explain that rules should be reasonable, since the child will obey them 'from motives of affection and duty', just like adults follow the rule of God: 'Has our Great Parent given to *us* a single law of which we cannot understand and approve the reason; and if *He* so far condescends to lay open before us the principles of his government, why should not we govern our children by the same equitable rule?' ([1]1838, p. 97). Although he does not lose sight of 'the virtues of self-denial and self-control' ([3]1860, p. 135), these can only grow in a happy surrounding:

Macmillan, London/Basingstoke.

> Happiness is the atmosphere in which all good affections grow – the wholesome warmth necessary to make the heart-blood circulate healthily and freely; unhappiness the chilling pressure which produces here an inflammation, there an excrescence, and worst of all, "the mind's green and yellow sickness – ill-temper". Make a child unhappy by continually thwarting him, chiding him, and punishing him, and ten to one he will soon show an evil temper of his own, and a distortion of his moral nature. (^{3}1860, p. 134f.)

Although the authors of health guides explain the influence of happiness (unless it is excessive, when it can cause 'sudden death') in similar terms, most of them seem to have a concept of childhood which is based not on individual freedom but on the notion that children should do what their parents tell them. Thus Bray's emphasis on individual character and liberty differs from other conduct book and advice manual writers and their calls for a greater degree of obedience, and consequently stress emotional control more than the need for the expression of the feelings. It is this liberal approach to education which receives greatest praise from 'C.S.H.', the reviewer in *The Westminster Review* (1850), who speaks of the pleasure of being taught the right things at the right age, and the pain which results from forced and 'unnatural work' at school, once again evoking the pain-and-pleasure dichotomy so favoured by writers on the feelings.[45] Interestingly, the review is followed by a short text about Fröbel, Pestalozzi and the '*Kinder Gürten*', as the reviewer calls them, and the notion of teaching children 'in harmony with nature'. Fröbel's ideas were to become more and more popular towards the late 19th century; in England, his ideas were spread by the educationalist Emily Shirreff, an author whose novel *Passion and Principle*, written with her sister Maria Georgina Grey, is one of the key texts of the following chapter.

That the emotional education of children (and adults) was not only a concern of non-fiction writers can be illustrated by Charles Dickens's novel *Hard Times* (1854).[46] The 'keynote', as Dickens calls it, of the Coketown world dominated by Gradgrind and his followers, whose names are equally telling, appears to be a rigorously utilitarian approach to life: 'Fact, fact, fact, everywhere in the material aspect of the town; fact, fact, fact everywhere in the immaterial' (p. 29). Thomas Gradgrind teaches his

---

45 C.S.H. (1850), 'Education', p. 615.

46 Charles Dickens (1995) *Hard Times For These Times*, Penguin, Harmondsworth. The page references are to this edition.

children never to 'wonder', as the narrator comments: 'Herein lay the spring of the mechanical art and mystery of educating the reason without stooping to the cultivation of the sentiments and affections. Never wonder' (p. 54). Gradgrind's room is used to sum up not only his approach to life but also his character:

> Although Mr Gradgrind did not take after Blue Beard, his room was quite a blue chamber in its abundance of blue books. Whatever they could prove (which is usually anything you like), they proved there, in an army constantly strengthening by the arrival of new recruits. In that charmed apartment, the most complicated social questions were cast up, got into exact totals, and finally settled – if those concerned could only have been brought to know it. As if an astronomical observatory should be made without any windows, and the astronomer within should arrange the starry universe solely by pen, ink and paper, so Mr Gradgrind, in *his* Observatory (and there are many like it) had no need to cast an eye upon the teeming myriads of human beings around him, but could settle all their destinies on a slate, and wipe out all their tears with one dirty little bit of sponge. (p. 98f.)

Typical for Dickens is the comic effect he produces by animating objects – the blue books are turned into new recruits of an 'army' – and also the use of objects to represent and describe his characters. But in spite of Gradgrind's penchant for facts and statistics, a thinly veiled attack on the social reformers of the 19th century who worked along such positivist lines, not all is well in his world. His daughter Louisa incites her brother Tom to join her in their investigation of Sleary's circus, the counterworld that Dickens sets up. Although she is a model pupil and has crammed her head full of facts and one 'Ology' after another, as her feeble-minded, invalid mother says (p. 201), Louisa is still attracted by the 'other' world she perceives in the circus, since in her can be found 'a light with nothing to rest upon, a fire with nothing to burn, a starved imagination keeping life in itself somehow' (p. 19). The traditional 'pressure-cooker' concept of emotion in the shape of the image of the smouldering fire accompanies Louisa's description, and it is the 'fire' she continuousely watches which will burst out of her when she realises that she has wasted her life on intellectual pursuits almost entirely devoid of feeling and affection.

The circus people's world is governed by quite different principles.[47]

---

[47] Cf. Kate Flint (1995), 'Introduction' in the Penguin edition of *Hard Times* on the complex nature of this counterworld, pp. xi-xxxii.

Although they, too, have to rely on financial income to survive, their main aim in life is not material, their support is emotional: they help each other, they enjoy their work and afford their audience pleasure. Dickens expresses considerable sympathy even for their unorthodox relations. They do not live according to the model family with retiring females in the background, but rather as a group of people all willing to help one another, with working women at that. In spite of their untidy appearance,

> ... there was a remarkable gentleness and childishness about these people, a special inaptitude for any kind of sharp practice, and an untiring readiness to help and pity one another, deserving, often of as much respect, and always of as much generous construction, as the everyday virtues of any class of people in the world. (p. 41)

The contradictions and limits of Gradgrind's world become evident when Sissy Jupe, the clown's daughter, becomes part of the Gradgrind household. She openly expresses her emotions – her sorrow at her father's absence and the pain of parting from her circus friends – and with her naive approach to seemingly simple questions, shows up the immorality of the utilitarian approach Dickens satirises in *Hard Times*. When asked, concerning arithmetics, '"What is the first principle of this science?"' by the aptly named teacher M'Choakumchild, Sissy answers: '"To do unto others as I would that they should do unto me"' (p. 60). In spite of Gradgrind's adverse reaction to Sissy's apparent lack of progress, he is affected by her:

> Somehow or other, he had become possessed by an idea that there was something in this girl which could hardly be set forth in a tabular form. Her capacity of definition might be easily stated at a very low figure, her mathematical knowledge at nothing; yet he was not sure that if he had been required, for example, to tick her off into columns in parliamentary return, he would have quite known how to divide her. (p. 95f.)

Later, Sissy will take on the crucial role of reconciling the circus world with Gradgrind, by asking her circus friends to save Tom from being put on trial for the bank robbery he has committed. Her friends help to hide Tom – fittingly enough impersonating a black clown, the complete opposite or 'other' of the successful young middle class bank clerk he used to be – so that Gradgrind may send him abroad to avoid public shame.

Tom, of course, is the worst outcome of the Gradgrind system – only interested in his own success, morally weak, easily impressed (by James Hearthouse in particular), with little emotion save that for his sister, and even that is hidden by his egoism to such an extent that he only expresses his love for her when he lies dying in foreign parts. His death – the just reward for not achieving the ideal of unselfish muscular masculinity – is paralleled by Louisa's fire bursting out in the wrong place, before it is subdued for ever, since after her separation from Bounderby Louisa remains single for the rest of her life. In other words: the Gradgrind-system is shown to have failed entirely but at least Louisa and her father are allowed to change under Sissy's influence: they accept that 'fancy' and 'feeling' are essential elements of human relations and that 'facts' alone cannot solve all problems – on the contrary, they may even create them. Particularly the example of Louisa is pertinent here. Because she is unable to suppress all her feelings she is trapped by James Hearthouse who plays with her emotions in order to advance his own cause.

That the sole reliance on 'facts' and the absence of feeling is dangerous to the individual is amply illustrated in *Hard Times*. But what of the social consequences? Obviously, another Victorian favourite approach to life – self-help, as it was shortly to be propagated by Samuel Smiles – is exposed and criticised by Dickens with the help of the wind-bag Bounderby. In order to impress his fellow citizens, Bounderby has created his own story: by relying solely on his own resources, he claims, he has become 'Josiah Bounderby of Coketown', a fact which he brags about constantly. Early on, the narrator indicates how the readers are to judge Bounderby:

> It was one of the most exasperating attributes of Bounderby, that he not only sang his own praises but stimulated other men to sing them. There was a moral infection of clap-trap in him. Strangers, modest enough elsewhere, started up at dinners in Coketown, and boasted, in quite a rampant way, of Bounderby. They made him out to be the Royal arms, the Union-Jack, Magna Charta, John Bull, Habeas Corpus, the Bill of Rights, An Englishman's house is his castle, Church and State, and God save the Queen, all put together. (p. 49)

Because Bounderby is only interested in himself, he denounces his mother and lacks understanding of his 'hands', as the working classes are called by the master of the mill. In assuming that they want what he wants – riches – he accuses them of making outrageous demands. Quite apart from the fact that Bounderby marries a girl thirty years his junior because she seems so suitable, not because he loves her. And because he is so full of himself, he does not even notice how she falls for another man. Bounderby's rejection of Stephen Blackpool's plea for help with his divorce procedures is crucial here. If Bounderby had helped him, disaster could have been averted.

But for all the criticism of mid-Victorian complacency, of belief in facts, in the good to come from machines and industrialised production processes, for all the tensions and contradictions which one can find in *Hard Times*, Dickens remains within the boundaries of middle class views of the emotions. They have to be controlled – otherwise the passionate, animal-like mob threatens to swallow the middle classes[48] – but not suppressed, since affection and feeling are necessary to maintain social order. Social order consists of a benevolent relationship between masters and workers, and in the upholding of gender relations. Although *Hard Times* is full of dysfunctional families and odd relationships like the one between Bounderby and his housekeeper Mrs Sparsit, Dickens firmly endorses the typical view that women are the educators of the heart, if one lets them assume that role. Rachael, the 'angel in the house' who saves Stephen from murdering his wife, and helps clear his name of the alleged bank robbery, is almost too good to be true. And Sissy, too, embodies the ideal female character – selfless, affectionate, with an intuitive knowledge of good and bad, right and wrong. And even Louisa, whose perverted heart nearly leads her astray, shows great affection for her brother. However, with Mrs Gradgrind even this system seems to be questioned by Dickens. She is so feeble and so weak that she is totally ineffective, and, naturally, dies. It seems to be that the future lies with Sissy, so fond of fiction and fancy that she read fairy-tales and novels to her father – much to Gradgrind's horror.[49] As the final paragraph explains, slightly ambiguously:

> But, happy Sissy's happy children loving her; all children loving her; she, grown learned in childish lore; thinking no innocent and pretty fancy ever to be despised; trying hard to know her humbler fellow-creatures, and to beautify their lives of machinery and reality with those imaginative graces and delights,

---

[48] The workers themselves are treated sympathetically in the novel, although they are described as rather easily led, but the political agitator Slackbridge appears beast-like, he 'froths and fumes', declaims himself into a 'violent heat', clenches his fists and sets his teeth (p. 142, 145).

[49] For the intricate relation of 'fiction' and 'fact' in *Hard Times*, cf. Valentine Cunningham (1994), *In the Reading Gaol. Postmodernity, Texts and History*, Blackwell, Oxford, pp. 133-151.

> without which the heart of infancy will wither up, the sturdiest physical manhood will be morally stark death, and the plainest national prosperity figures can show, will be the Writing on the Wall, – she holding this course as part of no fantastic vow, or bond, or brotherhood, or sisterhood, or pledge, or covenant, or fancy dress, or fancy fair; but simply as a duty to be done ... (p. 297f.)

It appears that fiction, fancy and feeling win over facts in the end. Expression of the emotions, albeit in strict boundaries, is vital according to Dickens and his fellow middle class writers during the middle of the 19th century. The dangers of the industrialised world and of the machine age, the moral dilemmas, cannot be overcome and solved without fancy and feeling, but industrialisation itself is not questioned. As Gradgrind understands at the end of the novel, there is 'a wisdom of the Head, and there is a wisdom of the Heart' (p. 226) and only both together will ensure that middle class values will persist.

Just as Dickens is obviously interested in maintaining order in a disordered world, Bray's overall aim – in spite of the ambiguities that characterise *The Education of the Feelings* – is similar. That it is order which lies at the centre of Bray's educational project can also be illustrated by his use of a popular school of 'scientific' thought: phrenology, which serves as just one example of the convergence between explicit calls for emotional and consequently social order, and the performance and production of symbolic order on the discursive level. Bray bases his advice manual on the phrenological classification system of 'feelings', 'propensities' and 'sentiments'.[50] He came across phrenology by mistake, as he explains in his autobiography. Instead of Andrew Combe's text on *physiology* that he had ordered, he received George Combe's book on *phrenology* and in spite of his prior reservations, he was converted on the spot (p. 21f.). Phrenology was developed by Franz Joseph Gall (1758-1828) and his pupil Johann Caspar Spurzheim (1776-1832), who coined the term. In the first half of the 19th century, it attracted interest all over Europe, not least because Gall was accused of materialism and atheism and had his courses in Vienna forbidden by the Austrian emperor, which led to his emigration and travels throughout Europe. Gall's concept of innate moral and intellectual faculties, depending on the morphology of the brain, the main organ consisting of many different organs to which the different

50 See chapter 2 for the differences between these three terms.

faculties are directly linked, developed from 18th-century organological ideas attempting to replace all metaphysical speculation by materialist and physiological explanations for human activities. A matter of contention between Gall and Spurzheim, and later followers, was the question of 'nature' and 'nurture', i.e. the degree to which the phrenological make-up of a person determined his or her future behaviour. Gall identified twenty-seven 'primitive forces', to which he later added another five, all of which had their specific region of the brain attributed to them. And although phrenology's association with materialism and atheism first led to its being sceptically observed and its advocates persecuted, it nevertheless became all the rage in Europe, proof of which can be found in periodicals, caricatures and illustrations, and in many popular and serious novels. In Britain, it was the text *Constitution of Man Considered in Relation to External Objects* (1828 etc.) written by the Scottish lawyer George Combe (1788-1858) which was to be the source of popular phrenological knowledge. It consists of a 'lay decalogue which prescribed virtues and duties: temperance, hygiene, the discipline of labour, the right of possession, the primacy of the family', as Claudio Pogliano has put it.[51] And it is here that the reason for phrenology's success in Britain can be found: in its uses for self-improvement and self-help. While physiognomy 'was an extension of theology; phrenology, in its English incarnation, was based on a materialist system of the mind and was linked to a specific political and social platform', as Sally Shuttleworth has explained.[52] In contrast to essentialist and idealist notions on which physiognomy was based, and the belief that outer form directly embodied inner characteristics, phrenology 'treated the external only as a system of signs to be decoded to determine what lay below: the sign itself was not directly expressive of inner quality, but was only an indicator of quantity'.[53] In addition, phrenologists in Britain followed a programme of social change

---

51 '... un décalogue laïc qui prescrivait vertus et devoirs: la tempérance, l'hygiène, la discipline du travail, le droit à la propriété, la primauté de la famille'. Claudio Pogliano (1994), 'Entre forme et fonction: une nouvelle science de l'homme', in *L'Ame au corps. Arts et sciences 1793-1993*. Catalogue réalisé sous la direction de Jean Clair, Galeries nationales du Grand Palais 19 octobre – 24 janvier 1994, Gallimard/Electa, Paris, pp. 238-265, quotation p. 262. My translation, G.S.

52 Sally Shuttleworth (1996), 'Reading the mind: physiognomy and phrenology', in id., *Charlotte Brontë and Ninteenth-Century Psychology*, Cambridge UP, Cambridge, pp. 57-70.

53 Op. cit., p. 61.

in education, care for the insane, factory legislation and penal reform that conforms with Charles Bray's ideas on the *Education of the Feelings*.[54] Phrenology appealed to 'socially marginal and upwardly mobile groups', as Shuttleworth has demonstrated, – exactly that group to which Bray himself belonged as a lapsed Non-conformist and rising member of the commercial middle class, with an interest in co-operatives and Owenism, and an unorthodox private life. The phrenologists' preference for a social hierarchy which did not threaten the existing order but instead emphasised self-improvement for all classes[55] matched Bray's ideas perfectly.

How then is phrenology related to the education of the emotions? Bray summarises his phrenological view of the feelings in the third edition of *The Education of the Feelings, or Affections*: '... the mind and body are so intimately related, that it is quite impossible to separate moral from physical training' (^{3}1860, p. 3). In Bray's opinion, this assumption concerning the relation between body and mind can be followed even though phrenology is not accepted everywhere and people may not believe in the individual elements of such a system (loc. cit.).[56] But the system must have held an added attraction, apart from the explicit ideas it is based on: namely the possibility of self- as well as social control and the symbolisation of order. In its visualisation of order and as a classification system bordering on the excessive, the phrenological approach to the feelings (and the intellect) performs just that kind of order which the explicit discussions call for. The 'Names of the Phrenological Organs', taken from George Combe's successful *Outlines of Phrenology* (^{5}1835), whose first date of publication is unknown, illustrate this scientistic method but also symbolise how dearly Victorian thinkers loved order and classification. Combe's earliest book on phrenology appeared in 1819 and this representation of the 'phrenological organs' was reprinted in many phrenological books (fig. 4.1).

Scientistic classification schemes for the emotions, the recurrent use of

---

54 Op. cit., p. 63.

55 Op. cit., p. 64.

56 His own doubts on the subject can be observed when comparing the different editions. Not only does he follow the extended phrenological account in the first edition with a defence in the third edition, explaining the necessity for 'dry nomenclature' which always accompanies classification (^{3}1860, preface, p. v), but he leaves it out altogether in the fourth edition 'as the technicality has been found to interfere with the usefulness of the work' (^{4}1872, preface, p. iv). What one can observe here is phrenology's decline in popularity throughout the 19th century.

the same keywords and metaphors, the circumscription of the discourses on emotions by virtually invariable moral, religious and social assumptions – all these features of the Victorian discourses on emotions help to perform what middle class writers demand: individual and social order, on which 'social happiness' depends, as Sarah Ellis argues in her book of advice *Education of the Heart: Woman's Best Work* (1869).

Further up the scientific scale, and based on Associationism[57] and not on phrenology, Alexander Bain's textbook *The Emotions and the Will* (1859 etc.) is a prime example for just this overlap between explicit calls for self-control and social order, and its discursive performance or creation. Since Bain focuses not only on the painful expression of the emotions, but also on their pleasures, he does not call for simple repression to uphold individual and social control.

Its use of excessive classification, its implicit morality and the predominance of conventional gender stereotypes make his long treatise similar to many texts on the emotions in this period. Bain's sentences not only verbalise the notion of emotional expression and emotional control, e.g. in the frequent use of words such as 'current', 'stemming', and 'channelling' for the feelings. Bain's metaphors also highlight how the process of control is more and more internalised in this period. His discussion of morality in relation to the feelings is especially instructive in this context. Implicit moralisation is typical of the discourses on emotions in the 19th century, i.e. the feelings can only be talked about in certain contexts, two of the most important ones being religious values and gender relations. One can also observe examples which deal with social order, for instance when Bain says of the need for consistency: 'without consistency – in the various shapes of punctuality, fulfilment of promises, correspondence of statement with fact – the operations of daily life would be frustrated, and every society pass into disorganization' ([2]1865, p. 169). But apart from this implicit moralisation, Bain also explicitly discusses 'the ethical emotions; or, the moral sense'. He enumerates all possible sources of moral behaviour: 'The will of the Deity, Propriety, Right Reason, the Fitness of Things, the Decision of the Civil Magistrate, Self-

57 Associationism was a dominant trend in British psychology in the first half of the 19th century. Its development can be traced from John Locke via David Hartley, Thomas Reid, Thomas Brown, William Hamilton, James Mill, John Stuart Mill and Alexander Bain to Herbert Spencer and Charles Darwin. Cf. William S. Sahakian (1975), *History and Systems of Psychology*, John Wiley & Sons, New York etc., pp. 44-70.

Interest, the unreasoning Dictates of a Special Faculty called the Moral Sense or Conscience, Utility or the Common good of Mankind' (^{2}1865, p. 255), but none of them satisfy him. His approach to morality is firmly relativist in that he is aware of 'place and time' which influence what is considered moral and what is considered immoral. The utilitarian aim of moral behaviour is the preservation of the individual and society, or, in other words: of social order. Bain rejects the 18th-century notion of an innate moral sense and stresses the social context as an important source for the internalisation of moral rules and the preservation of this social order: 'Social security must be maintained as the highest necessity of men's existence in common fellowship; and whatever militates against it must be considered wrong' (^{2}1865, p. 274). And in the ultimate performative move, he relates external order and internal control, or 'government', in the following metaphorical description of the internalisation of moral rules: 'Conscience is an imitation within ourselves of the government without us' (^{2}1865, p. 283).

The place where children were taught to imitate this 'government without' and to internalise the actual and symbolic order was the family, or the 'domestic sphere'. Since this 'sphere' is intimately linked to the third major element on which the 19th-century middle class habitus is based – namely, gender – it is discussed in the following section in which I examine the function and attraction of the 'domestic affections'.

Gender: The domestic affections

That Charlotte Brontë uses a gender framework to discuss the emotions in *Shirley* is no idiosyncrasy on the part of a female author, but rather a feature of the discourses on emotions in general. All writers implicitly link emotionality and gender, for instance by making women blush much more often than men, or by classifying anger as an aberration in women but not necessarily in men. But more importantly, virtually in no text on the feelings is the issue ignored. On the contrary, the majority of writers spend an inordinate amount of time discussing the relation between emotion and gender. From health guides and conduct books to dictionary articles, scientific studies on the feelings, and fictional texts – all genres supplied Victorian readers with gendered concepts of emotion. Two discourses intersect here: the separate spheres discourse which attributes social roles to each gender, and the discourses on emotions which ascribe certain feelings and their appropriate expression either to men or to women. In the following passages I shall analyse the reasons for this overlap, explore the tensions accompanying it, and I shall argue for a limited agency resulting from this discursive convergence which allowed women the advancement of their own causes.

The discursive construction of a domestic sphere in which women operate and a public one in which men are said to be the sole agents is based on the notion of biological difference. One of the conduct book authors whose use of emotionally expressive language I have already mentioned in the section on religion, and who writes on both the feelings and separate spheres, is Mary Ann Stodart. Her texts shall serve as my major examples for the overlap between these two discourses and the contradictions this encounter produces, supplemented by a look at her better-known fellow conduct book author, Sarah Ellis. Both authors are interesting because their texts simultaneously affirm and in their occasional inconsistency also question the separate spheres view of the feelings.

Mary Ann Stodart was also a poet – a fact which was honoured by her poems being anthologised in her lifetime – but her conduct book output seems to have been greater. Her *Hints on Reading* (1839), *Christ Our Law*,[58] *Every Day Duties: In Letters to a Young Lady* (1840) and *The Female Writers: Thoughts on Their Proper Sphere and on Their Powers of Usefulness* (1842) were all published in cheap editions by G. Seeley, an important London publisher.[59] Stodart invests a lot of energy into her project of drumming 'every day duties' into the heads of her prospective (female) readership. In the preface to her letters to 'young ladies on leaving school' she is unequivocal as regards women's position: 'The author's deep conviction is, that the part of woman is one of subordination and dependence; and that her duty in social life is, commonly speaking, to be expressed in one word "obedience", qualified by one single adjunct "in the Lord"' (p. vii f.). After having got this out of the way, Stodart begins her fourteen letters addressed directly to 'My Dear Young Friend', alternating them with her own poetry. In the second letter, 'Home, the True Sphere of

---

58 This title, for which no date is given, is advertised in *Female Writers* but appears neither in the British Library catalogue nor in the Pre-1920 catalogue of the Bodleian Library. I have therefore been unable to consult it.

59 *Hints on Reading* was available for 3*s* 6*d*, *Christ our Law* cost 6*s*, *Every Day Duties* 4*s* 6*d*, and *Female Writers* was available for 4*s* 6*d*.

Woman', she explains where women's sphere of action and influence lies by drawing on biblical authority:

> And believe it, – though the sphere of man is varied; and the church, the senate, the court, the bar, the army, the navy, may offer to him a wide field for the exercise of his powers, yet the province of woman may be told in one word – a word of true English birth and English growth, – a word eminently and peculiarly English, and which expresses, in heart-language, our most cherished feelings, – the precious, precious word of HOME. ... We limit her energies and powers within a circle, but it is a circle of gold. The adaptation of the faculties and constitution of woman to her home-sphere, and her home-duties, may be considered a beautiful instance of the wisdom and goodness of God, as displayed in the creation. It is her part to soothe, to solace, and to sympathize, and they who would elevate her above her real station, would, in so doing, destroy the beauty of her character, as well as the usefulness of her position, for there is a beauty in appropriateness, a gracefulness in consistency. (p. 16f.)

By using a nationalist language, not unusual in the discourses on emotions (or any other 19th-century discourse, for that matter), but probably also influenced by her own brand of Ulster Protestantism and patriotism, she puts women in their place.[60] Her favourite shorthand word for the feelings, the heart, features prominently and is the basis of her arguments: women's peculiar sensibility is said to predestine them to provide a safe haven for men who will find 'soothing', 'solace' and 'sympathy' there. This 'soft' place for emotional recreation, accentuated by Stodart's alliterative language, can only be created with the help of women's specific qualities – '[q]uietness, humility, gentleness, submission' (p. 18). Stodart naturalises

---

60 A disparaging review of Stodart's patriotic poetry (*National Ballads, Patriotic and Protestant*) appeared in *The Athenæum* No. 760, 21 May 1842, p. 449, written by Thomas Kibble Hervey, the editor of *The Athenæum* between 1846 and 1855: 'The volume is one of those disgraceful attempts to prostitute the Muse to the cause of sectarian rancour; to which, happily for both Truth and Poetry, the Muse never lends herself. All the old watch-words which, in darker days, were reverenced as the phylacteries of the British Constitution, and formed an eminent portion of "the wisdom of" some of "our ancestors", are here as confidently and authoritatively repeated as if education had not desecrated them, and they were still "spells to conjure with". For such teaching as this volume offers, there is a daily decreasing public; and no Muse sits by the fountain which yields such polluted waters. Time has been when such books might have done their small part towards lighting the Fires of Smithfield – a consideration which, opportunely, suggests a use to which this volume may be turned in any household to which, by chance, it has, unhappily, obtained admission' (p. 449).

this order of things as the 'steady lustre of a planet' which is more stable 'than the fitful blaze of the rapid and mysterious comet' (p. 20). One of her favourite examples of a female 'comet', Germaine de Staël, makes her first of many appearances here. In this instance, the famous French author and enemy of Napoleon is used as an example for a woman who has too public a character. Stodart again uses a naturalising metaphor to explain why women are not suited to public life:

> There is a delicacy in the female character which renders it peculiarly liable to injury; and injury not easily repaired. It is not difficult to strike the plumes from the butterfly's wing, or to remove the bloom from the luscious plum, but what human hand can replace the lost beauties? Something may be added, but nothing can give again the charm that is lost. .... the first fragrant bloom ... should be guarded with the most sedulous care and the most jealous eye, just as we watch over a tender plant, in stormy and wintry weather. We screen such a plant from biting winds, as well as guard it from nipping frosts. Women also require to be *housed*; .... (p. 21f.)

She continues her criticism of women who transgress these explicit boundaries and move into the sphere reserved for men, by attacking Harriet Martineau's series of political tales[61] as 'wanting [something] which "the heart looks for in woman"' (p. 23). Again the heart is invoked as the measure of gender roles, and in this case it is found wanting. The first indication that all is not well in Stodart's binary world comes at the end of the letter in which she explains that she now no longer regrets 'as I once did in the wild dreams and baseless visions of childhood, that the senate, the cabinet, and the field, are closed against our entrance ...' (p. 25). She exerts herself in distributing men and women across the social spheres and uses the alleged greater emotional capacity of women as her main argument to uphold this social division. But her own acknowledgement that women do dream of more than their domestic role, as well as the ambivalent case of Germaine de Staël who appears as both model and negative example, subvert Stodart's own efforts. Her attempt at this social division which she goes on to elaborate in the remaining letters and poems is wishful thinking more than representation of actual facts. This becomes apparent in the poem closing the letter, entitled *Stanzas. Home, the True*

---

61 Harriet Martineau's (1832-34) *Illustrations of Political Economy*, 9 vols., London, n.p., put her on the map as a serious writer.

Sphere of Woman. The poem is written in the *modus potentialis*, thus performing a feeling rule instead of representing 'actual' feelings (of the author or her poetic persona). As is to be expected, it is once again 'woman's heart' which has the final word:

> I ask not in the stately hall
> To mingle in the festival;
> To join the dance, and lead the song,
> Amid a gay and giddy throng;
> From scenes like these my heart would roam,
> And pine for a secluded home.
> ...
> A humble, quiet path be mine!
> I ask to cheer and not to shine;
> Around the fire and social board,
> To hear and speak the gladd'ning word;
> And in home-labours, day by day,
> Calmly pursue my pilgrim way.
> ...
> And let it be our aim, our boast,
> To labour humbly at our post,
> Ne'er wandering on forbidden ground,
> But safe and blest in duty's bound,
> And thankful for the joys that come,
> To woman's heart in peaceful home.
> (p. 26f.)

Historians have shown that 19th-century women of the middle classes, at whom the separate spheres argument is mainly directed, did not in fact follow the many similar publications by male and female authors. What appears to be the norm on paper soon becomes blurred when compared with what is known of actual women's occupations. There is a danger of falling for the Victorian construction of clearly divided spheres of occupation for middle class men and women. While women may have worked unpaid in their capacities as doctor's assistants, charity workers and bazaar organisers, this sort of activity nevertheless resulted in their appearance in public. Arguably, these roles were simply extensions of that of the wife and helpmeet but nevertheless women were not as invisible as

Stodart's 'circle of gold' seems to imply.[62] But the point of this analysis is not to show that women went beyond their prescribed role but rather to find out why the discourses on emotions and the separate spheres debate are linked in the inextricable manner that they are.

Their overlap is nowhere more obvious than in discussions of the 'domestic affections', that favourite Victorian emotion, and its epitome: maternal love. Again, one can observe the implicit rules of the discourse at work. Mothers serve as the preferred and most frequent example of certain emotions for all kinds of writers, leaving no doubt as to the feminisation of the emotions which has become apparent in Stodart's texts.[63] It is rather ironic that in her essay 'Woman in France: Madame de Sablé' (1854) even George Eliot, a woman who was to practice birth control so as not to become a mother (although she did behave in maternal fashion towards George Henry Lewes's children), praises the 'maternal feelings' and makes them the prime point of distinction between women and men.[64] Alexander Bain and Charles Darwin, in spite of their attempts at producing scientific studies of the emotions, are further cases in point. Darwin tries to resist

---

62 Cf. Amanda Vickery (1993), 'Golden Age to Separate Spheres? A Review of the Categories and Chronology of English Women's History', in *The History Journal*, vol. 36 (2), pp. 383-414; Leonore Davidoff (1993), '"Alte Hüte". Öffentlichkeit und Privatheit in der feministischen Geschichtsschreibung', in *L'Homme, Zeitschrift für feministische Geschichtswissenschaft*, 4th year, no. 2, pp. 7-36; Anne Digby (1990), 'Victorian Values and Women in Public and Private', in *Proceedings of the British Academy*, vol. 78, pp. 195-215, and Catherine Hall (1990), 'Private Persons versus Public Someones: Class, Gender and Politics in England, 1780-1850', in Terry Lovell (ed), *British Feminist Thought. A Reader*, Blackwell, Oxford, pp. 51-67. Cf. also Anne-Charlott Trepp (1996), *Sanfte Männlichkeit und selbständige Weiblichkeit. Frauen und Männer im Hamburger Bürgertum zwischen 1770 und 1840*, Vandenhoeck & Ruprecht, Göttingen for an approach to emotion history which tries to differentiate between emotionology and emotions by looking beyond the conventions of the separate spheres debate.

63 This term is taken from Francesca M. Cancian (summer 1986), 'The Feminization of Love', in *Signs*, vol. 2, pp. 692-709.

64 'Under every imaginable social condition, she [woman] will necessarily have a class of sensations and emotions – the maternal ones – which must remain unknown to man; and the fact of her comparative physical weakness, which, however it may have been exaggerated by a vicious civilization, can never be cancelled, introduces a distinctively feminine condition into the wondrous chemistry of the affections and sentiments, which inevitably gives rise to distinctive forms and combinations.' George Eliot (1968) [October 1854], 'Woman in France: Mme de Sablé', in Thomas Pinney (ed), *Essays of George Eliot*, Routledge and Kegan Paul, London, pp. 52-81, quotation p. 53, repr. from the *Westminster Review*, vol. 62, pp. 448-473.

contextualising his discussions of emotional expression and only relatively rarely allows himself a moral judgement. But it is consistent with Darwin's notion that '[n]o emotion is stronger than maternal love ...' that his first example in his chapter on love is the love of a mother.[65] And in a section in which Alexander Bain explicitly deals with the relation which in his view 'is most replete with tender feeling', he uses physiological terminology to explain the great impact of maternal love which even women who are not mothers cannot resist:

> The Lacteal secretion of women no doubt co-operates with the lachrymal, as a physical basis of tender feeling. Even without the stimulus of maternity, the mammary glands may be supposed to be in a state of fluctuating activity, and any rise in the degree is likely to be accompanied with a genial feeling, entering into the aggregate of tenderness, and consummated by finally squeezing some living object to the breast. If this be so in the ordinary state, we can imagine the increased development given to it in the mother giving suck to the child.[66]

A fitting illustration of motherhood can also be found in visual contributions to the discourses on emotions. In E.T. Parris's coffeetable-style book *Gems of Beauty, Displayed in a Series of Twelve Highly Finished Engravings of the Passions* (1838), accompanied by verses written by the Countess of Blessington, three out of twelve engravings show mothers with their children. As an illustration of 'Affection', a

---

65 Apart from the many examples involving mothers and the 'maternal feelings', the implicit gender assumptions of the discourses on emotions can also be observed in the use of other examples. Darwin e.g. explains tears and crying by giving the example of a boy who cries because he is vaccinated, whereas the girl does so because she is teased or because she is frightened by a dog, Charles Darwin (1872), *The Expression of Emotions in Man and Animals*, John Murray, London, quotation p. 78, examples p. 215, p. 191.

66 Bain (^{2}1865), *The Emotions and the Will*, p. 78, p. 74. In fairness to Bain one has to acknowledge that he is one of the few writers to include an explicit statement on paternal love as well as on motherhood. In his opinion, '[t]he Paternal relationship involves essentially the same modes of feeling and acting, with some few variations. If there is less of personal contact, there is the damming up of the excitement for stronger outbursts; and if the maternal temperament is more alive to tenderness, the father is more struck with the effect of contrast,' p. 80. This rather obscure passage cannot be considered as a true revision of the notion that mothers have a greater capacity to feel than men, since most of Bain's other examples focus on women and mothers, rather than fathers. It is interesting to note, though, that he is aware of the possible dangers of excessive maternal feelings since complete selflessness may result in 'the permanent loss to herself', p. 114.

mother, her two daughters and a dog are depicted in a Madonna-like image (fig. 4.2). The three figures form a triangle, emphasised by the younger daughter's upward gaze, and would seem to create a world unto themselves if the elder daughter did not draw the viewer into the picture by her gaze. This gaze, as well as certain parts of the image which have been highlighted, provide a subtext for the image which runs dangerously close to sexual allure. By feminising the emotions, authors and artists also risked sexualising them, in spite of all professions of 'pure hearts' and the absence of desire in domestic affections.

In view of this tendency to sanctify motherhood, ineffectual or bad (substitute) mothers such as the unsympathetic Mrs Tulliver in *The Mill on the Floss*, Pip's brutal sister in *Great Expectations*, Mrs Gradgrind in *Hard Times*, idle Lady Ethelwode in *Passion and Principle*, the profligate and heartless Mrs Ashton in *The Ruling Passion* who abandons her two children, the childish young Mrs Rothesay in Dinah Mulock Craik's novel *Olive*, and initially even the 'unnatural' Mrs Pryor in *Shirley* who likewise leaves her daughter Caroline, appear to be even more negative characters than they do anyway. That maternal love and properly functioning families were perceived to be vital for children's mental and physical well-being can also be illustrated by the many orphan plots which dominate Victorian novels. It is often the death or absence of mothers which results in their husband or children becoming involved in conflicts that endanger their emotional health. This is the consequence if the *Education of the Heart* is left in the wrong hands (or indeed in none at all), as one might conclude with Sarah Ellis, who gave just this title to one of her many publications on women and their duties.

Dissenting voices in this strictly circumscribed discourse are rare. One example can be found in James Henry Powell's lecture on the universality of feeling in *The Poetry of Feeling and Poetry of Diction*. Powell was a self-educated working class writer and his other publications such as *Woman, at Home and Abroad: A Glance At Her Domestic and Social Condition* (1861) or *Phases of Thought and Feeling, Poems and Lyrics* (1857) do fit a separate sphere paradigm.[67] But in his lecture, delivered at

---

[67] James Henry Powell describes himself as an itinerant worker who received encouragement from his wife, his employers and his colleagues in his intellectual pursuits. His writings are overtly political and focus on what Powell calls 'the want of *true freedom*' in England. Although this emphasis characterises him as working class, and therefore reminds one of Richard Carlile (see chapter 3), his ideas on self-

the Wolverhampton Mechanics' Institution in 1853, he does not genderise the feelings. On the contrary, he states that 'The Poetry of Feeling ... is universally the property of Man' (p. 6). Due to his Universalist Christian beliefs he does not limit creativity, emotionality or other human abilities and characteristics to any sex or class. He contrasts 'the poetry of feeling' and 'the poetry of diction' in the following manner: the 'Poetry of Feeling' is universal and 'calls forth our sympathy for suffering and sorrow ...' and it 'lead[s] to Patriotism and individual exertion, self-denial and suffering, endurance, for the good of Humanity' (p. 6). By contrast, the 'Poetry of Diction' is a power which only the poet can command, since he or she can give 'an existence, in burning and glowing language, to the ideal musings of his mind, so that other minds may realize the same emotions, the same aspirations as himself' (p. 17). Poets provide others with 'a surer guide and a more developed theory of the human heart; – for the poet's mission principally is to record the teachings, forebodings, and ecstasies of the human heart, and to prophecy for humanity the coming events – the future of the world' (p. 18). It is remarkable that although Powell also relates poetry to its alleged emotional impact he does not link this to the female sex. He even includes a few female poets as examples (e.g. Eliza Cook), a far cry from Keble's exclusively male list of true poets and true feelings, discussed in the following chapter. Apart from this rare exception, the majority of 19th-century writers place the feelings in a gendered framework.

In contrast to the consecration of maternal love, the opposite tendency can also be observed with regard to certain emotions. Obviously firmly within a separate spheres context, Herbert Spencer explains his system of the 'moral sentiments',[68] among which he counts justice as the highest

improvement and his complaints against fashion and commerce bring him closer to middle class opinion as expressed by Charles Bray or Mary Ann Stodart. In his publication concerning women, Powell uses the separate spheres argument for a working class purpose: not only does he explain that women need to stay at home because this is their natural calling, but also that the absence of mothers leads to more poverty and neglect, as well as to male unemployment. This indicates how pervasive the concept of the innate differences between men and women was, but also that it could be adapted to specific agendas which were not identical with middle class aims. That middle class readers could accept Powell's basic notions as well as his poetry can be gathered from the extracts of reviews of his works, included on the back page of *Phases of Thought and Feeling*, which praise the 'taste and feeling' of his writings.

68 Herbert Spencer (1855), *The Principles of Psychology*, Longman, Brown, Green and

emotion. Unfortunately, women cannot attain the heights of human development (just like children and savages) because their nature does not allow for the 'abstract' feelings such as justice.[69] In line with his evolutionary model of the emotions, Spencer is convinced that women are more emotional than men because the development of their physical energy has been arrested earlier due to the cost of reproduction which requires such a preservation of 'vital power'.[70] Although Spencer also uses maternal love as a frequent example, he stresses the danger of excess that can result from it and the negative impact of strong feelings in general: 'emotion of every kind and degree disturbs the intellectual balance ...'.[71] In spite of a rather bleak picture which he paints of the relations between men and women he does, however, allow for the possibility that they might proceed to a greater similarity some time in the future: 'it is inferable that as civilization re-adjusts men's natures to higher social requirements, there goes on a corresponding re-adjustment between the natures of men and women, tending in sundry respects to diminish their differences'.[72]

Why the discourses on emotions naturalise the emotions by feminising them can be explained fairly easily. In post-Romantic times, the importance of the feelings can no longer be ignored and it is impossible to repress them altogether. But by relegating them to the 'female sphere', a sphere allegedly closed off from male pursuits, they find a safe place. Public judgement will not be coloured by feeling, as Sarah Ellis is convinced would happen if women appeared in public and took part in parliamentary debates: 'I cannot help thinking if women should obtain as some desire for them, the high privilege of a seat in the senate ... that their presence in the house would overwhelm the manly element there, and would consequently be of very limited duration.'[73] Feeling is nevertheless

---

Longmans, London, in particular chapter VIII, 'The Feelings'. See also Spencer (1 April 1871), 'Morals and Moral Sentiments', in *Fortnightly Review*, pp. 419-432 and Spencer ([13]1887) [1873], *The Study of Sociology*, Kegan Paul, Trench & Co., London, in particular chapter VII, 'Subjective Difficulties – Emotional' and chapter XV, 'Preparation in Psychology'.

69 Spencer ([13]1887), *The Study of Sociology*, p. 374ff.

70 Op. cit., p. 373.

71 Op. cit., p. 147, p. 160ff.

72 Op. cit., p. 378.

73 Spencer argues along similar lines: 'And this difference between their ways of estimating consequences, affecting their judgements on social affairs as on domestic affairs, makes women err still more than men do in seeking what seems an immediate

available at home but since it is firmly 'enclosed' by being both private and female (and at least on the level of discourse under man's control), it offers no great threat. On the contrary, its total absence or at least the absence of the 'tender feelings' may result in individual and social danger, as the above discussion and the preceding chapter have shown. By using the separate spheres paradigm, writers on the emotions also shore up this discursive construction intended to legitimise the division of labour which developed so markedly at the end of the 18th and during the most part of the 19th century.

It is more difficult to explain why the participants in the separate spheres debate use the emotions as their pivotal argument. That women's and men's social roles should be distinguished is not an 18th-century, let alone a Victorian invention. Women's alleged inferiority has always been a hotly contested topic, and the origins of the gender debate known as the *Querelle des femmes* can be traced to the late Middle Ages. Male and female writers, engravers and artists argued about women's (and men's) abilities and respective positions, and quarrelled over actual and symbolic issues of power.[74] But after the comparatively short-lived period of discursive gender equality during the late Enlightenment and in the context of the French Revolution,[75] it may have become difficult to use extremely

---

public good without thought of distant public evils'. Op. cit., p. 380; Ellis (1869), *The Education of the Heart*, p. 32.

74 For an introduction to the European *Querelle des femmes*, see Gisela Bock and Margarete Zimmermann (1997), 'Die europäische Querelle des Femmes. Eine begriffs- und forschungsgeschichtliche Einführung', in id. (ed), *Die Europäische "Querelle des Femmes". Geschlechterdebatten seit dem 15. Jahrhundert* (Querelles. Jahrbuch für Frauenforschung, vol. 2), Metzler, Stuttgart/Weimar, pp. 9-38.

75 Cf. Ina Schabert (1997), *Englische Literaturwissenschaft aus der Sicht der Geschlechterforschung*, Alfred Kröner, Stuttgart, and Jane Rendall (1985), *The Origins of Modern Feminism: Women in Britain, France and the United States, 1780-1860*, Macmillan, Basingstoke. For an account of the 'gender order' as maintained by the separate spheres debate cf. also Claudia Honegger (1996) [1991], *Die Ordnung der Geschlechter. Die Wissenschaften vom Menschen und das Weib 1750-1850*, dtv, Munich. See also Karen Offen's overview of Enlightenment feminism *avant la lettre*, which highlights not only the complexity of 18th-century debates over sex and gender but also illustrates once again that the major topics of the Victorian women's movement were already bones of contention in the 18th century (e.g. mothers as educators and marriage). She also makes clear that although the Enlightenment appeared as a short phase of (contested) discursive equality, the emphasis on sexual difference although accompanied by a rejection of sexual hierarchy and a belief in rationality for both women and men, paved the way for the separate spheres view of gender relations. Karen

misogynist and pejorative views of women, focusing on their alleged abject and deceitful character or on their irredeemable stupidity and obtuseness. An argument had to be found which, although it would still allow a strict division between women and men, would not imply such negative connotations as to be totally useless as a means of justification. Although 19th-century writers make it abundantly clear that excessive sensibility is dangerous, they make it equally clear that the absence of emotionality is almost as problematic. The answer to the problem was to find a 'place' for the emotions to operate safely. The feelings also serve as a 'positive' point of distinction between women and men, thus posing no threat to male prerogatives while at the same time not laying male writers open to accusations of disparaging women.

For women writers, on the other hand, what seems at a superficial reading to limit women's activities to the domestic sphere, also allowed them a certain form of agency. Although the norms and institutions (the family, unpaid women's work) of the middle classes are not subverted, women writers use the emotionalised separate spheres debate for their own purposes. Sarah Ellis is a perfect example. She never actually transcends the ideal middle class habitus and does not denounce middle class values and institutions, except when she objects to excessive materialism, which by the middle of the century had become a standard criticism. But she uses the separate spheres argument to call for women's education and in turn for their role as (professional) educators, thus empowering them to a certain but not insignificant extent. Much more radical proponents of the women's movement went a lot further in their campaigns for female education and colleges for women but for the majority of middle class women, this was not a realistic option.

Sarah Ellis's advice manual *The Education of the Heart: Woman's Best Work* was first published in the woman's magazine *Leisure Hour* before appearing as a single volume in 1869 (Hodder and Stoughton) and in a second, identical, edition in 1872. In many respects, *The Education of the Heart* is a conventional assertion of – at the time of publishing – traditional middle class values,[76] expressed in the metaphorical shape of the 'heart'

Offen (1998), 'Reclaiming the European Enlightenment for Feminism. Or Prolegomena To Any Future History of Eighteenth-Century Europe', in Tjitske Akkerman and Siep Stuurman (eds), *Perspectives on Feminist Political Thought in European History from the Middle Ages to the Present*, Routledge, London/New York, pp. 85-103.

76 The interpretation of *The Education of the Heart* presented in Almaric Rumsey's (?) (11

which is in need of training if the emotions are not to 'flow' uncontrolled and into the wrong 'channels', thus endangering social order. Less radical in its demands than Bray's *Education of the Feelings*, Ellis's publication nevertheless shares a number of aspects with Bray's advice manual. Ellis expresses a strong belief in progress and improvement through education, just as Bray does (p. 23f.) and this sense of achievement and advancement is not limited to the individual, her main addressee, but extends to society in general (preface, p. v). Ellis shares with Bray and Dickens the conviction that the 'heart' is just as much in need of training as the 'head', if not more so, because it influences human behaviour: 'The one, if neglected, leaves only a blank – a state of ignorance, of not knowing what ought to be known; the other, if neglected, leaves the field of action open to passion and inclination, and the whole character becomes a ruin' (p. 113).

Although on the whole Ellis is more severe since she speaks of 'negative' passion more than Bray does, she does share his opinion that the 'heart' needs training, not just simple repression (p. 30). And like Bray, Ellis locates the 'enemy' within, in spite of her social criticism (centring on crime, materialism, immorality, indulgence and excessive luxury), and emphasises the dangerous effects of selfishness (for the individual and society) more than she criticises social or political reality (p. 56, p. 130, p. 151, p. 117). But in spite of these similarities, there is less tension in *The Education of the Heart* than in *The Education of the Feelings*. Ellis is not interested in changing the general structure of society and comes nowhere near acknowledging the increasing importance and power of the working classes, nor does she express radical views on capital punishment or poverty. On the contrary, she repeatedly stresses the need for order. It is worth quoting the final passage of her chapter on 'Law and Order' in which one can once again observe the convergence of explicit calls for

---

June 1870) review in *The Athenæum* (No. 2224, p. 771) reads the book as an assertion of female modesty: 'This little work is written with good intentions, very different from those ambitious impulses which prompt some people now-a-days to urge women to win the places hitherto occupied by men in the various transactions of life.' The reviewer recommends the book to 'young parents' and praises Ellis's criticism of girls' schools, never realising that she actually demands paid work for women, thereby arguing for just that occupation of the positions held by men which she is not interested in, according to the reviewer. The review reads *The Education of the Heart* rather selectively in its sole focus on education for girls – that Ellis is almost as interested in the education of boys does not come out at all.

order and its implicit literary-linguistic performance, but this time in the shape of the ambiguous metaphor of the 'rolling river':

> It seems a little thing, when the rolling river first began its course, that it fell drop by drop from fields of snow in the far-off mountain solitudes, and it seems a little thing, that near its commencement there stood a rock whose sharp edge turned the little sill towards the south, or the north, or which ever way it went. But far down in the valley where the sill has become a stream, or farther still, where the stream has become a broad river, we see that nothing can stop its flow or change its course. The little drops, so insignificant that no traveller would have observed them, came first from the melting snow, the rock stood out and turned them as they fell into that precise direction according to which the sill became a stream of bounty to plains and villages and cities, its course so marked and so unalterable as to form the boundary line of separate nations. (p. 208)

What is most striking in this passage is the tendency to naturalise social and cultural constructs. This tendency is particularly pronounced when Ellis reaches her main topic: the role of women, and in particular of mothers, as the prime educators of the heart. She describes the split into two separate spheres as an 'harmonious working', a natural element of 'creation', with little awareness of the possible costs or ambiguities of this construction, as one finds them in Mary Ann Stodart's publications:

> Men have their appropriate place in creation, and women have theirs. It is absurd to compare them as being superior or inferior on either side; or to say that in one there is more mental capability required than in the other. But it must still be of a different order, and directed to different purposes, otherwise the whole structure, the harmonious working, the happiness and the beauty of our social constitution would be destroyed. (p. 17)

Associating women and feeling, or the 'heart' as she prefers to put it, comes natural to Sarah Ellis and like so many other Victorian writers, she attributes to women a universal, God-given and 'natural fitness' (p. 117, p. 36) for motherhood: 'It is an interesting fact, a provision designed no doubt for the preservation of helpless infancy, that all women seem to have by nature more or less of the maternal instinct ready to be called forth ...' (p. 218). Yet this 'life of the heart' is not free from pain:

> All the learning in the world cannot quench the vitality of this life, scarcely alter its conditions. It does not consist in knowledge, in science, in calculation, in the adaptation of means to ends. Its hunger and thirst, its very existence, is supplied by sustenance altogether distinct from these. It has joy and sorrow for its daily food, the sweet and the bitter; and the measure in which these are appropriated, as well as the sources from whence they are derived, constitute what we understand as character in woman. (p. 34f.)

That a woman's character is largely 'natural' is emphasised by the metaphors of bodily needs and physical experience (hunger, thirst, food), contrasted sharply with learning, knowledge, science and 'calculation'. By implication, the latter are associated with the male sphere. But education and learning should not be absent from a woman's life. Nor should she be totally 'swallowed up in her nursery', 'absorbed by the claims of ... external society', or forget that she is a wife (p. 217, p. 213). How then does Sarah Ellis imagine women's role as educators of the heart?

First of all, she asserts that a 'condition of human life' exists which is 'absolute – that women have the care of childhood ...' (p. 1). But what she is interested in is not education in the sense of instruction at school, since she believes that women need not be 'great scholars' to be good mothers (p. 224). But two years before the Education Act made elementary schooling compulsory,[77] she does acknowledge the need for better education, in particular for girls, and accepts the criticism that it is often characterised by 'shallowness, frivolity, and want of practical worth' (p. 3). She is also aware of possible causes for this situation: girls' schools are too expensive so that many girls are kept at home on the grounds that they are considered less worthy 'objects' of investment and therefore do not benefit from their peers.[78] This means that girls cannot learn how to overcome hardship and 'how to share the common lot' (p. 4ff.). That many teachers are also unfit to teach girls properly is a result of their own insufficient training. Ellis therefore calls for a greater number of inexpensive schools and 'plain and solid teaching' (p. 10f.), both of which should be publicly supported. Schooling should prepare women for their two possible

[77] The 1870 Education Act made elementary schooling compulsory, but apart from the fact that state schools were only slowly established and at the beginning frequented mainly by lower (middle) class pupils, girls continued to receive a rather patchy education and usually were taught at home or in private finishing schools, if parents could afford to send them there. See Budde (1994), *Auf dem Weg*, p. 328ff.

[78] On the reality of middle class education for girls see Budde (1994), op. cit., p. 227ff.

situations in later life: marriage or spinsterhood.

Ellis accepts that many women cannot marry, if only because there are more women than men (correct at the time of writing), and considers education a useful means of counteracting their disadvantages. And: 'they would be saved from that terrible temptation of marrying only for a maintenance and a home' (p. 14). But this would only work if society 'welcome[d] to its honoured places those women who maintain themselves' (loc. cit.). It is here that Ellis departs from Mary Ann Stodart's stance and even goes beyond Bray's call for mothers as educators of the heart. Ellis actually demands that jobs are found for women, without however wanting to endanger male employment which would only exacerbate the inequality between men and women in terms of numbers (p. 14ff.). She considers education (for girls and boys) the appropriate field for women to work in and it is quite clear that she means paid work. Education should not make women 'masculine in their attainments' (p. 16) and if a woman does acquire 'those masculine attainments which are now considered so desirable for her' she needs to accompany this by her own education of the heart, prior to becoming an educator herself (p. 18). What would result is an increase in happiness and value in the world (p. 20) because these women are immensely important as future mothers (and sisters). Ellis waxes lyrical when she describes how this process of educating the heart would work:

> And whether, in the achievements to which these [the men] devote themselves, their work will be established on right principles or wrong, on truth or falsehood, will depend very much upon the early basis given to their characters by that young girl whose fingers we saw gliding swiftly over the strings of her harp, by her who sat in the garden shade wreathing herself with flowers, by her who sang the fairy song, or by her who, wearied with the dance, fell asleep in a cloud of her own dishevelled hair. (p. 22f.)

Surprisingly, Ellis does not represent moral teaching here, or exemplary behaviour, let alone a school-scene, but creates a distinctly eroticised image of conventional feminine accomplishments. Such an idealised feminine realm, exuding its 'ethereal' spirit, cannot be effective when 'the care-taker of childhood forgets to do her part, [and] nature asserts her claim, and passion and self-will seize the victim for their own' (p. 23). But Ellis prefers following her idealised or perhaps even utopian vision which poses little threat to men:

> Rather let us look forward to the dawn of a happier day, when the education of the heart shall keep pace with that of the head; and when women shall faithfully maintain their legitimate place in the training of youth, so as that one generation after another shall be marked by greater dignity and worth of character, and each, with God's blessing, be more noble, happier, and better than the last. (p. 23f.)

This 'legitimate place' for women still limits them to a nurturing role. But Ellis's assertion of feminine influence and her criticism of male teachers for women (p. 31) stakes a claim for women's work, however much it may be coloured by conventional metaphors ('heart-work', p. 160) which associate femininity and emotionality.[79]

In summary, then, one can conclude that the feminisation of the emotions may have had empowering as well as restricting consequences. By placing the emotions in the 'female' domestic sphere, their expression as well as their (discursive) control could be ensured – a healthier option than complete repression. Here, they could function as a support for the development of middle class Christian values deemed so important for the creation and preservation of a middle class habitus and social order. One might, in fact, argue with Armstrong and Tennenhouse for the more efficacious form of control not through institutions such as the police or law courts, but through representations of gender.[80]

By making women the 'educators of the heart', the 'judicious trainers of the feelings', the negative results of ruthless middle class enterprise, materialism and selfishness, could be alleviated.[81] To quote Charles Dickens in the guise of Thomas Gradgrind, educated by Sissy Jupe in *Hard*

---

79 The entry on Sarah Ellis in Janet Todd (ed) (1989), *The Dictionary of British Women Writers*, Routledge, London, contains a salutary warning neither to exaggerate the inconsistencies in Ellis's books, nor to underestimate the achievements of this 'unconventional woman' on the grounds that it is difficult to ascertain to which degree Ellis accepted the submission of women.

80 Nancy Armstrong and Leonard Tennenhouse (1987), 'The literature of conduct, the conduct of literature, and the politics of desire: an introduction', in id. (eds), *The Ideology of Conduct. Essays on Literature and the History of Sexuality*, Methuen, New York etc., pp. 1-24, in particular p. 16.

81 Jane Rendall (1985) has shown that the debate on female education and on the alleged special moral qualities of women has its origin in the 18th century – again an indication that the Victorian discourses on emotions are characterised more by discursive continuity than by change. See her chapter 'Educating Hearts and Minds', in id., *The Origins of Modern Feminism*, pp. 108-149.

Times: '"Some persons hold ... that there is a wisdom of the Head, and that there is a wisdom of the Heart. I have not supposed so; but, as I have said, I mistrust myself now. I have supposed the Head to be all-sufficient. It may not be all-sufficient. ..."'[82]

Women, the feelings and 'home' would also provide a safe haven for men whose constant conflicts with the lower classes were seen as endangering male middle class (individual and social) health. Finally, women could also teach the lower classes middle class values by providing them with examples of Christian behaviour and feeling. And if middle class feeling could be married to aristocratic wealth, then even excessively proud and uncaring, selfish aristocrats – like the pseudo-aristocrat Mrs Sparsit in Dickens's *Hard Times* who asks not for payment or 'terms' for her services which would smack of the middle classes, but for an 'annual compliment',[83] could be made to reform in time.

How this 'education of the heart' relates to non-fictional and fictional narrative is the focus of the next chapter, in which I will also look at the way women writers of fiction used the separate spheres argument to establish themselves in the literary field.

---

82 Dickens (1995) [1854], *Hard Times*, p. 226.
83 Op. cit., p. 108.

5 Plot and Passion: Narrating the Heart

The spontaneous overflow of powerful feelings, or, Politics, Poetics and Poetry

That 'plot and passion' go together, as the title of a popular story and play by John Lang (1817-1864) implies, has been a matter of debate since Plato's and Aristotle's times.[1] But in spite of recurrent arguments relating literature to emotionality, it is the period-specific characteristics of this quarrel which interest me. Nineteenth-century writers concentrate particularly on poetry in their texts on the relation between feeling and writing. That more than just poetic quibbling is at stake becomes obvious when this critical controversy is considered in the wider context of the Victorian discourses on emotions.

Explicit discussions of the relation between 'plot and passion' can be found in health guides, treatises and novels and in poetic texts. Poetry is regarded as the genre *par excellence* which gives expression to the emotions. Once again it is the dialectic relationship between emotional expression and emotional control which lies at the heart of these poetic investigations. Since Wordsworth is a point of reference for many Victorian writers, a short overview of the Wordsworthian ideal of poetry and feeling will serve as an introduction to the debate. And in accordance with the opposition set up by the Victorian critics themselves, this chapter will pursue the argument by looking at the emotional functions attributed to both poetry and prose. Since novels are not only attacked by

---

1 The short little story *The Secret Police; or, Plot and Passion* is set in Paris during the reign of Napoleon, shortly after the Revolution and focuses on a kind of secret police involved in political intrigue. The stage adaptation ends with a tableau-scene and a summary of the story's and play's moral: '"If from the whirl of passion, plot, / and play, / My storm-tossed bark seeks wedded life's calm bay, / What tamed the gambler's passion in my heart? / What 'gainst the plotter turned his own deep art? / What made weak hands strong for a giant's fall? / The master-passion, Love – 'that still is lord of all"'. John Lang and Tom Taylor (1854), *Plot and Passion*, Lacy's Acting Edition vol. 13, Thomas Hailes Lacy, London, p. 56.

19th-century critics, but also considered useful for didactic purposes, I have investigated how paradigm scenarios in fictional but also in non-fictional texts may have fulfilled these didactic aims. A common type of paradigm scenario or plot focusing on the education of the heart can be found in many novels, and it is these intertextual relations that I am most interested in. In a final section the connection between the education of the heart and the nation is traced, since this thematic link simultaneously affirms and subverts the Victorian discourses on emotions and indicates in which direction they may have moved towards the end of the 19th century.

In his famous and controversial preface to the second edition of *Lyrical Ballads* (1802), William Wordsworth justifies his definition of poetry.[2] His famous explanation of the relation between poetry and emotion runs as follows:

> For all good poetry is the spontaneous overflow of powerful feelings: and though this be true, Poems to which any value can be attached, were never produced on any variety of subjects but by a man, who being possessed of more than usual organic sensibility, had also thought long and deeply. For our continued influxes of feeling are modified and directed by our thoughts, which are indeed the representatives of all our past feelings; ... we shall describe objects, and utter sentiments, of such a nature, and in such connection with each other, that the understanding of the Reader must necessarily be in some degree enlightened, and his affections strengthened and purified. (p. 387f.)

The passage contains several important arguments which later writers were to take up. Poetry is considered as the expression of feelings but nevertheless this emotional expression is moderated by thought. In a later paragraph, Wordsworth stresses the need to 'temper' poetic renderings of the passions by selecting an adequate language: 'He will depend upon this

---

2 William Wordsworth (1944) [1802], 'Preface to the Second Edition of Several of the Foregoing Poems, Published, with an Additional Volume, Under the Title of "Lyrical Ballads"', in E. de Selincourt (ed), *The Poetical Works of William Wordsworth*, Clarendon Press, Oxford, pp. 383-404. By permission of Oxford University Press. All page references are to this edition. For two fairly recent discussions of feeling and its role for Romanticism see Lore Metzger (1990), 'The Role of Feeling in the Formation of Romantic Ideology', in Syndy McMillen Conger (ed), *Sensibility in Transformation. Creative Resistance to Sentiment from the Augustans to the Romantics*, Associated University Presses, London/Toronto, pp. 172-194, and David S. Miall (summer 1992), 'Wordsworth and *The Prelude:* the Problematics of Feeling', in *Studies in Romanticism*, vol. 31, pp. 233-253.

for removing what would otherwise be painful or disgusting in the passion' (p. 394). That the ability to express these feelings is not universal is another point which Wordsworth raises: the poet is equipped with a special 'sensibility' and this allows for the specific associations that he will represent in his poetry. Such a concept of the poet is élitist since it limits this special ability to a small number of people. Nevertheless, the poet only differs from other people in degree, not in kind: 'But these passions and thoughts and feelings are the general passions and thoughts and feelings of men' (p. 397). The aim of such passionate poetry is to enlighten the reader and to 'purify' his 'affections'. Wordsworth later adds that the poet should 'take care, that, whatever passions he communicates to his Reader, those passions, if his Reader's mind be sound and vigorous, should always be accompanied with an overbalance of pleasure' (p. 401). He intends to distinguish his own poetry from the popular poetry of his day, interested only in 'action and situation' which gives importance to the feelings, and criticises 'gross and violent stimulants' (p. 389) which the growing mass of people crave.

The notion that the representation of passion needs to contain more pleasure than pain (p. 395f.) also lies at the heart of the distinction that Wordsworth draws between poetry and prose. Both have as their object 'the great and universal passions of men' (p. 398) but poetry has a special task to perform:

> The end of Poetry is to produce excitement in co-existence with an overbalance of pleasure; but by the supposition, excitement is an unusual and irregular state of the mind; ideas and feelings do not, in that state, succeed each other in accustomed order. If ... the images and feelings have an undue proportion of pain connected with them, there is some danger that the excitement may be carried beyond its proper bounds. Now the co-presence of something regular ... cannot but have great efficacy in *tempering and restraining the passion* by an intertexture of ordinary feeling, and of feeling not strictly and necessarily connected with the passion. ... there can be little doubt but *that more pathetic situations and sentiments, that is, those which have a greater proportion of pain connected with them, may be endured in metrical composition, especially in rhyme, than in prose.* (p. 399) (My emphasis, G.S.)

In other words: although prose may also give an adequate representation of passion, the dangers of expression can only be properly contained by poetry because its metrical foundation will always serve to restrain the 'spontaneous overflow of powerful feeling'. And only then can poetry perform its special task of counteracting the danger of a 'blunt[ed]' and torpid public taste (p. 389).

That emotion is best expressed by poetry soon becomes a cliché, repeated by many fellow poets and critics such as John Keble, John Stuart Mill, Matthew Arnold and Charles Mackay. Again, the continuity inherent in the discourses on emotions is conspicuous in the repetition and expansion of Wordsworth's central arguments.[3] John Keble dedicates his lectures on poetry, held between 1832 and 1841, when he was Oxford Professor of Poetry, to Wordsworth, 'who by the special gift of man or of nature failed not to lift up men's hearts to holy things ... '.[4] Keble begins his lectures with a warning against current political developments echoing Wordsworth's anxiety about mass culture (1, 1, p. 14),[5] but in his later expositions on the relation between poetry and politics, his extremely conservative world-view becomes obvious: he argues against the dangers of revolutions and the threat posed by 'passionate restless men' (1, 12, p. 240) and explains that what he calls 'primary poets' usually do not like popular governments (1, 13, p. 256f.). The relation between poetry and politics is thus made even more explicit than in William Wordsworth's 'Preface'. Keble follows Wordsworth in his defence of the capacity to feel which he also attributes to 'simple country folk' (1, 2, p. 29). And although 'unconscious poetry' is present in wider circles (1, 2, p. 27), his hierarchy of primary and secondary poets makes it clear that the ability to write poetry is limited to a special group of people: true poetry has to come from the heart (1, 4, p. 65). Again and again, Keble uses the metaphor of the heart or the soul as the source for 'good' poetry (2, 14, p. 103) which has to be pure and simple in order to meet his critical standards. He paraphrases the Wordsworthian concept of recollected emotion as the source for poetry: 'Whosoever, by some charm of recollection or by some

---

3 In her study of Sir Walter Scott's Waverley novels, Ina Ferris argues along similar lines when she considers the early decades of the century as constitutive for the manner in which fiction was viewed in the later 19th and even in the 20th century. Ina Ferris (1991), *The Achievement of Literary Authority. Gender, History, and the Waverley Novels*, Cornell UP, Ithaca/London, p. 5.

4 John Keble (1912), *Keble's Lectures on Poetry, 1832-41*, transl. by Edward Kershaw Francis, 2 vols., Clarendon Press, Oxford, verso of the Latin title page. For a discussion of the continuity between Romanticism and Tractarian aesthetics see Gregory H. Goodwin (summer 1987), 'Keble and Newman: Tractarian Aesthetics and the Romantic Tradition', in *Victorian Studies*, vol. 30 (4), pp. 475-494.

5 The first number in brackets refers to the respective volume, the second one to the respective lecture.

natural instinct, are carried spontaneously away to country or wood, must necessarily feel their minds moved by the mere mention of the loved objects, almost as if they saw them immediately before their eyes' (2, 31, p. 292). But Keble takes Wordsworth's ideas further in his emphasis on control. Although even Wordsworth stresses the need for tempering the emotions, Keble makes the need for 'modest reserve' his main focus. The need of the Victorian writer to contain the idealised Romantic concept of the feelings as a source of 'natural' humanity is clearly discernible here. Poetry gives comfort, soothes emotion and steadies the mind, it gives 'healing relief' and allows the ordering and control of the passions. The best poetry is that which also answers 'the needs of modest reserve' (1, 1, p. 22) and it is metrical verse rather than mere skill in story-telling (2, 28, p. 220) which may calm 'troubled feelings ... as children are by the croonings of their nurses' (2, 24, p. 100). The use of medical terms indicates not only that the body is a troubled terrain but also that keeping the expression and control paradigm in a balance has perhaps become more difficult.

At the other end of the critical scale with no pretensions to high culture, Charles Mackay prefaces his successful poetry anthology *The Home Affections* (1858 etc.) with a comparable concept of true poetry which needs to 'spring from the hearts of the writers' in order to affect the reader (p. vi). The collection contains poems for 'the most refined and fastidious, as well as those ... who are not critical, provided their hearts be touched and their generous sentiments aroused' (p. viii). Emotional refinement is again the aim of poetry which has the 'duty of celebrating the beauty and the purity of Affection, and of linking the two great principles of Love to God and Love to Man' (p. v). In accordance with popular taste, the volume concentrates on love or the 'Domestic Affections' which can be found in examples 'drawn from the cottage or the palace, from the forests and wilds of the savage, or from the cities of civilized man ...' (p. v), thus creating a vision of social order and harmony which fits the less troubled political and social climate of the mid-century years, compared to the upheaval of the period following the French Revolution and during the 1830s and '40s.

That poetry ought to represent not 'the outward man' but the 'inward man', i.e. that the object of poetry is the human soul, is also maintained in Matthew Arnold's prefaces to his poetry collections dating from 1853 and 1854. He recommends that the poet 'penetrate' himself with the feeling for the situation and 'everything else will follow' (1853, p. xxiii). Actions are the 'eternal objects of Poetry', in particular those 'which most powerfully appeal to the great primary human affections: to those elementary feelings which subsist permanently in the race, and which are independent of time' (1853, p. xix f.). Arnold also stresses the need for restraint and simplicity, to be learnt from the ancients, as opposed to mere expression (1853, p. xxvii f.).

A further essay on poetry, John Stuart Mill's 'What Is Poetry?' (1833, 1867),[6] illustrates how Wordsworth's argument is continued in the Victorian period, before two authors shall be heard whose texts pose a challenge to the orthodox view of poetry as the medium for emotional expression and control. Mill takes up Wordsworth's attempt to attribute a special place to poetry by distinguishing it from science, prose and eloquence or oratory.[7] He sets up a hierarchy with poetry in the top position. In his opinion, poetry works by moving, not by convincing; since prose also addresses the feelings, both genres are somewhat similar (p. 344). What distinguishes them is the difference between mere incident in prose and the truth of human emotion, to be found almost exclusively in poetry. Poetry is again considered as the best medium to give expression to the feelings and only if the source for this is the inner soul of man and not materialistic interests can it be true poetry. In Mill's opinion, 'poetry is *over*heard', it 'is feeling confessing itself to itself' while eloquence or oratory is written with an audience in mind, it is heard, not overheard (p. 348). This concept of emotion and poetry related to solitude and contemplation is akin to Wordsworth's and Keble's conviction that true poetry has to come from the heart, the inner recesses of the soul.

Mill famously discovered poetry comparatively late in life since his father had not considered fictional literature a suitable element of his education. During his intellectual and mental crisis, Mill came to the conclusion that the 'maintenance of a due balance among the faculties, now seemed to me of primary importance. The cultivation of the feelings

---

6 John Stuart Mill (1981) [1867], 'Thoughts on Poetry and Its Varieties', in John Mercel Robson and Jack Stillinger (eds), *The Collected Works of John Stuart Mill*, vol. 1, University of Toronto Press, Toronto, Routledge & Kegan Paul, London, pp. 343-365. All page references are to this edition.

7 For a more detailed discussion of Mill's attitude to poetry and the significance it had for his life, see Peter F. Morgan (winter 1982), 'Mill and Poetry: The Central Years', in *The Wordsworth Circle*, vol. 13 (1), pp. 50-56, Patrick Creevy (1986), 'J.S. Mill and James Martineau: Possibilities and Limitations of an Associationist Aesthetics', in *Victorian Poetry*, vol. 24 (2), pp. 115-129, and Michele Green (summer 1991), 'Sympathy and the Social Value of Poetry: J.S. Mill's Literary Essays', in *University of Toronto Quarterly*, vol. 60 (4), pp. 452-468.

became one of the cardinal points in my ethical and philosophical creed.'[8] Like Dickens's Thomas Gradgrind, Mill learns to consider 'poetry and art as instruments of human culture' and this may go some way to explain the importance he grants poetry, and the fact that contrary to the majority of the other critics already quoted on this topic, he is less interested in the control of emotional and poetic expression, but rather in its sincerity and truth. Truth assures the positive effects of poetry, while mere eloquence and audience-orientation does not, on the contrary, it may result in the vain and self-dependent type of culture that Mill attributes to France and French literature (p. 353).

Poetry, I would argue, is chosen as the genre *par excellence* because it suits the expression and control paradigm that governs the Victorian discourses on emotions. This becomes obvious in the central metaphor that poetry and emotionality share in these discourses: that of a flowing current, stemming from the heart, in need of channelling or controlling but equally in need of an expressive outlet.[9] Poetry is the 'spontaneous overflow of powerful feeling' (Wordsworth), just as it is a 'fountain-head', a 'flow from the heart', a 'stream' (Keble/Powell) and a 'river' (Arnold), while emotion is a 'rush' (Keble), or a 'full tide' (Grey and Shirreff), it needs to be poured through a 'channel' (Ellis), it can suddenly 'gush' or 'pour out river-like' (C. Brontë), it can be a 'copious fountain', a 'flood always ready to overflow' and a 'current' which needs 'restraint' (Bain). Thus, the perfect vehicle for 'stem[ming] the torrent of excessive emotion' (Bain) which simultaneously leaves enough room for its expression is – at least on the level of (poetic) discourse – metrical composition. By taking up an 18th-century concept, namely the aesthetic as a specially marked off area, Romantic and Victorian writers provided the emotions with a 'safe' place. In such a concept, the feelings are contained but at the same time are given free play. The conjunction of expression and control not only in Victorian poetry but in Victorian culture in general shows 'that the longer-term positive impact of sensibility depended upon its assimilating the critique it

---

8 John Stuart Mill (1873), *Autobiography*, Longmans, Green, Reader, and Dyer, London, p. 143f. Note the phrenological terminology and the emphasis on 'balanced' mental faculties.

9 Isobel Armstrong (1977), 'The Role and the Treatment of Emotion in Victorian Criticism of Poetry', in *Victorian Periodicals Newsletter*, vol. 10 (1), pp. 3-16, quotation p. 8: 'And naturally enough, critics tend to think of emotion in terms of the dead metaphor of flow, current, springs, wells, outlet, just as Wordsworth did when he talked of the spontaneous "overflow" of feeling. But now the "overflow" of feeling has to be controlled in proportion to its depth or even suppressed before it *can* overflow.'

provoked', as Michael Bell has explained with regard to 18th-century sensibility and aesthetics. In a culture which could afford to set aside more and more time for the luxury of self-contemplation and reflection upon the value of the emotions, it was no longer a matter of choice between either emotionality or its opposite, complete containment, but rather an urgent requirement to reconcile the two.[10]

Challenges to some of the elements of the Wordsworthian concept of poetry, and its Victorian variations, come from two directions. Firstly, a text by a non-middle class author – Powell's *The Poetry of Feeling and Poetry of Diction* (1853) – already briefly touched upon in the preceding chapter, indicates that the model is essentially a middle class one and cannot claim to appeal to all classes. And secondly, when gender issues are confronted with poetics, as in Mary Ann Stodart's *Female Writers: Thoughts on Their Proper Sphere and on Their Powers of Usefulness* (1842), the implicit analogy between masculinity and poetry is threatened.

In his small pamphlet, of which only 400 copies were printed so that it cannot lay claim to great influence, Powell implicitly questions the élitism inherent in the concept of the poet as a particularly sensitive creature, endowed with more sensibility than the average man. Although he admits that the poet has power over others (p. 17), he repeatedly emphasises that the 'poetry of feeling', i.e. the ability to appreciate beauty in nature and in art, is universal (p. 6f.) and that both poetry and religion are innate (p. 17). As a self-educated worker, speaking before his fellow workers at the Wolverhampton Mechanics' Institution, it is not surprising that he does not join Keble in his objection to 'popular government'. On the contrary, Powell champions freedom and the rights of man (p. 8) Nevertheless, his description of the 'Poetry of Feeling' which 'calls forth our sympathy for suffering and sorrow' and the need for 'patriotism, self-denial, and endurance for the good of humanity' (p. 6) are close enough to the middle class ideal of the patriotic and sympathetic individual who represses every selfish impulse for the 'good of humanity'.

When it comes to the 'Poetry of Diction' which can 'rouse all the faculties of the mind and can lift the soul and expands the hearts' (p. 18), Powell comes even closer to the middle class critics' concept of poetry as the expression of the inner self and the poet as a 'guide': 'Diction is to the Poet that which language is to all Men – namely, the expression of that which is within – the agent by which he distributes to Others that which he

---

10 Michael Bell (2000), 'Adam Smith and Friedrich Schiller: The Luxury of Sensibility and the Aestheticising of Emotion', in *REAL*, vol. 16, pp. 105-116.

feels himself' (p. 17). Although he is firmly on the side of the 'moderns' by praising contemporary poets, he also has the effects of poetry uppermost in his mind: it can teach lessons and can rouse sympathy for others (p. 27). Refining the heart, or 'purifying' the affections, as Wordsworth put it, can best be achieved with the help of poetry.

Mary Ann Stodart, who has already appeared as one of my main witnesses for the separate spheres debate, is also relevant in this context. She would surely have agreed with Powell's proposition since she was also convinced that poetry has 'power over the human heart'.[11] But in her treatise on *Female Writers* Stodart introduces gender issues and these complicate matters further. Poetry is now no longer implicitly the prerogative of the male poet but is feminised as 'she', an effect which is further accentuated by the use of lexeme combinations explicitly marked as feminine in the discourses on emotions:

> The domain of poetry is wide; *her* power over the human heart immense. It is *hers* to describe ... those objects which are too vast, and those which are too minute for ordinary ken; ... And it is *hers* too to embody and give permanence to those *delicate, evanescent emotions* which pass over the mind like the *blush* over the *maiden's brow*, and which can no more be distinguished by the powers of an ordinary mind, than the blending and intermingling of the rain-bow tints. It is the province of poetry to arouse by *her* trumpet-call to vigorous action, and to melt by her *plaintive warblings* to *gentle* and *tender emotion* ... . (p. 83f.) (My emphasis, G.S.)

At least with regard to certain subject matters, Stodart considers poetry to be especially suited to the woman writer who can even outdistance Shakespeare in specific instances:

> It is not within our province to dive into the deep recesses of the human heart with that myriad-minded man, our own Shakespeare, and to drag into the open day-light the hidden secrets of the soul. No! but there are light and delicate movements which a woman's pen may express, and which Shakespeare, though unrivalled amid poets for his knowledge of women's heart, has not even guessed. We have struck on the point where lies the true poetic power of woman. It is in the heart – over the heart – and especially in the peculiarities of her own heart. (p. 88)

---

11 M.A. Stodart (1842), *The Female Writers: Thoughts on Their Proper Sphere and Their Powers of Usefulness*, G. Seeley, London, p. 83. Subsequent page references are to this edition.

By associating poetry and femininity so closely, Stodart threatens the stable gender identity of the poet who is suddenly confronted with 'feminine' qualities. Just as much as the danger of madness, implied by the concept of flowing emotions as the source of true poetry – another 'feminine' element, if one thinks back to the obsessive debates centring on the body, the emotions and hysteria briefly described in chapter 3 – feminised poetry may also destabilise by its 'power over the heart'.[12]

This confrontation of gender and poetry constitutes a kind of paradox. By strictly adhering to the separate spheres principle, clearly distinguishing male and female characteristics and activities, Stodart clears a space for the woman writer, comparable to Sarah Ellis's coupling of separate spheres-arguments and the call for women's education. From the concept of the woman as the more emotional human being follows the subject matter which she may write about. But by creating such a space – which incidentally many women writers, including herself, consciously and unconsciously attempted to leave behind them[13] – Stodart also paradoxically threatens exactly that binary distinction on which the separate spheres principle rests. When poetry is feminised and its main source, 'the heart', is so closely associated with femininity, I would assume that this may have resulted in a threat to the gender identity of male writers.

The majority of the critics quoted above, with the exception perhaps of Powell, overcome this paradoxical situation by relegating women to the utterly unpoetic domestic sphere. No woman writer is ever mentioned (except Sappho, and she receives short shrift) and the weight of male authority in the shape of ancient authors such as Virgil or Homer is repeatedly emphasised. Feminine feeling is identified with novel reading, and although the male poet also attempts to move the heart, it is quite

---

12 Cf. Jane Wood (2001), *Passion and Pathology in Victorian Fiction*, Oxford UP, Oxford, 'The Disorders of Literary Men', pp. 59-77.

13 One female poet who confidently overstepped the 'mark' for literature written by women is Elizabeth Barrett Browning (1806-61). In an early long poem entitled *An Essay on Mind* (1826), Barrett Browning discusses the role of poetry, the emotions, learning and the mind. According to her, poetry and poets convince the intellect 'through the heart' (line 944ff.) but this effect is not limited to male writers as her poem and in particular her later work were to show. Cf. Gesa Stedman (2000), '"Private" Passions in Public Places – Women's Poetry on the Feelings', in Sabine Coelsch-Foisner and Holger Klein (eds), *Private and Public Voices in Victorian Poetry*, Stauffenburg Verlag, Tübingen (Studies in English and Comparative Literature, vol. 16), pp. 149-160.

obviously not the same kind of heart that sensational novels are said to influence.[14]

Avoiding undue excitement: The Dangers of Novel Reading

It is therefore not by chance that John Stuart Mill sets poetry off against 'the most trashy productions of the Minerva press',[15] those sensationalist novels written by 'Silly Lady Novelists', whom George Eliot hated enough to write an important essay about them.[16] While poetry is seen as a safe genre for the expression of the feelings, the potential for boundless emotion in novels – at least in a certain kind of novel – is considered dangerous and novels are objects, and reading novels a practice, against which many writers issue the strongest warnings. The author of the popular health guide *Health for the Million* (1858) gives the following advice which is typical in its juxtaposition of text, reading and the female body. After first focusing on physical symptoms, the author moves to the 'deranged mind' and then recommends not only medical treatment but different reading matter (history) and a different lifestyle as remedies. In the whole passage, a fear of (feminine) disorder prevails:

> *Among the bad habits to which many young persons, chiefly females*, are addicted, we may mention *novel reading*. ... Dr. Mason Good observes that he had several patients, chiefly ladies, who had spent their nights and days over captivating novels, till they gave evident proofs that they were of a mind occasionally deranged. In such cases there are usually headaches, indigestion, costiveness, wandering nervous pains, flatulence, ringing in the ears, flushings

---

14 For an analysis of Wordsworth's poetry and its relation to gender and feeling see Adela Pinch (1996), *Strange Fits of Passion. Epistemologies of Emotion, Hume to Austen*, Stanford UP, Stanford, in particular chapter 3, 'Female Chatter', pp. 72-110 and Susan J. Wolfson (1994), '*Lyrical Ballads* and the Language of (Men) Feeling: Wordsworth Writing Women's Voices', in Thaïs E. Morgan (ed), *Men Writing the Feminine. Literature, Theory and the Question of Genders*, State University of New York Press, Albany, pp. 29-57.

15 Mill (1981) [1867], 'Thoughts on Poetry and Its Varieties', p. 346.

16 George Eliot (October 1856), 'Silly Novels by Lady Novelists', in Thomas Pinney (ed), *Essays of George Eliot*, Routledge and Kegan Paul, London, pp. 300-324, reprinted from *The Westminster Review*, vol. 61, pp. 442-461. For a description of the Minerva Press and its writers, see Nigel Cross (1985), *The Common Writer: Life in Nineteenth Century Grub Street*, Cambridge UP, Cambridge/New York, p. 170ff.

> in the face, alternate sensations of burning and coldness in the hands and feet, and all the numerous attendants of nervous derangement.[17]

What might be considered the excessive opinion of a deluded doctor who recommends reading history instead of novels, and talking walks in fresh air, is in fact a traditional motif whose origins, in particular concerning the connection between women and reading, go back a long way.[18]

In the hierarchy that Mill sets up, narrative is inferior to poetry, although it also has its uses. In spite of the fact that both genres are said 'to act upon the emotions', narrative only represents incident and 'gives a true picture of life', whereas poetry's truth 'is to paint the human soul truly'. Fondness for narrative is associated with children and savage states 'like ... the Tartars and Arabs at this day'. Once again a Wordsworthian echo can be heard in Mill's rejection of the 'trashy productions of the Minerva press'[19] – Wordsworth held that 'our elder writers ... are driven into neglect by frantic novels, sickly and stupid German tragedies, and deluges of idle and extravagant stories in verse'.[20]

Mary Ann Stodart is also violently opposed to novel reading and writing for women. In her letters on *Every Day Duties* (1840), she associates reading with ingestion and disease, two key elements of the 'trope of female reading' (Ferris) and compares novel reading to smoking, drinking and taking opium and calls it a 'bad and ruinous habit' from which young women can only be saved by total abstention:

> Let no vain pretence of historical novels, or religious novels, prevail upon you, to break through your resolution. ...
>
> I warn you against religious novels, that froth and scum upon which thousands of professed Christians feed, or rather starve their minds. A valued friend of mine said to Mrs. Hannah More, on the publication of Cœlebs,

---

17 Anon (1858), *Health for the Million; Including Hints on the Physical Training of Youth, and the Treatment of Invalids and Old Age: With Observations on Unhealthy Employments*, W. Kent & Co., London, p. 197f. I have been unable to unearth the anonymous author's background. Italics in the original. For other examples of this kind of argument see Ferris (1991), *The Achievement*, p. 42.

18 Cf. Kate Flint (1993), *The Woman Reader*, Oxford UP, Oxford, in particular pp. 28-31, and Ferris (1991), *The Achievement*, in particular her analysis of 'female reading', considered as a great danger, and 'feminine writing' which appears in the form of the 'proper novel' (p. 35).

19 Mill (1981) [1867], 'Thoughts on Poetry and Its Varieties', p. 344, p. 346, p. 345.

20 Wordsworth (1944) [1802], 'Preface', p. 389.

> 'You do not know the mischief you have done. You have opened the flood-gates to religious novels, and we shall be carried away with the torrent.'[21]

Being 'carried away by the torrent' can only be avoided if 'fiction and fable' are replaced by 'truth and reality', i.e. natural history.[22] The greatest danger in what Stodart calls the 'bane of woman' lies in the weakening of her character: 'This accounts perfectly for what has often been considered anomalous, how a lady can weep over a novel, and turn away from a case of real distress without making any effort for its relief. ... It is not sickly sensibility that we want ..., you must work, act, do.'[23] Obviously, not only the threat to the individual woman is important here, but what is endangered by this kind of indulgence is her social role as daughter, wife, mother or benevolent helper. In Eliza Armstrong's anthology *Affection's Token* (c. 1850), a story by an anonymous author, possibly written by the editor herself, illustrates the problem. The protagonist of 'The Still Small Voice' sends her son Frank away when he asks her whether he will have to die, like the person whose funeral he is observing from the window, in order to have time to read the latest novel 'upon her luxurious cushions'. She has to think of her child's question in spite of herself, but soon forgets the problem and plays the harp instead. As is to be expected, Frank falls ill shortly afterwards and dies. Only then does the mother repent and regrets that instead of thinking of her duty as a mother, and of God and religious matters, she chose to immerse herself in novels.[24]

In spite of this gloomy view of narrative, some writers do consider 'stories' to be of some worth in relation to the emotions, in fact, they express the opposite opinion, in particular concerning children and young

---

21 Stodart (1840), *Every Day Duties: In Letters to a Young Lady*, G. Seeley, London, p. 122f.

22 Op. cit., p. 141. Excessive images such as the 'torrent' of novels or the 'rabble rout of abominations' are common in 19th-century critical discourse, in particular during the early decades. Cf. Ferris (1991), *The Achievement*, p. 15.

23 Op. cit., p. 146f. In her *Hints on Reading: Addressed to a Young Lady*, published by R.B. Seeley and W. Burnside in 1839, Stodart recommends a reading programme for women (historical and religious works, as well as books on natural history). Her advice to women writers to avoid what is not suitable for them follows similar lines, expressed in chapter VIII of *Female Writers*.

24 Eliza Armstrong (ed) (c. 1850), *Affections Token: A Selection of Prose and Poetry from the Best Writers*, Thomas Allman & Son etc., London, pp. 40-43. Novel reading was associated with luxury and sensuality, as opposed to 'upright reading' in the study or library. Not only the content but the bodily act of reading is sexualised, as Ferris (1991), *The Achievement*, p. 40, explains.

people. The anonymous author of *The Young Man's Mentor*, a series of letters addressed to young men,[25] stresses the positive effects of reading: 'The more special tendencies of literary habits are, to meliorate the disposition – to soften and melt down rancorous feelings – to elevate and enlarge the mind – to encourage benevolence of sentiment, and a ready sympathy with generous conduct.'[26] And although he too warns against the dangers of romance,[27] Charles Bray also emphasises the emotional refinement that can be accomplished with the help of poetry and stresses in particular the use of narrative for the emotional instruction of children: 'The extreme eagerness with which children listen to 'a tale', particularly if it appeals to the wonderful, points it out as a most valuable vehicle for instruction, and for the exercise of our best feelings.'[28]

I would argue that certain novels win the day precisely because they are 'a valuable vehicle for instruction, and for the exercise of our best feelings'. To quote Charles Dickens's *Hard Times* once again

> Utilitarian economists, skeletons of schoolmasters, Commissioners of Fact, genteel and used-up infidels, gabblers of many little dog's-eared creeds, the poor you will have always with you. Cultivate in them, while there is yet time, the utmost graces of the fancies and affections to adorn their lives so much in need of ornament; or, in the day of your triumph, when romance is utterly driven out of their souls, and they and a bare existence stand face to face, Reality will take a wolfish turn, and make an end of you![29]

It is worthwhile to take a look at those paradigm scenarios that are the most prevalent in the 'tales' told by writers of non-fictional and fictional texts on the emotions and to explain why some novels could become successful in spite of the genre's negative image.

---

25 That the author thinks it safe to recommend literature as a means for moral improvement may be explained by his intended male readership, constitutionally less in danger of succumbing to 'excessive sensibility'. Cf. also Wood (2001), *Passion and Pathology*, p. 96, on the recommendation of a curriculum for boys excluding fiction in order to control emotion and the imagination, which she, perhaps, foregrounds too much.

26 Anon (1842), *The Young Man's Mentor, on his Entrance Into Life*, T.M. Cradock, London, p. 58.

27 Bray ([1]1838), *The Education of the Feelings*, p. 142.

28 Bray ([2]1849) *The Education of the Feelings*, p. 93f. and Bray ([1]1838), *The Education of the Feelings*, p. 133.

29 Dickens (1995) [1854], *Hard Times*, p. 165f.

Feeling Shakespeare: The 'Literary' Education of the Heart

In *Shirley*, Caroline Helstone tries to teach Robert Moore to be more humble and less proud by reading Shakespeare's *Coriolanus* with him. Although she fails at first, the course of events in the novel finally make her achieve her goal, and she does not only educate his heart in the process, but also her own. In *Passion and Principle*, a text on which the section on novels focuses, a piece of writing has a crucial role to play in the rearrangement or synthesis of two formerly opposing emotional habitus. And in a number of novels which retell the French novel *Corinne*, analysed in the same section, performing drama or creating and reciting poetry are emotionally charged acts on which the central problematic of the creative but nevertheless 'feminine' woman centres. But before the function of these fictional paradigm scenarios become my focus, I will briefly discuss those scenarios contained in non-fictional texts, since all texts on the feelings in the 19th century share the use of narrative in their attempts to educate the heart. Although some fictional texts are more complex than non-fictional ones with respect to these paradigm scenarios, they are remarkably similar in the emotional values they recommend to their readers.

The injurious fruit of ungoverned passion: Non-fictional Texts

Non-fictional texts on the emotions are related to fictional texts in three ways: firstly, their authors frequently quote or allude to fictional texts, and use authors of fiction, notably Shakespeare, as their authorities.[30] Secondly, their analyses of the feelings are interpolated with short narrative passages, usually based on cases that the author alleges to have come across. Thirdly, authors give examples or stories which they invent to illustrate their argument. The second and third type of narrative is not always easy to distinguish, in particular since the authors usually assume that the reader believe the implied referentiality of the story, without being able to actually verify this. And although by the use of literary quotations authors actually refer to another story, these in realist terms non-referential narratives or quotations are cited as evidence in a manner which resembles the insertion of allegedly referential case stories. This indicates how

---

30 This is a feature of Victorian scientific writing in general. See Gillian Beer (1996), 'Parable, Professionalization, and Literary Allusion in Victorian Scientific Writing', in id. *Open Fields. Science in Cultural Encounter*, Clarendon Press, Oxford, pp. 196-215.

difficult (and perhaps futile) it is to mark the boundaries between fictional and non-fictional texts. This type of overlap also puts into question referentiality as the standard feature for the distinction between the two types of text. It is not so much a characteristic of the text, but of the context. A writer and publisher of a specific type of text marks this text as belonging to a certain category, e.g. a book of advice, and can have expected its readership to react to it as such. Expectations then would have influenced all participants in the process of book production and consumption to read everything contained in such a publication as true, regardless of the constructed or fictional character of the text. Conversely, since realism was such a dominant trend in 19th century fiction, fictional tales could equally well be read as true in the sense of 'possible', since they made clear how much they also referred to and relied upon their immediate surroundings. The answer to the problem, then, lies in the uses non-fictional and fictional stories and publications were put to; and since these are similar, perhaps it is best to focus on these – the didactic aims, the recommendation of a balance between emotional expression and control – rather than on the possible differences between the two types of text.

The health guide *Health for the Million* (1858) combines all three types of allusion. The text begins with a poetic 'Invocation to Health'[31] by the Scottish doctor and poet John Armstrong (1709-1779), a favourite medico-poetic source of quotations for the authors of health guides. In the section on vice and 'evil tendencies' in the chapter on 'Habits Prejudicial to Bad Health', the author quotes long passages from Charles Lamb's (1775-1834) 'The Confessions of a Drunkard' (from the *Essays of Elia*, 1823) as a 'case' of alcoholism, and recommends abstinence as 'the only means of safety and immunity'.[32] The chapter on the 'Government of the Passions' begins with a Spenser quotation on the 'raging passion' which '[r]obs reason of her true regality', followed by a passage from Crabbe on the 'insolent and strong' passions. The introduction to this section ends with Armstrong and the 'greatest art of life' which lies in managing 'the restless mind'.[33] No sources are given and the literary allusions are inserted into the running text. Finally, allegedly true cases are quoted, e.g. 'obstinacy of temper' which the Stuarts suffered from, with the exception of Charles II,

---

31 Anon (1858), *Health for the Million*, Kent & Co., London, p. xvi.
32 Op. cit., p. 190.
33 Op. cit., p. 275.

resulting in the 'fatality which attended the house of Stuart'.[34] A further example of the overlap between literary allusion and the citing of an alleged 'case' can be found in Cassell's *Hand-Book of Health and Physiology* (1863) which quotes Shelley as an authority on the relation between 'violent passions' and certain foods.[35]

Two reasons for the inclusion of fictional elements in non-fictional texts can be distinguished. By quoting literary authorities writers could express their learning and raise their status. This was particularly important for medical writers since doctors did not have a reputation for being learned.[36] William Cooke's expanded version of his treatise on the emotions (1852) testifies to this anxiety, he worries that 'nothing will be found tending to dishonour the profession in the view of its members, or of the public'.[37]

This reason which seems to be extrinsic to the discourses on emotions since it applies to all kinds of non-fictional writing in the 19th century,[38]

---

34 Op. cit., p. 279.

35 Anon (c. 1863), *Hand-Book of Health and Physiology* (Cassell's Elementary Handbooks), Cassell, Petter, and Galpin, London, p. 82.

36 Beer (1996), 'Parable, Professionalization ...' explains the use of citing classical (and English) authors by focusing on the continuity with the past that this technique creates, and on the cohesion that results from such an appeal to shared education. In addition, she considers the 'direct pleasures of reading' as a further reason for authors like Darwin and Lyell to have included literary quotations and allusions (p. 210). She names Milton and Wordsworth as the most frequently quoted authors, Shakespeare merely comes third (p. 211). In the texts that I have studied, Shakespeare is by far the most frequently quoted author, perhaps because he has a reputation for being unrivalled in his dramatic representations of emotional states.

37 W. Cooke (1852), *A Commentary of Medical and Moral Life; or Mind and the Emotions, Considered in Relation to Health, Disease, and Religion*, Longman, Brown, & Co., London, p. xi. Cooke uses both editions of his treatise to distinguish himself and the medical profession from fashionable alternative approaches to healing, e.g. 'animal magnetism' and homeopathy. Evidently, his disparagement of these approaches to illness which he considers so dangerous, in particular for women, that patients may be drawn into the 'vortex' or the 'whirlpool of error from which they may be floated into an abyss where the fine influence of science and truth, and the nobler influence of moral character may perish together', Cooke, (1839), *Mind and Emotions in Relation to Health and Disease*, Longman & Co., London (p. 36), is motivated by the wish to establish and consolidate doctors as the only legitimate providers of curative medicine. For a description of the medical profession during the Victorian period, and its status in relation to quackery, see W.F. Bynum (1992), 'Medical Values in a Commercial Age', in *Proceedings of the British Academy*, vol. 78, pp. 149-163.

38 Gillian Beer (1996), *Open Fields*, has shown how closely 'the discursive strategies of scientist and poets' (p. 149) are related in 19th-century discourse, and stresses the interchange and mutual influence between both seemingly separate discourses since

can be distinguished from one intrinsic to these discourses. Inserting narrative passages that read like miniature melodramatic tales or like the plots of sensationalist novels is not specific to the Victorian discourses on the emotions.[39] It is nevertheless specifically Victorian to use narrative since the notion was extremely widespread that visual and verbal representations had to contain a moral and the best way to drive this moral home was to build a story around it. But it is also the 'nature' of the topic, the emotions, that requires narrative frameworks or paradigm scenarios since writing about the emotions in the abstract will not reach the reader. In order to convince or to move him or her, the feelings have to be 'attached' to a narrative framework, ensuring the effectiveness of any warning against the emotions, or recommendation as to their employment. Such passages do not work simply as illustrations, but may in a Foucauldian sense be said to be constitutive of their object.[40]

In *The Emotions and the Will* (^{2}1865) Alexander Bain gives a slightly different explanation for the attraction of stories, or what he calls the 'Literature of Plot-interest':

> The position of the spectator of moving events, is greatly enlarged by language, which can bring before his mind, scenes witnessed by other men; and, in so far as he is able to conceive what is thus related, he catches the fire of the actual witness. This is the interest of story, which is such a widely-spread source of excitement.

Literary plots, in other words, also serve as a medium to 'discharge ... the pent-up currents' of emotion, they have a positive function, but fortunately, the 'poet or romancer' is not bound by fact, as the historian is, and can 'cast ... about also for the class of events best able to awaken agreeable

---

'they share the moment's discourse' (p. 168 and p. 171). She relates this discursive overlap to the Victorian conviction of 'the mother tongue', i.e. a shared language and shared knowledge transcending disciplinary boundaries (p. 173 and p. 203).

39 This feature can also be found in earlier treatises, e.g. in Walter Charleton's genre-transcending treatment of the passions. Cf. M. Müller (1999), *'These Savage Beasts Become Domestick': The Discourse of the Passions in Early Modern England With Special Reference to Non-Fictional Texts*, D.Phil. Thesis, unpublished ms., University of Oxford, p. 213ff., p. 238 and p. 249f.

40 Cf. Jürgen Schlaeger (1999), 'Introduction', in J. Schlaeger and Gesa Stedman (eds), *Representations of Emotions*, Gunter Narr, Tübingen, p. 10; and Ronald de Sousa, (1980), 'The Rationality of Emotions', in Amélie Oksenberg Rorty (ed), *Explaining Emotions*, University of California Press, Berkeley etc., pp. 127-151.

emotions in a story; ...'.[41] Bain does not explain what these 'agreeable emotions' are but from the preceding discussion of his aesthetic criteria (harmony, order) and the general moral and political notions on which his study rests, one can gain an impression what they may be (e.g. pleasure, 'tender emotion', ordered behaviour etc.).

Case studies and invented but allegedly true case stories in non-fictional texts on the feelings are based upon unsophisticated plot structures and use stereotypical characters. Simple causal links are established in order to explain why lack of emotional control may lead to poverty, death or suicide (the 'injurious fruits of ungoverned passion', in Cooke's terminology) and why goodness, benevolence or religiously inspired faith may help to overcome adversity.

Occasionally, stories of the dangers of repression are included in the non-fictional texts on the emotions, but the majority of writers prefer the stories of excess leading to disaster.[42] An example would be the 'case' that Cooke includes in both his editions of *Mind and Emotions in Relation to Health and Disease* which tells the story of a successful merchant who becomes so prosperous that his activities increase to such an extent that he falls mad and dies.[43] Had he shown moderation in his business affairs, Cooke argues, his health would not have suffered; lack of control led to uncontrolled nervous excitement.[44] Herbert Spencer's examples

---

41 Bain, (^{2}1865) [1859], *The Emotions and the Will*, Longmans & Co., London, p. 160 and p. 161.

42 This may be explained by the profession of many writers: doctors, that is the authors of health guides and medical treatises, needed to argue their own case and if neither body nor mind were endangered by excessive emotion, the doctors themselves would become superfluous or at least would loose a considerable part of their income (e.g. for treating 'hysterics'). But it is important to note that these warnings against excessive emotionality were by no means restricted to women, as Wood (2001) seems to imply in *Passion and Pathology*, p. 53, p. 60.

43 In Dinah Mulock Craik's best-selling novel *Olive* (1850), the protagonist's father dies suddenly when his business fails (although a prior illness is hinted at) and in Grey and Shirreff's novel *Passion and Principle* (1842/1853), one of the two protagonists is orphaned when her father succumbs to shock when he realises that all his investments have been lost (also after a physical illness has been diagnosed). Both fictional accounts motivate these cases of 'sudden death' by some form of bodily disturbance but the emphasis is laid on the mental shock that business affairs – failures in these instances – can bring on.

44 Cooke (1839), *Mind and Emotions*, p. 7f. Beer (1996), *Open Fields*, p. 156f., sees a parallel in the predictable outcome of narrative and the text of scientific discovery which is in fact a process of disclosure of something whose aim is already known: 'The enterprises of scientist and of writer both act out the paradox that narrative implies

concentrate on the same issues. In one case, he reminds his readers of a kind of communal hysteria which broke out after a murder had occurred on the North London Railway, inducing people to avoid using the train although the probability of such a case happening again was very small. He concludes that 'emotion of every kind and degree disturbs the intellectual balance'.[45]

Characters in these stories and 'cases' are often hysterical women, selfless mothers or their opposite, negligent mothers, possessive or overambitious business men, grieving widows as in Cooke's story quoted in the preceding chapter, and upright and moral men. Good and bad is clearly distinguished in these exempla and depending on the optimistic or pessimistic perspective of the author, redemption or death is the outcome.

One of Cooke's rarer positive stories of an alleged case he treated recounts the woes of a young girl said to have simulated hysteria but after his treatment she became able to fulfil her task as a domestic governess and later even became a wife and mother. In other words, the influence of moderated emotions instead of boundless hysterical feelings ensured that she would take up her allotted place in society.[46]

The simplistic plots, stereotypical characterisation, the binary moral world-view and the emphasis on excess suggest an affinity between these case stories and melodrama which uses similar elements to achieve its effects.[47] In summary, one can say that the stories emphasise the centrality

---

teleology even when its argument denies it. The acknowledgement of the foreknown in the imprinting of writing; the process of discovery which has now become disclosure; the fact that the book ends (even when the argument of the ending is peremptory and unresolved): all this makes for an organization in which the future is already disposed, and is thus apparently under the control of the writer's description at least, if not of his free choosing. Narrative implies successful prediction.'

45 Herbert Spencer ([13]1887) [1873], *The Study of Sociology*, Kegan Paul, Trench & Co., London, p. 147.

46 Cooke (1839), *Mind and Emotions*, p. 103. Cf. also Wood (2001), *Passion and Pathology*, p. 41.

47 Cf. Peter Brooks (1976), *The Melodramatic Imagination. Balzac, Henry James, Melodrama and the Mode of Excess*, Yale UP, New Haven/London. This type of simplicity is not necessarily restricted to non-fictional texts. G.P.R. James's *A Book of the Passions* (1838-39) contains stories modelled on the same paradigm scenario: uncontrolled emotion is dangerous and results in disaster. Brotherly rivalry leads to death, extreme jealousy to the loss of a lover and future wife etc. Interestingly, the review in *The Athenæum* (No. 583, December 29, 1838, p. 930) criticises James for the banality of his stories (and the 'inferior' quality of the accompanying engravings), since a writer of his ability should be able to paint a more complex picture of human behaviour. Perhaps the stories were intended more as a vehicle for the images, and since

of the emotions for mental and physical health and for 'earthly' life in general.

The texts in my corpus which do not contain any narratives of this kind use other devices to affect their readers: conduct books are often collections of letters, addressed to an alleged friend of the author's. Since they are written in an intimate mode, they may not require further offers to identify with specific cases studies, because an affinity with the reader is already established. Serious scientific treatises such as Darwin's publication on emotional expression contain more detached examples and only a few stories of the melodramatic kind. But he uses literary examples to make up for his subject's potential inaccessibility, and significantly he chooses Shakespeare and Dickens, two writers whose vivid language ensures that he can carry his point. That he used literary allusions at all indicates that a purely scientific approach to the emotions was not entirely satisfactory. As Gillian Beer explains: 'Parable and allusion not only worked as tactic and resource in Victorian scientific writing. They could also harbour anxieties and insights that tapped the further implications of current scientific theories, beyond the range for which experiment could vouch.'[48]

The following passages concentrate on novels and the didactic aims and discursive limits of 'tactic and resource' in fictional texts. As has already been mentioned and illustrated in the analysis of *Shirley*, novels tend to be more complex in their treatment of emotional expression and control than non-fictional texts. But in them, too, writers warn against the dangers of emotional expression if it is not counterbalanced by emotional control and it is this problem, in particular when confronted by women (writers), that is the main concern of the final sections of this chapter.

Using fable as the vehicle of truth: Fictional Texts

Not only poets wanted to reconcile the demands of emotional expression and control. Novelists grappled with the same problem, most obviously

---

they afford visual pleasure they counteract to some extent the stories' moralistic overtones (see chapter 3 for two examples). I have been unable to discover the author of the review. The difference in dates between the review and the publication date indicates that an earlier version of *A Book of the Passions* must have appeared in 1838, although the catalogue of the British Library and the copy of the book I consulted in the Bodleian Library both give 1839 as the year of publication.

48 Beer (1996), *Open Fields*, p. 215.

perhaps in novels whose very titles demonstrate what was at stake: *Sense and Sensibility* (1811), *Five Years of Youth, or Sense and Sentiment* (1831), *Temper and Temperament* (1846) and *Passion and Principle* (1842/1853).[49] The latter shall serve as one of the main texts of the following passages. Not only because its title conveniently summarises what I contend to be the main concern of the Victorian discourses on emotions but also because it is part of an intertextual 'system' of novels by women writers. *Passion and Principle* and its textual relations occupy a discursive space similar to that of *Shirley* (albeit further down the scale of originality and proto-feminist explicitness), which allows me to take up some points already raised in chapters 3 and 4: namely the ambiguous relation between gender and emotion. *Passion and Principle* also has an interesting publication history which is instructive in terms of women's access to the literary field, an issue which forms part of the gender-and-emotion nexus in the 19th century because it is linked to the problem of the passionate, creative woman.

Three issues are relevant in this context: how women can be equipped with the necessary prerequisites for their role as chief educators of the heart, how this role can be reconciled with their own needs of expressing their feelings, creatively or otherwise, and how this expression of feeling is linked to 'national' characteristics. These three major points are discussed in the new mode of the 'proper novel' (Ferris) written by women, a mode of writing which is not only used by women writers to advance their own (limited) cause, but which also provides the most adequate literary form for the expression-and-control paradigm, based as it is on the combination of passion and principle. The explicit focus on women writers in the following section is a consequence of the discourses on emotions themselves. From the affirmation of the separate sphere's notion of women as the more emotional gender, follows – albeit somewhat paradoxically – that women are especially equipped to write about affairs of the heart. This

49 The model for the titles, if not the plots of these novels, is of course Jane Austen's *Sense and Sensibility. Five Years of Youth, or Sense and Sentiment* was one of Harriet Martineau's early publications and the influence of Jane Austen's novels is obvious. The story of two sisters, one of whom is sensible whereas the other indulges in excessive sensibility and consequently suffers, is a didactic tale for young girls. *Temper and Temperament; or, Varieties of Character* by Sarah Ellis is a set of three separate stories, published together in two volumes. As is to be expected of a conduct book writer, these tales are thinly veiled instructions on how to moderate excesses of temper and serve to illustrate Sarah Ellis's convictions which she expressed more successfully in her various books of advice.

view is confirmed by literary critics, e.g. by George Henry Lewes in his essay 'The Lady Novelists', when he states unequivocally that '[w]oman, by her greater affectionateness, her greater range and depth of emotional experience, is well fitted to give expression to the emotional facts of life, and demands a place in literature corresponding with that she occupies in society; ... '.[50] Men, of course, were equally in danger of suffering from an imbalance of emotional expression and control. Too much (Reginald Ireby) or too little feeling (Thomas Gradgrind) could lead to a male identity crisis not always easily resolved. But the women's dilemma in relation to emotion seems to have been more dramatic and more pressing, not only because more writers – male and female ones – focused on it. Women had less room to manoeuvre, in fiction as in real life, if they failed to fulfil their socially prescribed role. The dilemma of the creative woman trying at the same time to follow the model put so succinctly by G.H. Lewes is particularly interesting in this respect. In the fictional representations of creative women, femininity is simultaneously affirmed and questioned and it is these tensions which I am most interested to uncover and explain in the context of the discourses on emotions.

Passion and Principle When *Passion and Principle* first came out in 1842,[51] published as a three-decker by Henry Colburn, its reviewer in the *New Monthly Magazine* immediately questioned the alleged 'authorship' (or editorship) of Captain Frederick Chamier, to whom the novel is attributed on the title page: '... we must observe that the writer of this excellent novel is, if we do not greatly mistake her quality (about her sex there can be no mistake), at the very least as well entitled to edit as to be edited ... '.[52] In his monograph on the naval officer and writer of adventure stories Frederick Chamier, P.J. Van der Voort also speculates about the author of the novel but is unable to find the answer to the problem, in spite of his doubts which focus on the unusual topic for a writer of naval stories, the emphasis on female characters, and on the fact that Chamier is only mentioned as the editor at a time when he was already a successful

---

50 G.H. Lewes (July 1852), 'The Lady Novelists', in *The Westminster Review*, vol. 58 o.s., pp. 129-141, quotation p. 132.

51 There is some doubt as to the exact publication date of the first edition of *Passion and Principle*. While the *DNB* entry (1897) gives 1841 *The English Catalogue* and the catalogue of the British Library both list 1842 as the year of publication. References in my text are to the edition published in 1853 by George Routledge, London.

52 Anon (1842), *New Monthly Magazine*, LXV, p. 427.

novelist, thus hiding the true author behind the mask of semi-anonymity. The keyword is of course 'semi-anonymous' which in addition to the novel's content points towards female authorship.[53] By comparing the two novels of the same title, one published in 1842 and the other in 1853, which the British Library catalogue lists, it is not too difficult to discover that they are virtually identical. One can therefore safely assume that the authors of the second edition of the novel, the sisters Emily Shirreff and Maria Grey, née Shirreff, are also the authors of the first edition. Emily and Maria Shirreff may have met Captain Chamier through their father William Henry Shirreff (1785-1847) who was a rear-admiral in the navy.[54] Since by the 1830s Chamier was a fairly well established author, he may have offered them his services as an 'editor' to help them gain access to the publishing world without being immediately identified as young and inexperienced (female) authors.

Although the reviews in *The New Monthly Magazine* and *The Gentleman's Magazine* are full of praise, the first edition appears to have been slightly less successful than the two later ones.[55] *Passion and*

---

53 The novel contains startling elements indeed for a male author of adventure stories. While male writers have been known to focus on female protagonists (e.g. William Thackeray in *Vanity Fair*), the emphasis on a father-daughter relationship, the struggle for a suitable occupation for women and the emphasis on women's education, as well as the rare and fairly explicit inclusion of a baby's birth would argue strongly for female authorship. Although the latter scene ends with the convention of 'innate' maternal feelings, the emphasis on pain is unusual: 'At length her hour came. She bore her long and dreadful suffering with a woman's bravery, but there was despair in her silent endurance. She had no hope then; she felt sure that her child would not live; and it was not till she heard its first feeble cry that she would believe her attendant's assurance of its safety. That cry seemed to restore to the mother the life she had given her child; pain, fear, sorrow, the weary suffering of so many months were all forgotten, as that first faint cry thrilled to her inmost heart, and told her that she was indeed a mother' (p. 216).

54 Van der Voort lists Chamier's service stations but the dates of these trips do not coincide with the periods that the Shirreffs spent in Gibraltar. P.J. Van der Voort, (1972), *The Pen and the Quarter-Deck. A Study of the Life and Works of Captain Frederick Chamier, R.N.*, Leiden UP, Leiden, Appendix II, p. 154. Yet he may have known Rear-admiral Shirreff, or he might have met the two sisters when they returned to London. Ellsworth's monograph on the Shirreff sisters does not explain the details of the novel's publication. Cf. Edward W. Ellsworth (1979), *Liberators of the Female Mind: the Shirreff Sisters, Educational Reform and the Women's Movement*, Greenwood Press, Westport., Conn., p. 16.

55 Although Victorian bibliography specialists disagree on the average length of time it took a three-decker novel to be republished as a single volume, eleven years are definitely a long period to lie between both forms of publication. Cf. Simon Eliot (1985), 'The Three-Decker Novel and Its First Cheap Reprint, 1862-94', in *The Library*,

Principle was translated into German in 1843[56] and in 1853, Routledge & Co. published an abridged version of the novel in their successful series of popular literature as part of the one-shilling Railway Library. A second edition followed a year later and the two sisters found themselves in the company of such well-known writers as James Fenimore Cooper, G.P.R. James, Captain Marryat, Mary Brunton and Jane Austen, whose most popular titles were also published in the Railway Library-series. The association between *Passion and Principle* and the last two authors is particularly fitting since both Mary Brunton's widely-read novels *Self-Control* (1811) and *Discipline* (1814), as well as Jane Austen's *Sense and Sensibility* (1811) and *Pride and Prejudice* (1813) obviously inspired *Passion and Principle*.[57]

Passion and Principle tells the story of two young girls, Louisa and Ellen, and their respective 'education of the heart'. While principled Louisa has to fight an unsuitable passion for the immoral Arthur St John and only later learns to love her childhood friend Reginald, impetuous Ellen breaks off her engagement with her childhood sweetheart, the clergyman Edward Annesley, and falls for cold Lord Caldwell and a loveless marriage. Edward forgives her desertion in the end and remains unmarried while Ellen is reconciled to Caldwell and ends as his nurse and helpmeet.

Both Louisa and Ellen undergo a development and both have to learn to overcome adversity in love. But as the title indicates, they embody two different ways of dealing with their problems. Emily Shirreff and Maria Grey use this device – distributing two attitudes to emotionality onto two characters – effectively to make their point that in the end it is principle which has to conquer passion, although some space has to be allowed for feeling. The most obvious intertextual models are the works of Mary Brunton, Jane Austen, and to a slightly lesser extent Staël's novel *Corinne, ou l'Italie*. These models extend their influence right across the board of Victorian fiction and therefore deserve a place in an account of the most common emotion paradigm scenarios in Victorian (fictional) discourse.

6th series, vol. VII, pp. 38-53.

56 Van der Voort (1972), *The Pen*, p. 150, gives the following details which I have been unable to verify, since no German library catalogue for the 19th century mentions this title: *Leidenschaft und Grundfasz. Ein Roman* [sic], 4 vols., Braunschweig 1843, translated by W. Schulze.

57 In the *Times*-obituary for Emily Shirreff, *Passion and Principle* is tellingly misquoted as 'Passion and Prejudice' (*The Times*, 24 March 1897, p. 8).

The novels' influence can be explained by the manner in which they combine plot action with self-exploratory heroines (with the exception of Jane Austen as regards action), by the way in which they simultaneously give room to feeling but make morality and control persevere in the end, thus combining the thrilling elements of more down-market novels with middle class notions of propriety.[58] And finally, Staël's *Corinne* even supplies the arguments needed to move the discourses on emotions' boundaries, indicating that the delicate balance between emotional expression and control was from the beginning a precarious one.

Mary Brunton and Jane Austen: Self-Control and Sensibility Substantial elements of *Passion and Principle's* plot are taken from Mary Brunton's two successful novels *Self-Control* (1811) and *Discipline* (1814), whose titles refer to that side of the expression-and-control paradigm embodied by 'principled' Louisa Conway in Grey and Shirreff's novel. The other side of the coin – passionate Ellen Perceival in *Passion and Principle* – appears as 'proud, petulant, and rebellious' Ellen Percy in *Discipline*. Not only do the latter two protagonists share a name, their moral development is similar, too. Both have to learn how to overcome vanity, pride and passion, while Louisa Conway and Laura Montreville, the main character in *Self-Control*, share their struggle of principle over passion for an attractive but unsuitable, immoral lover who threatens to seduce and conquer them. Significantly, neither Brunton, nor Austen, nor Grey and Shirreff focus on married life – as the ideal balance for emotional expression and control – but rather on the protagonists' and their partners' requisite education of the heart which precedes marriage.

That Maria Grey and her sister were inspired so obviously by Mary Brunton's two novels does not only testify to the latter's success and influence. It also indicates that what Brunton developed as a model – a combination of an 'action-packed' plot and the moral development of her protagonists – proved to be exceptionally effective for didactic stories focusing on the education of the heart.[59] Drawing on the conventional

---

58 Combining action and morality is of course not a 19th-century invention. But Samuel Richardson's model, for all its paradigmatic influence on later female characters (the 'Pamela-type'), significantly lets the originally immoral aristocrat win while in Brunton's and all subsequent novels the dangerous bigamist or otherwise immoral lover does not obtain the heroine as a wife.

59 See Ann H. Jones (1986), *Ideas and Innovations. Best Sellers of Jane Austen's Age*, AMS Press, New York, pp. 79-113.

metaphor of 'poison' for fiction, Brunton explains in her preface to *Discipline* how this new mode of writing could provide a suitable antidote:

> The appetite for fiction is indeed universal, and has unfortunately been made the occasion of conveying poison of every description into the youthful mind. Why must the antidote be confined to such forms as are sure to be rejected by those who need it the most? There is high authority for using fable as the vehicle of important, even of solemn truth; and to this purpose it is here applied without hesitation.[60]

Ann H. Jones explains the effects of this mode of writing:

> Thus, while all that Mary Brunton was trying to do at this stage in her career was to show that, though the way of Christian principle was not an easy one, with self-control it could be followed, in this one respect her religious purpose aided rather than hindered her as a novelist. Laura wrestles with her own desires, foreshadowing struggles like Jane Eyre's over Mr. Rochester and Maggie Tulliver's over Stephen Grant, though she lacks the passion of these heroines ... .[61]

Or, one might add, like Louisa Conway's management of her own passion for Arthur St John, Alice Bryant's struggle against passion for Conrad in Geraldine Jewsbury's *The Half-Sisters* (1848), or even Eleanor Dashwood's rather unsuccessful 'conquering' of her feelings for Edward in *Sense and Sensibility*, and like Caroline Helstone's equally ineffective attempt at repressing her love for Robert Moore. The similarities between these novels do not only prove 'just how far Jane Austen was in the mainstream of the novel of her day and how far she was ahead of her contemporaries in artistry', as Ann H. Jones asserts.[62] Austen's and Brunton's novels are also examples of a new mode of writing, developed in the early 19th century, which would provide the model for much of the Victorian novelistic output to come.[63]

---

60 Mary Brunton (1814), *Discipline*, Manners and Miller, Edinburgh, p. v f.

61 Jones (1986), *Ideas and Innovations*, p. 89.

62 Op. cit., p. 96. Cf. also John Halperin (1974), *Egoism and Self-Discovery in the Victorian Novel*, Burt Franklin, New York, in particular chap. 1 'The Victorian Novel and Jane Austen', pp. 1-30, and B.C. Southam (ed) (1995) [1968], *Jane Austen. The Critical Heritage*, 2 vols., Routledge, London/New York, for contemporary and Victorian reviews of Austen's novels which, although always present throughout the 19th century, became more popular from the mid-19th century onwards

63 Another important author in this context is Hannah More (1745-1833), whose pious and

This new mode of writing, although also used by male writers, is closely associated with women writers. By replacing the 'dangerous' type of narrative fiction which Mary Ann Stodart saw as 'the bane of woman' with the serious, moral novel, women writers achieved two things[64]: they entered the literary field so far dominated mainly by men, and they could use this space to advocate not only moral and religious issues, fictionalised in education-of-the-heart-type plots, thus underlining their alleged moral and emotional superiority. By claiming this space in the literary field, they could also voice concerns such as the need for women's education which would aid women in their task as self-controlled, disciplined educators of the heart.

In *Passion and Principle*, two things help Louisa Conway to achieve her goal: moral and intellectual education, and creativity, while the humbling of her financial prospects, among other events, lead to her transformation from a proud young girl to a sensible young woman (another Jane Austen echo). It is precisely the lack of education of any kind that results in Ellen's downfall, and only through the offices of her principled friend Louisa, and her own experience is she later enabled to lead a life governed less by selfish passion than by regard for the feelings of her relatives and friends.

Sir Charles Conway's affection for his daughter and the manner in which he educates her are important in this context, because it provides the model for Louisa's later marriage with Reginald. When Reginald finally proposes to Louisa, he is not passionate but tender:

> As he spoke these words in a low, earnest voice, trembling with emotion, Louisa murmured some almost inarticulate sounds; and, seeing her agitation, he passed his arm round her, and gently raising her from her drooping position, he drew her towards him. (p. 241)

Similar words are used to describe the father's reaction to Louisa's crisis when she learns that St John is as immoral as Reginald had alleged he was and after a further encounter with St John (p. 133, p. 140). Her father does not only provide her with a means of expressing her feelings (verbally and

---

didactic tales were widely read.

64 Ferris (1991), *The Achievement*, p. 52ff., explains how the 'proper novel', or feminine writing, was used as a corrective to 'female reading', and was praised for its restraint and didactic objectives. It is interesting to note that the novelists considered to be exemplary by contemporary (male) reviewers were all women.

non-verbally), he has also ensured three vital guiding aspects: affection, piety, and knowledge – the three elements missing from Ellen Perceival's neglected education. His 'woman's tenderness' is explained as a result of his wife's death and the need for consolation which he finds in his daughter.[65] It is interesting to note the use of emotion words which are clearly marked as feminine:

> Sir Charles did not get tired of the task he had undertaken. With a *woman's tenderness*, and the clear, firm judgement of a man, he watched over and trained that young and tender main. He gave, with a father's wisdom, the guidance and instruction needed by his child, and fostered, with a *mother's brooding love*, each good and noble quality of her soul. (p. 2f.) (My emphasis, G.S.)

His attentions have resulted in Louisa's somewhat unusual characteristics which will stand her in such good stead in her struggle against St John: '... her strength of mind, her cultivated intellect, her fervent but enlightened piety, and the nobleness of a spirit incapable of one mean or ungenerous impulse' (p. 4). One reason for St John's attraction to Louisa is precisely her intellectual ability. It is this training of the mind, together with a pious upbringing, which ensure that reason conquers passion, expressed in conventional metaphorical guise as a 'madness' and a 'storm':

> In such moments as these, judgement and reason are suspended; the feelings are roused and reign alone, and fearful is their empire. But Louisa's mind was all too unused to such a yoke, to bow beneath it long; and gradually, as the night wore away, her thoughts became more collected. She blessed God, on her knees, that the temporary madness was over, and prayed, that never might that fearful storm of passion sweep over her soul again. (p. 141)

And in contrast to deprived Maggie Tulliver in *The Mill on the Floss*, Louisa even uses this cultivated mind as a resource to overcome financial problems and poverty. Coupled with her creative abilities, her intelligence ensures that she manages to make a living for herself and her maid Sarah.

Louisa's attempt at publishing her work are thwarted because the publishers do not want to take up a nameless author.[66] In its focus on

---

65 Cf. John Tosh (1999), *A Man's Place: Masculinity and the Middle-Class Home in Victorian England*, Yale UP, New Haven/London, for accounts of tender fathers openly expressing their feelings for their children.

66 How she achieves this position as a painter and writer is another element which points towards female authorship of the novel: the detailed account of the difficulties of finding

mental imprisonment ('galling chains', 'cage'), the following passage, although written in a more formulaic manner, is similar to Caroline Helstone's longing for useful occupation:

> It is only women who can know such solitude as hers, which her conventional position converted into a dreary prison-house. No ties of business connected her with her fellow-creatures – no community of interests, such as a man, however abject his poverty, might rejoice in, as he discusses public news in the resorts of his fellow-men. She had been truly alone in thought and spirit; for Sarah's affection, strong as it was, could not teach her to sympathize with Louisa's mental sufferings – with the conflict of an aspiring mind struggling in vain against its invisible but galling chains – the wild longing of a spirit, full of energy and consciousness of power, to find a scope for its exertion, ere it could sink withering in its cage and be still. (p. 200f.)

The 'Christian's' reward for all this hardship is 'internal peace' but Louisa is fortunate enough to receive material rewards as well. She reads an attack against Reginald in the paper and answers it anonymously to great success, and this leads to her work as a writer and alleviates the more severe consequences of poverty (p. 201). Significantly, it is a piece of writing which brings Reginald and Louisa back together. But before exploring this link between female creativity and passionate women further, a look at the parallels between Grey and Shirreff's non-fictional *Thoughts on Self-Culture* and *Passion and Principle* will illuminate how they imagined women should gain principled self-culture to avoid Ellen's unfortunate experience.

Thoughts on Self-Culture: Morally Superior Educators of the Heart The plea for women's education and self-reliance formulated in *Passion and Principle* makes it unlikely that the novel should have been written by a man. It brings to mind the issues already discussed with regard to *Shirley*: the absence of a suitable occupation for women and the dangers of superficial education. Education is also famously the desire of Maggie Tulliver in *The Mill on the Floss* for whom no 'blissful' return to marriage lay in store, a fate perhaps befitting her violent passion (for learning and occupation) which could not be contained otherwise than in death.[67]

---

a publisher and the suffering of a woman trying to find an outlet for her own creativity emphasises the particular difficulty that a woman encounters in such a situation. These passages also invite an autobiographical reading.

67 A further difference between *The Mill on the Floss* and *Passion and Principle* lies in the

In *Passion and Principle*, moral and religious superiority as well as self-reliance are the main resources which enable Louisa not only to conquer her own passion for St John, and to make Reginald transform his wounded pride into humility. These 'sterling' qualities also rub off on Ellen Perceival. Louisa can thus be considered a 'multiple' educator of the heart who fulfils that role which Grey and Shirreff recommend to women in their *Thoughts on Self-Culture*, published in 1850.

In *Self-Culture*, the two sisters express their belief in separate spheres and sexual difference. But they deplore women's frivolity and argue the case not only for single women but also for a better preparation for both marriage and spinsterhood. A sound education, to replace what they metaphorically call the 'patch-work begun without aim, fashioned without method, and flung aside, when half-finished, as carelessly as it was begun' (1, p. 54) will ensure that women will be able to live a self-reliant life. Together with self-control and conscience, inspired by religious values, they will no longer have to 'slave at the needle' (1, p. 65), but will be prepared for their role as chief educators of the heart. Shirreff and Grey firmly believe in this 'vocation' for women, since the 'regeneration of society must begin at the fountain head' (1, p. 37), the fountain head being women's greater force of feeling which is needed in particular for the education of boys. Although the sisters' social criticism is more explicit than (and several years in advance of) Sarah Ellis's similar complaints, Grey and Shirreff are not yet calling for schools for girls, let alone for women as professional, paid educators (1, p. 8). This was to change in the course of their lives. But in the decade between writing *Passion and Principle* and *Thoughts on Self-Culture* it is the moral development and the education of the self which is uppermost in their minds. Significantly, they argue for education as a means of fostering independent thinking, not education as the acquisition of knowledge (1, p. 55, p. 67 and volume 2 for its practical appliance). And from *Self-Culture* one can gather that their novel is a fictionalised version of their beliefs. They are critical of novels which describe principled and intelligent characters as ugly and boring and so cannot convince their readership that this is the course to follow:

> In these works, though the broad distinctions of morality may not be lost sight of, yet the being led astray by passion is invested with all the charms of a

---

ineffectiveness of religion. Maggie Tulliver attempts to overcome her longing for education and a position in the world by following religious principles and being meek and submissive. This turns out to be an illusion and fails to satisfy her.

> romantic interest; love or compassion are excited for the erring woman or the guilty man, while the character of those who steadfastly follow the dictates of principle are represented as unattractive or unamiable .... (1, p. 139)

That is why they have invested Louisa with so many positive qualities and attractions while Ellen is the victim of what the sisters consider to be the most eloquent 'voice' – that of passion: '... each time that inclination has been allowed to call in question the decision of conscience, it grows more importunate, till at length headstrong passion oversways the mind, and the course of duty is not discerned till it is perhaps too late for everything but repentance' (1, p. 142). Because she is so selfish, and does not act according to 'the principles of justice, truth, and benevolence' (1, p. 123), Ellen falls into the hand of Lord Caldwell. The two sisters recommend either remaining single – a state for which they make a surprisingly strong case (1, p. 23ff., p. 274ff.) – or if a woman marries, not to opt for passion, like Ellen does. Rather, a woman 'must learn to choose her lover, and consequently her husband, as she would choose her friend, for those moral qualities that are the only solid basis of love, and to feel that any misery is preferable to marriage without esteem' (1, p. 271). There it is again – the keyword 'esteem' which is considered the basis of friendship and marriage, just as in Louisa's and Reginald's marriage in the novel, the type of marriage which is held up as the ideal in *Self-Culture*:

> We believe, on the contrary, that the happiest marriages are often those formed (after the fervour of youthful feeling is over) upon sober choice, grounded on respect and esteem. The warmth of feeling which may at first be wanting, will soon spring up under the influence of common interests and common ties, and when it does arise, will combine all the strength with more than all the tenderness of friendship. (1, p. 272)

Grey and Shirreff assert that proper education as they define it will ensure two things: women will be able to function as the indispensable educators of the heart (in particular of their children). And it will ensure that whether they remain single or whether they marry, in both states it is not passion (for an unsuitable lover turned husband or for a different fate) which will govern their life but feeling tempered by reason. This is the consequence they envisage for the Ellens and Louisas to which *Thoughts on Self-Culture* and *Passion and Principle* were addressed: 'And the blessing will not fail to come even to us at last, – the peace of a heart that has won the victory over itself, that has subdued passion to principle' (1, p. 280).

Women who are able to follow these guidelines will be principled and morally superior emotional guides. But the question remains how they are to express their own passions if tender friendship does not fulfil their emotional needs. In *Passion and Principle*, the mental and material struggle a woman may have to survive if she tries to express her feelings creatively is only briefly hinted at. Yet this connection between a woman's creative expression of passion (in art or literature) and the need to remain not only a respectable but an effective educator of the heart is a major focus of a number of novels. They are paradigmatic for the Victorian discourses on emotions since they express and dramatise the tensions that characterise these discourses. As the texts derive their inspiration from Staël's novel *Corinne, ou l'Italie* (1807), the next section will focus on two major points: how do English writers adapt the *Corinne*-plot to their own needs to allow the creative expression of their feelings and the preservation of moral superiority? And how is this emotional expression associated with nationality or with national 'otherness'? For both of these important 19th-century concerns, *Corinne* supplies the initial arguments allowing women (writers) to extend the boundaries of accepted emotional and social behaviour while at the same time following the implicit and explicit rules that order the 19th-century discourses on emotions. In other words, *Corinne* provides the major expression-and-control plot which would be re-written countless times in the Victorian period.

Corinne Maria Grey and Emily Shirreff could have used only one of the two Mary Brunton-plots, but they chose to combine them. Once again, the dangers of emotional repression, and the threat of uncontrolled passion, are enacted by two female characters. A similar principle – although inherently more ambiguous – can be found in Brontë's *Shirley*, in Martineau's rather schematic *Sense and Sentiment*, in Jewsbury's *The Half-Sisters*, in George Eliot's *The Mill on the Floss* and numerous other Victorian novels[68] influenced by Germaine de Staël's *Corinne, ou l'Italie*. *Corinne* was first published in 1807 and translated into English in the same year.[69] The novel

---

68 See Ellen Moers (1977), *Literary Women*, W.A. Allen, London, and Gill Frith (1997), 'Playing with Shawls: George Eliot's Use of Corinne in The Mill on the Floss', in John Rignall (ed), *George Eliot and Europe*, Scolar Press, Aldershot, pp. 225-239, for more examples.

69 The catalogue of the British Library lists two translations of *Corinne* for 1807 (one three-volume and one five-volume one, published by Colburn and Tupper respectively), another one for 1822, the 1833-version by Isabel Hill which contains an introduction to Germaine de Staël, and the verse passages by Letitia Elizabeth Landon ('L.E.L.'), a

tells the story of the Anglo-Italian singer and poet Corinne and her struggle to reconcile creative talent with the love for her Scottish suitor, Oswald, Lord Edgermond. *Corinne* had an immediate impact on its international readership, not least in England and Scotland, in particular in Edinburgh, where academics are alleged to have stopped each other in the street to discuss the novel.[70] A contemporary critic from *The Monthly Review* regarded it as 'something out of the beaten track' and especially praises the 'accuracy of information and depth of reflection on the antiquities, arts, language, literature, music, climate, and manners of the people of Italy...'.[71] Apart from translation mistakes, the reviewer criticises the love story. The critic writing in *The Edinburgh Review* also mixes praise with criticism. Again, it is the Italian scenes which have pleased the writer most, while the plot is considered somewhat improbable. Nevertheless, *Corinne* is described as an exemplary story:

> From the history and fate of the amiable and accomplished Corinna, the reader may learn to watch over a passion which, if left to itself, may become one of the worst distempers of the mind, blasting and consuming even the noblest faculties. One may learn, too, the necessity of conformity to those rules that restrain the intercourse of the sexes, ...[72]

Whether this is really the main thrust of the novel's argument is debatable, and later critics and writers of fiction seem to have been attracted by *Corinne* not because it shows how not to behave, but rather because it provides them with a model for feminine creativity coupled with truth of feeling.

Contemporary English critics focused either on Staël's alleged personal defects and apparent immoral behaviour,[73] or, with regard to her work, on

---

further 'new translation' for 1883, and the edition by George Saintsbury, 1894, which is based on one of the two 1807-translations. All her other works were also translated soon after publication and her life, as well as her work, remained objects of considerable interest throughout the 19th century.

70 An account of this appears in Abel Stevens's (1881) *Madame de Staël. A Study of Her Life and Times: The First Revolution and The First Empire*, 2 vols., John Murray, London, vol. 2, p. 8.

71 Anon (1807), *The Monthly Review*, vol. 54, ser. 2, pp. 152-159.

72 Anon (October 1807), *The Edinburgh Review*, vol. 11, p. 194.

73 Invectives against her can only be partly explained by a general anti-Romantic impulse. The focus on her looks and her alleged absence of maternal feelings, as well as the fixation with her various lovers, indicate that it also a misogynous impulse which is at work here. A typical strategy of denigrating women writers or women who move beyond

its lack of didacticism: 'Few people, we are persuaded, have risen from her compositions with their taste purified, or their principles strengthened,' writes the author of the obituary in *The Times*.[74] But Germaine de Staël's critical reception was to change considerably throughout the 19th century, and in the later decades not only her person but also her work were again and again held up as shining examples. While the Italian scenes which seem interminable to modern readers are no longer regarded so highly towards the middle and end of the century, praise is heaped on the love plot (and on Germaine de Staël herself, who is now no longer judged an immoral and forward bluestocking, but a maternal, loving, if intellectually exceptional woman). This new approach to her person and her work may have been instigated by Lord Byron's tribute, written after her death, and quoted in Isabell Hill's 1833-translation of *Corinne*, published by Richard Bentley:

> Corinna has ceased to be a woman – she is only an author; ... She will enter into that existence in which the great writers of all ages and nations are, as it were, associated in a world of their own, and, from that superior sphere, shed their eternal influence for the control and consolation of mankind. ... The mother tenderly affectionate and tenderly beloved, – the friend unboundedly generous, but still esteemed, – the charitable patroness of all distress, cannot be forgotten by those whom she cherished, and protected, and fed.[75]

Byron was to set the tone for later critical appraisals. He appears to have been one of the first writers to confuse Staël with her fictional character Corinne[76] – a confusion which may well have been influenced by a portrait of Germaine de Staël, painted by Elisabeth Louise Vigée-Lebrun in 1808. It shows Staël 'en Corinne' (fig. 5.1), wrapped in an Indian shawl, playing the lyre with bare arms. Making the author and her character, both 'women of genius', converge may have given the author a strategic advantage by placing her in the same realm as her fictional character. Equally, the strategy to make her fate resemble that of Corinne would also have amounted to a containment of Staël's power as an author, since Corinne

---

prescribed boundaries of accepted behaviour is to focus on their person rather than on their work, and in particular on their external appearance.

74 Anon (19 July 1817), *The Times*, p. 2, col. 4.

75 Germaine de Staël (1833) [1807], *Corinne, or Italy*, trans. by Isabel Hill, Richard Bentley, London, p. xlv f.

76 See Robert Escarpit (1954), *L'Angleterre dans l'oeuvre de Madame de Staël*, Marcel Didier, Paris, for a 20th-century example of the same rather unprofessional attitude.

perishes in the end. Obviously, several performative levels are at work at the same time, and it is difficult to distinguish between self-invention and subsequent attributions by (male) readers and critics. Byron does not only stress Staël's importance as a writer, rather than as a mere socio-political celebrity, he also describes her as a woman whose alleged feminine characteristics leave nothing to be desired. This tendency to 'feminise' women according to the dominant Victorian model of femininity is widespread during the 19th century.[77] Abel Stevens, the author of a two-volume study of Staël's life, comments in a similar vein:

> This feminine sensibility, this predominance of her womanly heart over her manly intellect, is one of the most admirable charms of her character. In her hours of happiness it rendered her irresistibly fascinating. She gave herself up to her spontaneous sentiments; ... .[78]

The late 19th-century edition of *Corinne* is no longer interested in Staël as a person. The introduction by George Saintsbury praises *Corinne's* 'higher moral tone', compared to Staël's other novel *Delphine*, and is particularly taken by the 'truth' of the representation of emotion. It is obviously her manner of depicting feeling which fascinated other writers of fiction, as opposed to critics. Staël's contemporary Romantic readers would have been interested in the general relation between emotion and 'genius'[79] but it is the woman of 'genius' which seems to have influenced the novel's reception by Victorian writers of fiction and poetry.[80] Being a

---

77 See Gesa Stedman (1999), '*Channel Crossings*: Zum Verhältnis englischer und französischer Autorinnen im 19. Jahrhundert', in Renate Kroll and Margarete Zimmermann (eds), *Gender Studies in den romanischen Literaturen: Revisionen, Subversionen*, dipa, Frankfurt a.M., pp. 256-276.

78 Stevens (1881), *Madame de Staël*, p. 186.

79 See John Clairborne Isbell (1994), *The Birth of European Romanticism. Truth and Propaganda in Staël's "De l'Allemagne", 1810-1813*, Cambridge UP, Cambridge, for Staël's influence on European Romanticism.

80 'Dieses Buch [*Corinne*, G.S.] wird zu einer identitäts- und gemeinschaftsstiftenden Erzählung für dichtende Frauen im 19. Jahrhundert'. Ina Schabert (1997), *Englische Literaturwissenschaft aus der Sicht der Geschlechterforschung*, Alfred Kröner, Stuttgart, p. 463. See also Julia Kavanagh's (1862) discussion of *Corinne* in her volume *French Women of Letters: Biographical Sketches*, Hurst and Blackett, London, pp. 295-319, which emphasises not only how much Byron was indebted to Germaine de Staël (p. 301), but also discusses the novel in terms of female creativity. Kavanagh concludes that the novelist is less 'wonderful' than the 'eloquent critic, the acute thinker, the clear though dogmatic politician' (p. 318), thereby reinstating Staël as a creative woman transcending the boundaries of Victorian concepts of femininity.

writer without violating Victorian ideals of femininity was one of the major concerns of female authors in the 19th century and a problem which English writers may have found the most difficult to overcome, in view of the rigidity of English gender norms.[81] Using a model with a doubly 'foreign' background (written in French and with a half-Italian protagonist) may have had several reasons. The French tradition of literature by women goes back longer than the English one, which may have influenced English women writers because their own heritage perhaps did not have enough weight for them to draw upon. It is more likely that a foreign model was needed because the relative geographical and symbolic distance inherent in *Corinne* allowed the English women writers to see their own concerns more clearly. A 'safe' novelistic environment was required to debate dangerous issues (it is only 'foreign' women who transgress 'our' (gender) norms) which in an entirely English setting might have proved too difficult to handle. 'France' and/or 'Italy' have always had this symbolic function in English literature and culture, and in a period in which the concept of national differences was becoming more and more popular, its influence on women writers does not come as a surprise.[82]

In their construction of Germaine de Staël as a person and as a female author, and in *Corinne*, Victorian women writers found a model and a plot which was to help them work through their particular dilemma. That this had perhaps become even more pressing in the 19th century than in the 18th century with its short-lived period of discursive gender equality can be explained by two developments. On the one hand, gender norms were becoming increasingly rigid in the course of the late 18th and early 19th century. And on the other hand, the increase of women writers in the 19th century posed a threat. By their sheer numbers, women writers potentially undermined the concept of the domesticated middle class woman. The following passages therefore discuss how Victorian women writers attempt a compromise between these two seemingly irreconcilable roles.

The intensity of intertextual links between *Corinne* and Victorian novels and poems is remarkable, as is the extent of references which may range from brief quotations to complete re-tellings of the original plot,

---

81 Christiane Planté's (1989) study *La petite soeur de Balzac. Essai sur la femme auteur*, Seuil, Paris, shows that French women writers had similar problems.

82 See Ceri Crossley and Ian Small's (1988) collection of essays and in particular their introduction, *Studies in Anglo-French Cultural Relations: Imagining France*, Macmillan, Basingstoke, for the various symbolic uses of 'France' by their English/British neighbours.

thereby creating a 'system' of intertextual links which in its turn, in addition to references to *Corinne* as the foundational text, was used by women writers as a point of departure. In Rhoda Broughton's novel *Not Wisely But Too Well* (1867), which tells the story of an unhappy passion between Kate Chester and the married Captain Dare Stamer, a short reference to *Corinne* is used as an ironic comment on the narrow-mindedness of English tea parties: 'And this was the sort of improving, edifying conversation that was going on, not much more interesting to an averagely intelligent hearer than that of Lady Edgermond's circle in *Corinne*.'[83]

The most trivial form of allusion to *Corinne* is the use of the Æolian harp as a metaphor for creativity which gives expression to the woman's love for a man, e.g. in a poem entitled 'The Æolian Harp', from a collection by a Mrs Spencer, called *Commemorative Feelings* and published in 1812. Here, the conflict between the woman's love and the social restrictions she suffers from as a writer have disappeared from the text. The use of the image of the broken harp or lyre became so widespread that it even provoked parody and obviously, over time, it lost any critical impact it may originally have had.[84]

A number of Sappho/*Corinne*-poems also use one of the two names in their titles for their take on the struggles of the creative woman. These poems all focus on the death of the creative woman, although in some cases her creativity is celebrated at length, before her suicide or death end it, e.g. in Felicia Hemans's two poems which separate the pain and the pleasure into two poems. One focuses on the success of the writer, the other on her loneliness and suffering (*Corinne at the Capitol* and *The Last Song of Sappho*).

A partial retelling of *Corinne* can be found in Craik's novel *Olive*, which this time allows the angelic character not only a love story with a happy ending but also a successful career as a painter. Interestingly, the direct reference to Germaine de Staël's novel in *Olive* emphasises domesticity and not creativity: 'A Michelangelo can stand alone with his genius .... But there scarce ever lived the woman who would not rather sit meekly by her own hearth, with her husband at her side, and her children at her knee, than be the crowned Corinne of the Capitol.'[85] Finally, Elizabeth

---

83 [Rhoda Broughton] (1993) [1867], *Not Wisely But Too Well*, Alan Sutton, Stroud, p. 149.

84 See Schabert (1997), *Literaturgeschichte*, p. 468f.

85 Dinah Mulock Craik (1996) [1850], *Olive*, Oxford UP, Oxford/New York, p. 126.

Barrett Browning's long poem or verse-novel *Aurora Leigh* (1856) is a complete adaptation of *Corinne*, as is Jewsbury's *The Half-Sisters*, both with a more optimistic ending than the original.

The majority of references to *Corinne* are explicit, naming the novel's title or main characters. In some cases, the book as a physical object actually appears in the English novels, e.g. in *The Half-Sisters* or in *The Mill on the Floss*, where Maggie Tulliver famously refuses to continue reading it since she is fed up with the 'blond haired women' always winning the day.[86] On the scale of possible intertextual links, this type of reference is the most explicit and the most obviously marked one.[87] It illustrates two things: on the one hand, writers could safely assume that their readership shared their own knowledge of the French original – as Geraldine Jewsbury puts it in *The Half-Sisters*, 'The first reading of "Corinne" is an epoch a woman never forgets.'[88] On the other hand, the authors were obviously not afraid of invoking Staël as their model. By 'victorianising' and 'feminising' her more controversial traits and again and again asserting her femininity and by largely ignoring her political and philosophical importance, Victorian critics paved the way for writers of fiction who could safely and even proudly expose their indebtedness to Germaine de Staël.[89]

Yet writers of fiction were not content to simply retell the French original's plot, and not all English adaptations pick up the same elements. They all focus on the problems a 'woman of genius' has to overcome, but not all of them force the same fate on their creative and passionate heroine whose death or suicide has – I think erroneously – also been read as the ultimate act of the creative woman's self-expression.[90]

86 George Eliot (1985) [1979] [1860], *The Mill on the Floss*, vol. 2, ch. 'Another love scene', Penguin, Harmondsworth, p. 433.

87 See Manfred Pfister (1985), 'Konzepte der Intertextualität', in Ulrich Broich and Manfred Pfister (eds), *Intertextualität. Formen, Funktionen, anglistische Fallstudien*, Max Niemeyer Verlag, Tübingen, pp. 1-30, in particular p. 26ff.

88 Geraldine Jewsbury (1994) [1848], *The Half-Sisters*, Oxford UP, Oxford/New York, ch. XI, p. 60.

89 19th-century women writers did not only refer to Staël but also to each other, by dedicating poems to each other or by writing memorial poems, e.g. Elizabeth Barrrett Browning's poems on Felicia Hemans, Letitia Elizabeth Landon and George Sand. It is obvious that these cross-references are intended to create a 'literature of their own' (Showalter) and serve to reinforce and back up the precarious situation of the woman writer in a century which saw any move into the 'public sphere' (even if this move only occurred in writing) as a potential transgression of ideal feminine behaviour.

90 For this reading see Joan DeJean (1991), 'Portrait of the Artist as Sappho', in Madelyn

One type of *Corinne* adaptation significantly creates a compromise in the form of marriage which may end the conflict and balance the claims of emotional expression and control. If one of the two antagonists dies, it is not the creative character inspired by Corinne but her angelic counterpart. Admittedly, marriage can be considered as a partial death, since the creative woman stops being creative, and turns into a wife. But both *Olive* (which lets all the major players in this context stay alive) and *The Half-Sisters*, as well as Grace Aguilar's story 'The Authoress' (1853) spend so much more time on the woman as writer or actress, than on her as the loving wife, that for the reader, the attractions of creativity may have eclipsed the possible boredom of marriage.

Geraldine Jewsbury's novel *The Half-Sisters*, published by Chapman and Hall in 1848, is a particularly interesting example. It was immediately associated with its French predecessor, as can be gathered from the review in *The Athenæum*, written by Jewsbury's friend Henry Fothergill Chorley. Chorley is not wholly satisfied with Jewsbury's second novel. He demands that she 'examine herself closely' because she attacks respectability and its restricting influence on creativity: 'Inasmuch as we would have it [Genius, G.S.] rule, are we bold to assert that its supremacy can only be assured when it clothes itself with "the form and the order", the charities, nay, and with the "respectabilities" – which it has been too much the habit to satirize.' Jewsbury is told that 'it rests with herself to do good service to the wide world of workers and dreamers',[91] thus clearly implying that she has so far fallen short of this task. Yet it is precisely her relative lack of didacticism and her ironic 'Arnoldian' treatment of middle class niceties which make *The Half-Sisters* interesting.

Jewsbury is scathing in her attack on middle class notions of propriety (p. 13).[92] A second element that sets *The Half-Sisters* off from other versions of the Sappho-*Corinne* story is the success that Bianca Pazzi is allowed to enjoy in England. Although it is her mixed background which have resulted in her 'southern' looks, and her acting talent is associated with her Italian origin, she is not smothered by English antipathy to Italian

---

Gutwirth et al. (eds), *Germaine de Staël. Crossing the Borders*, Rutgers UP, New Brunswick, N.J., p. 122-137, in particular p. 133ff.

91 [Henry F. Chorley] (18 March 1848), *The Athenæum*, p. 290.

92 The description of shallow conversation amongst respectable middle class women at a dinner party also includes a reference to 'Mrs Ellis's novels' which Jewsbury obviously thought little of (*The Half-Sisters*, p. 50). It is this kind of thinly veiled attack on middle class shallow earnestness which Chorley probably had in mind when he criticised Jewsbury's emphasis on the restrictions that result from 'respectability'.

'genius', like Corinne is. On the contrary, Bianca is transformed into the leading London actress and regularly brings the house down. The English are redeemed (they are less averse to real talent than is implied in *Corinne*) and the possibility of being a creative woman and a 'pure' woman at the same time is not discounted. Bianca's success and the effect she has on her audience is extraordinary, because not a cool 'English' reception with one round of applause but a burst of enthusiasm is the reaction to her talented performance:

> The curtain drew up! the play began. She was received with immense applause, and called before the curtain at the end of the first act. The enthusiasm went on increasing to the end, when it seemed to exceed all bounds; bouquets, bracelets, wreaths, every possible missile of admiration were flung at her in profusion. (p. 171)

And in spite of remarks and innuendo spread by the crowd of admirers and hangers-on, Bianca never succumbs to her passion for her suitor Conrad or is involved in any 'improper' way with another man.

When Conrad's passion for Bianca has finally died, and he decides that his type of woman is closer to what he sees in dreamy, delicate and modest Alice, Jewsbury inserts an extraordinary discussion on professional women into the narrative. Conrad and Lord Melton exchange their views and while Conrad deplores working women, Lord Melton defends them to a certain extent. Conrad argues that a professional life like Bianca's 'unsexes' a woman: 'A public life must deteriorate women ...; they lose all the beautiful ideal of their nature, all that is gentle, helpless, and confiding; they are obliged of necessity to keep a keen eye to their own interests ... and are reduced to cunning' (p. 216).

But most dangerous of all is their loss of virtue, not necessarily in the literal sense, 'but, in their dealings with men, they use their sex as a weapon; they play with the passions of men to some degree like courtesans' (loc. cit.). The paradox inherent in these arguments eludes Conrad – for how can a woman be at once 'unsexed' and 'like a courtesan'? But his emphasis on the dangerous attraction of passion is significant, because not the individual danger of passion is foregrounded, but rather the public consequences: women behaving like prostitutes, and men falling for their fake charms. The threat to his rigid idea of a gendered order of society is the point, since his ideal woman is supposed to be rational yet inferior to him, 'looking to me for guidance; a gentle, graceful timidity keeping down all display of her talents, a sense of propriety keeping her from all eccentric originality, either of thought or deed, her purity and delicacy of mind keeping her from all evil...' (p. 218).

Melton characterises this concept of femininity as 'a mixture of Oriental notions and European customs' (loc. cit.) and then goes on to voice his own opinion. Jewsbury makes him the spokesman for a programme that reminds one of Grey and Shirreff in its insistence on the need for guidance for women, but not on the grounds of inferiority, but because they are restricted by convention. Again, it is not votes for women or complete independence that he argues for (p. 222), but individual development of talent:

> Women are put under plenty of conventional restraint, there is plenty of punishment in store if they go astray, but no broad principle is ever given on which they may take their stand; ... Women from their birth are kept from that knowledge which contact with the actual things of life alone can give; they are placed in a state of pupillage; ... they do need guidance – they call for it earnestly and passionately, and what is the guidance they find? – an appeal to their sense of gracefulness! ... no higher motive is ever suggested to them than that of being agreeable to us; ... A woman is a rational being, with reasonable soul and human flesh subsisting, and yet she is never educated for her own sake, to enable her to lead her own life better; her qualities and talents are not considered sacred personalities; but are modified, like the feet of Chinese women, to meet an arbitrary taste. (p. 218f.)

With the image of the tied Chinese feet, Jewsbury has found an extraordinarily strong metaphor for what she here makes a male character deplore: the restrictions placed upon (talented) women and the lack of 'higher principles' and education which would ensure their development.

In the end it is not passion coupled with creativity but affection and the prospect of motherhood which lie in store for Bianca. Passion kills, as is illustrated by Alice's disastrous attachment to Conrad which is formed once Conrad has rejected Bianca. Again, as in *Passion and Principle*, gradual friendship and tenderness are the feelings which Jewsbury seems to recommend by making Bianca slowly realise her love for Lord Melton. But in spite of this watered-down variety of emotion, feeling is not described as creativity's killer, since Bianca's talent does not die with her love for Conrad. It is not the power of feeling that provokes a crisis, as in *Corinne*, where the protagonist slowly loses her powers even before Oswald rejects her. Rather it is the fact that Conrad does not return Bianca's feelings which make it difficult for her to continue her career.

And once she has realised that she loves Lord Melton, it is the insecurity which distracts her from her chosen task of elevating her profession to one of the 'fine arts' (p. 254), because she fears that she has offended Melton and that he will never return to her (p. 354). And although she herself no longer acts after her marriage, she ensures that her own talents are handed on to a younger version of herself, the singer Clara Broughton (who also marries). And just like the silver lining on *Corinne's* horizon, embodied by Oswald's and Lucile's daughter Juliette, the image of a brighter future for the creative woman is at least hinted at: 'It is a great mistake to suppose that genius is shown in one special mode of manifestations alone; – it inspires its possessor, and enables him to feel equal to all situations' (p. 391).

This sense of compromise and optimism, in spite of the descriptions of hardship and anguish for women, can also be observed in Grace Aguilar's story 'The Authoress', taken from the enormously successful collection *Home Scenes and Heart Studies* (1853), published in London by Groombridge & Sons.[93] Grace Aguilar, also the author of a complete Corinne-adaptation entitled *Women's Friendship* (1850 or 1851), defends the woman-as-author in her story. The talented writer Clara Stanley, the opposite of the frivolous scribbling lady, is rejected by Dudley Granville because his notion of literary women was modelled on his mother, 'one of those shallow pretenders to literature which throw such odium upon all its female professors' (p. 229). Clara does not sacrifice morality, modesty or reason to her talents since she believes in 'making her talents a source of usefulness as well as of pleasure' (loc. cit.). She is so successful that she becomes a household name but has to move to the country to become a teacher where she works as the epitome of the educator of the heart because her family has a 'horror of blueism' (p. 232, 238). Meanwhile, Dudley Granville has made a bad marriage with a frivolous women who soon dies. His child is sent to the boarding school where Clara happens to teach, and his daughter falls dangerously ill (p. 238f.). Of course it is Clara who 'devoted herself, day and night, to the young sufferer. Her affections had never before been so warmly enlisted; ... it seemed as if the child must be something nearer to her than in reality she was' (p. 239). This is indeed the case: Dudley Granville reappears and learns that it was Clara who saved his daughter. They fall in love again and marry but Clara continues to write, not without explaining to Granville that at her age she is no longer

93 Subsequent page references in my text are to this edition.

a woman he might mould to his wishes: 'I cannot draw back from my literary path, for I feel it accomplishes good' (p. 243). But how has she convinced the declared hater of literary women who has observed her and wonders how she can combine 'so perfectly the literary with the domestic characters?' (p. 242). She answers with a bold assertion of the usefulness of her chosen career and spells out the terms of the compromise which the story celebrates as the ideal of the woman writer: '"... it is impossible to divide [the literary and the domestic characters]. Perfect in them, indeed, I am not; but though I know it is possible for woman to be domestic without being literary ... to my feelings, it is not possible to be more than usually gifted without being domestic"' (p. 242).

This sense of compromise was not to last: the assertive *fin-de-siècle* women writers were no longer interested in reconciling domesticity, morality and tender feeling with creativity, as one can for instance observe in Vernon Lee's story 'Lady Tal' (1896).[94] An effeminate novelist helps Lady Tal rewrite her manuscript *Christina*. The encounter of this large-boned, cigarette-smoking, independent and somewhat slapdash amateur author with the repressed Henry-James-type 'artist' ends in an offer of marriage that she makes him. He is unable to resist Lady Tal's ambiguous attractions and significantly it is he who needs her as a creative inspiration, but not just as his muse, but as his writing partner. As she explains to him: '"We ought to write that novel together, because I've given you the ending – and also because I really can't manage another all by myself, now that I've got accustomed to having my semicolons put in for me –"' (p. 261). Although she offers him marriage as well, it is the writing partnership which she focuses on as the future basis of their relationship. He will be responsible for 'putting in the semicolons', while she will be the main creator – and no hint of duty, caring or submission is included.

With this bold assertion of feeling and creativity no longer in need of control, the move away from the 'proper novel' and its amalgamation of feeling and duty, expression and control, is complete. But *Corinne* also supplied another possibility for women writers to focus on the tensions inherent in the concept of the emotional woman, and the compromise between domesticity and emotion: feeling and 'national' character. This is a staple element of the discourses on emotions which does not automatically subvert them, on the contrary, many 19th-century writers use

[94] Reprinted in Elaine Showalter's (1998) [1993] anthology of *fin-de-siècle* stories, *Daughters of Decadence. Women Writers of the Fin-de-Siècle*, Virago, London, pp. 192-261.

nationalist notions to bolster their idea of the superior English middle class habitus. But since in some instances the idea of the national 'other' can be used to question some of the elements of this habitus, the final section of this chapter explores the possibilities created by the woman as passionate 'other'.

Olive Varcoe This Eastern twist in her character seemed in English eyes a moral blindness, whence might spring all manner of sins and cruelties. And the passion, the leaven of fire in her nature, still further startled the calmer, colder hearts around her. ... A strange girl, dangerous to herself and others; vindictive, yet generous; false, yet fascinating and tender; a girl whom it was impossible to hate, and perilous to love.[95]

This is how in her Cornish thriller *Olive Varcoe* (1868) the author F.E.M. Notley introduces the female protagonist. The novel takes up what is first dramatised in *Corinne*: the conflict of the passionate woman in a national context. The 'Eastern twist' in Olive Varcoe's character goes together with 'passion, the leaven of fire' and both are modelled on the opposition set up by Staël between 'England' and a national 'other'. In *Corinne*, both 'England' and 'Italy' are used to symbolise certain values. Whereas 'England' is represented simultaneously as narrow-minded, traditional, aristocratic and socially restrictive, in particular for women, it is also the country of order and reason. 'Italy' by contrast is described as warm-hearted, emotional, artistic, inspirational, less narrow-minded but also as more chaotic, more volatile. This contrast can be explained not only by Germaine de Staël's European background, her republican ideals and her personal experience of England and Italy.[96] It is also typical for a period during which a topic that was to dominate much of the 19th century gained momentum: national character and nationalism.[97]

References to national 'characteristics' are common in the discourses

---

[95] Derrick, F. [= Frances E.M. Notley], (1872) [1868], *Olive Varcoe: A Novel*, new edition, Virtue & Co., London, Virtue & Yorston, New York, p. 27.

[96] Cf. Doris Y. Kadish (1991), 'Narrating the French Revolution: The Example of *Corinne*', in Gutwirth et al. (eds), *Germaine de Staël*, pp. 113-121 on *Corinne* as a republican text and Corinne as the ideal embodiment of aristocratic and bourgeois values, and Gill Frith (1995-96), 'Embodying the Nation: Gender and Performance in Women's Fiction', in *New Formations*, vol. 27, pp. 98-113.

[97] For an account of the rise of the nation since the 1780s, and its importance for the 19th century, see Eric Hobsbawm (1992) [1990], *Nations and Nationalism Since 1780. Programme, Myth, Reality*, new and revised edition, Cambridge UP, Cambridge and Linda Colley (1992), *Forging the Nation 1707-1837*, Yale UP, London/New York.

on emotions. A medical publication such as William Cooke's *A Commentary of Medical and Moral Life; or Mind and the Emotions* contains a distinction based on character and emotions which contrasts the 'uncivilised' Chinese with the more 'advanced' Europeans.[98] A similar opposition is used by Herbert Spencer when he explains how 'moral sentiments' cannot be expected in countries where 'savages' live.[99] John Stuart Mill's essays on poetry attribute different emotional reactions to poetry and narrative to 'Tartars and Arabs' and 'civilized' people respectively.[100] And he contrasts 'French sentiment' and culture with the more sober and less audience-oriented English variety.[101] These examples illustrate how widespread was the notion that nations differ, that some were considered superior to others, and that 'national character' was often believed to be innate and unchanging.

One can conceive of two possible connections between 'nation' and emotion.[102] Firstly, following Benedict Anderson's constructivist concept of nations as 'imagined communities', much of the idea of distinct nations relies on an affective tie with an entity which its adherents and members

---

98 'Perhaps there are no people less interesting, as a race, than the Chinese, and they are reported to have a remarkable similarity of physical and mental character. ... Nor is this sameness confined to the body, it extends also to the mind. *Constitutional bluntness of feeling*, grossness in their enjoyments, and little capacity for mental delight, are ascribed to them in general; but exceptions exist, and it is allowed that, even among them, there are found persons actuated by noble sentiments' (p. 92f., my emphasis, G.S.). Herbert Spencer ([13]1887) [1873] also uses the Chinese as an example of the national 'other' in *The Study of Sociology*, Kegan Paul, Trench & Co., London, p. 365, as well as France and French sentiment (p. 153f., 157, 158, p. 175), in particular with regard to the 'passions' excited by the French Revolution. The Chinese also turn up in Alexander Bain's ([2]1865), *The Emotions and the Will*, Longmans & Co., London, p. 110, and he also criticises 'excessive Oriental politeness' (op. cit., p. 123) and contrasts it with his preferred English reserve.

99 Herbert Spencer (1 April 1871), 'Morals and Moral Sentiments', in *Fortnightly Review*, pp. 419-432, in particular p. 427.

100 Mill (1981) [1867], 'Thoughts on Poetry and Its Varieties', in particular p. 345.

101 Op. cit., p. 353. That the French are most often used as a contrast to English culture and 'character' can be explained by the impact of the French Revolution and the Napoleonic Wars which once again brought the old rivalry between England and France to a head. When the reference to other cultures and countries is European, France is the most common example mentioned in the texts studied for this book.

102 See the useful collection of essays *Nation und Emotion*, edited by Etienne François et al. (1995), Vandenhoeck & Ruprecht, Göttingen (Kritische Studien zur Geschichtswissenschaft, vol. 10), for an introduction to this topic. For the relation between emotion, nation and the national 'other', see Robert C. Young (1995), *Colonial Desire. Hybridity in Theory, Culture and Race*, Routledge, London/New York.

have to create and recreate in their minds and hearts at any given time.[103] Secondly, Victorian national(ist) discourses (and practice) can also be considered as a further 'safe place' for emotionality, perhaps comparable to the 19th-century concept of religious experience, certain circumscribed areas such as the Victorian theatre with its emphasis on cathartic melodrama, and the domestic sphere. In addition, nationalism could contribute to the emergence and bolstering of a middle class habitus because it translates collective belonging into individual physico-emotional experience. This can be observed in Sarah Ellis's description of the 'aggregate force' of patriotism influenced by moral power. Again, the use of conventional emotion metaphors ('fire', 'pulsation of a kindred heart') in this passage from *The Education of the Heart* (1868) indicates that here emotionality may find an outlet. As with ecstatic religious feelings, the need for control is less important, since 'the fire already burning' is directed not at another human being but towards a higher aim:

> It is then that the grasp of a hand, the flashing of an eye, the pulsation of a kindred heart, doubles and redoubles the fire already burning, kindles new life and energy to join the ranks of the enterprise, and serve and struggle and die, if it must be, in the good cause.[104]

Her emotionalised representation of patriotic feeling is more soberly described in John Abercrombie's definition of patriotism, which he considers 'the result of a combination of the other affections' and not as a distinct human principle. Abercrombie explicitly associates patriotism with social and moral order, indicating how 'zeal' for one's own country can be combined with social control.[105] Implicitly, Abercrombie supports the assumption that Britain's 'prosperity' needs the support of its people, and that social and moral order are indispensable for Britain's advancement. When Sarah Ellis argues in like manner for Britain's superiority, the emphasis lies less on internal support (patriotism) than on external distinction (nationalism): '... in a race of competition England has no cause to be afraid' and '[a]s a nation England stands proudly forth as the advocate of improvement – of progress, of all that tends to advancement,

---

[103] See Benedict Anderson (1983), *Imagined Communities. Reflections on the Origin and Spread of Nationalism*, Verso, London.

[104] Sarah Ellis (1869), *The Education of the Heart: Woman's Best Work*, Hodder and Stoughton, London, p. 85f.

[105] John Abercrombie (1833), *The Philosophy of the Moral Feelings*, John Murray, London, p. 76f.

so that the present may be better than the past, and the future better still'.[106]

But in the following passages my focus lies on a different aspect. Writers seem to have explored the space created by this 'nationalist' discourse for a more specific purpose, apart from the pervasive need to distinguish the English 'imperial race' from the more 'savage' and emotionally less controlled natives in the colonies, and the morally less reliable Continentals. By using elements of the conventional national(ist) discourses, they create a fictional space for passion, thereby pushing the discourses on emotions to its limits. For women writers, using the nationalist discourse to create passionate female protagonists allowed them another opening for unusual characters, sometimes linked to the topic explained in the context of *Passion and Principle*: the call for female education, useful occupation and an unrestricted outlet for female talent.[107]

Again, it is Staël's novel *Corinne* that provides the model for this creative use of a common element in the Victorian discourses on the feelings. In novels such as Charlotte Brontë's *Jane Eyre* (1847), but even more so in Dinah Mulock Craik's *Olive* (1850) and in F.E.M. Notley's *Olive Varcoe* (1868), the discourses on emotions are simultaneously affirmed and subverted in the attempts at redefining passion and femininity on the basis of 'national characteristics'. How 'national otherness' and creativity was combined in the eyes of many writers and painters can be illustrated by an exotic image by Ingres, entitled 'Odalisque and Slave' (1842) (fig. 5.2). In the background one can see a Black slave, a dark beauty – the Odalisque – playing a string instrument and a white woman, sprawling almost naked on a bed. Passionate emotion is represented by one woman and creativity by another one, but in their exotic context both together evoke the power of 'foreign' female passion, dangerously paired with indolence and music-making.

If one confronts the two groups of characters that all the novels inspired by *Corinne* are based on, an interesting pattern emerges. Corinne herself, as well as Bianca Pazzi in *The Half-Sisters*, Aurora Leigh, and Maggie Tulliver in *The Mill on the Floss* (and many more of the countless Sapphos and Corinnes in the various poems on the topic) are all half-Italian, or in Maggie Tulliver's case, at least symbolically related to a non-English

---

[106] Ellis (1869), *The Education of the Heart*, p. 150, p. 49.

[107] Isobel Armstrong has shown that women poets made use of the same strategy: Isobel Armstrong (1993), '"A Music of Thine Own": Women's Poetry', in id., *Victorian Poetry. Poetry, Poetics and Politics*, Routledge, London/New York, pp. 318-377, in particular p. 325.

'race', namely the gypsies.[108] Passion is closely associated with national 'otherness', but also with intelligence and creativity. Some of the novels which belong to the same group change the pattern. In *Passion and Principle*, Louisa is less passionate than Ellen and better able to control her feelings, but it is she who is creative, and both are English.

In *Olive*, exotic passion is embodied by a more positive version of Charlotte Brontë's Bertha Mason in *Jane Eyre*, named Christal Manners, also a 'half-caste'. But her creative counterpart is her entirely Anglo-Scottish half-sister Olive Rothesay, who belongs more to the other group of fictional women, the domestic and angelic variations on Corinne's half-sister Lucile (Lucy in *The Mill on the Floss*, Alice in *The Half-Sisters* and Eleanor Maristowe in *Olive Varcoe*).

But while in *Jane Eyre* the mad and passionate woman has to be shut up in the attic and then dies, and a number of the above-mentioned black-haired Corinnes commit suicide or perish in other ways, in *Olive Varcoe* the passionate woman is given more space. The reasons for this lie in the subversive potential offered by the female protagonist after whom the novel is named. Olive Varcoe comes back to 'haunt' her English family, she upsets their aristocratic values with her unconventional attitudes (although Notley does not go as far as George Eliot in combining 'otherness' with calls for specific advances for women). What at first appears to be an affirmation of 'Englishness' as represented by proud Sir Hilton and insipid Eleanor, because Olive's 'Eastern' fashion seems so inferior to their controlled behaviour, is later transformed. Englishness is shown to be dangerous because it is repressive. Although the novel's protagonist undergoes a development and ends up being less passionate than at the outset, her rival not only dies, it is the 'half-caste' Olive who wins her man and educates a number of hearts as she goes along. So much room is given to a passionate woman that the attractions of depicting her outweigh the conventional happy ending with its subdued emotionality, tenderness, and marriage.

Olive Varcoe, written by Frances Eliza Millett Notley, first came out in 1868 (serialised in the *Family Herald* and then published as a three-decker) and had a second single-volume edition in 1872, published by Virtue & Co in London and in New York by Virtue & Yorston.[109] It was later translated

---

108 Eliot (1985) [1979] [1860], *The Mill on the Floss*, 1, chap. 11, 'Maggie Tries to Run Away from her Shadow', p. 168ff.

109 My analysis is based on the version published in 1872; page references are to this edition.

into several languages and dramatised three times, without however being performed. The novel draws on several conventions: the sensation novels and plays of the 1860s,[110] early crime fiction, Pre-Raphaelite imagery, the regional novel, stories of female rivalry and aristocratic pride. Olive Varcoe is clearly indebted to characters like Corinne, Christal Manners, Bianca Pazzi, Aurora Leigh and Maggie Tulliver in the presentation of its female protagonist.[111] Although the novel is not very original and Notley even occasionally loses sight of minor plot lines, it is even for a modern reader quite a thrilling read and contains some idiosyncratic and effective elements, e.g. the multiple narrative perspectives, the Cornish setting, a surprising lack of interest in maternal figures and most of all the fascination with the woman of passion.[112]

---

110 Cf. Ann Cvetkovich (1992), *Mixed Feelings. Feminism, Mass Culture, and Victorian Sensationalism*, Rutgers UP, New Brunswick, N.J., on the function of emotions in sensation novels: 'The readers who are excited by the sensational lure of their mysteries [the sensation novels' mysteries, G.S.] are provided with experiences of affect that are ultimately regulated and controlled. The solution to the mysteries rationalizes intense affect and makes it safe. In the process of explaining the affective dilemmas of private life, the sensation novel performs the cultural work of representing social problems as affective problems and hence confirming the importance of emotional expression to middle-class life' (p. 7).

111 An emphasis on black hair, the power to 'bewitch' and seduce are the shared traits of all these characters. These images belong to the tradition of the 'dark lady' or the demonic woman. But what might at first glance seem to carry negative connotations is used in *The Mill on the Floss* (and many other Victorian novels) as the sole possible expression for strong and passionate female characters. The 'demonic code' is the only code available to authors who wanted to go beyond the conventions of the angel in the house, as Kim Reynolds and Nicola Humble (1993) have convincingly argued in their study *Victorian Heroines. Representations of Femininity in Nineteenth-Century Literature and Art*, Harvester Wheatsheaf, Hemel Hempstead, p. 89ff. and in particular p. 92f. Similar imagery and descriptions can also be found in Elizabeth Barrett Browning's *Aurora Leigh* of which George Eliot thought so much, and it is the inherently erotic nature of the dark, passionate, talented woman to which the Victorian readership reacted. In particular the focus on sensuality was not to the taste of many reviewers (but perhaps one reason for the success of *The Mill on the Floss* or Rhoda Broughton's less intellectual but racier novels). See for instance the anonymous review of *The Mill on the Floss* in *The Saturday Review* 9, 14 April 1860, pp. 470-471, which criticises Eliot, Charlotte Brontë and a third source for sensuous women, George Sand, for 'linger[ing] on the description of the physical sensations that accompany the meeting of hearts in love'. Reprinted in Stuart Hutchinson (ed) (1996), *George Eliot. Critical Assessments*, vol. 1, Helm Information, Mountfield, pp. 118-122, quotation p. 121, which contains many more such reviews of *The Mill on the Floss*.

112 Geraldine Jewsbury (5 December 1868) reviewed the novel in *The Athenæum*, No. 2145, pp. 750-51, and again did not discover that the author is a woman. She criticises

Olive Varcoe tells the story of the Cornish gentleman Sir Hilton Trewavas and his brother John. Trewavas is torn between his cousin – Olive Varcoe, of Eastern origin – and the more suitable Eleanor Maristowe, whom his brother John secretly loves. Eleanor is murdered and everybody suspects Olive who has to flee the country. After many turns and twists of plot it is revealed that it was John, who dies of madness, who murdered Eleanor because he could not love her. Trewavas and Olive are reconciled and marry but only after he has shed his excessive pride and she has left some of her passionate nature behind.

From the start Olive Varcoe is represented as a seductive Eastern beauty, whose 'large black eyes', 'glossy black hair' and 'ripe lips' (p. 2f.) all affect her cousin Hilton Trewavas so much that he is tempted to succumb to her charms, instead of continuing in his suit for Eleanor Maristowe. His attempt at controlling Olive's seductive manner towards him, which she emphasises by saying '"[w]ords are so tame, they never say anything that I want to express with my whole heart"' (p. 4), is scorned by her: 'Olive's dark eyes flashed at Sir Hilton's words, and she flung his hand away with an angry gesture. "There, you have undone your kindness now", she said. "I understand you; I have not acted up to your stiff English notions of propriety ..."' (loc. cit.). The difference between English behaviour and her foreign background is used as the force that drives the plot. Olive's origins are not glossed over: she is Lady Trewavas's nephew's daughter, probably born by a slave from Smyrna (p. 7f.). She appears to John Trewavas as a witch with superhuman abilities (p. 9) and is told off for her tendency to lie. Olive defends the outbreaks of her 'Eastern blood': '"You know, if I am neither Cornish nor English, I cannot help it, can I?"' (p. 24).

The narrator places Olive's character traits firmly within a context of national difference. Inventing things 'Eastern fashion' is considered 'un-English', yet her 'opponents', as they are called by the narrator, are not

---

Olive Varcoe as a 'flashy tale' but acknowledges that its author 'has the power to do something better ...'. Although Jewsbury admits that the novel is exciting, she thinks little of its 'practical impossibility' and improbability, and its 'high-coloured exaggeration of sentiment'. But she does admit that *Olive Varcoe* is cleverly written and that the representation of passion and distress 'are well given' and praises the interest in character rather than 'mere incident'. Jewsbury's unease seems to go beyond a distaste for 'common and vulgar incidents of a detective-police affair'. On the whole, the ambivalent nature of this review reflects the ambivalence that readers must have felt when confronted with Olive Varcoe, someone with 'such questionable endowments and antecedents' (p. 751).

angry with her: '... it was permitted her to do and say things that in an English lady would be inadmissible' (p. 27). It is her mixed origin which simultaneously allows Olive more space and which is the cause for her ambivalent nature, represented in the quotation opening this final section. Her passionate nature, her intensity of feeling, her unusual combination of tenderness and vindictiveness, generosity and falsehood are explicitly contrasted with the 'calmer, colder hearts around her' (loc. cit.) and expressed in the familiar metaphorical shape of 'flashing eyes', hands 'burning hot' and 'a glow like fire on her cheeks' (e.g. p. 24f.). When the tension rises after Eleanor's body has been discovered, Olive's alleged 'evil temper', the murder and the weather are associated in a passage in which passion is used as the metaphorical origin of a storm:

> The day closed in storm, with a north-west wind, rolling in upon the beach a heavy sea, which echoed and thundered far inland. ...
>
> As the darkness grew intense, as the winds rose, and the rain fell, a fear and a gloom that the sunshine had held back crept through corridor and hall, gathering the servants into groups, and chilling the hearts of the stoutest. Each one knew that a murderer hid amongst them; ...
>
> The desire in the hearts of all that the murderer should be discovered and taken grew in intensity, and the suspicions gathering like shadows round the figure of Olive crept closer to her, pointing her out as a mark for indignation and loathing. (p. 153f.)

Olive represents a destabilising element, in that she literally and symbolically questions the seemingly clear-cut boundaries of Englishness, illustrating that what constituted English 'national identity' was by no means a foregone conclusion, but rather a process of constant refashioning. As it turns out, the 'Eastern' character is not only necessary to reaffirm Englishness, but rather to remould it, so that true feeling instead of mere family pride will become the leading principle. It is not difficult to discover that this type of education of the heart is inspired by the middle class criticism of empty aristocratic feeling which requires the transformation that Olive, as a representative of a different culture, initiates. Interestingly, the middle class concept of 'true feeling' here needs help from a 'foreigner' to be brought to bear on the stubborn landed gentry from Cornwall.

The death of Olive's opponent Eleanor in a cold pond, Ophelia-style, is all the more fitting in view of her emotional coldness contrasting with Olive's 'Eastern' passion. The gothic discovery scene reminds one of John

Everett Millais's famous 'Ophelia' (1851-52) which highlights the virginal body of the dead young woman. In the novel, this innocence is later revealed to have screened a manipulative woman, playing with her femininity and seeming weakness, which ultimately results in her death (fig. 5.3). The perspective of Olive's neighbour and suitor, Charles Vigo, is chosen to represent the first view of the dead girl:

> ... the dead face of Eleanor Maristowe floated upwards, pale and pure, just beneath the surface of the water. A huge beech branch lying level, with leaves dipping in the pool, hid her body; but between the shining green gleamed the lilac robe, and the small white hands crossed on her bosom.
>
> Done to death, cruelly murdered, there she lay, wonderfully beautiful, the expression on her face calm as might be an angel's sleeping in Paradise.
>
> Stooping and holding by the branch, Charles Vigo raised her in his right arm. Then he saw her fair hair streaming over her shoulders, and the crimson cord that Olive had worn tied about her wrists. (p. 113)

But as it turns out, Olive's 'crimson cord' is only tied about her wrists because Olive had lost it after their quarrel, and John used it in his mad frenzy to win power over Eleanor.

Although passion is in a way responsible for Eleanor's murder, it is not simply Olive's 'Eastern blood' which is the cause of the disaster. On the contrary, it will emerge that for all her strong emotions, she will be the one to teach Hilton to be more humble and admit that his pride had something to do with the crisis. If he had acknowledged his feelings for Olive and had let Eleanor, although she would have made him the more 'suitable' wife, be taken by John, no murder would have had to be committed. Nevertheless, John's passion is indeed conceptualised conventionally as a danger to himself and to others: '"Passion, and anger, and jealousy, have wrought an evil work among us – a work that will take him for its next victim ..."' (p. 174), as Olive explains, and she is right, since John goes mad and dies. John is an interesting case of a man who, unable to marry the woman he loves and then unable to control his passion, succumbs to the violence of emotion and ultimately his weak nerves.[113]

Although Olive takes some of the blame, because out of spite she egged John on (p. 363) as she says, and is transformed into a much more domesticated creature by the end of the novel, the transformation of power

[113] Cf. also Wood (2001), *Passion and Pathology*, 'Nervous Sensibility and Ideals of Masculinity', pp. 59-109.

relations between her and Hilton are the more significant change in the text. Olive, the narrator states, '[w]ho, as a poor relation, despised and dependant, had fought with fiery impatience against her chain; she who, when galled and miserable, had been proud, fierce, and impetuous – is now the gentlest of women' (p. 425). But Sir Hilton has had to undergo an even more significant development, and it is not only told in a few paragraphs, but shown in a sequence of passages, a narrative technique which has more impact than mere telling.

Shortly after the murder, Hilton has his first insight into the part he played in the drama. But his reflection is taken over by the narrator who explains the power of passion. Significantly, not the passions themselves are vilified – they are shown to be 'earnest and true; weapons for good or evil' but it is the misuse of them which is criticised. 'Crushing' a heart for pleasure is the root of suffering, as the narrator explains in language rich in imagery (passions 'ooze upwards', and may 'sow[ ] seeds ... of sorrow and of sin') – something that Hilton only realises at the very end of the novel:

> Vainly he might tell himself that hundreds of men and women had done idly what he had done, and no tragedy, no deed of blood had followed. No, his conscience answered; not visibly, perchance, had crimes come, but surely sorrow has been heaped upon sorrow through the sins of heartless vanity .... Not always certainly with the dagger and the bowl, and the red hands of murder, but such things are. And at times, when they ooze upwards through the smiling surface of life, and appear in our daily journals, they startle for a moment the idle and careless into a passing thought of fear. For one brief instant a light flashes through the soul, showing that human passions are earnest and true; weapons for good or evil, and that man, or that woman who dares for pleasure, or for vanity, to crush a heart, and fling it away bruised and bleeding, sows seeds in it of sorrow and of sin, of which fleshy eye may not see the root, but which the spirit of the sufferer feels, as he curses in bitterness the hand that planted them. (p. 123)

Hilton asks Olive to flee the country, which she refuses. She in turn asks for a final mark of affection between them, a touch of his hand or a kiss which he declines (p. 184). Olive appears humbled and ashamed when during the same scene she accepts Charles Vigo's offer of support and marriage (p. 189). Although Hilton tries to intervene, she is adamant and defends her decision. Significantly, she argues with an embodied notion of feeling, stating that '"His flesh and blood are not stone and ice, like yours. His heart is not narrow, and hard, and unbelieving"' (p. 191). But when it comes to their final parting, he asks for her hand or a cousin's kiss, which she now refuses, in the first of several passages which highlight the inversion of power between them: 'Sir Hilton's face was scarcely less pale than hers, as he stood before her irresolute and trembling. Small, fragile as she was, she was more powerful to subdue him than a lion, and he dared not put forth his hand and touch her' (p. 191f.). The importance of the scene is also indicated by their physical reaction, as well as by the use of animal imagery.

Although after her many trials in Ireland and Paris, Olive is subdued and ill, she knows that she has saved Hilton Trewavas, and most of all his pride, by keeping quiet about her knowledge of the murderer, and appearing to take the blame herself (p. 351). When Hilton comes to visit her, he acknowledges his share in Eleanor's death and promises to 'forgive' her for the murder, thereby showing how strong his family pride still is. This hinders them from meeting on an equal footing:

> It seemed to him that they had changed places, and she was the accuser now, while he stood, humbled and abashed, before her, she was no longer the wilful, petted child, or the passionate girl, whose humble, caressing tenderness he had first encouraged, then rejected. No; she was a woman now, chastened and subdued – by a sense of guilt, he thought – and prouder and colder in her repentance than he would have deemed it possible that the fiery and loving Olive Varcoe could ever be .... (p. 367)

It is not her guilt, of course, that has changed her, but her continuing love and passion for the Trewavas family which is the cause for her suffering. She has changed, but although she may have shed that side of her passionate nature which was potentially disruptive (her vindictiveness and jealousy), strong feeling is still present. When Hilton finally realises this, the inversion of power relations and his education of the heart is completed as he acknowledges Olive's greater power in bowing to her 'as one bows to a queen'. Again, the transformation of power relations is described as embodied and it is noteworthy that Olive, for all her seemingly more subdued feeling, as the representative of the 'East' is allowed the role of 'queen' which underscores once again the fragility of Hilton's 'English' concept of feeling: 'As Olive turned her head she met Sir Hilton's gaze, and he bowed to her as one bows to a queen. To him all worth on earth was enshrined in her – the little, weak, passionate creature, whom he had once deemed too mean to love' (p. 383).

In the end, Vigo gives up Olive and marries her former pupil instead. Olive finally realises that Hilton has changed, that his name and his house and his pride are no longer important to him, and that although she considers her own actions unimportant, he finally values them. In spite of the narrator's assertion that happiness does not make a story, again an indication that writers thought the process of educating the heart more important than its outcome, the readers do get a final romantic scene which leaves nothing to the imagination in terms of the happiness that Olive and Hilton may expect. What may appear as a conventional scene in which the man asks the woman to be his wife again illustrates the transformation: Hilton has to ask Olive to return to him. And befitting such an important scene, the narrator barely intrudes, and lets non-verbal communication with a final emphasis on Olive's foreign origin ('her large dark eyes') carry the message:

> "Will you come to Trewavas, Olive?"
> "Yes, I will come", replied Olive, in a low voice.
> "As a daughter, Olive?" he asked.
> She did not answer in words; but as her large dark eyes met his, Sir Hilton gathered her in his arms and kissed her. (p. 423)

Olive Varcoe illustrates how far the boundaries of the discourses on emotions could be pushed. Indebted more to sensation novels than to the 'proper novel', Notley spends more time with the attractions of passion than with its control, although she still decides to use the education-of-the-heart plot to provide her readers with a conventional 'Victorian' ending. The novel shows that the discourses on emotions move gradually towards an emphasis on expression, and leave control more and more behind. This tendency could already be observed in Darwin's text on expression, which, in spite of some features typical for the discourses on emotions, already indicated a gradual shift, not only in terms of new scientific paradigms being confirmed (evolution, physiology), but also in a relative lack of concern with order and control. In particular with regard to the central role of the body, it is obvious that by mid-century Keble's 'modest reserve' is being pushed more and more into the background. It has to make room for 'bodies' succumbing to passion, a passion which would become more and more sexualised towards the end of the century, and less and less in need of the national 'other' as its permitted embodiment: for instance in Joseph Conrad's *Heart of Darkness* (1902), passion may still be associated with a 'savage' nation, but it is an Englishman or at least a European man who is affected by it. But perhaps most interesting in *Olive Varcoe* is the destabilising of 'Englishness' and the stress that is laid on the need to transform the ‘cold-hearted’ habitus of the landed gentry. This can only be achieved with the help not just of any passionate woman, but of a foreign passionate woman. For all the popularity of the idea of the superior English or British nation, even a middle-brow novel such as *Olive Varcoe* can contain startling elements which question an apparently stable ‘imagined community’ and empower the Eastern ‘other’ by using its alleged greater capacity of feeling.

6 Modern Passion? Concluding Remarks

> I submit that the introduction of machinery, the diminution of the sense of personal dealing out of commercial transactions, and the perfecting of our administrative system, establishing everywhere the triumph of the laws, are what may be termed mechanical influences operating with gradually increasing effect in enforcing a comparative inaction of the passions, and that in the repose of the feelings this secured religion may be expected to have freer scope than it has ever had previously – the two causes conjoined pointing to a degree of civilization far beyond the range of our present conception. Men will necessarily grow milder, and life will be embellished by the quieter feelings, purified and enlarged, while the rougher, turbulent emotions will die away.[1]

This surprising and optimistic hypothesis, published in *The Cornhill Magazine* under the heading 'Machinery and the Passions', seems to confirm the view that the 19th century is a period of rapid change on all levels.[2] And it appears to support what I began with: the initial contention that in a period of social and political upheaval the discourses on emotions would have to react and reflect upon these transformations. Only slightly later, in 1868, an anonymous journalist made similar claims. 'Modern Passion', he says in *Once a Week*, is 'of a milder type than [that] of our forefathers' and characterised by 'the fear of ridicule, the sensitive deference to public opinion, the sure and speedy retribution attending any act of violence, the strong dislike to scenes and fuss ...' – in other words: by (internalised) control.[3] These journalists go even further than my

---

1 Anon (1865), 'Machinery and the Passions', in *The Cornhill Magazine*, vol. 11, pp. 541-47, quotation p. 547.

2 According to the *Wellesley Index of Victorian Periodicals*, the author of the article was William Cyples (1831-82), a philosophical writer. It is interesting to note that Cyples argues against two common 19th-century opinions: Carlyle's classic opposition to the 'Age of Machinery' (*Signs of the Times*, 1829) which many writers, e.g. Dickens, were to take up, and Herbert Spencer's ([13]1887) [1873] liberal attitude which criticised state intervention and saw its administrative system as counterproductive and dangerous. *The Study of Sociology*, Kegan Paul, Trench & Co., London, p. 169.

3 Anon (1868), 'Modern Passion', in *Once a Week*, vol. 2, pp. 570-572, quotation p. 570.

original hypothesis: they believe that actual emotional experience changed in the 19th century. While the emphasis on Victorian innovation and historical difference may or may not have been an accurate representation of mid-Victorian feelings, my emotionological analysis has led to the emergence of a different pattern and it is on this level only that I am able to argue.

In terms of Victorian emotionology, then, it is not change but continuity which distinguishes the discourses on emotions. Key emotion words taken over from previous periods, in particular the 18th century, continue to be used in all texts on the feelings, be they novels or treatises, poems or pamphlets. Although one can observe semantic shifts over the centuries, the meanings of the words affection, emotion, feeling, passion, sensibility and sentiment remain surprisingly stable in the period covered in this book. But specific meanings have not disappeared entirely – the concept of commotion inherent in the older meaning of 'emotion' is for instance still present in the wider semantic context of the discourses on emotions: the emphasis on social and political order in relation to feeling is not only explicitly demanded but also implicitly performed in many texts. This performative element is characteristic of the discourses on emotions. In their predictable repetitiveness, the semantically and discursively contextualised keywords work like 'veiled instructions', like feeling rules *en miniature*, thus performing what many authors explicitly call for in their texts on the emotions.

What they demand is again influenced by continuity more than by change, new invention, unheard of topics or novel contexts. The central paradigm that orders the discourses on emotions in the 19th century is the relation between expression and control, and linked to it, pain and pleasure. Some authors are aware of the fact that many emotions do not fall neatly into either category. But the repetition of this Aristotelian dichotomy emphasises the need to stabilise what exceeds stabilisation. The need to control the topic extends from the use of recurrent key emotion words and central metaphors to explicit rules recommended to keep the 'storms of passion' and their effects at bay. But in equal measure the need to express the feelings is given room. The attempt at balancing both these claims results in the manifold tensions and contradictions of the Victorian discourses on emotions.

These tensions can best be observed when fictional texts are read along with non-fictional ones, and when canonical material is confronted with lesser-known or seemingly inferior texts and images. And from this a contextualised approach naturally follows which situates the Victorian discourses on the feelings in their period and relates them to topical concerns. Although a slight development towards expression with less emphasis on control can be observed throughout the early 19th century, the need to 'have their cake and eat it' continues to drive Victorian authors. Not least in their use of common, almost dead emotion metaphors can one see that discursive stability was consciously or unconsciously used to 'stem the torrent' of potentially excessive emotionality and everything else that was going on outside discourse. In this sense, William Cyples's association of machinery and passion is typical: the discourses on emotions in the 19th century are inextricably linked to their context, either by explicitly discussing it, or by ignoring it which makes an even stronger case for its subliminal presence.

On the level of the individual, emotional expression was considered essential for individual health, as long as it was kept in strict bounds. Excessive passion without this control was seen as one of the main causes of mental and physical danger and could lead to 'sudden death'. This view of the passions and the body is expressed in metaphors conceptualising the body as 'a rotten carcass' and as an unpredictable source of instability, in particular for women who were considered to be in danger of succumbing to their 'excessive sensibility'. But equally, authors of health guides and conduct books, as well as novelists, saw too great a control of the feelings as unnatural and dangerous. Not only the individual needed to be able to show grief by crying, shame by blushing, or love by trembling, using the body as the 'medium' of non-verbal communication. More importantly, if the rapidly increasing members of Victorian mass society did not express and show their feelings, they might become totally inscrutable to their middle class observers, intent on social distinction, and thus become even more dangerous and uncontrollable. This need to distinguish oneself socially from those above and below fuelled the debate led mainly by middle class writers. The social or the body politic was therefore never far from the minds of the writers studied in this book. I have explained the intricacies of individual and social expression and control with the help of Charlotte Brontë's novel *Shirley*: individual repression of the feelings nearly results in the death of Caroline Helstone. If she and Robert Moore had each succeeded in repressing their love, the social consequences would have been dire indeed, and the same goes for the love between aristocratic Shirley Keeldar and the middle class intellectual Louis Moore. Only after the education of the hearts of the protagonists has been completed can a sense of compromise between individual and social expression and control be achieved. How difficult this is, in particular for women who where often at the receiving end of prescriptive emotional rules, can be illustrated by the torturous process that Caroline (and to a lesser extent Shirley) has to undergo before she can reconcile her longing for a suitable occupation with her love for Robert.

It is no accident that Charlotte Brontë focused her contribution to the debate on women and their attempts at dealing with the central problem of expression and control. An important element in the Victorian discourses on emotions is the use of the feelings for the creation of a stable middle class habitus with its three mainstays of gender relations, social order and religion. These three aspects are not only explicitly discussed, they also function as implicit rules ordering the boundaries and strategies of the Victorian discourses on emotions.

Christianity is the basis on which rest the main values characteristic for the age: thrift, piety, humility, the absence of pride, selfishness and greed. Being able to follow these moral guidelines relies on the individual coming to terms and managing passions which go against this set of rules. But religion also allows emotional expression, not only its control. Because all religious feeling is directed towards God and not to earthly, let alone sexual, matters, it is a safe 'place' for the expression of the feelings. Not surprisingly then, they can be represented in emotion metaphors normally reserved for the dangerous aspect of passion: torrents and channels, swelling and throbbing hearts.

A second assumption which orders what could and what could not be said about the feelings in the 19th century is the need to create social distinctions between the middle classes and the aristocracy and the 'untutored masses' or the 'mob'. For this purpose, feeling is used as the touchstone of true moral behaviour. If the right balance is struck between expression and control by adhering to religious principles and maintaining order, then Victorian writers give a fictional character or actual people and cases their approbation. But if an aristocratic younger son like Reginald Ireby in *The Ruling Passion* cannot overcome his pride and his greed, his fate is sealed: he has to die (even though he repents before perishing), since passion which has not been 'channelled' properly can only lead to death and damnation. This kind of individual and social order is not only explicitly demanded, it is also implicitly performed and expressed in many of the texts in my corpus. By classifying the emotions, setting them in strict hierarchies, ordering them along sets of binary distinctions, using the same metaphors and expressions again and again, and inventing and applying new scientistic models for them, authors like Charles Bray, for all his innovations, represent the 'heart' of the matter: the emotions have to be circumscribed if individual and social order is to be maintained.

If Reginald Ireby's kind of fate is to be averted, a process of special education is needed to teach children how actual and symbolic order is to be achieved. But who is to undertake this education? It is here that women come into their own, according to male and female writers alike. The separate spheres ideology already developed in the 18th century becomes more and more rigid in the 19th century and permeates all texts on the emotions. Apart from the fact that actual Victorian women and men did not fit the discursively constructed dichotomy quite as neatly as the proponents of men in 'public' and women in 'private' would have it, the separate spheres view of the world did not only restrict women. The constant invocation of motherhood and the 'domestic affections' paradoxically limited women and created a space for the emotions but also for specific female activities. By relocating the feelings to a strictly limited sphere, the expression of the emotions and their individual and social value was ensured and acknowledged. But in this construction, passion would not influence and colour public and political life directly. Yet indirectly, it would work its positive way into society from the 'fountainhead' downwards: through the influence of mothers, the epitome of the most favourite Victorian emotion: affection. By providing their children, and in particular their sons with moral guidelines, women would achieve two things. On the one hand, their alleged greater capacity for feeling would 'soften' their sons' rough edges. But on the other hand, this special task would ensure their moral superiority and it also allowed the cautious call for female occupation. What started as the claim for better education for women for their own sakes could turn into the necessity to train them as professional educators so that they could fulfil their role as prime educators of the heart, as Sarah Ellis demands. This type of ambiguity, obvious to modern eyes but not necessarily to Victorian readers, is typical of the discourses on emotions: they simultaneously limited emotional expression and created new spaces for it.

Educating the heart, balancing expression and control, had to be taught and how better to do this than through fiction? But matters were not quite as simple as that, since fiction, in particular novels, were eyed with great suspicion by many Victorian critics. The indulgence and the sensuousness which were associated with novels are repeatedly made the target of novel criticism. Writers like M.A. Stodart or even J.S. Mill thought novels were dangerous, in particular for women readers, because they tended to be 'carried away' by excessive feeling. Many authors preferred poetry as the genre best suited to express the 'passions' while remaining in command of them, since metrical composition provided the best means of ordering the feelings. This Romantic legacy of authentic self-expression in feeling, combined with hankerings after Neo-classic orderliness, is a further example of the close relation between expression and control in the 19th century. Again, writers like Keble or Mill seem not to have been aware of the possible tensions that this kind of joking-together would also have produced. Nevertheless, some writers, e.g. Charles Bray, also considered fiction a suitable vehicle for conveying moral values and good behaviour. This would only work in a specific mode of writing, that of the 'proper novel' (Ferris), or in the case of non-fictional texts, if the plot rested on the same kind of paradigm scenario that constitutes the plots of the 'proper novel'.

Fiction and non-fiction converge in the discourses on emotions (and in other Victorian discourses as well), because literary quotations allowed non-fiction authors to express what exceeded their rigid 'scientific' classification or physiological description. In addition, this indication of *Bildung* could confer on them a rise in status. But mini-melodramas and narrative passages in treatises and tracts were needed because the emotions themselves are virtually inaccessible, if they cannot be coupled to a paradigm scenario illustrating what happens if one succumbs to the sway of passion. Interestingly, narrative in non-fictional texts focuses more on repression and its dangers than the more complex fictional texts in my corpus tend to do.

Typical paradigm scenarios illustrate the education of the heart of the protagonist in a novel or case story, who has to learn to shed pride or passion, in order to combine it with principle or self-control. The 'proper novel', although also used by male writers, is the domain which allows women writers to enter the literary field. This results from their alleged moral and emotional superiority: if they have more and better feelings, they are the ones best adapted to write about the 'heart' and its requisite education. Women writers followed this programme, but again they made use of the space created for and by them to further their own causes: better education and suitable occupation. This demand is the centre around which revolves a group of novels which were all influenced by Germaine de Staël's paradigmatic novel *Corinne, ou l'Italie*, rewritten and adapted countless times in the 19th century. It provides the central expression-and-control plot which tries to reconcile femininity with passion, creativity with domesticity. But it also sets this problem in a nationalist context, by contrasting a symbolic 'Italy' with an equally symbolic 'England'.

The discourses on emotions, just like all other Victorian discourses, are shot through with references to national 'characteristics' and difference. Again, patriotic feeling could be used as a further safe 'space' for emotional expression, directed as it was to 'higher' aims and not just to individual happiness. But this conventional element of the discourses on the feelings was used by women writers to reset the discourses' boundaries, a further indication that what appears at face value to be repressive or questionable, like the concept of separate spheres, also allowed new openings, however small. *Corinne* supplies the model for the foreign, passionate woman. Combined with the 'demonic code' of the dark lady, this potent mixture allowed women writers the creation of memorable female protagonists who move beyond the angelic mode. The attractions of passion outweigh the need to control it and the focus for that kind of attraction is again the body. This illustrates that by mid-century, under the influence of sensation novels and advances in physiology, representations of the body were slowly moving away from associating it with ill-health and danger, and gaining in attraction. The sensuous descriptions of Rhoda Broughton (or George Eliot at the other end of the aesthetic scale) share the outrage they provoked in their readers. But they also illustrate that the balance between emotional expression and control, if it had ever existed in the first place, was fast becoming difficult, if not impossible towards the middle and end of the century. And these novels belie Cyples's hope that life in the 19th century would actually be 'embellished by the quieter feelings', as he conjectures in 'Machinery and the Passions'.

Thus, in spite of my emphasis on continuity rather than change, slight movements can be detected in the Victorian discourses on emotions. Whether these also indicate a change in emotional experience is not for me to say – it would require another study to find an answer to this question. Whoever embarks on such a study would have many options from which he or she could choose: a full-scale comparative approach to intercultural and intertextual German and French influences on the discourses on emotions; an analysis of the visual representations of the feelings, which should read images as more than mere illustration; the role that the emotions played for the different religious groups in the 19th century; a 'long-shot' view of the discourses on emotions spanning the ages and including longer periods than studied in this book; the use of even less well-known material, including for instance more working class and aristocratic authors and a systematic analysis of the rich material from Victorian periodicals; 'close-ups' of actual emotional experience in the 19th century, in whatever way one would approach 'objects' of study which are only available in representations heavily influenced by literary conventions; and a look at individual emotions and their representations which have emerged as problematic for the Victorians, such as anger, pride or selfishness. However – I agree with Perceival Leigh, the author of the article "Comicalities of the Feelings": The present subject is inexhaustible. 'But we fear that by protracting it we shall try the reader's philosophy, rather than increase it.'[4]

4 Perceival Leigh (1842), 'Comicalities of the Feelings', in *Bentley's Miscellany*, vol. 11, pp. 51-55, quotation p. 55.

Appendix: Biographical Notes

John Abercrombie (1780-1844). Physician. Obtained a degree in medicine from Edinburgh University (1803), continued his studies at St George's Hospital (London), before opening a practice in Edinburgh (1804). Abercrombie always showed an interest in the mental aspects of medical science, but was also involved with work for the poor. Became fellow of the College of Physicians (1824) and obtained the complimentary appointment of 'physician in ordinary to the King in Scotland'. His popular works were widely read and also published in America but his concept of the mind relies largely on early-19th century theories, derived from Stewart, Reid and Brown and, according to contemporary reviewers, convinced the general public rather than his fellow scientists. Received the degree of doctor of medicine from Oxford (1835) and became rector of Marischal College in Aberdeen (1836).[1]

Grace Aguilar (1816-1847) was of Spanish Jewish descent. One of the first women to write openly as a Jew about Jewish history and religion. Published novels and stories which were posthumously published or edited by her mother. Aguilar died young because her health had been impaired by an early attack of measles. Her highly popular novel *Home Influence, a Tale for Mothers and Daughters* (1847) was the only novel to appear during her lifetime.[2]

Eliza Armstrong No details available. Edited *Affection's Token*, one of the many Victorian anthologies of popular verse.

Alexander Bain (1818-1903), born in Scotland as the child of a strict Calvinist farmer and weaver. Self-taught. Spent three months at a grammar school and obtained a bursary for Marischal College (later to become one of the colleges of the University of Aberdeen) at the age of eighteen. Graduated in 1840 and began contributing to *The Westminster Review*. Met Lewes, Carlyle, George Grote and John Stuart Mill whose manuscript for *Logic* he revised and later reviewed in *The Westminster Review*. Studied

1 Cf. the *DNB* for details.

2 For more information see the *DNB* and Virginia Blain et al. (eds) (1990), *The Feminist Companion to Literature in English*, Yale UP, New Haven/London (henceforth abbreviated as *The Feminist Companion*).

phrenology at the instigation of Mill, and after a few failed attempts to gain professorial chairs – there were doubts as to his religious orthodoxy since he was an agnostic – he came to London and became assistant secretary to the metropolitan sanitary commission in 1848. Also lectured at the Bedford College for Women and continued his writing and married Frances A. Wilkinson in 1855. Published *The Senses and the Intellect* (1855) and *The Emotions and the Will* (1859). Both works are considered as the first British textbooks of psychology because they are based on physiology, define the scope of psychology clearly and grasp the requirements of scientific method. Both were used as standard texts throughout the 19th century, until they were replaced by Stout's *Manual of Psychology* in 1898. Was made professor of logic and English at the United University of Aberdeen on the recommendation of the home secretary. Published his major work, *Mental and Moral Science, a Compendium of Psychology and Ethics* (1868), *Logic* (1870) and *Body and Mind* (1872). Bain also assisted in the editing of Grote's *Aristotle* in 1873 and was instrumental in founding the periodical *Mind* for which he was financially responsible until 1892 and to which he contributed regularly. Was elected Lord Rector of Aberdeen University (1880), continued to write (on James and John Stuart Mill, and various philosophical topics). His *Autobiography* was published posthumously in 1904.[3]

Alexander Melville Bell (1819-1905), Scottish authority on the physiology of the voice, elocution and on 'phonetics'. Became professor of elocution in London, following his father, and was in his turn followed by his son, Alexander Graham Bell (1847-1922), the inventor of the telephone. The Bells emigrated to Canada in 1870, and A.G. Bell was later naturalised as an American.[4]

Sir Charles Bell (1774-1842), nerve specialist, physiologist. Son of a Scottish Episcopal clergyman. Received his chief literary education from his mother. Studied at the University of Edinburgh where his talent for drawing soon became known. First published *A System of Dissections* while still a student (1798) and soon became a surgical attendant at the Edinburgh Infirmary. Left for London in 1804, where he was already known for his various works on physiology. He had already written his

3 Cf. the *DNB*, L.S. Hearnshaw (1964), 'Bain and his Background', in id., *A Short History of British Psychology 1840-1940*, Methuen, London, pp. 1-14, and William S. Sahakian (1975), *History and Systems of Psychology*, John Wiley & Sons, New York etc., pp. 51-63.

4 Cf. the *DNB* under Alexander Graham Bell for more details.

Anatomy of Expression by that time, but only published it in 1806. His more important discoveries relating to the nervous system were made in the years after the publication. His investigations were completed in a series of papers he gave before the Royal Society from 1821 to 1829. Before this time, nothing much was known about the nervous system, so that Bell's discoveries concerning the relations of the nerves and muscle action can be considered crucial to 19th-century science. His main discovery was the concept of two kinds of nerves, one sensory and one motor. Returned to Scotland in 1836 when he was offered the chair of surgery at the University of Edinburgh. Died in 1842.[5]

Elizabeth Bonhote (1744-1818), novelist, poet and writer of conduct books from Suffolk. Her moralising novels such as *The Fashionable Friend* (1773, epistolary novel) or Hortensia (1777) met with approval. Married a solicitor sometime between 1770 and 1774. The first of her publications to be published under her name was *The Parental Monitor* (1788), written for her children. Bonhote became a best-selling writer for the Minerva press.[6]

Charles Bray (1811-1884), son of a well-to-do Coventry ribbon manufacturer who was educated at boarding schools in the country and in London, before being 'articled' at a large warehouse in London at the age of 17. Brought up on Methodist principles, later converted to Evangelicalism. Succeeded his father in his business in 1835. A crisis of faith led to his renunciation of any fixed creed. Set up an infant school in Coventry and defended non-sectarian schools in general, was interested in Robert Owen's utopian socialism and co-operative management, started a working man's club and founded the Coventry Labourers' and Artisans' Society, helped in setting up the Coventry Mechanics' Institute and also bought a local paper in 1846 which he owned until 1876, enabling him to spread his ideas on education and self-help further. His belief in phrenology was shared by Marian Evans, later to become George Eliot, for whom Bray's undogmatic Coventry circle of family and friends was to be important from an early age. Bray retired from business in 1860 but continued his charitable works and attempts at establishing co-operative communities. Remained married but kept a mistress, with whom he had several children, and his wife was apparently also romantically involved with another man.[7]

---

5 Cf. the *DNB* for more details.

6 For further details cf. *The Feminist Companion*.

7 For more biographical details, cf. the *DNB*, Bray's (c. 1884) autobiography, *Phases of*

Rhoda Broughton (1840-1920), niece of Joseph Sheridan Le Fanu, in whose *Dublin University Magazine Not Wisely But Too Well* (written in 1862-63) was serialised. Before it was reissued, her second novel *Cometh Up As A Flower* (1867) came out in two volumes, published anonymously. Both novels were received by a shocked readership, surprised by Broughton's outspokenness, vivid dialogues and in particular by her unashamed fascination with sensuous passion. In addition, *Not Wisely* contains a description of fever-infested slums which would have been unusual reading material for the majority of middle class readers.[8]

Mary Brunton (1778-1818), daughter of Colonel Thomas Balfour of Elwick. Born Mary Balfour on the island of Barra, Orkney. Irregular education, but learned some French and Italian. After managing her father's household for four years she married the Rev. Alexander Brunton, who would later become professor of oriental languages at the University of Edinburgh. Together, they studied philosophy and history. Apart from the two novels, Mary Brunton wrote an unfinished story entitled *Emmeline*, which was published together with letters and some criticism in a memoir written by her husband (1819). Brunton died in childbirth. *Self-Control*, dedicated to Joanna Baillie (1762-1851), the author of the widely-read *Plays on the Passions* (1798, 1802, 1812), was published anonymously and caused such a sensation that its first edition sold out within a month. Two further editions appeared in the same year, and by 1812 it had already reached a fourth edition. *Self-Control* and *Discipline* were republished in Bentley's Standard Novels in 1832, and in another edition in 1837 as well as in Routledge's Railway Library in 1852.[9]

Richard Carlile was born in Devon and received only little formal education. First worked as a journeyman and tinplate worker between 1802 and 1817. Married in 1813 and had several children but the marriage was not a happy one. The Carliles moved to London where Carlile was to stay for most of the rest of his life although he believed in respectability and tried to avoid urban working class recreations. By 1819, Carlile had become a spokesman for the poor after coming into contact with radical

---

Opinion and Experience During a Long Life: An Autobiography, Longmans, Green, and Co., London, and for his private life cf. Elsemarie Maletzke (1993), *George Eliot. Ihr Leben*, Insel, Frankfurt a.M., pp. 39-43.

8 See *The Feminist Companion*, the *DNB* and the study by Marilyn Wood (1993), *Rhoda Broughton (1840-1920). Profile of a Novelist*, Paul Watkins, Stamford, for further details.

9 For more details cf. the entries in the *DNB* and *The Feminist Companion*.

reformers such as Cobbett and Hunt. Gave up tinplate working and became a full-time radical reformer, selling radical journals and a publisher. Spent several years in prison because of a refusal to pay fines but was unexpectedly freed in 1825. Wrote and published *Every Woman's Book* (1826), the most outspoken birth-control pamphlet to be published in England at the time. Other reformers, as well as conservatives, rejected Carlile's 'feminist' attitudes. His marriage ended in separation in 1832 and he died in 1843.[10]

Frederick Chamier (1796-1870) entered the navy in 1809 and worked as a midshipman before becoming commander of the Britomart sloop in 1826 and being paid off in England in 1827. Retired in 1833 but was promoted to captain in 1856. Pursued a literary career and wrote several quite popular novels in the style of Marryat. Also published travel books and edited James's *Naval History*. In 1832, he had married Elizabeth Soane, granddaughter of the architect Sir John Soane. Died in October 1870.[11]

William Cooke (1785-1873), London GP, worked as surgeon for the Protector Life Assurance and Widow's Annuity Societies. Other publications include an abridged English edition of Giovanni Battista Morgagni's *Seats and Causes of Diseases* (1822), *A Practical and Pathological Inquiry into the Sources and Effects of Derangements of the Digestive Organs* (1828/1831), and *A Brief Memoir of Sir William Blizard* (1835) who was a fellow Hunterian (see below). Cooke was also secretary, first treasurer and then president of the Hunterian Society of which he was a founding member. The Hunterian Society was a professional association of East-London doctors, founded in 1819. Its 70-odd members held meetings every fortnight, and from 1825 onwards an annual oration was delivered at a special dinner. Cooke's 1839-version of *Mind and Emotions* was such an annual oration which he later expanded to a book-length study.[12]

---

10 See Joel H. Wiener (1983), *Radicalism and Freethought in Nineteenth-Century Britain. The Life of Richard Carlile*, Greenwood Press, Westport, Conn./London.

11 Cf. the author portrait, anon. (1838), *Colburn's New Monthly Magazine*, vol. 52, pp. 508-510, the entry in the *DNB* and P.J. Van der Voort (1972), *The Pen and the Quarterdeck. A Study of the Life and Works of Captain Frederick Chamier, R.N.*, Leiden UP, Leiden, for further details.

12 Cf. anon. (1847), *The London Medical Directory 1847*, John Churchill, London, and Henry I. Fotherby (1869), *Scientific Associations, Their Rise, Progress, and Influence, with a History of the Hunterian Society. An Oration. Delivered on the Fiftieth Anniversary of the Above Institution, February 10, 1869*, Bell & Daldy, London.

Dinah Maria Mulock Craik (1826-87), daughter of an eccentric Irish Baptist preacher. Had to provide for the family after her mother's death since her father had been committed as a pauper lunatic in the 1830s. Lived in London and wrote for *Chambers Magazine*. Her first of over twenty novels, *The Ogilvies*, came out in 1849. *Olive* was published in 1850. In 1865, she married a younger man and adopted a daughter in 1869. Happily married but consistently focused on single life for women as a viable alternative to marriage, not least in her *Woman's Thoughts About Women* (1858).[13]

Robert James Culverwell London doctor, author of numerous health and anti-masturbation guides. Main source of income, apart from practising as a doctor and publishing cheap advice literature, were public baths. Member of the Royal College of Surgeons of England. In his grandiloquent (but boring) autobiography *The Life of Doctor Culverwell* (1852/1855) he not only explains his concept of public baths, but interestingly also announces that he treats patients by correspondence, another of his sources of income. One of his 'anti-vice' pamphlets went to one hundred thousand copies, his publication *Porneiapathology, or the Green Book* (c. 1847) on the treatment of venereal diseases to two hundred thousand copies and many of his general health guides went to more than one edition. His interest in sexual matters can also be gathered from *The Solitarian; or, the Physiology of the Passions, Their Use and Abuse* (1849).[14]

Sarah Ellis (1812-72), née Stickney, Quaker turned Congregationalist in her youth. Married the chief foreign secretary of the London Missionary Society, William Ellis, when aged 25. Both were involved in the work of Christian missions and both were strongly convinced of the temperance cause. They had no children but S. Ellis had many nieces to whom she remained close throughout her life. Edited annuals, wrote didactic novels, and founded a school, Rawdon House, for working-class women. Famous for her conduct books, e.g. *The Women of England, their Social Duties and Domestic Habits* (1839) (more than twenty editions), *The Daughters of*

13 Cf. *The Feminist Companion* and Cora Kaplan's introduction to the Oxford UP's Popular Fiction edition of *Olive* (1996), and Sally Mitchell (1983), *Dinah Mulock Craik*, Twayne Publishers, Boston, for more information.

14 See the British Library catalogue, the advertisements included in Culverwell's publications and in particular his autobiography for details of his interests (no birth and death dates are available for Culverwell).

England (1842), *The Mothers of England* (1843) and *The Wives of England* (1843), *The Education of the Heart: Woman's Best Work* (1868).[15]

For **Maria Georgina Grey** see **Shirreff**.

Alban J.X. Hart (d. 1879). Entered the novitiate but ill-health forced him to discontinue his chosen career. Became master of Sedgley Park School, travelled to the United States and on his return joined St Mary's College, Oscott. Died at Worcester on 13 April 1879, and apart from *Catholic Psychology*, an abridgement of larger works on psychology, he published *An Essay on Mental Philosophy* (New York 1853), some poetry, and an English grammar for beginners. The word 'catholic' in the title of *Catholic Psychology* refers less to his religious affiliation than to the universality of the subject. Hart's aim was to reconcile faith and reason, human and divine nature, and human feelings with God's guidance and laws.[16]

'Rainey Hawthorne' (1832-1906). Real name Charlotte Eliza Lawson but was known as Mrs J.H. Riddell, of Irish descent. Wrote to gain a living as a young woman after her civil engineer husband had fallen into debt. Prolific and quite successful writer. *George Geith of Fen Court* (1864) was dramatised at Scarborough and in Australia and earned her the comparatively high sum of 800*l.* from her publisher William Tinsley. During the 1860s and 1870s Mrs Riddell was one of the most popular women novelists. Fictionalised her experience of 'life in nineteenth-century Grub Street', (Cross) in the autobiographical novel *A Struggle for Fame* (1883). Also co-proprietor and editor of *St. James's Magazine*, edited a magazine called *Home* in the 1860s, and wrote tales for the Society for the Promotion of Christian Knowledge and Routledge's Christmas annuals. Was one of the first writers to receive a pension of 60*l.* a year from the Society of Authors (1901).[17]

George Payne Rainsford James (1799-1856). Son of a London physician and naval officer. Acquired an early taste for French and Italian literature and also travelled on the Continent as a young man. Gave up plans of a political career and became a writer of extremely popular

---

15 Cf. Joanne Shattock (1993), *The Oxford Companion to British Women Writers*, Oxford UP, Oxford/New York, *The Feminist Compqnion*, and the volume of letters compiled by her nieces in 1893: *The Home Life and Letters of Mrs Ellis*, J. Nisbet & Co, London.

16 See Joseph Gillow (c. 1888), *A Literary and Biographical History or Biographical Dictionary of the English Catholics*, 5 vols., repr. Burt Franklin, New York.

17 Cf. the *DNB*, Nigel Cross (1985), *The Common Writer: Life in Nineteenth-Century Grub Street*, Cambridge UP, Cambridge/New York, pp. 194-198, and Janet Todd (ed) (1989), *Dictionary of British Women Writers*, Routledge, London.

historical novels (influenced by Scott) and miscellaneous historical publications. Was appointed historiographer royal by William IV. His fantastic plots and fast-paced novels appeared in Routledge's Railway Library, catering to the taste of the middle classes. In the 1850s, James held several diplomatic posts in America, married an American and died on a diplomatic post in Venice in 1856.[18]

Geraldine Endsor Jewsbury (1812-1880) was the first woman to become a regular publisher's reader (for the publisher Bentley). But before pursuing her literary and critical career (she also wrote more than 1600 reviews for *The Athenæum*), Jewsbury had to take over the management of her father's household when her sister Maria Jane (1800-33) married. First novel *Zoë* (1845) caused a minor scandal because of the way it treated religious doubt and the relationship between a priest and a married woman. Apart from *The Half-Sisters*, which went into two single-volume editions during Jewsbury's lifetime (1854, Chapman and Hall; c. 1861, vol. 230 of the Parlour Library), the author published four further novels, children's stories and co-edited Lady Morgan's memoirs, with whom she had been friends. Remained single and died in Kent in 1880.[19]

Walter M.B. Johnson London doctor, son of the physician Edward Johnson, and former medical tutor at Guy's Hospital in London. Author of numerous publications on hydropathy, homeopathy, and, together with his father, on temperance and on the dangers of alcoholism.[20]

Julia Kavanagh (1824-1877), novelist and writer with strong French leanings, who had spent her childhood in Paris. Returned to London in 1844 and adopted literature as a profession, while caring for her aged and infirm mother at the same time. Later years were spent at Nice, where she died in 1877. Her novels are often set in France and in both the novels and her critical writing Kavanagh was interested in the limits of female creativity. It is thanks to her studies *Women in France* (1850) and *French Women of Letters* (1862) that the influence of French women's writing can be traced to Victorian novelists.[21]

John Lang (1817-1864) was a writer of popular novels and travel

---

18 See the *DNB* for more details.

19 For more details cf. the *DNB*, *The Feminist Companion*, and the introduction to the Oxford UP's World's Classics edition of *The Half-Sisters*, edited and introduced by Joanne Wilkes (1994), Oxford/New York.

20 No dates or further details are available for Johnson but see the British Library catalogue for the titles of his other publications.

21 Cf. the *DNB* and *The Feminist Companion*.

books who was born in Australia, lived in India and Europe and contributed to magazines such as *Household Words*.[22]

'Vernon Lee' (1856-1935) (Violet Paget). Spent most of her life in France, where she was born, and in Europe. Accompanied Singer Sargent and his mother to Rome, where she began to write with Mrs Sargent's help and assumed her pen name. Published a number of novels, travel books and works on aesthetics. 'Lady Tal' appeared in a collection of stories entitled *Vanities*, published by William Heinemann in London (1896).[23]

Charles Mackay (1814-1889). Scottish poet, composer and editor. Mackay was a lawyer, but made his career in the literary field, in particular with his work as editor of several periodicals, most notably of the *London Illustrated News*, of which he became the editor in 1852. In 1860, he established the *London Review* and became correspondent of *The Times* during the civil war in the 1860s. His poetry collections were very popular during the 19th century. In his later years, Mackay was more interested in Celtic philology. Died in London in 1889.[24]

Henry Longueville Mansel (1820-1871). Scholar. Read widely, studied at St John's College, Oxford. Soon became one of the leading private tutors at Oxford and became ordained as a deacon in 1844 and as a priest in 1845. Married in 1855 and was elected 'professor fellow' of St John's in 1864. Wrote on metaphysics and was appointed professor of ecclesiastical history in 1866 and appointed to the deanery of St Paul's by Disraeli.[25]

James Martineau (1805-1900), brother of Harriet Martineau, leading Unitarian clergyman of his time. His publications were widely read. Religious issues were the cause for the rift between Harriet and her favourite brother: she decided to leave behind her the Unitarian creed in which they had been brought up. James studied at the Unitarian Manchester College in York, took up various positions in England and Ireland, where his first hymn book was published and used by his own congregation. Became professor of mental and moral philosophy and political economy at Manchester New College which moved to London in the second half of the 19th century. Became principal in 1869 and was an

---

22 Cf. F. Boase (1892-1921), *Modern English Biography, Containing ... Memoirs of Persons Who Have Died Since ... 1850 ...*, 6 vols., Netherton & Worth, Truro and the British Library catalogue.

23 Cf. *The Feminist Companion* for more details.

24 Cf. the *DNB* for more details.

25 Cf. the *DNB* for more details.

active writer, teacher and preacher almost till the end of his life. Married in 1828 and had eight children.[26]

Frances Eliza Millett Notley (1820-1912) published the novel *Olive Varcoe* under the pseudonym 'Francis Derrick' but signed the second edition with her real initials (F.E.M.N.). Born in Landager, near Liskear in Cornwall. Educated in England and France, married George Notley of Combe, in Sydenham, Somerset (1843). Began writing in the 1850s, probably after her husband's death in 1855. Many of her stories are set in Cornwall. *Olive Varcoe* is her most successful novel but a number of her other publications also had more than one edition. Her last publication appeared in 1888 (*The Power of the Hand: A Novel*).[27]

Edmund Thomas Parris (1793-1873), successful painter who first exhibited at the Royal Academy in 1824. Known for his panorama paintings and for his portraits, in particular of women. His paintings became popular through engravings printed in annuals such as *The Keepsake*. Several combinations of engravings taken from his paintings with Lady Blessington's verses published in the 1830s met with popular approval. Parris also painted a coronation portrait of Queen Victoria and was entrusted with the restoration of paintings in St Paul's Cathedral. In 1832, Parris was appointed historical painter of Queen Adelaide, and was also known as the inventor of 'Parris's Medium', a kind of paint used for fresco-like surfaces mixed with oil.[28]

James Henry Powell Itinerant worker and occasional poet, about whom nothing is known except that he was married and that his numerous publications (poetry collections, lectures and pamphlets) were published in small editions by fairly insignificant publishers. Nevertheless, his poetry was reviewed in prestigious periodicals, as can be gathered from the advertisements printed on the backs of his pamphlets.

Emily Anne Eliza Shirreff (1814-1897) and her sister **Maria Georgina** (1816-1906) are today known less for their literary publications, a novel written by Maria, *Love's Sacrifice* (1868) dedicated to Emily, and the *Letters from Spain and Barbary* which they wrote together (1835), but for their treatises on education for women and their active support of kindergarten work and colleges for women. The sisters were friends with Mary Somerville, the famous woman scientist and with the influential

---

26 Cf. the *DNB* for further details.

27 Cf. *The Feminist Companion* and J.F. Kirk's (1882) [1859-71] supplement to *Allibone's Biographical Dictionary*, J.B. Lippincott & Co, Philadelphia, for further details.

28 Cf. the *DNB* for details.

geologist Charles Lyell. Herbert Spencer, Thomas Huxley and other eminent Victorian intellectuals were further members of their wider social circle. Emily was greatly affected by Maria's marriage to William Grey in 1841 but this did not hinder the sisters in their joint endeavours. In 1849, they finished writing *Thoughts on Self Culture*, published with W. Grey's help (second edition in 1854). Both sisters had to nurse various family members, W. Grey died in 1864 after a prolonged illness (fictionalised in *Love's Sacrifice*), and they only embarked on their public life, championing women's education and women's colleges (Girton among them) in the later decades of the 19th century. Both were involved in the setting up of training colleges for middle class girls and Emily was also important in bringing Fröbel's ideas on early education for children to a wider audience. Co-founders of the Fröbel Society, gave public talks on educational matters. Lived and worked in close association till Emily's death in 1897. Maria Grey died in 1906.[29]

Mrs Walter Spencer published two volumes of poetry, and according to the title page of the second volume, probably came from Manchester and was a Miss Jackson before her marriage. *Commemorative Feelings* (1812) was followed by *Poetical Trifles: or, Miscellaneous Poems on Various Subjects* (1831), and printed on the basis of a subscription list. Both collections are highly conventional but illustrate that even women poets writing according to their period's taste sometimes (inadvertently?) touched upon matters of wider significance, e.g. political issues. No further details are available.

Anne Louise Germaine (Necker), **Baronne de Staël** (1766-1817) always had close associations with England. Although her image of England was at first clouded by an early experience – she was to have married W. Pitt – she warmed to the English in later life, mainly due to her two stays in England and her experience as a political exile (1793, 1813-14). Was friends with Fanny Burney, later Mme d'Arblay, with whom she corresponded for a time; also corresponded with Lord Byron and Sir James Mackintosh and many other public figures. A number of her works were first published in London. Apart from *Corinne*, her treatise on the passions (*De l'influence des passions sur le bonheur des individus et des nations*, 1796) is remarkable since it is one of the very few philosophical treatises on the feelings written by a woman. It was translated into German and

---

29 Cf. the entry on Emily Shirreff in the *DNB* and Edward W. Ellsworth (1979), *Liberators of the Female Mind: the Shirreff Sisters, Educational Reform and the Women's Movement*, Greenwood Press, Westport, Conn. for further details.

English, received favourable notice from Goethe and Schiller, and was reviewed with interest in Britain.[30]

Hiram Miner Stanley No details are available for this author, who may have been an American. The British Library catalogue mentions *Essays on Literary Art* (Swan Sonnenschein & Co., London 1897) and *Psychology for Beginners* (Open Court Publishing Co., Chicago 1899) as further publications. The National Union catalogue also lists a cheap edition of *Studies in the Evolutionary Psychology of Feeling*, published in 1905.

Mary Ann(e) Stodart No birth and death dates are available for Stodart. In his reference work *Poets of Ireland* (1892), D.J. O'Donoghue lists Stodart as 'Mary Anne Stodart (Miss)'. Referring to her Northern Irish background she is described as an 'Orange poetess'. Some of her work apparently appeared in the second volume of poetry issued by the National Board of Education in Ireland (1849). Two further titles by Stodart herself are mentioned by O'Donoghue: *National Ballads, Patriotic and Protestant* (1814, second edition 1851) and *Scriptural Poems for Children* (1841). She also published *Principles of Education* in 1844.[31]

Mrs Stringer No details are available for this author and no other publication apart from *The Chain of Affection* is listed for her in the catalogue of the British Library.

---

30 No satisfactory study of Staël's relationship with England exists; Robert Escarpit's (1954) *L'Angleterre dans l'œuvre de Madame de Staël*, Marcel Didier, Paris is useful for factual details but biased in his judgement which is coloured more by 19th-century concepts of femininity than by critical distance. The best account of Staël's life and work is by Simone Balayé (1994), *Mme de Staël. Ecrire, Lutter, Vivre*, Droz, Geneva. See also Victor de Pange (1970), 'Le Rêve anglais de Mme de Staël', in *Mme de Staël et l'Europe* (colloque de Coppet 18-24 juillet 1966), Klincksieck, Paris, pp. 173-182 and Roswitha Böhm and Gesa Stedman, 'Reading Corinne is an epoch in every woman's life – Germaine de Staël in England', in Andrew James Johnston and Ulrike Schneider (eds), *Anglo-Romanische Kulturkontakte von Humanismus bis Postkolonialismus*, Dahlem UP, Berlin, forthcoming. For the treatise on the passions and its place within Romanticism and as another crucial expression-and-control text, see Madelyn Gutwirth (1983-85), 'Forging a Vocation: Germaine de Staël on Fiction, Power, and Passion', in *Bulletin of Research in the Humanities*, vol. 86 (3), pp. 242-254, and Gesa Stedman, 'Fundstück', in Ingrid Kasten, Gesa Stedman, Margarete Zimmermann (eds), *Kulturen der Gefühle in Mittelalter und Früher Neuzeit* (Querelles. Jahrbuch für Frauen- und Geschlechterforschung, vol. 7), Metzler, Stuttgart/Weimar, forthcoming.

31 Jane Rendall (1985) mentions Stodart as the editor of the *Christian Lady's Magazine* in *The Origins of Modern Feminism: Women in Britain, France and the United States, 1780-1860*, Basingstoke, Macmillan, p. 92. I have been unable to substantiate this claim (made on the basis of a secondary-source quotation), as the catalogues of the British Library and the Bodleian Library give two other names as editors for this periodical.

Robert Tyas (1811-1879), publisher, bookseller, clergyman and amateur naturalist. Studied theology at Queen's College, Cambridge and became a clergyman. Worked as a publisher (1838-44) and bookseller of works on health, general knowledge and on plants. Published an illustrated edition of Shakespeare in two volumes in 1839-43, produced extra illustrations for Dickens's works but became most famous for his series *The Sentiments of Flowers* whose attractive coloured illustrations must have influenced their considerable success.[32]

[32] See Boase (1892-1921), *Modern English Biography* and the catalogue of the British Library.

Select Bibliography

Primary Sources

Abercrombie, J. (1833), *The Philosophy of the Moral Feelings*, John Murray, London.

Aguilar, G. (1853), 'The Authoress', in id., *Home Scenes and Heart Studies*, Groombridge & Sons, London.

anon (1828), *The Book of Health; A Compendium of Domestic Medicine*, Vizetelly, Branston, and Co., London.

anon (c. 1832), *The Best Methods of Improving and Preserving Health and Invigorating Life. By a London Physician*, C. Kerbey, London.

anon [Robert Tyas?] (1840), *The Handbook of Health*, Robert Tyas, London.

anon (1842), *The Young Man's Mentor, on his Entrance Into Life*, T.M. Cradock, London.

anon (1842), 'Passion and Principle. Ed by Captain Frederick Chamier, R.N.', in *New Monthly Magazine*, vol. 65, pp. 427-428.

anon (1847), *The London Medical Directory 1847*, John Churchill, London.

anon (1858), *Health for the Household*, Jarrold and Son, London.

anon (1858), *Health for the Million*, Kent & Co., London.

anon (1858), *The Household Encyclopaedia; or Family Dictionary on Everything Connected with Housekeeping and Domestic Medicine* ..., 2 vols., W. Kent & Co. etc., London etc.

anon (c. 1863), *Hand-Book of Health and Physiology* (Cassell's Elementary Handbooks), Cassell, Petter, and Galpin, London.

anon (1868), 'Modern Passion', in *Once a Week*, vol. 2, pp. 570-572.

anon (1980) [1933], *The Brontës. Their Lives, Friendships and Correspondence*, 2 vols., Basil Blackwell, Oxford.

Armstrong, E. (ed) (c. 1850), *Affection's Token: A Selection of Prose and Poetry from the Best Writers*, Thomas Allman & Son etc., London.

Arnold, M. (1987) [1970] [February 1866], 'My Countrymen', in P.J. Keating (ed), *Matthew Arnold. Selected Prose*, Penguin, London, pp. 175-201. Repr. from *The Cornhill Magazine*.

Arnold, M. (1987) [1970] [1869], 'Culture and Anarchy', in P.J. Keating (ed), *Matthew Arnold. Selected Prose*, Penguin, London, pp. 202-300.

Austen, J. (1986) [1969] [1811], *Sense and Sensibility*, Penguin, London.

Austen, J. (1996) [1813], *Pride and Prejudice*, Penguin, London.

Bain, A. ([3]1868) [1855], *The Senses and the Intellect*, Longmans, Green & Co., London.

Bain, A. ([2]1865) [1859], *The Emotions and the Will*, Longmans & Co., London.

Bain, A. (1904), *Autobiography*, Longmans & Co., London.

[Barrett [Browning], E.] (1826), *An Essay on Mind with Other Poems*, James Duncan, London.

Barrett Browning, E. (1996) [1856], *Aurora Leigh*, W.W. Norton & Co., New York/London.

[Baynes, T.S.] (April 1873), 'Darwin on Expression', in *The Edinburgh Review*, vol. 137, pp. 492-528.

Beeton, S.O. (c. 1868), *Family Etiquette: A Complete Guide to Conversation, Parties, Travel, and the Toilette, with Hints on Domestic Affairs*, Ward, Lock, and Tyler, London.

Bell, A.M. (1852), *The Language of the Passions. A Selection of Expressive Extracts, Emphasized & Rhetorically Punctuated; Forming a Series of Emotive Elocutionary Exercises*, printed for the author and published by W.P. Kennedy etc., Edinburgh etc.

Bell, C. (^{3}1844) [1806], *The Anatomy and Philosophy of Expression as Connected with the Fine Arts*, John Murray, London.

Black, G. (1892), *The Family Health Book*, Ward, Lock & Co., London.

Blennerhassett, Lady (1889), *Madame de Staël. Her Friends, and Her Influence in Politics and Literature*, Chapman and Hall, London.

[Bonhote, E.] (1810), *Feeling, or, Sketches from Life; a Desultory Poem. With Other Pieces. By A Lady*, Manners & Miller, Edinburgh, Longman, Hurst, Rees & Orme, London.

Bray, C. (1836), *The Education of the Body. An Address to the Working Classes*, printed by Henry Merridew, Coventry.

[Bray, C.] (1838), *The Education of the Feelings*, Printed for Taylor & Walton, London, and Adam & Charles Black, Edinburgh.

Bray, C. (^{2}1849), *The Education of the Feelings*, Longman & Co., London.

Bray, C. (^{3}1860), *The Education of the Feelings*, Longman & Co., London.

Bray, C. (^{4}1872), *The Education of the Feelings*, Longmans & Co., London.

Bray, C. (c. 1884), *Phases of Opinion and Experience During a Long Life: An Autobiography*, Longmans, Green and Co., London.

Brontë, C. (1985) [1849], *Shirley. A Tale*, Penguin, Harmondsworth.

Brontë, E. (1941) [1837], 'Alone I sat; the summer day', in C.W. Hatfield (ed), *The Complete Poems of Emily Jane Brontë*, Columbia UP, New York, p. 48.

[Broughton, R.] (1993) [1867], *Not Wisely But Too Well*, Alan Sutton, Stroud.

[Broughton, R.] (1993) [1867], *Cometh Up As a Flower*, Alan Sutton, Stroud.

[Brunton, M.] (1811), *Self-Control: A Novel*, 2 vols., Manners and Miller, Edinburgh.

Brunton, M. (1814), *Discipline*, Manners and Miller, Edinburgh.

C.S.H. (1850), 'Education', in *The Westminster Review*, vol. 52, pp. 615-617.

Carlile, R. (1826), *The Philosophy of the Sexes, or Every Woman's Book*, Richard Carlile, London.

Carlyle, T. (1986) [1971] [June 1829], 'Signs of the Times', in Alan Shelston (ed), *Thomas Carlyle. Selected Writings*, Penguin, London, pp. 59-85. Repr. from *The Edinburgh Review*.

Chambers's Encyclopædia. A Dictionary of Universal Knowledge for the People ..., (1862-1868), W. & R. Chambers, London.

Chambers's English Dictionary. Pronouncing, Explanatory, and Etymological ..., (1872), W. & R. Chambers, London/Edinburgh.

The Complete Dictionary of Arts and Sciences in Which the Whole Circle of Human Learning is Explained ... (*Croker's Dictionary*) (1766), J. Wilson etc., London etc.

Cooke, W. (1839), *Mind and Emotions Considered in Relation to Health and Disease*, Longman & Co., London.

Cooke, W. (1852), *A Commentary of Medical and Moral Life; or Mind and the Emotions, Considered in Relation to Health, Disease, and Religion*, Longman, Brown, & Co., London.

Craik, D.M. (1996) [1850], *Olive*, Oxford UP, Oxford/New York.

Culverwell, R.J. (1844), *Guide to Health and Long Life*, published for the author, and sold also by Messrs Sherwood and Co., London.

[Cyples, W.] (1865), 'Machinery and the Passions', in *The Cornhill Magazine*, vol. 11, pp. 541-547.

Darwin, C. (1872), *The Expression of Emotion in Man and Animals*, John Murray, London.

Darwin, C. (^{3}1998), *The Expression of Emotion in Man and Animals*, ed by Paul Ekman, Harper Collins, London.

Derrick, F. [= Frances E.M. Notley] (1872) [1868], *Olive Varcoe: A Novel*, new edition, Virtue & Co., London, Virtue & Yorston, New York.

Dickens, C. (1985) [1970] [1846-48], *Dombey and Son*, Penguin, London.

Dickens, C. (1995) [1854], *Hard Times For These Times*, Penguin, Harmondsworth.

Dickens, C. (1993) [1860-61], *Great Expectations*, Oxford UP, Oxford.

Eliot, G. (1968) [October 1854], 'Woman in France: Mme de Sablé', in Thomas Pinney (ed), *Essays of George Eliot*, Routledge and Kegan Paul, London, pp. 52-81. Reprinted from *The Westminster Review*, vol. 62, pp. 448-473.

Eliot, G. (1968) [October 1856], 'Silly Novels by Lady Novelists', in Thomas Pinney (ed), *Essays of George Eliot*, Routledge and Kegan Paul, London, pp. 300-324. Repr. from *The Westminster Review*, vol. 61, pp. 442-461.

Eliot, G. (1985) [1979] [1860], *The Mill on the Floss*, Penguin, London.

Ellis, S. (1846), *Temper and Temperament; or, Varieties of Character*, 2 vols., Fisher, Son & Co., London.

Ellis, S. (1869), *The Education of the Heart: Woman's Best Work*, Hodder and Stoughton, London.

The Home Life and Letters of Mrs. Ellis. Compiled By Her Nieces (1893), J. Nisbet & Co., London.

Encyclopædia: or, an Universal Dictionary of Arts and Sciences (Chambers) (1728), R. & W. Chambers, London.

Encyclopædia Britannica, (^{3}1788-1797), A. Bell and C. Macfarquhar, Edinburgh.

Encyclopædia Britannica, (^{7}1830-42), A. and C. Black, Edinburgh.

Encyclopædia Britannica, (^{8}1853-1860), A. and C. Black, Edinburgh.

Gaskell, E. (1977) [1906] [1857], *The Life of Charlotte Brontë*, J.M. Dent, London.

Grey, M.G. and Shirreff, E. (1850), *Thoughts on Self-Culture, Addressed to Women*, 2 vols., Edward Moxon, London.

Grey, M.G. and Shirreff, E. (1853) [c. 1842], *Passion and Principle*, George Routledge, London.

Hart, A.J.X. (1869), *Catholic Psychology*, n.p., London.

Hawthorne, R. [= Charlotte Elizabeth Riddell] (1857), *The Ruling Passion*, 3 vols., Richard Bentley, London.

Hemans, F. (1812) *The Domestic Affections and Other Poems*, T. Cadell, London.

The Household Encyclopædia ..., (1858), 2 vols., W. Kent & Co., London.

James, G.P.R. (1838-39), *A Book of the Passions Illustrated with Sixteen Splendid Engravings* ..., Longman, Orme, Brown, Green, and Longmans, London and Delloy & Co., Paris.

Jewsbury, G. (1994) [1848], *The Half-Sisters*, Oxford UP, Oxford/New York.

Samuel Johnson, S. (1968) [1755], *A Dictionary of the English Language*, 2 vols., Georg Olms Verlagsbuchhandlung, Hildesheim.

Johnson, W.B. (1850), *The Morbid Emotions of Women; Their Origin, Tendencies, and Treatment*, Simpkin, Marshall and Co., London.

Kavanagh, J. (1862), *French Women of Letters: Biographical Sketches*, Hurst and Blackett, London.

Keble, J. (1912), *Keble's Lectures on Poetry, 1832-41*, transl. by Edward Kershaw Francis, 2 vols., Clarendon Press, Oxford.

Lang, J. (c. 1859), *The Secret Police; or, Plot and Passion*, Ward and Lock and Petter and Galpin, London.

Lang, J. and Taylor, T. (1853), *Plot and Passion*, Lacy's Acting Edition vol. 13, Thomas Hailes Lacy, London.

Lee, V. [Violet Paget] (1998) [1993] [1896], 'Lady Tal', in Elaine Showalter (ed), *Daughters of Decadence. Women Writers of the Fin-de-Siècle*, Virago, London, pp. 192-261. Repr. from *Vanities*, William Heinemann, London.

[Leigh, P.] (1842), 'Comicalities of the Feelings', in *Bentley's Miscellany*, vol. 11, pp. 51-55.

Lewes, G.H. (1990) [1850], 'Currer Bell's Shirley', in Barbara Timm Gates (ed), *Critical Essays on Charlotte Brontë*, G.K. Hall & Co., Boston, Mass., pp. 217-223. Repr. from *The Edinburgh Review*, vol. 91, pp. 153-173.

Lewes, G.H. (1852), 'The Lady Novelists', in *The Westminster Review*, vol. 58 o.s., pp. 129-141.

Mackay, C. (1841), *Memoirs of Extraordinary Popular Delusions*, 3 vols., Richard Bentley, London.

Mackay, C. (1858 etc.), *The Home Affections*, George Routledge, London.

Martineau, H. (1831), *Five Years of Youth, or Sense and Sentiment*, printed for Harvey and Darton, London.

Martineau, J. (^{5}1846) [1840], *Hymns for the Christian Church and Home. Collected and Edited by J.M.*, printed for the editor and sold by Chapman, Brothers, London.

Mill, J.S. (1981) [1867], 'Thoughts on Poetry and Its Varieties', in *The Collected Works of John Stuart Mill*, vol. 1, ed. by John Mercel Robson and Jack Stillinger, University of Toronto Press, Toronto, Routledge & Kegan Paul, London, pp. 343-365.

Mill, J.S. (1873), *Autobiography*, Longmans, Green, Reader, and Dyer, London.

The Oxford Encyclopædia; or, Dictionary of Arts, Sciences, and General Literature (1828), printed for Thomas Kelly, London/Oxford.

Parris, E.T. (1838), *Gems of Beauty, Displayed in a Series of Twelve Highly Finished Engravings of the Passions*, Longman, Orme, Brown, Green & Longmans, London.

The Penny Cyclopædia of The Society for the Diffusion of Useful Knowledge (1833-58), 29 vols., Charles Knight, London.

Powell, J.H. (1853), *The Poetry of Feeling and Poetry of Diction. A Lecture*, Geo. De Fraine, Chronicle and Gazette Office, Ailesbury.

Powell, J.H. (1857), *Phases of Thought and Feeling. Poems and Lyrics*, Partridge & Co., London.

Powell, J.H. (1861), *Woman, at Home and Abroad: A Glance at her Domestic and Social Condition*, Wertheim & Macintosh, London, William Simpson, Brighton.

Reece, R. (1808), *A Practical Dictionary of Domestic Medicine* ..., Longman, Hurst, Rees, and Orme, London.

Ryland, F. (⁷1897), *Psychology. An Introductory Manual for the Use of Students*, revised and largely rewritten, George Bell and Sons, London.

[Spencer, Mrs] (1812), *Commemorative Feelings or Miscellaneous Poems, Interspersed with Sketches in Prose on the Sources of Pensive Pleasure*, White, Cochrane and Co. etc., London.

Spencer, H. (1855), *The Principles of Psychology*, Longman, Brown, Green and Longmans, London.

Spencer, H. (1 April 1871), 'Morals and Moral Sentiments', in *Fortnightly Review*, vol. 1, pp. 419-432.

Spencer, H. ([13]1887) [1873], *The Study of Sociology*, Kegan Paul, Trench & Co., London.

de Staël, G. (1985) [1807], *Corinne, ou l'Italie*, Gallimard, Paris.

de Staël, G. (2000) [1796], *L'Influence des passions sur le bonheur de l'individu et des nations*. Suivi de *Réflexion sur le suicide*, Rivages poche, Paris.

Stanley, H.M. (1895), *Studies in the Evolutionary Psychology of Feeling*, Swan Sonnenschein, London.

Stevens, A. (1881), *Madame de Staël. A Study of Her Life and Times: The First Revolution and The First Empire*, 2 vols., John Murray, London.

Stodart, M.A. (1839), *Hints on Reading Addressed to a Young Lady*, R.B. Seeley and W. Burnside, London.

Stodart, M.A. (1840), *Every Day Duties: In Letters to a Young Lady*, G. Seeley, London.

Stodart, M.A. (1842), *The Female Writers: Thoughts on Their Proper Sphere and Their Powers of Usefulness*, G. Seeley, London.

Stodart, M.A. (1844), *Principles of Education*, G. Seeley, London.

[Stringer, Mrs] (c. 1830), *The Chain of Affection; A Moral Poem and Other Pieces. By A Lady*, printed for J. Darnill, Richmond.

Sully, J. (1892), *Outlines of Psychology*, new rev. ed. Longmans, Green, and Co., London.

Tuke, D.H. (ed) (1892), *A Dictionary of Psychological Medicine ...*, J. & A. Churchill, London.

[Tyas, R.] (1836 etc.), *The Sentiment of Flowers*, Charles Tilt, London.

Wordsworth, W. (1944) [1802], 'Preface to the Second Edition of Several of the Foregoing Poems, Published, with an Additional Volume, Under the Title of "Lyrical Ballads"', in E. de Selincourt (ed), *The Poetical Works of William Wordsworth*, Clarendon Press, Oxford, pp. 383-404.

Secondary Sources

Allibone, S.A. (1882) [1859-71], *A Critical Dictionary of English Literature and British and American Authors, Living and Deceased ...*, J.B. Lippincott and Co, Philadelphia.

Anderson, B. (1983), *Imagined Communities. Reflections on the Origin and Spread of Nationalism*, Verso, London.

Armstrong, I. (1977), 'The Role and the Treatment of Emotion in Victorian Criticism of Poetry', in *Victorian Periodicals Newsletter*, vol. 10 (1), pp. 3-16.

Armstrong, I. (1993), '"A Music of Thine Own"', in id., *Victorian Poetry. Poetry, Poetics and Politics*, Routledge, London/New York, pp. 318-377.

Armstrong, N. and Tennenhouse, L. (1987), 'The literature of conduct, the conduct of literature, and the politics of desire: an introduction', in id. (eds), *The Ideology of Conduct. Essays on Literature and the History of Sexuality*, Methuen, New York etc., pp. 1-24.

Assmann, A. (1999), *Erinnerungsräume. Formen und Wandlungen des kulturellen Gedächtnisses*, C.H. Beck, Munich.

The Athenæum Index of Reviews and Reviewers, 1830-1870: http://www.cs.city.ac.uk/~asp/v2/home.html

Averill, J.R. (1990), 'Inner feelings, works of the flesh, the beast within, diseases of the mind, driving force, and putting on a show: Six Metaphors of Emotion and Their Theoretical Extensions', in David E. Leary (ed), *Metaphors in the History of Psychology*, Cambridge UP, Cambridge, pp. 104-132.

Baader, R. (1986), *Dames de lettres. Autorinnen des preziösen hocharistokratischen und 'modernen' Salons (1649-1698): Mlle de Scudéry – Mlle de Montpensier – Mme d'Aulnoy*, Metzler, Stuttgart.

Balayé, S. (1994), *Mme de Staël. Ecrire, Lutter, Vivre*, Droz, Geneva.

Barker, J. (1994), *The Brontës*, Weidenfeld and Nicolson, London.

Beer, G. (1996), 'Parable, Professionalization, and Literary Allusion in Victorian Scientific Writing', in id., *Open Fields. Science in Cultural Encounter*, Clarendon Press, Oxford, pp. 196-215.

Bell, M. (1983), *The Sentiment of Reality: Truth of Feeling in the European Novel*, Unwin, London.

Bell, M. (2000), 'Adam Smith and Friedrich Schiller: The Luxury of Sensibility and the Aestheticising of Emotion', in *REAL*, vol. 16, pp. 105-116.

Bennett, T. (1990), *Outside Literature*, Routledge, London/New York.

Blain, V. et al. (eds) (1990), *The Feminist Companion to Literature in English*, Yale UP, New Haven/London.

Boase, F. (1892-1921), *Modern English Biography, Containing ... Memoirs of Persons Who Have Died Since ... 1850 ...*, 6 vols., Netherton and Worth, Truro.

Bock, G. and Zimmermann, M. (1997), 'Die europäische Querelle des Femmes. Eine begriffs- und forschungsgeschichtliche Einführung', in id. (eds), *Die Europäische 'Querelle des Femmes'. Geschlechterdebatten seit dem 15. Jahrhundert* (Querelles. Jahrbuch für Frauenforschung, vol. 2), Metzler, Stuttgart/Weimar, pp. 9-38.

Böhm, R. (1998), 'Vom *code galant* zum *code tendre*. Freundschaftsentwürfe im Kreis der Madame de Sévigné', in Sabine Eickenrodt and Cettina Rapisarda (eds), *Freundschaft im Gespräch* (Querelles. Jahrbuch für Frauen- und Geschlechterforschung, vol. 3), Metzler, Stuttgart/Weimar, pp. 125-136.

Bonheim, H. (1980), 'Word Invention and the History of Affect', in Gunter Brettschneider and Christian Lehmann (eds), *Wege zur Universalienforschung (Festschrift für Hansjakob Seiler)*, Gunter Narr, Tübingen, pp. 521-528.

Bonheim, H. (1999), 'Die Variable Geschlecht im Wortschatz der Emotionen', in Andrea Gutenberg and Ralf Schneider (eds), *Gender – Culture – Poetics. Zur Geschlechterforschung in der Literatur- und Kulturwissenschaft (Festschrift für Natascha Würzbach)*, WVT, Trier, pp. 31-46.

Bourdieu, P. (1985) [1977], *Outline of a Theory of Practice*, transl. by Richard Nice, Cambridge UP, Cambridge [French original 1972].

Bowler, P.J. (1992), 'Darwinism and Victorian Values: Threat or Opportunity?', in *Proceedings of the British Academy*, vol. 78, pp. 129-147.

Briggs, A. (1958), 'Private and Social Themes in *Shirley*', in *Brontë Society Transactions*, pp. 203-219.

The British Library General Catalogue of Printed Books to 1975 (1979), Clive Bingley etc., London.

Brooks, P. (1976), *The Melodramatic Imagination. Balzac, Henry James, Melodrama and the Mode of Excess*, Yale UP, New Haven/London.

Bruder, K.-J. (1993), 'Psychologie der Emotion. Der psychologische Diskurs über die Gefühle', in id., *Subjektivität und Postmoderne. Der Diskurs der Psychologie*, Suhrkamp, Frankfurt a.M., pp. 167-201.

Budde, G.-F. (1994), *Auf dem Weg ins Bürgerleben. Kindheit und Erziehung in deutschen und englischen Bürgerfamilien 1840-1914*, Vandenhoeck and Ruprecht, Göttingen.

Bynum, W.F. (1992), 'Medical Values in a Commercial Age', in *Proceedings of the British Academy*, vol. 78, pp. 149-163.

Caine, B. (1997), *English Feminism 1780-1980*, Oxford UP, Oxford.

Cancian, F.M. (1986), 'The Feminization of Love', in *Signs*, vol. 2, pp. 692-709.

Chartier, R. et al. (eds) (1987), *La sensibilité dans l'histoire*, Gérard Monfort, Brionne.

Chartier, R. (1995), 'L'Histoire culturelle entre "Linguistic Turn" et Retour au Sujet', in H. Lehmann (ed), *Wege zu einer neuen Kulturgeschichte. Mit Beiträgen von Rudolf Vierhaus und Roger Chartier*, Wallstein Verlag, Göttingen, pp. 29-58.

Chew, S. and Altick, R. (^{2}1967), *The Nineteenth Century and After (1789-1939)* (A Literary History of England, vol. 4, ed by Albert Croll Baugh), Appleton-Century-Crofts, New York.

Christ C.T. and Jordan J.O. (eds) (1998), *Victorian Literature and the Victorian Visual Imagination*, University of California Press, Berkeley.

Codell, J.F. (1986), 'Expression Over Beauty: Facial Expression, Body Language, and Circumstantiality in the Paintings of the Pre-Raphaelite Brotherhood', in *Victorian Studies*, vol. 29 (2), pp. 255-290.

Codell, J.F. (1992), 'Sentiment, the Highest Attribute of Art: The Socio-Poetics of Feeling', in *Dickens Studies Annual*, vol. 21, pp. 233-251.

Colley, L. (1992), *Forging the Nation 1707-1837*, Yale UP, London/New York.

Cosslet, T. (1988), *Woman to Woman: Female Friendship in Victorian Fiction*, Harvester Press, Brighton.

Courtine, J.J. and Haroche, C. (1988), *L'Histoire du visage. Exprimer et taire ses émotions XVe – début XIXe siècle*, Rivages, Paris.

Cross, N. (1985), *The Common Writer: Life in Nineteenth Century Grub Street*, Cambridge UP, Cambridge/New York.

Crossley, C. and Small, I. (eds) (1988), *Studies in Anglo-French Cultural Relations: Imagining France*, Macmillan, Basingstoke.

Cunningham, V. (1994), *In the Reading Gaol. Postmodernity, Texts and History*, Blackwell, Oxford.

Cunningham, V. (1999), 'Readers Beside Themselves: Particular Pleasures and Generic Controls', in Jürgen Schlaeger and Gesa Stedman (eds), *Representations of Emotions*, Gunter Narr, Tübingen, pp. 43-57.

Cunningham, V. (2000), 'The Poetry and Poetics of Violent Feelings', in *REAL*, vol. 16, pp. 186-198.

Cvetkovich, A. (1992), *Mixed Feelings. Feminism, Mass Culture, and Victorian Sensationalism*, Rutgers UP, New Brunswick, N.J.

Daston, L. (1998), 'Die Kultur der wissenschaftlichen Objektivität', in Otto Gerhard Oexle (ed), *Naturwissenschaft, Geisteswissenschaft, Kulturwissenschaft: Einheit – Gegensatz – Komplementarität?*, Wallstein Verlag, Göttingen, pp. 9-39.

Davidoff, L. (1993), '"Alte Hüte". Öffentlichkeit und Privatheit in der feministischen Geschichtsschreibung', in *L'Homme. Zeitschrift für feministische Geschichtswissenschaft*, 4th series, vol. 2, pp. 7-36.

Davidoff, L. and Hall, C. (1987), *Family Fortunes. Men and Women of the English Middle Class, 1780-1850*, Hutchinson, London.

DeJean, J. (1991), *Tender Geographies. Women and the Origin of the Novel in France*, Columbia UP, New York.

DeJean, J. (1991), 'Portrait of the Artist as Sappho', in Madelyn Gutwirth et al. (eds), *Germaine de Staël. Crossing the Borders*, Rutgers UP, New Brunswick, pp. 122-137.

DeJean, J. (1997), 'A Short History of the Human Heart', in id., *Ancients Against Moderns: Culture Wars and the Making of a Fin de Siècle*, University of Chicago Press, Chicago, pp. 80-123.

The Dictionary of National Biography on CD-ROM (1985), Oxford UP, Oxford.

Digby, A. (1990), 'Victorian Values and Women in Public and in Private', in *Proceedings of the British Academy*, vol. 78, pp. 195-215.

Digby, A. and Searby, P. (1981), *Children, School and Society in Nineteenth-Century England*, Macmillan, London/Basingstoke.

Dinzelbacher, P. (1993), 'Emotionen', in *Das andere Mittelalter. Emotionen, Rituale und Kontraste*, Kunsthalle Krems 1993, pp. 101-110.

Duden, B. (1995), 'Anmerkungen zur Kulturgeschichte des Herzens', in Faridah Akashe-Böhme (ed), *Von der Auffälligkeit des Leibes*, Suhrkamp, Frankfurt a.M., pp. 130-141.

Eagleton, T. (1975), *Myths of Power. A Marxist Study of the Brontës*, Macmillan, Basingstoke/London.

Eagleton, T. (1990), 'Class, Power and Charlotte Brontë', in Barbara Timm Gates (ed), *Critical Essays on Charlotte Brontë*, G.K. Hall and Co., Boston, Mass, pp. 50-60.

Ekman, P. (1998), 'Introduction', in Charles Darwin, *The Expression of Emotion in Man and Animals*, Harper Collins, London, ed by Paul Ekman, pp. xxi-xxxvi.

Elias, N. (^{19}1995) [1936], *Über den Prozeß der Zivilisation*, 2 vols., Suhrkamp, Frankfurt a.M.

Eliot, S. (1985), 'The Three-Decker Novel and Its First Cheap Reprint, 1826-94', in *The Library*, 6th series, vol. 7, pp. 38-53.

Eliot, S. (1995), 'Some trends in British book production, 1800-1919', in John O. Jordan and Robert L. Patten (eds), *Literature in the Marketplace. Nineteenth-Century British Publishing and Reading Practices*, Cambridge UP, Cambridge, pp. 19-43.

The English Catalogue of Printed Books (1914), Publisher's Circular, London.

Erickson, R.A. (1997), *The Language of the Heart, 1600-1750*, University of Pennsylvania Press, Philadelphia.

Febvre, L. (1953) [1941], 'Comment reconstituer la vie affective d'autrefois? La sensibilité et l'histoire', in id., *Combats pour l'histoire*, Librairie Armand Colin, Paris, pp. 221-238. Reprinted from *Annales d'Histoire Sociale* 3.

Ferris, I. (1991), *The Achievement of Literary Authority. Gender, History, and the Waverley Novels*, Cornell UP, Ithaca/London.

Fischer-Lichte, E. (2000), 'The Body as Sign and as Experience: On the Effect of Theatre Performance', in *REAL*, vol. 16, pp. 117-131.

Flint, K. (1993), *The Woman Reader*, Oxford UP, Oxford.

Flint, K. (2001), *The Victorians and the Visual Imagination*, Cambridge UP, Cambridge.

Foster, S. (1985), *Victorian Women's Fiction: Marriage, Freedom and the Individual*, Croom Helm, Beckenham.

Foucault, M. (1991), *Der Wille zum Wissen. Sexualität und Wahrheit 1*, Suhrkamp, Frankfurt a.M., [French original 1976].

Foucault, M. ([7]1995), *Archäologie des Wissens*, Suhrkamp, Frankfurt a.M., [French Original 1969].

Foucault, F. (1996) [1991], *Die Ordnung des Diskurses*, Fischer, Frankfurt a.M., [French original 1972].

François, E. et al. (eds) (1995), *Nation und Emotion* (Kritische Studien zur Geschichtswissenschaft, vol. 10), Vandenhoeck and Ruprecht, Göttingen.

Frith, G. (1995/96), 'Embodying the Nation: Gender and Performance in Women's Fiction', in *New Formations*, vol. 27, pp. 98-113.

Frith, G. (1997), 'Playing with Shawls: George Eliot's Use of *Corinne* in *The Mill on the Floss*', in John Rignall (ed), *George Eliot and Europe*, Scolar Press, Aldershot, pp. 225-239.

Gallagher, C. (1987), 'The Body Versus the Social Body in the Works of Thomas Malthus and Henry Mayhew', in Catherine Gallagher and Thomas Laqueur (eds), *The Making of the Modern Body. Sexuality and Society in the 19th Century*, University of California Press, Berkeley, pp. 83-106.

Gay, P. (1984-1998), *The Bourgeois Experience. From Victoria to Freud*, 5 vols., Oxford UP, Oxford, W.W. Norton and Co., New York/London.

Gerhards, J. (1986), 'Soziologie der Emotionen. Ein Literaturbericht', in *Kölner Zeitschrift für Soziologie und Sozialpsychologie*, vol. 38, pp. 760-71.

Gerould, D. (1990), 'Representations of Melodramatic Performance', in *Browning Institute Studies*, vol. 18, pp. 55-71.

Gilbert, S.M. and Gubar, S. (1984) [1974], 'The Genesis of Hunger, According to *Shirley*', in id., *The Madwoman in the Attic. The Woman Writer and the Nineteenth-Century Literary Imagination*, Yale UP, New Haven/London, pp. 372-398.

Gillis, J.R. (1988), 'From Ritual to Romance. Toward an Alternative History of Love', in Carol Z. Stearns and Peter N. Stearns (eds), *Emotion and Social Change: Toward a New Psychohistory*, Holmes and Meier, New York/Oxford, pp. 87-121.

Gillow, J. (c. 1888), *A Literary and Biographical History or Bibliographical Dictionary of the English Catholics ...*, 5 vols., reprinted Burt Franklin, New York.

Göbel, W. (1996), 'Conflicting Definitions of the Culture of Sensibility', in Jürgen Klein and Dirk Vanderbeke (eds), *Anglistentag 1995 Greifswald. Proceedings. XVII*, Max Niemeyer Verlag, Tübingen, pp. 93-104.

Goodwin, G.H. (1987), 'Keble and Newman: Tractarian Aesthetics and the Romantic Tradition', in *Victorian Studies*, vol. 30 (4), pp. 475-494.

Graham, J. (1961), 'Lavater's *Physiognomy* in England', in *Journal of the History of Ideas*, vol. 22, pp. 561-572.

Green, M. (1991), 'Sympathy and Social Value of Poetry: J.S. Mill's Literary Essays', in *University of Toronto Quarterly*, vol. 60 (4), pp. 452-468.

Gutwirth, M. (1983-85), 'Forging a Vocation: Germaine de Staël on Fiction, Power, and Passion', in *Bulletin of Research in the Humanities*, vol. 86 (3), pp. 242-254.

Hall, C. (1990), 'Private Persons versus Public Someones: Class, Gender and Politics in England, 1780-1850', in Terry Lovell (ed), *British Feminist Thought. A Reader*, Blackwell, Oxford, pp. 51-67.

Hansen, K.P. (ed) (1990), *Empfindsamkeiten* (Passauer Interdisziplinäre Kolloquien, vol. 2), Wissenschaftsverlag Richard Rothe, Passau.

Hardy, B. (1986) [1985], *Forms of Feeling in Victorian Fiction*, Methuen, London.

Harré, R. (1986), 'An Outline of the Social Constructionist Viewpoint', in id. (ed), *The Social Construction of Emotions*, Basil Blackwell, Oxford, pp. 2-14.

Harrison, J.F.C. (1971), *The Early Victorians, 1832-1851*, Weidenfeld and Nicolson, London.

Hempfer, K.W. (1990), 'Zu einigen Problemen einer Fiktionstheorie', in *Zeitschrift für französische Sprache und Literatur*, vol. 100, pp. 109-137.

Herrlinger, W. (1987), *Sentimentalismus und Postsentimentalismus. Studien zum englischen Roman bis zur Mitte des 19. Jahrhunderts*, Max Niemeyer Verlag, Tübingen.

Hirschman, A.O. (1977), *The Passions and the Interests. Political Arguments for Capitalism before its Triumph*, Princeton UP, Princeton.

Hobsbawm, E. (1992) [1990], *Nations and Nationalism Since 1780. Programme, Myth, Reality*, new and revised edition, Cambridge UP, Cambridge.

Hobsbawm, E. (1995), 'Die englische *middle class* 1780-1920', in Jürgen Kocka (ed), *Bürgertum im 19. Jahrhundert*, vol. 1 (*Einheit und Vielfalt Europas*), Vandenhoeck and Ruprecht, Göttingen, pp. 85-112.

Honegger, C. (1996) [1991], *Die Ordnung der Geschlechter. Die Wissenschaften vom Menschen und das Weib 1750-1850*, dtv, Munich.

Houghton, W.E. et al. (eds) (1966-1989), *The Wellesley Index of Victorian Periodicals 1824-1900*, 5 vols., University of Toronto Press, Toronto.

Jöckel, S. (1984), *'Nouvelle histoire' und Literaturwissenschaft*, Schäuble, Rheinfelden.

Jones, A.H. (1986), *Ideas and Innovations. Best Sellers of Jane Austen's Age*, AMS Press, New York.

Kadish, D.Y. (1991), 'Narrating the French Revolution: The Example of *Corinne*', in Madelyn Gutwirth et al. (eds), *Germaine de Staël. Crossing the Borders*, Rutgers UP, New Brunswick, N.J., pp. 113-121.

Kaplan, F. (1987), *Sacred Tears. Sentimentality in Victorian Literature*, Princeton UP, Princeton.

Kemper, T. (1993), 'Sociological Models in the Explanation of Emotions', in Michael Lewis and Jeannette M. Haviland (eds), *Handbook of Emotions*, The Guilford Press, New York/London, pp. 41-51.

Korte, B. (1993), *Körpersprache in der Literatur. Theorie und Geschichte am Beispiel englischer Erzählprosa*, Francke, Tübingen.

Kucich, J. (1990) [winter 1985], 'Passionate Reserve and Reserved Passion in the Works of Charlotte Brontë', in Barbara Timm Gates (ed), *Critical Essays on Charlotte Brontë*, G.K. Hall and Co., Boston, Mass., pp. 68-88. Repr. from *ELH*, vol. 52, pp. 913-937.

Lakoff, G. and Johnson, M. (1980), *Metaphors We Live By*, Chicago UP, Chicago.

Leary, D.E. (1990), 'Psyche's Muse: The Role of Metaphor in the History of Psychology', in id. (ed), *Metaphors in the History of Psychology*, Cambridge UP, Cambridge, pp. 1-78.

Le Goff, J. (1985), 'Préface', in id., *L'imaginaire médieval. Essais*, Gallimard, Paris, pp. I-XXI.

Lewis, M. and Haviland, J.M. (1993), 'Preface', in id. (eds), *Handbook of Emotions*, The Guilford Press, New York/London, pp. ix-x.

Lorenz, M. (2000), *Leibhaftige Vergangenheit. Einführung in die Körpergeschichte*, edition diskord, Tübingen.

Luhman, N. (1982), *Liebe als Passion*, Suhrkamp, Frankfurt a.M.

Lutz, C. (1990), 'Engendered Emotion: Gender, Power, and the Rhetoric of Emotional Control in American Discourse', in Catherine Lutz and Lila Abu-Lughod (eds), *Language and the Politics of Emotion*, Cambridge UP, Cambridge, pp. 69-91.

Lutz, C. (2002), 'Emotion and Feminist Theories', in Ingrid Kasten, Gesa Stedman, Margarete Zimmermann (eds), Kulturen der Gefühle in Mittelalter und Früher Neuzeit (Querelles. Jahrbuch für Frauen- und Geschlechterforschung, vol. 7), Metzler, Stuttgart/Weimar, pp. 104-121.

Lutz, C. and Abu-Lughod, L. (eds) (1990), *Language and the Politics of Emotion*, Cambridge UP, Cambridge.

Lutz, C.A. and White, G.M. (1986), 'The Anthropology of Emotions', in *Annual Review of Anthropology*, vol. 15, pp. 405-436.

Lyon, M. and Barbalet, J.M. (1994), 'Society's body: emotion and the "somatization" of social theory', in Thomas J. Csordas (ed), *Embodiment and Experience. The Existential Ground of Culture and Self*, Cambridge UP, Cambridge, pp. 48-66.

Madden, W.M. (1963-64), 'The Victorian Sensibility', in *Victorian Studies*, vol. 7 (1), pp. 67-97.

Metzger, L. (1990), 'The Role of Feeling in the Formation of Romantic Ideology', in Syndy McMillen Conger (ed), *Sensibility in Transformation. Creative Resistance to Sentiment from the Augustans to the Romantics*, Associated University Presses, London/Toronto, pp. 172-194.

Miall, D.S. (1992), 'Wordsworth and *The Prelude*: the Problematics of Feeling', in *Studies in Romanticism*, vol. 31, pp. 233-253.

Mills, S. (1998), *Discourse*, Routledge, London.

Mitchell, S. (1983), *Dinah Mulock Craik*, Twayne Publishers, Boston.

Moers, E. (1977), *Literary Women*, W.A. Allen, London.

Morgan, P.F. (1982), 'Mill and Poetry: The Central Years', in *The Wordsworth Circle*, vol. 13 (1), pp. 50-56.

Mosse, W. (1995), 'Adel und Bürgertum im Europa des 19. Jahrhunderts. Eine vergleichende Betrachtung', in Jürgen Kocka (ed), *Bürgertum im 19. Jahrhundert*, vol. 3 (*Verbürgerlichung, Recht und Politik*), Vandenhoeck and Ruprecht, Göttingen, pp. 9-47.

Müller, M. (1999), *'These Savage Beasts Become Domestick': The Discourse of the Passions in Early Modern England With Special Reference to Non-Fictional Texts*, D.Phil. Thesis, unpublished ms., University of Oxford.

O'Donoghue, D.J. (1892-93), *The Poets of Ireland. A Biographical Dictionary with Bibliographical Particulars*, D.J. O'Donoghue, London.

Oexle, O.G. (1984), 'Geschichtswissenschaft im Zeichen des Historismus. Bemerkungen zum Standort der Geschichtsforschung', in *Historische Zeitschrift*, vol. 238, pp. 17-55.

Offen, K. (1998), 'Reclaiming the European Enlightenment for Feminism. Or Prolegomena To Any Future History of Eighteenth-Century Europe', in Tjitske Akkerman and Siep Stuurman (eds), *Perspectives on Feminist Political Thought in European History from the Middle Ages to the Present*, Routledge, London/New York, pp. 85-103.

Oxford English Dictionary on CD-ROM (^{2}1994), Oxford UP, Oxford.

Perkin, J. (1988), *Women and Marriage in Nineteenth-Century England*, Routledge, London.

Perrot, P. (October 1987), 'La richesse cachée: pour une généalogie de l'austerité des appararences', in *Communications*, vol. 46, pp. 157-179.

Pfister, M. (1985), 'Konzepte der Intertextualität', in Ulrich Broich and Manfred Pfister (eds), *Intertextualität. Formen, Funktionen, anglistische Fallstudien*, Max Niemeyer Verlag; Tübingen, pp. 1-30.

Pinch, A. (1996), *Strange Fits of Passion. Epistemologies of Emotion, Hume to Austen*, Stanford UP, Stanford, Cal.

Planté, C. (1989), *La petite sœur de Balzac. Essai sur la femme auteur*, Seuil, Paris.

Pogliano, C. (1994), 'Entre forme et fonction: une nouvelle science de l'homme', in *L'Ame au corps. Arts et sciences 1793-1993. Catalogue réalisé sous la direction de Jean Clair, Galeries nationales du Grand Palais 19 octobre – 24 janvier 1994*, Gallimard/Electa, Paris, pp. 238-265.

Porter, R. (1991), 'History of the Body', in Peter Burke (ed), *New Perspectives on Historical Writing*, Polity Press, Cambridge, pp. 206-232.

Porter, R. (1991), 'Bodies of Thought: Thoughts about the Body in Eighteenth-Century England', in Joan H. Pittock and Andrew Wear (eds), *Interpretation and Cultural History*, Macmillan, Basingstoke and London, pp. 82-108.

Reddy, W.M. (June 1997), 'Against Constructionism. The Historical Ethnography of Emotions', in *Current Anthropology*, vol. 38 (3), pp. 327-351.

Reichardt, S. (1997), 'Bourdieu für Historiker? Ein kultursoziologisches Angebot an die Sozialgeschichte', in Thomas Mergel and Thomas Welskopp (eds), *Geschichte zwischen Kultur und Gesellschaft. Beiträge zur Theoriedebatte*, C.H. Beck, Munich, pp. 71-93.

Rendall, J. (1985), *The Origins of Modern Feminism: Women in Britain, France and the United States, 1780-1860*, Macmillan, Basingstoke.

Reynolds, K. and Humble, N. (1993), *Victorian Heroines. Representations of Femininity in Nineteenth-Century Literature and Art*, Harvester Wheatsheaf, Hemel Hempstead.

Robling, F.-H. (1995), 'Probleme begriffsgeschichtlicher Forschung beim Historischen Wörterbuch der Rhetorik', in *Archiv für Begriffsgeschichte*, vol. 38, pp. 9-22.

Russell-Hochschild, A. (1983), *The Managed Heart. Commercialization of Human Feeling*, University of California Press, Berkeley, etc.

Sahakian, W.S. (1975), *History and Systems of Psychology*, John Wiley and Sons, New York etc.

Schabert, I. (1997), *Englische Literaturwissenschaft aus der Sicht der Geschlechterforschung*, Alfred Kröner, Stuttgart.

Schabert, I. (1999), 'Eros und Erotik: Das Modell *Corinne*', in Andrea Gutenberg and Ralf Schneider (eds), *Gender – Culture – Poetics. Zur Geschlechterforschung in der Literatur- und Kulturwissenschaft* (*Festschrift für Natascha Würzbach*), WVT, Trier, pp. 13-30.

Schlaeger, J. (1999), 'Introduction', in Jürgen Schlaeger and Gesa Stedman (eds), *Representations of Emotions*, Gunter Narr, Tübingen, pp. 9-18.

Schlaeger, J. (1999), 'The Politics of Taste', in Jürgen Schlaeger and Gesa Stedman (eds), *Representations of Emotions*, Gunter Narr, Tübingen, pp. 77-85.

Schultz, H. (1979), 'Begriffsgeschichte und Argumentationsgeschichte', in Reinhart Koselleck (ed), *Historische Semantik und Begriffsgeschichte*, Klett-Cotta, Stuttgart, pp. 43-74.

Sennett, R. (1974), *The Fall of Public Man*, Alfred J. Knopf, New York.

Shapiro, A. (winter 1968), 'Public Themes and Private Lives: Social Criticism in *Shirley*', in Barbara Timm Gates (ed) (1990), *Critical Essays on Charlotte Brontë*, G.K. Hall and Co., Boston, Mass., pp. 223-232. Reprinted from *Papers on Language and Literature*, vol. 4 (1), pp. 74-84.

Shattock, J. (1993), *The Oxford Companion to British Women Writers*, Oxford UP, Oxford/New York.

Showalter, E. (1987), *The Female Malady: Women, Madness and English Culture, 1830-1980*, Virago, London.

Showalter, E. (1999) [1977], *A Literature of Their Own. British Women Novelists from Brontë to Lessing*, expanded ed., Princeton UP, Princeton, N.J.

Shuttleworth, S. (1984), *George Eliot and Nineteenth-Century Science: The Make-Believe of a Beginning*, Cambridge UP, Cambridge.

Shuttleworth, S. (1996), *Charlotte Brontë and Ninteenth-Century Psychology*, Cambridge UP, Cambridge.

Shweder, R.A. (1984), 'Anthropology's Romantic Rebellion Against the Enlightenment, or There's More to Thinking Than Reason and Evidence', in R.A. Shweder and Robert A. LeVine (eds), *Culture Theory. Essays on Mind, Self, and Emotion*, Cambridge UP, Cambridge, N.Y., pp. 27-66.

Small, H. (1996), *Love's Madness. Madness, the Novel and Female Insanity, 1800-1865*, Clarendon Press, Oxford.

Sommers, S. (1988), 'Understanding Emotions: Some Interdisciplinary Considerations', in Carol Z. Stearns and Peter N. Stearns (eds), *Emotion and Social Change. Toward a New Psychohistory*, Holmes and Meier, New York/London, pp. 23-38.

de Sousa, R. (1980), 'The Rationality of Emotions', in Amélie Oksenberg Rorty (ed), *Explaining Emotions*, University of California Press, Berkeley etc., pp. 127-151.

Starobinski, J. (1974), 'La littérature. Le texte et l'interprète', in Jacques Le Goff and Pierre Nora (eds), *Faire de l'histoire*, vol. 2, Gallimard, Paris, pp. 225-244.

Stearns, C.Z. and Stearns, P.N. (1988), 'Introduction', in id. (eds), *Emotion and Social Change: Toward a New Psychohistory*, Holmes and Meier, New York/Oxford, pp. 1-21.

Stearns, P.N. (1993), 'History of Emotions: The Issue of Change', in Michael Lewis and Jeannette M. Haviland (eds), *Handbook of Emotions*, The Guilford Press, New York/London, pp. 17-28.

Stearns, P.N. with Stearns, C.Z. (1985), 'Emotionology: Clarifying the History of Emotions and Emotional Standards', in *American Historical Review*, vol. 90, pp. 813-36.

Stedman, G. (1999), 'Mind, Matter and Morals – The Emotions and Nineteenth-Century Discourse', in Jürgen Schlaeger and Gesa Stedman (eds), *Representations of Emotions*, Gunter Narr, Tübingen, pp. 125-135.

Stedman, G. (1999), '*Channel Crossings*: Zum Verhältnis englischer und französischer Autorinnen im 19. Jahrhundert', in Renate Kroll and Margarete Zimmermann (eds), *Gender Studies in den romanischen Literaturen: Revisionen, Subversionen*, dipa, Frankfurt a.M., pp. 256-276.

Stedman, G. (2000), '"Private" Passions in Public Places – Women's Poetry on the Feelings', in Sabine Coelsch-Foisner and Holger Klein (eds), *Private and Public Voices in Victorian Poetry* (Studies in English and Comparative Literature, vol. 16), Stauffenburg Verlag, Tübingen, pp. 149-160.

Stedman, G. (2000), 'Pleasurable Pictures – The Delights of Visual Excess', in *REAL*, vol. 16, pp. 149-162.

Stedman, G. (2002), 'Fundstück', in Ingrid Kasten, Gesa Stedman, Margarete Zimmermann (eds), *Kulturen der Gefühle in Mittelalter und Früher Neuzeit* (Querelles. Jahrbuch für Frauen- und Geschlechterforschung, vol. 7), Metzler, Stuttgart/Weimar, pp. 241-259.

Straub, J. (1999), 'Personale und kollektive Identität. Zur Analyse eines theoretischen Begriffs', in Aleida Assmann and Heidrun Friese (eds), *Identitäten. Erinnerung, Geschichte, Identität*, vol. 3, Suhrkamp, Frankfurt a.M., pp. 73-104.

Strongman, K.T. ([3]1993), *The Psychology of Emotion*, John Wiley and Sons, Chichester etc.

Sutherland, J. (1976), *Victorian Novelists and Publishers*, Athlone Press, London.

Thoits, P.A. (1989), 'The Sociology of Emotions', in *American Review of Sociology*, vol. 15, pp. 317-341.

Thompson, F.M.L. (1988), *The Rise of Respectable Society: A Social History of Victorian Britain, 1830-1900*, Fontana, London.

Todd, J. (1986), *Sensibility: An Introduction*, Methuen, London.

Todd, J. (ed) (1989), *The Dictionary of British Women Writers*, Routledge, London.

Tosh, J. (1999), *A Man's Place: Masculinity and the Middle-Class Home in Victorian England*, Yale UP, New Haven/London.

Trepp, A.-C. (1996), *Sanfte Männlichkeit und selbständige Weiblichkeit. Frauen und Männer im Hamburger Bürgertum zwischen 1770 und 1840*, Vandenhoeck and Ruprecht, Göttingen.

Treuherz, J. (1993), *Victorian Painting*, Thames and Hudson, London.

Van der Voort, P.J. (1972), *The Pen and the Quarter-Deck. A Study of the Life and Works of Captain Frederick Chamier, R.N.*, Leiden UP, Leiden.

Vaughan, W. (1999), *British Painting. The Golden Age from Hogarth to Turner*, Thames and Hudson, London.

Veeser, A. (1989), 'Introduction', in id. (ed), *The New Historicism*, Routledge, London/New York, pp. ix-xvi.

Vester, H.-G. (1991), *Emotion, Gesellschaft und Kultur. Grundzüge einer soziologischen Theorie der Emotionen*, Westdeutscher Verlag, Opladen.

Vester, H.-G. (1999), 'Emotions in Postemotional Culture', in Jürgen Schlaeger and Gesa Stedman (eds), *Representations of Emotions*, Gunter Narr, Tübingen, pp. 19-27.

Vickery, A. (1993), 'Golden Age to Separate Spheres? A Review of the Categories and Chronology of English Women's History', in *The History Journal*, vol. 36 (2), pp. 383-414.

Vrettos, A. (1995), *Somatic Fictions. Imagining Illness in Victorian Culture*, Stanford UP, Stanford.

Wagner, P. (1999), 'Fest-Stellungen. Beobachtungen zur sozialwissenschaftlichen Diskussion über Identität', in Aleida Assmann and Heidrun Friese (eds), *Identitäten. Erinnerung, Geschichte*, Identität, vol. 3, Suhrkamp, Frankfurt a.M., pp. 44-72.

Wehler, H.-U. (1998), 'Pierre Bourdieu. Das Zentrum seines Werks', in id., *Die Herausforderung der Kulturgeschichte*, C.H. Beck, Munich, pp. 15-44.

Wehler, H.-U. (2000), 'Emotionen in der Geschichte: Sind soziale Klassen auch emotionale Klassen?', in id., *Umbruch und Kontinuität. Essays zum 20. Jahrhundert*, C.H. Beck, Munich, pp. 251-64.

Wiener, J.H. (1983), *Radicalism and Freethought in Nineteenth-Century Britain. The Life of Richard Carlile*, Greenwood Press, Westport, Conn./London.

Wiener, M.J. (1992) [1981], *English Culture and the Decline of the Industrial Spirit, 1850-1980*, Penguin, London.

Wierzbicka, A. (1986), 'Human Emotions: Universal or Culture-Specific?', in *American Anthropologist*, vol. 88, pp. 584-94.

Williams, M. (1985), *Women in the English Novel, 1800-1900*, Macmillan, London.

Williams, R. (1988) [1983] [1976], *Keywords. A Vocabulary of Culture and Society*, rev. and exp. ed., Fontana, London.

Wolfson, S.J. (1994), '*Lyrical Ballads* and the Language of (Men) Feeling: Wordsworth Writing Women's Voices', in Thaïs E. Morgan (ed), *Men Writing the Feminine. Literature, Theory, and the Question of Genders*, State University of New York Press, Albany, pp. 29-57.

Wood, J. (2001), *Passion and Pathology in Victorian Fiction*, Oxford UP, Oxford.

Wood, M. (1993), *Rhoda Broughton (1840-1920). Profile of a Novelist*, Paul Watkins, Stamford.

Young, R.C. (1995), *Colonial Desire. Hybridity in Theory, Culture and Race*, Routledge, London/New York.

Index